THE INTELLECTUALS AND McCARTHY:
THE RADICAL SPECTER

THE INTELLECTUALS AND McCARTHY: THE RADICAL SPECTER

MICHAEL PAUL ROGIN

THE M.I.T. PRESS
MASSACHUSETTS INSTITUTE OF TECHNOLOGY
CAMBRIDGE, MASSACHUSETTS, AND LONDON, ENGLAND

Copyright © 1967 by
The Massachusetts Institute of Technology

Set in Linotype Times Roman
and printed and bound in the United States of America
by Halliday Lithograph Corporation

First M.I.T. Press paperback edition, August 1969
Third printing, August 1971
Fourth printing, August 1978

Library of Congress catalog card number: 67–16489
ISBN: 0–262–68015–7

In Memory of
Ethel Lurie Rogin
1908–1966

PREFACE

Grant McConnell, Duncan MacRae, Jr., and the late Morton Grodzins supervised the preparation of this manuscript in its initial form, and the undertaking would have been literally impossible without their assistance. Each contributed specific and continuing commentary. More important, Grant McConnell made American politics intelligible to me; Duncan MacRae, Jr., and John M. Butler performed the same function with the statistical techniques which, thanks only to their perseverance, can appear here.

J. David Greenstone, Jerry Mandel, and Paul Roazen contributed the kind of detailed intellectual and editorial criticism one has no right to expect even from friends. In addition, the following people read some version of the manuscript, entirely or in part, and left their imprint on its final form: Arthur Lipow, Seymour Martin Lipset, Hanna Pitkin, Nelson W. Polsby, Donald S. Rothchild, Leslye Russell, Michael N. Shute, and Aaron Wildavsky. Nancy Poling of The M.I.T. Press contributed invaluable editorial assistance. The book also owes much to the students at Berkeley.

Miss Helen Smith of the University of Chicago, Inter-Library Loan, helped me procure valuable and esoteric election returns. Duncan MacRae, Jr., contributed from a grant the money which made the statistical work possible. Nancy

McCullough and the staff at the Institute of Governmental Studies, University of California at Berkeley, kindly typed the bulk of the manuscript; various secretaries in the political science department also lent their assistance.

Finally and most important, my wife has been a constant source of intellectual and emotional sustenance throughout the development of this book.

MICHAEL PAUL ROGIN

Berkeley, California
October 1966

CONTENTS

Anarchy is not the principal evil that democratic ages have to fear, but the least. For the principle of equality begets two tendencies: the one leads men straight to independence and may suddenly drive them into anarchy; the other conducts them by a longer, more secret, but more certain road to servitude. Nations readily discern the former tendency and are prepared to resist it; they are led away by the latter, without perceiving its drift; hence it is peculiarly important to point it out.

Alexis de Tocqueville
Democracy in America
Volume II, Book IV, Chapter 1*

* Translated by Francis Bowen and Phillips Bradley (New York: Alfred A. Knopf, 1944).

INTRODUCTION

In the decade that has elapsed since Joseph McCarthy of Wisconsin dominated American politics, the atmosphere of the McCarthy years has tended to fade from the public consciousness. But to forget the impact of McCarthyism is a mistake for two reasons. In the first place, the facts of McCarthy's power over public policy and private life in America bear repeating. Richard Rovere has written,

> He held two presidents captive — or as nearly captive as any Presidents of the United States have ever been held; in their conduct of the nation's affairs, Harry S. Truman and Dwight D. Eisenhower, from early 1950 through late 1954, could never act without weighing the effect of their plans upon McCarthy and the forces he led, and in consequence there were times when, because of this man, they could not act at all. He had enormous impact on American foreign policy at a time when that policy bore heavily on the course of world history, and American diplomacy might bear a different aspect today if McCarthy had never lived. In the Senate, his headquarters and his hiding place, he assumed the functions of the Committee of the Whole; he lived in thoroughgoing contempt of the Congress of which he was a member, of the rules it had made for itself, and — whenever they ran contrary to his purposes — of the laws enacted for the general welfare.[1]

McCarthy's impact on public policy hardly exhausted his influence. Directly or indirectly he shattered countless lives and seemed to inflict a mood of fear and suspicion on Amer-

1

ican life as a whole. Rarely has one man in this country cast so long or so dark a shadow.

McCarthy's power, if overwhelming, was comparatively short-lived. But his impact on the intellectual community has lasted far longer. There are those who charge that the McCarthy atmosphere continues to stifle intellectual dissent. But McCarthyism has not so much suppressed opinions as changed them; it has significantly altered the tone of intellectual discussion about politics in general and American politics in particular.

A loosely coherent social theory, substantially concerned with comprehending McCarthyism, emerged in the 1950's. My interest is in that social theory, as it explains McCarthy, as it reinterprets the reform tradition, as it refracts American history through the myopia of a traumatized intelligentsia.

When McCarthy first became prominent, most liberals interpreted the danger he posed in fairly straightforward terms. To them McCarthy was simply the most successful of a number of conservative Republicans capitalizing on the Communist threat to attack the New Deal at home and the Fair Deal abroad. "McCarthyism" was a synonym for smear attacks on liberals, its roots were in traditional right-wing politics, and its principal targets were innocent individuals and liberal political goals. Liberals hardly minimized McCarthy's political importance, although they had little difficulty explaining either his roots or the danger he posed.

But to many writers such traditional analysis failed to account for McCarthy's strength. In their eyes, McCarthy was getting support not from the established groups with which traditional conservatism had been associated but rather from the dispossessed and discontented. One had to wonder about any inevitable association between popular discontent and support for progressive movements of economic reform. Moreover, McCarthy continually appealed to the mass of people for direct support over the heads of their elected leaders. And the established eastern elite, unsympathetic to the

Wisconsin senator, was one of his important targets. All this suggested that popular democracy constituted a real threat to the making of responsible political decisions. McCarthy appeared not in the guise of a conservative smearing innocent liberals but in the guise of a democrat assaulting the political fabric.

If faith in democracy suffered from the McCarthy period, sympathy for radicalism hardly fared better. Both the more orthodox liberal analysts of McCarthyism and those with the newer view recognized that McCarthy dominated America while traditional radical movements lay dormant. To the old-fashioned liberals, McCarthyism symbolized the death of radical protest in America. In the newer view, McCarthy was the bearer of the historical radical mission — challenging, like earlier radicals, the established institutions of American society. The McCarthy years thus ushered in a new fear of radicalism among growing numbers of intellectuals. One can date from the McCarthy period the rise of such terms as "radical Right" to go with radical Left, and left-wing "fundamentalism" to coincide with right-wing extremism.

In this new view, McCarthyism was a movement of the radical Right that grew out of movements of the radical Left. For traditional liberals, the New Deal and contemporary liberalism had grown out of the protest politics of the pre-Roosevelt years. The newer view produced a very different history. Left-wing protest movements, democratic in their appeal to the popular masses, radical in the discontent they mobilized, had borne fruit in McCarthyism. To some, McCarthy was directly descended from an agrarian radical tradition. To others he had conservative roots as well, but his power derived from his ability to form an alliance between traditional conservatism and agrarian radicalism.

The term agrarian radicalism refers to the movements of rural protest that flourished between the end of the Civil War and the New Deal epoch — the Grangers, the Greenbackers, the Farmers' Alliances, the Populists, the progressives, and the Non-Partisan League. Not all these movements were exclusively rural. Progressivism in particular had an important urban wing, although it is well to remember that in state and national politics progressives most continually triumphed in rural areas.

Aside from being predominantly rural, pre-New Deal protest movements had important geographic sources of continuity. Outside the South, these movements flourished along the settled frontier. From the 1880's to the 1930's, left-wing protest politics were strongest in the West and the western Middle West.[2] Populism outside the South received most of its support from the plains states and those bordering on them. The Non-Partisan League of 1916 to 1924 had been strongest there too. Pre- and post-World War I progressivism tended to be strong in the Middle West and West and weak in the East.

Agrarian radicalism thus flourished in the states of the trans-Mississippi West. Political leaders in these states were most vociferous in their support of McCarthy and supplied him with most of his votes against the senatorial censure resolution of 1954. In particular, senators from states that had supported the Populist presidential candidate in 1892 or La Follette for President in 1924 disproportionately voted against the McCarthy censure.*

* In 1892, Populist presidential candidate Weaver received more than 37 percent of the vote in eight states. All provided at least one vote for McCarthy on the censure resolution. (The only other state in which Weaver received as much as 25 percent of the vote was Alabama.) Cf. John D. Hicks, *The Populist Revolt* (Omaha, Neb.: University of Nebraska Press, 1961), p. 263.

The coincidence of support for La Follette and McCarthy goes beyond the fact that both were from Wisconsin. In the censure vote, McCarthy got the support of two Republican senators in only five states — Indiana, Idaho, North Dakota, Nevada, and California. In all but Indiana, La Follette had gotten more than 30 percent of the vote in 1924; his national average (by states) was 17 percent. The one Republican senator in seven other states voted against the McCarthy censure. La Follette had exceeded his national average in all seven. Including Wisconsin, McCarthy got support on the censure

Certainly the geographic coincidence of support for McCarthyism and agrarian radicalism can be exaggerated. The South opposed both La Follette and McCarthy, but party loyalty was more crucial than ideological commitment. Since the Populist revolt, agrarian radicalism was not strong in the eastern Middle West; but this area produced strong Republican support for McCarthy. The trans-Mississippi West, however, supported both McCarthyism and agrarian radicalism. A look at the map thus provides concrete evidence linking McCarthy to agrarian radicalism. The interpretation of McCarthy as radical democrat appears persuasive. The new view of politics implied by that interpretation seems supported by the evidence.

The present study challenges the notion that McCarthy had agrarian radical roots. Examination of the empirical evidence finds no correlation between support for agrarian radicals and support for McCarthy; consideration of the reform tradition uncovers no unique reform appeals on which McCarthy capitalized. Investigation of the McCarthy movement discloses no agrarian radical flavor but rather a traditional conservative heritage. Analysis of the new social theory questions its relevance to American history.

Let it be clear at the outset, then, that I do not share the view of McCarthyism and agrarian radicalism presented here and in the chapter following. I only insist that that view be taken seriously. It has gained wide currency in the intellectual world, receiving the support of such prominent and thoughtful writers as Richard Hofstadter, Seymour Martin Lipset, Talcott Parsons, Edward Shils, David Riesman, Nathan

resolution from twenty states. Fourteen of the eighteen states that gave La Follette more than 17 percent of their vote were among those twenty. Cf. Herbert Parzen, "A Comparative Study of the Progressive Presidential Campaigns of 1912 and 1924," unpublished Master's thesis, Department of Political Science, Columbia University, 1926, pp. 1–7; "McCarthy's Strength Centered in West, Midwest," *Congressional Quarterly* (December 3, 1954), p. 1409. No Democrats voted against the censure.

Glazer, Oscar Handlin, Peter Viereck, Will Herberg, Daniel Bell, William Kornhauser.[3] Before they wrote, McCarthyism meant something like character assassination, and Populism was the name of a particular historical movement for social reform at the end of the nineteenth century. Through their influence Populism has become an example of and a general term for anomic movements of mass protest against existing institutions — the type of movement typified by McCarthyism.

Those connecting it with the earlier movements see McCarthyism, first, as a democratic revolt of dispossessed groups against the educated, eastern elite. Like McCarthyism, agrarian radicalism is also said to have substituted moralistic, irrational appeals for a rational politics. For many writers, these movements embody a nativist mystique which, glorifying the ordinary folk, threatens the civilized restraints of a complex society.

For these writers, both movements "reject the traditional cultural and educational leadership of the enlightened upper and upper-middle classes." Populism and La Follette progressivism identified the will of the people with justice and morality. Holding a plebiscitarian view of democracy, agrarian radicals placed the popular will above the autonomy of institutions and the desires of the various strata in the society. Since political leaders cannot function in an atmosphere of plebiscites and exposures, agrarian radicalism crippled responsible political leadership and endangered privacy. In this sense, "McCarthy is the heir of La Follette." McCarthyism and agrarian radicalism exhibit "the tendency to convert issues into ideologies, to invest them with moral color and high emotional charge [which] invites conflict which can only damage a society." "Beneath the sane economic demands of the Populists of 1880–1890 seethed a mania of xenophobia, Jew-baiting, intellectual baiting, and thought-controlling lynch spirit." McCarthyism is the "same old isolationist, Anglophobe, Germanophile revolt of radical Populist lunatic-

6

fringers against the eastern, educated, Anglicized elite."
"McCarthyism appealed to the same social groups as did
'left-wing' Populism."[4]

Clearly such charges rest on a particular view of politics —
one involving suspicion of the people, fear of radicalism,
friendliness to established institutions, re-examination of the
American past. The fear of mass democracy and radical
protest that grew in the McCarthy years eventuated in theories
of mass society and pluralism. Much of the effort to connect
McCarthyism and agrarian radicalism appears mysterious
until the theories which underlie that effort are comprehended.
Moreover, in the light of the new theories the problem of
McCarthyism and agrarian radicalism transcends its particular historical significance and becomes relevant to general
questions of social change and democratic politics.

The aim of this study, then, is fourfold. There is first the
effort to comprehend and criticize a dominant strand of social
science theory. That effort opens and closes the book and
provides the backdrop for the arguments of the historical
and statistical chapters. There is, second, in Chapter 2, such
discussion of American operating political ideas as seems
necessary to frame the analyses of McCarthyism and agrarian
radicalism. There is, third, a reinterpretation of American
reform, informed by the analysis of voting returns in three
states (Chapters 3 to 5) and the explicit subject of Chapters
6 and 7. There is, finally, the analysis of McCarthyism. The
statistical chapters seek to discover whether agrarian radicalism created a tradition of political support that moved from
Populism, progressivism, or the Non-Partison League into
right-wing Republicanism in general or McCarthyism in particular. Chapter 8 then discusses the nature of the McCarthy
phenomenon.

RADICALISM
AND THE RATIONAL SOCIETY:
THE PLURALIST VIEW

The Social Roots

Modern pluralism emerged as American intellectuals, mainly ex-radical, responded to the events of their youth and the pressures of the 1950's. The rise of communism and fascism in Europe had forcefully suggested the similarities between the extreme Right and the extreme Left and the dangers of mass movements. The moderate New Deal, on the other hand, succeeded in giving American capitalism a reasonable and stable basis. Thus drastic social change seemed not only terribly dangerous but also unnecessary.

But many of the thinkers with whom we are concerned remained critical of American society as a whole through World War II, perhaps sustained by the hopes for a new world pervasive during that war as during the previous one. These hopes soon exhausted themselves as the cold war and the rise of McCarthyism finally deadened the radical impulses of the pluralists:[1] the country now had to be defended against attack from without and within. McCarthy threatened the stability of the society to which the pluralists were becoming reconciled; in his attack on intellectuals he threatened the rapprochement itself. The pluralists now sought values in traditions of mainstream America with which they could

9

identify. They attributed to peripheral, radical movements the diseases they had previously located at the heart of the American ethos.[2]

The Intellectual Heritage

Writing at the height of the McCarthy hysteria, Edward Shils located the danger of McCarthyism in the "populist" tradition; American pluralism, he felt, saved us from the Senator and his following. A few years later, in *The Politics of Mass Society*, William Kornhauser echoed this counterposition between the Populist-McCarthy heritage and the pluralist tradition.[3] Many others who have connected McCarthyism to agrarian radicalism have also defended pluralism.[4]

An elaborate pluralist theory would inevitably include doctrines that individual pluralists would reject. Nevertheless, those placing McCarthy in an agrarian radical tradition seem to share certain common assumptions and underlying preoccupations. The effort here is not so much to be faithful to the ideas of each individual pluralist as it is to analyze an "ideal-typical" pluralism.[5]

Modern pluralism, I will argue, is not simply a defense of shared power or a sympathy for diverse values but also a theory of history in which industrialization is the major actor. Industrialization destroys traditional stability, but the success of industrialization enables group politics to dominate a society. Mass politics is defined by its orientation to the institutions and norms of industrial society. Group politics does not eliminate political moralism but rather directs it to its proper concern — social cohesion in a constitutional, industrial society. Group politics is the conflict not among groups but among group leaders, socialized into the dominant values and associations of industrial society. Pluralism does not extend its tolerance for diversity to mass movements and anti-industrial attitudes felt to threaten the conditions of diversity.

The pluralist defense of modern industrial society brings

10

together three strands of political thought. From traditional liberalism — through Weber — it borrows the concern for rationality. Liberalism united an impersonal society with self-interested individuals, and pluralism values this combination. From traditional conservatism — through Durkheim and mass theory — it borrows the need for an ordered society. Like conservatism, pluralism fears the unattached individual. From traditional pluralism — Figgis, Laski, Cole — it borrows the reliance on groups. It combines these elements to arrive at a normative and descriptive social theory aimed at the stability of the social system.

But each of these traditions was double-edged and pointed in the direction of liberty as well as order. The liberals, in atomizing society, aimed to liberate the individual from a multiplicity of group coercions. The conservatives feared that the rationalization of society destroyed the freedom that was preserved in the interstices of a hierarchical and traditional order. The traditional pluralists favored groups not to discipline their members and provide cohesion but to defend the liberty of their members against a powerful state. Modern pluralism accepts the liberal rationalization of traditional freedom, the conservative ordering of liberal freedom, and the group discipline of individual freedom.[6]

Consider first the pluralist transformation of mass theory. Finding roots in the conservative reaction to the French Revolution, writers such as Ortega y Gasset feared the rise of a state of the masses. In Ortega's view, nonprivileged groups in traditional society knew their place. Enmeshed in specific primary group loyalties, they recognized the special competence of elites in cultural and political affairs. The revolt of the masses threatened to destroy the privileged elites and the civilized values they preserved.[7]

Ortega had moral and aristocratic trepidations that modern pluralism has left behind. The revolt of the masses, he argued, would destroy culture and trivialize the quality of life for everyone. Modern pluralists like Bell and Shils specifically reject this version of mass theory.[8] Moreover, in government as in the arts Ortega feared the exertion of the "material pressure" of the masses.[9] Governing required the special skills of a political elite; there was no room for the pressure group politics of pluralism.

These differences between mass theory and pluralism have a common root. For Ortega, modern industrial society ushered in the revolt of the masses; he looked to America with horror. Tearing individuals from their traditional moorings, industrial society would produce mass extremist revolts. For the modern pluralists, industrial society destroys old loyalties and groups; but it also creates new ones. The new groups are more associations than communities, the new loyalties more utilitarian than traditional. But the functions they perform are similar. Thus, although the secondary associations of industrial society operate directly in politics, the pressure they exert is not equivalent to the mass pressure Ortega feared but rather a substitute for it. By putting new facts into the old analysis, the pluralists have arrived at a defense of industrial society instead of an attack on it. They stand the traditional theory of mass society on its head. Developed industrial countries like America are thus pluralist; they are not mass societies.[10]

How can theorists like Ortega who feared industrial society be used to promote its acceptance? The pluralist treatment of industrialization and bureaucratization is rooted in Max Weber's concern with the demystification of the world. By demystification, Weber meant the replacement of magical, emotional, evaluative, and traditional components of life by systematic, rational, practical modes of thought and activity.

Bureaucracies stressed norms of efficiency and impersonality. They dealt with individuals only in specific, job-oriented terms; the customer's total personality and his social position were equally irrelevant. Here is the meaning of formal equality, and it suggests that Weber's demystification of the world was in a peculiar sense also its depersonalization. Similarly, the Protestant ethic directed individuals to systematic subordination of means to ends in the accumulation of worldly goods. Capitalism depended structurally on a bureaucratic organization of the work force and psychologically on an instrumental orientation to worldly activity. A bureaucratic and capitalist society limited the permeation of everyday activity by ultimate moral standards. Those with an instrumental orientation judged everything by its use as a means. Moreover, means themselves became more rational. An instrumental society not only avoided questions of ultimate ends; it also minimized commitment to irrational means. Individuals became more concerned with discovering rational ways to achieve their ends. This concern permeated politics as well as personal affairs. Political groups became less likely to make self-contradictory demands, irrational in the specific and dangerous sense that the means would not achieve the ends. In Weber's instrumental society, political opponents could be "reasoned" with because their efforts to seek their ends were rational. Bargaining and compromise became possible.[11] As long as the society worked in a practical sense, those who had accepted an instrumental (*zweck-rationalität*) orientation would not threaten its stability. The political implication of this is that there is no basis within such a society for revolutionary values. The ultimate questions of justice were no longer to be the business of politics.

For Weber, the instrumental character of industrial society was unrelieved. Here he followed in the footsteps of the Enlightenment conception of a liberal society.

The Enlightenment thinkers favored a society of individuals uncoerced by group or traditional ties. According to the old theorists of mass society, such a conception atomized society, resulting in social disorganization, mass movements, and totalitarianism.[12] This paralleled the view of Emile Durkheim.

Durkheim thought that while traditional societies had a "mechanical solidarity" (common beliefs, and traditions) modern societies joined individuals together only on the basis

13

of diverse functions in a common division of labor. This organic solidarity atomized the individual from his group ties and destroyed his commitment to ultimate and stabilizing values. Durkheim saw Weber's rational society but found the individuals in it isolated and lost. The society produced not instrumental activity but social disorganization and anomie.

Durkheim's cure for anomie was not a return to mechanical solidarity but the perfection of organic solidarity. When each individual knew his place in the new rational society, personal and social disorders would cease.[13] A society rational in Weber's sense would also acquire organic solidarity in Durkheim's sense. Attacks on that society would not only be irrational, they would also tear at a social fabric of great value.

Empirical research has suggested how Durkheim's theoretical supplement to Weber works in practice. Modern industrial sociologists have transformed Weber's formal and spare bureaucracy into a network of group affiliations. Modern political scientists and sociologists have discovered the importance of formal and informal groups in a bureaucratized society. In sum, industrial society produces both capitalist and bureaucratic structures and an instrumental orientation; these make rational politics possible. It creates as well the groups that integrate individuals into the rational order. Weber's society solves Durkheim's problem; modern pluralism grows out of this synthesis.

For the modern pluralists, a constitutional regime requires "traditions of civility" that tolerate a variety of interests, traditions, life-styles, religions, political beliefs, and economic activities. This diversity is safeguarded when power is shared among numerous groups and institutions. Groups provide individuals with specific channels for realizing their demands, focusing their members on the practical desires that can be realized in ordinary democratic politics. At the same time, even nonpolitical groups provide isolated individuals with a home, integrating them into the constitutional order. Moreover, when an individual belongs to many groups he cannot act in an extreme fashion in support of one group without threatening his commitment to another. He thus becomes committed in general to the society and is unable to threaten that commitment through the support of a particular extremism.

Without groups, disorder and totalitarianism are real threats according to the pluralists. Lacking a sense of community and alienated from the total society, individuals are vulnerable to mobilization by mass movements. These movements rather than focusing on concrete group demands to improve the individual's position in the society play upon generalized resentments stemming from the deeper layers of the personality. Mass movements arise from the desperation, rootlessness, and irrational longings of isolated individuals. Their targets are scapegoats, and the solutions they propose are either harmless but pointless panaceas or else threaten to destroy the constitutional regime. Mass politics involve irrationality and chaos; group politics produce sensible and orderly conflict.*

The intellectual heritage of pluralism suggests that the theory is not simply a defense of diverse groups sharing power but also an analysis and defense of tendencies within modern industrial society. Pluralism requires more than diversity; it requires as well the consensus and orientations of modern industrial society to protect and limit that diversity. Herein

---

* Politics in industrial society is rational for the pluralists in four interrelated senses. First, political demands are not rationalizations for underlying frustrations. Since their manifest content is what counts, they can be handled rationally. Second, people are rational about means. They seek those that will achieve their ends; they think instrumentally. Third, individuals concern themselves with short-run, self-interested goals; rationality and self-interest become synonymous here. Finally, political ends are not utopian; they can be achieved within the framework of the existing social order. The politics of those who long for the return of the traditional, preindustrial way of life are irrational on all four counts; and this desire is at the root of much political irrationality.

15

lies the key to certain difficulties apparent in a more detailed examination of pluralism itself. Three problems are of particular concern — the relations between groups and the public interest, between groups and mass movements, and between multiple group affiliations and political moderation. In each case, the explicit analysis focuses on groups, but industrialization is the often inarticulate major premise. In each case, explicit reliance on groups produces apparent contradictions resolved only when industrial society as a whole enters the picture.

Group Politics and the Public Interest

For a wing of liberalism that extends from Adam Smith to David Truman, politics is rational when no one worries about social goals.[14] Individuals and groups pursuing their own interests preserve social cohesion in the good society.

In Smith's world, there is no politics because there is no power; the laws of the market are supreme. Truman's world seems eminently political for is not the essence of politics bargaining, compromise, and the reconciliation of group differences? But in a larger sense, Truman's group equilibrium corresponds to the invisible hand. Since power is shared among many groups, the outcome of group conflict corresponds to the desires of the organized citizenry. There is no need for a specific political attention to the public interest because politics regulates itself.

Truman defines out of existence any conflict between groups and the public interest. Since groups are "shared attitudes," all political actors can be called groups. Since versions of the public interest can only be rationalizations for group goals, the public interest cannot exist apart from group interests. The pluralists I am concerned with reaffirm the common identity of group politics and the public interest not by definition but because they are terribly afraid of the catastrophic conesquences of nongroup politics. Kornhauser, for

16

example, distinguishes between mass politics, concerned with general, remote, and moral objects, and pluralist politics, concerned with immediate and particular objects. The alternative to group determination of public policy is the influence of the irrational mass.[15] Similarly, Bell has contrasted "market" and "ideological" decisions. The former are based on the rational self-interest of the individual or group, the latter on a purpose clothed in moral terms and deemed important enough to override individual self-interest. The danger "is that political debate moves from specific interest clashes, in which issues can be identified and possibly compromised, to ideological tinged conflicts that polarize the groups and divide the society."[16]

Finally, Lipset and Hofstadter have distinguished between class and status politics. Class politics is any kind of economic group politics, whether of broad, economic classes or narrow, economic interest groups. In either form, it is group-based and economically self-interested, lacking the ideological, revolutionary connotations provided by Marx. By contrast, status politics is not the politics of organized groups but of status groups — the young, the downwardly mobile, the third-generation Americans, the ancient New England families. Status politics is, in Hofstadter's words, "the clash of various projective rationalizations arising from status aspirations and other personal motives." To the pluralists, vague feelings of status insecurity explain the support for such movements as the Ku Klux Klan in the 1920's and McCarthyism in the 1950's. Specific political programs to meet status resentments are generally difficult to envision; it is not a simple economic matter of wanting higher minimum wages or subsidies to the ship industry. Status concerns therefore tend to result in irrational political programs, whose manifest content has little relation to the fears that produced them.[17]

Status politics are seen as ideological mass politics; class politics are the politics of the market world and the group process. Politics divorced from group self-interest endangers

17

constitutional stability. The defense of self-interested politics seems at the heart of pluralism and is reinforced, paradoxically enough, by pluralist psychology.

Pluralist psychology is rooted in the studies of the authoritarian personality first prominent in the book of that name.[18] The psychology of *The Authoritarian Personality* has specific psychoanalytic roots which need not concern us here. In general, the pluralists are indebted to Freud for uncovering the hidden, nonrational layers of the human personality. For the pluralists, the unconscious explains the great human capacity for extreme and antirational behavior — from fascist sadism and mass murder to episodes of mob violence to milder forms of hero worship and political emotion. Nothing seems further from the behaviorist utilitarian psychology of the Smith, Bentham, Bentley tradition. In two ways, however, pluralist psychology goes back to that tradition.

In the first place, the concern for psychology has meant a shift away from more strictly political and structural concerns. Psychological attitudes become a main basis for predicting social behavior. Political programs, even positions in the political arena, become less important. Thus Lipset relies on psychological evidence of authoritarianism to demonstrate working-class political authoritarianism. That there should be a vital connection between the psychological makeup of individual workers and the political demands of workers and their organizations is not immediately obvious; yet Lipset virtually assumes the relevance of the psychological material.[19]

The psychology is different, but the method of analysis goes back to the utilitarians. The utilitarians also paid little attention to tradition, history, or position in the social structure in explaining political behavior. A knowledge of human psychology was sufficient to understand and arrange political institutions; the pleasure-pain calculus was at the root of politics. But if both the pluralists and the utilitarians have a psychological model of political behavior, then the resulting

18

political analyses, based as they are on such contrasting psychologies, must be very different.

Here the pluralists discard utilitarian individualism in order to reaffirm its rationalistic premises. They argue that political behavior in certain situations cannot be predicted directly from psychological attitudes. Where individuals are members of groups, group involvement and multiple group loyalties take over from depth psychology. In a structured situation, individuals are supplied with relatively well-defined roles; their psychological traits become less relevant. Moreover, groups direct the attention of their members away from the political satisfaction of deep-seated psychological grievances and toward bread-and-butter goals. In a meaningful psychological sense, groups control their members and make them rational.[20] By controlling individuals, groups permit the natural harmony of Adam Smith to be re-established on the group level. A society of competing groups not only solves the problem of isolation caused by the Smithian society; it also takes into account depth psychology without sacrificing the invisible hand. The invisible hand worked for Smith because men behaved rationally. For the pluralists men may be irrational, but groups impose rationality. The state therefore need not step in, and no politics of the public interest are necessary.

The psychology and sociology of the pluralists tell them that certain moral concerns are authoritarian and threaten existing institutions. But their psychology and sociology, used in the main to attack moralistic politics and defend groups, are also used crucially to defend a particular kind of moral politics. The moral politics defended are those resulting in the social cohesion of modern industrial society; the root pluralist fear is of mass passion over public policy, not of concern for the public interest per se.

For example, the pluralists praise the educated, eastern opponents of McCarthy for their commitment to law, established procedures, and social cohesion, devoid of any par-

19

ticular interests it serves for them. Similarly, the pluralists make the point that political conflicts have shifted from economic issues to matters of foreign policy, civil liberties, and so on. But this means that all politics concerned with these issues, not only McCarthyism, is status politics. If McCarthy is damned for concern with noneconomic questions, what can one say of his educated, eastern opponents? Indeed, Hofstadter's interpretation of the progressive movement in status political terms rests on the assertion that the progressives were afraid that new wealth was destroying old social institutions. Yet Hofstadter, and more clearly Riesman and Glazer, fear McCarthyism as a movement of new wealth against established institutions.[21] Their fear of McCarthyism parallels progressive anxieties. In thus reflecting progressive concerns, Riesman, Glazer, and Hofstadter not only exhibit status politics but the particular status politics of the progressives.

Because of their fear of the damage that an extremist movement can do, many of the pluralists seem to long for an autonomous political elite that stands above the group struggle and keeps that struggle from getting out of hand.[22] They desire a class for which the self-interested and nonmoral strictures do not apply. Questions which are remote to most people would be proximate to them. Thus Kornhauser quotes Schumpeter's description of a man's proximate objects as "the things under his personal observation . . . for which he develops the kind of responsibility that is induced by a direct relation to the favorable or unfavorable effects of a course of action.[23] For most people, this criterion excludes the broad questions of national and international politics. For the sophisticated political elite it would not. Are these broad questions with moral implications the legitimate group province of the pluralist elite? This elite is to be immune from "populistic" mass pressure. Is it not therefore insulated from the immediate pressures of group politics as well?*

* It could be argued that the pluralists favor intervention to safeguard the public interest only when the rules of the game of group

20

Group Politics and Mass Movements

In pluralist eyes, mass movements pose a major threat to social cohesion. But how are mass movements to be distinguished from groups when both end the anomie of isolated individuals? The distinction may seem obvious enough, but it is far from easy to categorize. Pluralist efforts to present such a distinction rely on contrasts in political demands, political styles, political methods, and in who is organized. The simplest contrast between mass movements and pressure groups focuses on their demands. Mass movements are said to make moralistic rather than economic demands, and to have broad programs rather than narrow, specific ones. They concentrate on matters remote from the daily experience of their members rather than on issues of "proximate" concern.[24] But such relatively straightforward distinctions are hardly satisfactory. The Townsendites and the Poujadists both exhibited "mass" characteristics in spite of their narrow, economic demands. On the other hand, groups organized on a narrow constituency — the AMA, for example — are often moralistic. The Anti-Saloon League, classic case of a single-issue pressure group, was both moralistic and extreme. And what could be of more "proximate" interest to the Luddites than the machines they smashed?

---

politics are threatened. But their own writing does not suggest so restrictive an interpretation. Moreover, the line between substantive and procedural intervention is far from easy to draw in practice, particularly when procedure is defined not in clear formal terms (secret ballot, majority election, and so forth) but in the less operational senses of tolerating opposition, following precedent, and respecting elite autonomy.

Consider foreign affairs, for example. In foreign policy, the nation as a whole and its interests are at stake; hence foreign policy may be included in the "nongroup" sphere of politics. Note that the school of political realism, which derides the concept of national interest at home, derides the possibility of anything else in foreign policy. "National interest" switches from a fuzzy rationalization to a hard political concept. This can be understood in terms of the two types of pluralist rational politics just sketched.

To distinguish mass movements from pressure groups by whom they organize also runs into difficulties. Mass movements are said to recruit the previously unorganized, those least integrated into the organizations and institutions of society.[25] On the other hand, they are said to make appeals that cut across existing political and economic cleavages, uprooting people from *existing* allegiances.[26] It may be that those who are uprooted were less involved in the first place, but this suggests the relevance, not simply of group involvement but of a general involvement in and allegiance to the norms of the wider society. Those more committed to the constitutional, industrial society are less mobilizable by mass movements.

Ultimately, pluralists distinguish groups from mass movements by their degree of commitment to constitutional values. Group politics is the politics of trial and error, compromise and restraint. It looks upon the political arena as a contrivance of human ingenuity, with many spheres outside of and irrelevant to politics. Mass movements are said to see a sole and exclusive truth in politics. Political ideals are part of a preordained system of philosophy, which it is the job of the movement to enforce. Mass movements are therefore intolerant of opposition, denying legitimacy to points of view other than their own. Emotional and supremely confident, mass movements love violence. They seek influence through direct action — riots, strikes, marches; suspicious of parliaments, mass movements prefer the streets. Their members participate directly in politics rather than relying upon organizational leaders. Masses of men ordinarily divided by their interests are united by hysteria and emotion.

Such efforts to distinguish mass movements from groups suggest that a pluralist society depends not only upon the existence of groups but upon their orientation as well. Ultimately, the difference between mass movements and pressure groups in the pluralist analysis is that the former reject the society, desire totally to transform it, and are, in a word,

22

radical. However narrow in focus or economic in approach, groups that attempt to retard the development of a sophisticated, industrial order have a "mass" character.

Group Politics and Political Moderation

There is still another important method of distinguishing mass movements from pressure groups. It might be argued that mass movements are not isolated from constitutional norms per se but first and foremost from other groups in society. An isolated group is one whose members are members of no other group. Isolated groups can thus exist even if there are numbers of groups in a society. Individuals must in addition be members of more than one group and free to move from one group to another.

Why would multiple group affiliations produce moderation? The argument is that those with several group memberships are pressured in different directions by the different groups and are therefore more moderate. Since group members lack total loyalty to a single group, they restrain leaders in the exercise of group pressure. This argument is superficially plausible; the evidence usually cited comes from the voting studies, which developed the notion of "cross-pressures." A cross-pressured person is one who is pressed in conflicting directions by competing loyalties. Multiple group affiliations are said to produce cross-pressures. These pressures from conflicting groups are said to moderate extremism.

But the actual evidence points in a narrower and very different direction. In the voting studies a cross-pressured person is one whose political views or social characteristics predispose him in conflicting directions with respect to his voting decision. He may be a rich Catholic or favor the Republican candidate and the Democratic issues; a woman may have a Democratic father and a Republican husband. In all cases, the cross-pressured person tends to be less likely to vote, less stable in his vote intention, less involved in political discus-

23

sion, and less knowledgeable about political issues. Far from being an independent moderating force, the cross-pressured person is very easily influenced. Moreover, he tends to misperceive the stands of candidates on issues. In general, cross-pressured people are not moderate through involvement but rather withdraw from politics because of conflict. Their multiple pressures lead not to rational moderation but rather to political withdrawal and confusion.[27]

The final irony is that cross-pressured people are not very likely to have multiple organizational affiliations. For example, those Democrats in Elmira in 1948 cross-pressured between Democratic party affiliation and candidate preference for Dewey were less likely to belong to organizations than the sample as a whole. And if cross-pressured people tend to misperceive the candidates' issue positions, those with organizational memberships tend to have a highly accurate picture of the candidates' positions.[28] If the cross-pressures hypothesis applied to those with multiple group affiliations, it would suggest the political apathy and irrationality of these people rather than their moderation; but it simply is not relevant to the organizationally involved.

Traditionally, the moderating influence of multiple group affiliations has been presented in terms of cross-pressured members limiting organizational leaders. However, as Stanley Rothman points out, relatively few Americans are in fact members of more than one or two groups. There is little evidence either that groups influence the attitudes of their members or that group members influence the conduct of their leaders. Members tend to be apathetic, attending few meetings and rarely participating in group deliberations. Decisions in fact are taken by self-perpetuating oligarchies.[29]

How, then, do multiple group affiliations promote constitutional stability? Apparently cross-pressured members do not moderate determined leaders. But the pluralists in fact rely not on the multiple affiliations of group members but on the characteristics of group leaders. The relatively small number of people highly involved in group life and belonging to many organizations tend to be the very leaders and activists themselves, not the public at large or the organizational rank-and-file. Leaders of organizations and voluntary associations are more likely to have multiple group affiliations than are the members. If overlapping group memberships check the leaders of organizations, this is not a check of members on leaders but a check of leaders on themselves and each other.

Indeed, it is more than that; it is a check of leaders on members. The pluralists here stand Robert Michels on his head. Michels argued that organizations produce leaders divorced from rank-and-file control and *embourgeoised* (socialized) into the values and associations of the wider society.[30] A revolutionary writing about socialist parties, Michels viewed this development with horror. But pluralists defend the independence of leaders from rank-and-file control. Leaders have better attitudes and are better informed than ordinary citizens.[31] Leaders tend to belong to more organizations. Because of their position, leaders are thought more likely than members to be willing to compromise; they are more exposed to the demands of other groups and to the obstacles in the way of achieving their own group goals. This is not so much because they are members of the other groups; rather the existence of these groups is in the forefront of their consciousness. Leaders have to deal with other groups; members do not. Leaders develop informal contacts with various political elites. In sum, for the pluralists leaders are more likely to be socialized into the dominant values and established institutions of their society.[32]

Ultimately, pluralism is not the politics of group conflict but the politics of leadership conflict. Are these simply the leaders of pressure groups such as the Farm Bureau and the Steel Workers? Or are they in addition those educated, informed, socially involved people (primarily in the urban middle and upper classes) whose specific organizational affiliations are less important than their knowledge and values in general? The problem of group politics and a pluralist elite has been referred to earlier; more than one road seems to suggest the elitist underpinnings of pluralist doctrine. Certainly pluralists rely less on the existence of groups than is apparent at first sight and more on the orientation of groups, on the presence of civilized values in society, and on the defense of those values by leaders equipped to protect them.

These more general considerations are also relevant in understanding why people join groups in the first place and which groups they join. Individuals may join groups which reinforce their attitudes rather than groups that overlap the relevant arena of conflict. Why does a right-wing Republican join only reinforcing groups; why does a French worker join a left-wing veterans group rather than the French equivalent of the American Legion? Indeed, how did Britain develop constitutional stability without, until recent years, the presence of cross-class organizations?[33] Overlapping group memberships seem a usual consequence rather than a cause of political stability. Is this not, in fact, what the pluralists believe — that the process of industrialization tends eventually to create values leading to overlapping group affiliation (at least among a small but vital segment of the population)?

Industrialization and Agrarian Radicalism

The relevance of pluralist theory to American history emerges most forcefully in Richard Hofstadter's *The Age of Reform*. Hofstadter's thesis is that reform movements before the New Deal were preoccupied with moral rather than "practical" questions. Populism and progressivism attempted "to save personal entrepreneurship and individual opportunity and the character type they engendered, and to maintain a homogeneous Yankee civilization." Trafficking in moral absolutes, they maintained an "exalted moral tone." Rural either in actual social composition or in roots, reformers were opposed to urbanization, industrialization, and the growth of an instrumental society. The opponents of Populism and progressivism, those who were industrializing the society, were practically rather than ideologically inclined.

With the New Deal, this relationship was reversed. According to Hofstadter, the New Deal scorned moral formulations, did not equate good politics with personal integrity, and "showed a strong and candid awareness that what was happening was not so much moral reformation as economic experimentation." It utilized organizations, the enemies of the individualistic rural reformers, to solve pragmatic problems. The opponents of the New Deal defended personal virtue and responsibility against practical actions. If once the progressives worried about the effect of money on moral character, now the conservatives opposed unemployment relief out of the same fear. In the past, conservatives had built factories and railroads and industrialized the society while the reformers raised moral objections. Now the New Deal fed the hungry, saved the banks, and rescued the industrial society from desolation, while the conservatives greeted these practical acts with moral indignation. Pre-New Deal reform shared with post-New Deal reaction a suspicious attitude toward industrial society.[34]

Pluralist history thus cements the connection between McCarthyism and agrarian radicalism. For the pluralists, McCarthyism and agrarian radicalism directed moralistic and "mass" appeals[35] against the development of an instrumental, bureaucratized industrial order. Many of the specific similarities identified by the pluralists grow out of the alleged anti-industrial character of the movements. Shils, for example, argues that both Populism and McCarthyism opposed established elites. Yet in the Middle West and particularly in the South, Populism challenged a rising elite.[36] This apparent contradiction can be reconciled by understanding that for Shils the new elite was an industrial elite, destined to become established. Similarly, Bell has written that both Populism and the radical Right appeal to "dispossessed" groups.[37] If this

27

word is to mean anything different from "discontented," it would seem to refer to once-secure groups that have lost status or power. Yet Bell goes on to identify *rising* elites as sources of support for the radical Right. But Bell's rising elites, unlike Shils', are alienated from status and power in a sophisticated, industrial order.

Without more ado, one may list other similarities between McCarthyism and agrarian radicalism alleged to flow from their mass, anti-industrial character. The movements made demands for a radical reorganization of society. They enlisted a mass following that split apart existing coalitions. They had an explosive character; that is, they came to prominence in a burst and disappeared as quickly. They believed that all opposition to them was illegitimate, had a low tolerance of ambiguity, and in general exhibited characteristics associated with the authoritarian personality. More particularly, the pluralists find the movements were for the people as a mass — for nationalism and Americanism. They were against both the traditional aristocratic elites and the newer industrial elites. They were against bureaucratization; intellectuals; science; cosmopolitanism; alien influences; privacy and civil liberties; the vested interests; instrumental activity in general; compromise; the disinterested performance of duties; established institutions and procedures. Suspicious of "overeducation," they believed that knowledge should be a means to Americanism rather than an end in itself. They were jingoist and nativist. They had a conspiracy theory of history and blamed political evil on individual morality rather than on the structure of society. They lacked faith in institutions of political representation.[38]

Thus far the pluralist argument is that McCarthyism and agrarian radicalism had similar preoccupations and were analogous political movements. Their appeal was not necessarily to the same groups of people but to people similarly discontented with industrialization and with an industrial society.[39] The movements might be similar in political character but different in specific social support. Thus Lipset points out that there is no authoritarian appeal per se; left- and right-wing authoritarian movements make similar appeals but not to the same types of people.[40]

This might suggest that Populist left-wing extremism and McCarthyite right-wing extremism had different bases of social support. Nevertheless, the pluralists argue that the same social strata supported McCarthyism and agrarian radicalism. These were movements not of the Right and Left but of the Center — that is, McCarthyism and agrarian radicalism had a middle-class base in common. Moreover, within the middle class, argues Lipset, isolated and poorly educated groups are particularly prone to support extremist movements.[41] The pluralists see agrarian radical roots in McCarthyism because the movements were *petit-bourgeois*. They received the support of the small, independent, old middle class.

Martin Trow discovered disproportionate support for McCarthy in Bennington, Vermont, among those opposed to big business and big labor. He called this view nineteenth century liberalism, relating it, in good pluralist fashion, to Populist fears of concentrated industrial wealth and power. Moreover, the social stratum in Bennington most sympathetic to McCarthyism was the small business class. In nineteenth century America, the vast majority of small businessmen were farmers. The small businessmen in Bennington, particularly those with a "nineteenth century liberal" ideology, seemed to prefer an older, rural America in which individual self-help had a more direct meaning than it does in a bureaucratized society.[42] Trow's findings suggest that those supporting agrarian radical movements moved with their ideology from Populism to McCarthyism.

In the pluralist view, certain specific similarities between McCarthyism and agrarian radicalism are due to the rural, small middle-class basis they shared in common. The movements were anti-British, anti-Wall Street, anti-international bankers, anti-eastern aristocracy. They were pro-German. They stood for the moral absolutes associated with agrarian virtue, such as personal integrity and religion. They were against bigness, favoring equal opportunity and the small producer. Calling upon the traditions of a rural, individualistic America, McCarthyism and agrarian radicalism threatened in the name of the popular will to destroy the pluralist society in which they lived.[43]

According to the pluralists, agrarian radicalism sought to reverse the processes of industrialization that would make America safe for democracy. McCarthyism challenged industrial society in the name of simpler, "purer" rural values. The specific concerns — economic hardship in the Populist case, communism for McCarthy — simply shielded the underlying hatreds and fears unleashed by McCarthyite and Populist appeals. The pluralists hardly favor outlawing such movements as McCarthyism and Populism, but they do locate these movements substantially outside the bounds of legitimate political controversy. These are movements radically challenging the rational, pluralist society.

In the abstract, the pluralist approach may seem compelling. But the conclusions of the present study fail to support it. Thus:

1. McCarthyism received the significant support of no social groups peculiarly inclined to support agrarian radicalism.

2. Populism was a mass movement but (*a*) its program and rhetoric were not anti-industrial and (*b*) its character was democratic, particularly in comparison with the industrializing "groups" that confronted it.

3. Moral indignation is not a peculiar feature of pre-New Deal reform movements but rather an essential element both of American politics in general and traditional conservatism in particular.

4. Reform moralism depended on and was related to practical proposals for social reform.

5. McCarthyism contained elements opposed to an industrial, cosmopolitan society, but these "mass" elements (*a*) composed the Senator's elite and not his mass following and (*b*) point toward McCarthyite roots not in agrarian radicalism but in traditional conservatism.

6. Unlike agrarian radicalism McCarthyism made little impact on the mass level; it influenced few voters and had its greatest success among (pluralist?) elites.

7. McCarthy's support at the popular level was the result of the cold and Korean wars in particular far more than anti-industrial sentiments and authoritarian preoccupations in general.

The present study finds little support for a simple "anti-industrial" interpretation of McCarthyism and agrarian radicalism. It fails to uncover significant agrarian radical roots in McCarthyism. These conclusions in themselves hardly invalidate pluralism as a whole. The theory is both too general and too diffuse for that. But the conclusions do suggest that pluralism, without significant refinements, distorts rather than illuminates our understanding of American politics. It is particularly ironic that pluralism, partially stimulated and rendered plausible by McCarthyism, fails to comprehend the Senator and his following.

LOCKEAN MORALISM
AND CONSERVATIVE IDEOLOGY

I

The pluralists find the roots of McCarthyism in left-wing radical movements that preceded the New Deal. These movements allegedly shared with McCarthyism a common approach to the world — one that was ideological in a particular rural and "populist" sense. This argument rests on a view of the rational and instrumental nature of industrial society. It rests on the belief that in pre-New Deal America a moralistic agrarian radicalism confronted instrumental and pragmatic classes allied with industrialization. This perspective misrepresents the nature of the industrializing ethic and therefore of the American liberal consensus because it attempts to split apart moral and pragmatic concerns. The bearers of industrialization were not instrumental automatons in the abstract but particular Americans. Both because they shared the Lockean ethic and because they desired to defend their positions of power, these men were no less moralistic than their opponents. Populism was hardly a moralistic flight from an environment in which everyone else was concerned with facts. The movement made an effort to come to grips with the transformation of American society. Simply because Populism faced the changes America was undergoing while other groups in part denied or repressed them, it is not therefore to blame for the more desperate political responses like McCarthyism.

Americans had drawn sustenance from a tradition of pre-industrial harmony, which functioned as myth where it was not fact. Industrialization created a new society which challenged important tenets of this liberal consensus. The transformation of America had an impact across the political spectrum; it affected everyone. The point is not that some groups were more moralistic in their response to industrialization and some more pragmatic (although there were often significant differences of degree along this dimension) but that moral and practical concerns interacted with and supported each other.

At times, certain groups seriously question the possibility of returning to the original consensus by any but the most desperate measures. The result is a politics of frustration in which the authoritarian elements of worldly asceticism become dominant. McCarthyism is the obvious example. In McCarthy's world, communism posed an imminent danger to American values; a threat requiring moral intransigence was being met instead, he asserted, by pussy-footing and compromise. Those who praised McCarthy as a moral savior revealed that the Senator satisfied their craving for values in a world where the old morality had seemed irrelevant. The content of a liberal public interest is fragile and uncertain. When it does not seem to provide meaningful pragmatic standards, the appeal to it may become moral in a frantic attempt to discover specific guides to action which are not obviously present. The failure of American moralism to provide operational standards thus results in moral absolutism. McCarthy's "solution" to this problem was hardly an attractive one; but the fear of a disintegrating consensus is endemic in American politics. Because the reformers also had to face this problem hardly makes their solutions the same as his.

Since I have used the terms "moralism" and "pragmatism,"

often employed in discussions of American politics, it is well to be as precise as possible about their meaning. As used here, "moralism" and "pragmatism" derive from the Weberian distinction between *wert-rationalität* and *zweck-rationalität*. A moral, or consummatory, outlook invests all decisions and activities with ultimate moral significance. An instrumental, or pragmatic, orientation shrinks the sphere of moral significance. Questions which had been moral become technical. If a pragmatic orientation stresses efficiency, results, getting the most output for the least input, a consummatory outlook rejects immoral activities and judges all actions by their intrinsic value in contributing to the moral worth of the individual. Politically, those with a pragmatic orientation are more willing to compromise since they do not perceive fundamental values to be at stake in immediate decisions. Whereas pragmatism tends to subordinate long-run consequences to immediate results, moralism looks always to the ultimate significance of the act. For example, farmers may decide between hoes on the basis of which will produce the most food for the least work or on the basis of which is more pleasing to the gods.[1]

In pluralist analysis, the consensus in a nonindustrial society is consummatory whereas that in an industrial society is pragmatic. A rural society may be politically stable, but since the stability is based on shared values, a challenge to that society will result in moralistic political conflict. Industrial society, on the other hand, contains political conflict within pragmatic grounds. Since reform movements are products of rural society, the argument continues, they will be moralistic; whatever the differences between Populism and progressivism, this fact unites them. True, progressivism was strong in cities, but its supporters looked backward to disappearing rural values. Therefore, implicit in pluralist interpretations is the view that reform movements and McCarthyism were moralistic rebellions against a pragmatic consensus[2] — or that moralism and pragmatism represent distinct halves of the American consensus, the one rural and radical, the other urban and industrial.

But there is a great difficulty in this view. The pluralists assert that politics and values in the United States have not changed essentially since the early days of the republic.[3] How is this possible if rural and industrial societies produce such a different politics? Moreover, if the rural American consensus was moralistic, why did such a rapid industrialization meet with so little opposition here compared to continental Europe?

One way out of these contradictions is to join other critics of pluralism in denying the notion of an operating American consensus.[4] In the view adopted here, however, a consensus has indeed configured American politics — a consensus which not only included the agrarian radicals but clearly dominated their approach. But that consensus is not simply pragmatic, nor does it contain moral and pragmatic elements in discrete compartments. Political tendencies in America cannot choose to be either consummatory or instrumental; they differ from each other in the way they combine the two orientations.

The Lockean Consensus

Alexis de Tocqueville, noting the absence of fundamental conflict in America, pointed also to the reason when he wrote, "As the United States was colonized by men holding equal rank, there is as yet no natural or permanent disagreement between the interests of its different inhabitants."[5] "Born equal," Americans did not have to overthrow a dominant feudalism. In *The Liberal Tradition in America,* Louis Hartz has developed from Tocqueville's basic insight a thoroughgoing, creative analysis of American political culture.[6] Hartz comes from an anti-Turner tradition and explicitly rejects the frontier explanation of American development. Yet his own theory, like Turner's, focuses on the American break with established institutions, procedures,

35

and hierarchies. Hartz has argued that the absence of feudal institutions in America created both a relative equality of condition and a fundamental social homogeneity. There was in America no extended family, little landed aristocracy, no peasant class, no nobility, no national established church, no hereditary officer caste.

Corresponding to American social hegemony, Hartz argues, went a consensus on "Lockean liberalism," produced by the middle-class character of America and by the absence of a struggle against feudalism. Hartz never defines Lockean liberalism precisely, but he clearly means the dominance of notions of individualism, property, natural rights, equality before the law and equality of opportunity, and the absence of strong attachments to social institutions of a *gemeinschaft* character. This was a society of individualists who lacked an emotional and moral attachment to prescriptive social institutions. The aim was mastery of the environment, with success the result of individual effort not special privilege.

In this glorification of means, efficiency seemed to become an end in itself. If Jefferson preferred rural capitalists to industrial ones, the ideology to which he subscribed preferred successful capitalists, whether from farms or cities. The American consensus was thus more instrumental than its rural roots might imply. Given this consensus, the ease with which industrialization could occur is clear. Prior to the actual fact of industrialization, the Lockean entrepreneurial ethic called it forth.

When in the face of industrialization, urbanization, and immigration social classes that looked like European social classes began to appear, the power of the Lockean consensus meant that they did not act like European classes. In America, both big business and a rising labor movement became assimilated into the liberal tradition. The uprooted, conservative European peasants who migrated to European cities produced a politics of revolutionary socialism. For those who settled in American cities, that same uprooting

36

migration from farms to cities resulted in a narrow, self-concerned machine politics. Lacking corporate feudal traditions, America had difficulty producing a corporate class consciousness. No *gemeinschaft* feudal stand meant no *gemeinschaft* capitalist or working class. In a Lockean society, the dream of individual success made common class action both difficult and apparently unnecessary. Hartz' analysis suggests the importance of a consensus in muting social conflict. With no basic conflict between powerful classes and traditional institutions in America, there was relatively little opposition to industrial change. Although the social and economic homogeneity of the early republic became diluted, the consensus that it had produced remained powerful.

This consensus dominated political approaches that at first blush may seem quite different. The American tradition of log-rolling and horse-trading for narrow political favors, symbolized by the machine, has a long and honorable tradition. Such a politics is viable only where individuals are satisfied with small favors. A narrowly pragmatic politics is not a substitute for ultimate values; rather it depends on agreement about those values.[7]

Political log-rollers are not the only ones in America whose appeal to facts makes sense only against a consensual background. When conservatives pointed to the self-made man and the material benefits allegedly brought by free-wheeling capitalism, they appealed to an audience that cared above all about the ability to acquire property. Sharing capitalist values, they could be influenced by the facts of capitalist success. On the other hand, reformers could disagree with those facts, and that disagreement was also a powerful political weapon. If conservatives had their "facts," reformers made use of a different set. Consider the Brandeis brief, persuasive only in a country where the disagreement was over facts and not over values. The New Deal was the ultimate in reform pragmatism. Since Roosevelt was not destroying capitalism but saving it — and businessmen, despite their

rhetoric, knew the difference between Roosevelt and Marx —
he could experiment with reforms and have his experiments
accepted.

Moreover, because ends were universally accepted, appeals to the public interest could be successful. An appeal to
the public interest is a moral appeal; where there is an implicit consensus on the public interest, it becomes practical
as well. To defend the natural right to acquire property was
not an alternative to pragmatic politics but a powerful political weapon itself. If conservatives used this appeal to attack
social legislation, reformers used it to attack a society in
which property rights were becoming restricted to the few. In
both cases, the appeal was to commonly held values, to a
public interest about which there was basic agreement.

The Moral-Material Paradox

Commitment to material success is a shared American
value, which can therefore serve as a moral standard.
Materialism also has moral underpinnings of a more thoroughgoing character.

The nature of this moral-material paradox has never been
spelled out better than in *The Protestant Ethic and the Spirit
of Capitalism*. Weber gave the name "worldly asceticism" to
the synthesis of moralism and pragmatism, idealism, and
materialism, found in the Protestant ethic. He argued that
the psychological mechanisms unleashed by Calvinist other-
worldly notions of a "calling," original sin, and predestination
promoted concern with worldly activities. According to
Weber, Calvinism required the individual constantly to prove
himself in the world. For the Calvinist to create the conviction of his own salvation, he had to do away with all
spontaneous enjoyment and subject his life to a systematic
self-control. A harsh rejection of all worldly pleasure thus
resulted in systematic worldly activity. The deep-rooted
Calvinist moralism caused a thoroughgoing materialism.

38

Weber's analysis and the consequent association of the Protestant ethic with industrializing capitalism are familiar historical themes. But their relevance to the American Lockean ethic must be stressed. Here is a transcendent, consummatory ethic of the subordination of material means to still further means. Worldly asceticism gives a moral justification to sacrifice, saving, and accumulation in the material world. It orients the individual to mastery of the material environment rather than to spontaneous enjoyment of it. Worldly asceticism provides a moral impetus for instrumental action.[8] In part, it is the presence of worldly asceticism in America that has turned potential into actual abundance. Just as the instrumental character of the American consensus impelled industrialization, so also did Protestant moralism.

But important characteristics of the Protestant ethic are not found undiluted in America. According to Weber, the original Protestant ethic had "a fundamental antagonism to sensuous culture of all kinds." Its individualism was of a "disillusioned and pessimistically inclined" character.[9] Moreover, Weber's description of Puritan ideology suggests its authoritarian character. The attempts to punish others for their sins and systematically to control desire, experience, and spontaneity reminds one of modern descriptions of the authoritarian personality.*

It is well to be reminded that American individualism, asserting the power of the will, is threatened by real individual difference and needs to master to feel secure. But at no time in American history has this been the whole story. As long as Americans could feel that the society they lived in belonged to them and was undivided by basic conflicts, they could feel less insecure. Confidence in the existence of external limits mitigated the need for mastery.

---

* Weber's treatment of the authoritarian theme is only implicit; Sven Ranulf's *Moral Indignation and Middle Class Psychology* gives extensive evidence of the authoritarian character of Puritan motivation and behavior.[10]

In Puritan New England, a community united by the reality of God provided a sort of peace for its members. In eighteenth- and nineteenth-century America, God became shadowy, replaced by more worldly preoccupations. The Americans of the Enlightenment and the democratic revolution still found limits on their striving in the world, but they relied on the spontaneous workings of society and on the artificial harmony created by political institutions to maintain these limits. And these spontaneous mechanisms instead destroyed the limits by promoting industrialization. The nature of these limits and the significance of their disappearance must be understood.

The Limits

Locke himself began by limiting a man's wealth to the goods he could use before they spoiled. Money, since it remained unspoiled indefinitely, destroyed this limit.[11] The American Lockeans had others: in their world, the nature of material resources prescribed the money any one man could make. Industrialization, corporations, and the revolution in technology destroyed that limit. Unchecked political and economic power had no place in a Lockean world: equal and independent producers flourished. Thanks to perfect competition, no individual could determine the conditions in which his fellows labored. The workings of the market prevented not only the unequal distribution of power but also the unequal accumulation of wealth. Those in disadvantaged occupations could move to new ones — an opportunity reinforced, symbolically if not otherwise, by the frontier. Indeed, the frontier itself provided a goal for instrumental activity. There was, after all, a continent to conquer. But as the continent was settled, the significance of this limit vanished. And the world of perfect competition, inexact a description of early America as it was, appeared totally foreign to the post-

Civil War world of giant corporations, urban poverty, and bureaucracy.

The most important guarantee of a society of independent producers was the ethic of self-help. It was not simply that one had to make more money; he had to make it through his own efforts. Liberty, because it meant the ability to help oneself, was synonymous with power. This followed Locke, for whom the essential characteristic of liberty was the power to acquire property. Although self-help hardly eliminated striving for success, it did provide a specific method of striving, a standard. But just as the limit on wealth provided little defense against a time in which limitless fortunes could be made, so the Lockean ideology did not foresee the time when self-help would not be the most efficient way to make money.

The limits on striving in early America were self-enforcing and self-evident; this was their sustaining and defeating quality. Liberalism rejected a state mechanism to enforce those values and relied instead on the American consensus, a constitutionally created political harmony, and the spontaneous actions of society. Liberalism did not reject a notion of justice; it rather assumed that facts could supply values. Thus the Jeffersonians believed that work and activity could justify themselves. They believed that the material world provided a realm of order, that facts had a transcendent reality, "that men's lives might be peaceful, orderly, and prosperous, even while there seemed no final hierarchy or systematic relation among ideas."[12]

From Jefferson to Brandeis to Thurman Arnold this reliance on facts has both assumed an underlying agreement on values and avoided the need for an inquiry into the nature of the correct values. In effect, liberal unanimity has at least partially validated the assumption that facts could supply values. But the peculiar absence of qualitative content in liberalism has made the avoidance of an inquiry into values all the more necessary. In other societies, religious or tradi-

41

tional norms provide substantive common standards. The liberal consensus defends individual rights but does not provide clear-cut obligations. The consensus works only if its content is not examined too closely for specific guides to action. Thus the result of American values has been a reliance on facts, on practicality — a self-conscious pragmatism.

Pragmatism was so central because the Lockean limits on instrumentalism — perfect competition, self-help, the primitive character of technology — were unenforceable. In Jeffersonian days, efficiency told the Lockean liberal how to help himself, and self-help told him how to be efficient. But with industrialization the symbiotic relationship between these values ended. In an urban, industrial, bureaucratic society the Lockean had to face the choice of abandoning self-help for a success achieved through bureaucratic means or maintaining personal control of his own destiny at the probable cost of success.

The Protestant ethic had located rationality in the individual; each person made his own decisions. The bureaucratization of society — again Weber's analysis is crucial — usurped rationality from individual control. It now became rational to follow orders; one obeyed the commands of a rational hierarchy, not the dictates of his own reason.[13] Was it more important to earn money in a bureaucratic corporation or to be your own boss? Could the bureaucratic state apparatus legitimately act in the service of individual independence? In short, was the original Lockean consensus relevant to the problems of an industrial society? This was the dilemma with which industrialization confronted American politics. For if the consensus had lost its relevance, the country would lose its mission, its reason for being, and its stability.

But Americans are hardly a people desperate over the loss of their past. Everyone knows they believe in the future instead, exhibiting a remarkably insistent optimism. This

optimism, an Enlightenment addition to the original Protestant ethic,* has been crucial in American politics. But it
is worth remembering that Americans locate their faith not
only in the future but in the past as well. The American
belief in progress depends on the prior assumption that the
Lockean consensus of the early Republic will continue to be
relevant in the changing society.

This confidence inhibits the punitive consequences of
jealousy and frustration.[15] Optimism thus allows a relaxation
of moral standards; it permits a pragmatic experimentation.
That is not all. The optimism produces a relaxation based not
only on experimentation but on moral certainty as well. This
certainty is that republican virtues will not be destroyed. In
Jacksonian times, the reality was close enough to those virtues that hope for their unadulterated return did not seem
absurd. In the progressive period, Enlightenment optimism
fostered a faith that basic changes in the character of America would end with a return to republican virtue.[16] The certainty that the old values would not be destroyed allowed a
reliance on spontaneity not countenanced by the original
worldly asceticism. Optimism that the moral consensus was
in operation relaxed the frenzied attempt to impose it.

But a politics that depends on optimism is not the most
secure ground for civilized values. Optimism may easily become embittered in an imperfect world, seeking scapegoats
on which to vent its rage. Hence the search for an American
tradition emancipated from consensual preoccupations and
optimistic visions. Cannot one imagine a politics that ap-
plauds the changes brought by industrialization and adjusts
to the "realities" of contemporary life? Many pluralists, for

* Contrast the Weberian capitalist — a cautious, pessimistic, rational calculator — with the nineteenth-century American entre-
preneur. Whether petty frontier capitalist before the Civil War or
robber baron afterward, this man was an optimistic, speculative,
daring adventurer.[14]

whom political optimism and dreams of a lost golden age are peculiarly reform vices, have turned to the conservative tradition.

II

During the McCarthyite period, such pluralists as Shils, Herberg, and Parsons discovered virtues in conservatism that they had heretofore minimized. Because of their closeness to the centers of power and their commitment to the status quo, conservatives were said to possess certain valuable political properties. As men in power, they had no illusions about mass democracy and did not make destructive attacks on existing institutions and elites. They had a recognition of limits, a sense of sin, an antiutopian and practical character not shared by the agrarian radicals. Moreover, the political conservatives in America formed the best educated group and were highly integrated members of society. They had the final virtue, in the pluralist view, of being the bearers of industrialization.

The purpose here is not to write another study of conservatism; several excellent ones are available.[17] Nor is it proposed to examine conservative political practice or the impact of industrialization and the bureaucratization of industry upon conservative ideology.[18] But if the pluralists have reinterpreted the reform tradition in the light of its proto-McCarthyism, American conservatism has benefited from a more charitable neglect. How does conservative ideology fare by the standards applied to Populist thought? Could McCarthyism have grown in traditional conservative soil?

The Federalists

Although our main concern is with the conservative contemporaries of agrarian radicalism, it is well to begin with the

Federalists. Because they do not appear to have shared Jeffersonian illusions about democracy and human nature, their stock has risen in recent years. The Federalists are said to be realistic, pessimistic, and constitutional rather than moralistic, optimistic, and plebiscitarian. Here, apparently, is an alternative to Lockeanism.

Only the most schematic treatment of the Madisonian-Federalist tradition is possible here. We shall argue first that the thinking of the founders falls clearly within the Lockean ideology; second that Federalist-style realism provides questionable security for constitutional rights; and third that the very sobriety with which the Federalists viewed democracy destroyed Federalism in American politics.

It is particularly important not to bypass the Federalists because their political outlook resembles that of the pluralists. Here is the same fear of an uprising of the masses, the same suspicion of democracy. Federalists and pluralists alike place a considerable reliance on responsible leadership. Both groups of thinkers are pessimistic about human nature and optimistic about the power of institutions to check and control human beings. Both are preoccupied with the importance of balance. Both rely heavily on a pluralism of interests and institutions. Both express powerful nationalistic sentiments while asserting the primacy and legitimacy of (mainly economic) individual self-interest. Both insist that political institutions must be rooted in social conflict, yet desire those institutions to stand apart from and mediate social conflict.*

* Many of the same dilemmas that inform pluralist writing were already encountered by the Federalists. Was Madison, for example, content to rely simply on the conflict of self-interested factions to achieve the public interest? The answer to this is by no means as clear-cut as a modern reading of *Federalist No. 10* would suggest. Adams, to take another instance, believed that political institutions should and must reflect distinct social classes. Yet in relying on a strong president above the battle, he sought to escape from the consequences of his social determinism of politics. Cf. Adams' *Thoughts on Government* and his *Defense of the Constitutions of Government of the United States of America*, in the *Works of John*

But for all the pessimism and institutional bias of Madison and the Federalists, they were hardly outside the Lockean tradition. Certainly their thinking bore little resemblance to that of European conservatives. Consider only: their search for an abstract and universal human nature; their belief in individual natural rights; their view of human nature in terms of rationalism and self-interest; their desire to limit power by external rather than internal checks; their analysis of the artificial nature of government; their faith in institution and constitution making; their mechanistic reliance on balance; their antipathy toward monarchy; their attack on social pretensions and feudal institutions; their lack of confidence in tradition; and their failure to treat America as a unique, organic, historical entity (as Burke, for example, treated England).[19]

It should be clear that the Federalists no more endorsed a politics of totally self-interested pragmatism than they shared the outlook of European conservatism. Like Locke, the founders believed in natural laws that placed limits on individual behavior and protected natural rights. They believed in "the permanent and aggregate interests of the community." The Madisonian-Federalist political perspective was distinctly Lockean.

If the Federalists adhered to a Lockean ideology, they cannot be the source of a nonideological strand in the American political tradition. On the other hand, if the Federalists were within the Lockean consensus, then their thinking may be relevant for future American politics. Is there not a viable tradition here which transcends narrow self-interest and concerns itself with ultimate values but does not exhibit the moralistic and democratic excesses of much of American politics?

The Federalists, however, were as implicated in consen-

Adams, Charles Francis Adams (ed.) (Boston, Mass.: Little, Brown, 1851–1865), Vol. 4, pp. 196–197; Vol. 6, pp. 64–66. We have already discussed, in Chapter 1, the pluralist version of these same difficulties.

sual preoccupations as the Jeffersonians. They equally feared the existence of irreconcilable conflict, but while Jefferson located his faith in the land and in the moral instincts of Americans, the Federalists located theirs in institutional and social arrangements. Rather than substituting pessimism for optimism, they simply transferred their optimism from people to institutions.[20]

Suppose, as Adams wrote, that a constitution really had to control "lions, [who] young or old, will not be bound by cobwebs." Suppose the class conflict in America really was as serious as the Federalists believed. It would then be the sheerest naïveté to hope that institutional arrangements alone could save the country from destructive individual and class conflict.[21] And the consequences of this desperate reliance on institutions would not be salutary. Those who fear human nature and political conflict tend to rely on institutional stability to preserve a constitutional regime. This combination of fear and faith often leads to repressive political acts. Institutions, so fragile and important, must be preserved at all costs. Thus the Federalists, fearing that opposition and political conflict threatened social stability, adopted such repressive measures as the Alien and Sedition Acts.

The punitive consequences of frustrated optimism were not alien to Federalist thinking. Sympathy with established institutions and fear of their dissolution can have repressive consequences; subsequent conservative practice made this clear, and echoes find their way into pluralist thought itself.[22]

Conservative "Populism"

In one way, however — in their attitudes toward democracy — the Federalists differed decisively from later American conservatives. The pluralists argue that agrarian radicals stressed the virtues of the people and attacked the independence of established elites. This weakened the power and authority of the elites and made leadership dependent on the erratic and irrational sentiment of masses of people. By attacking elite autonomy, the argument continues, the agrarian radicals undermined representative institutions. In his appeal to the people against constituted procedures and authorities, McCarthy inherited and exploited this "populist" tradition.

When agrarian radicals are compared with Federalists, they are clearly more "populist." But the Federalists eliminated themselves from political importance precisely because they were unwilling to accommodate themselves to democratic optimism.[23] The Federalists attempted to base their political rule on European ideas of deference. They failed to understand that in America there was no aristocracy to make such an ideology plausible. In their fear of the mob, in their effort to distinguish themselves from the common people, they simply made conservatives targets for the democracy triumphant in liberal America.

The Populists did not inaugurate "populism"; nor did they inherit a Jacksonian tradition which the Whigs had opposed. Whatever the merit of a noblesse oblige conservatism with corporate values and a tradition of high culture, conservatism in nineteenth-century America was not of that character.[24] The Whigs began to learn the lesson of the Federalist defeat. A conservative strategy that emphasized class distinctions could not succeed, but a conservatism based on American homogeneity had dazzling prospects. For, to paraphrase Jefferson, if we are all democrats, we are all capitalists as well. When the conservatives, reeling from the consequences of Federalist doctrine, overemphasized equality, this was not only a powerful political weapon but also an essential one. The real American "new conservatives" neither sought an aristocracy where none existed nor emphasized a genuine distinction between upper and lower middle classes. They rather submerged themselves among "the people," for only in this way could they dominate.[25] In pre-Civil War state politics, Whig and Jacksonian rhetoric was almost indistinguishable. According to both groups, "They and their party represented 'the people'; their opponents represented the 'aristocracy.' "[26]

Moreover, if the conservatives were "populistic" before the Civil War, they exploited the ideology of democratic capitalism even more successfully afterward. Carnegie's *Triumphant Democracy,* even to the title, well captures the flavor of this "populistic" conservatism. The dedication is "to the country which has removed the stigma of inferiority which his native land saw proper to impress upon him at birth, and has made him in the estimation of its great laws as well as in his own estimation (much the more important consideration), the peer of any human being who draws the breath of life, be he pope, kaiser, priest, or king — henceforth the subject of no man, but a free man, a citizen."[27]

Capitalist ideology in Lockean America could not surround property with Burkean prescription or family tradition; it had instead to defend it as the product of individual activity and personal accumulation. Special privileges and special advantages, whatever the facts, must be denied in the theory.[28] Reformers were called socialists, their sins were aristocratic — passing "class legislation" to give special privileges to those who could not help themselves. Any effort to treat people as if they were members of distinct groups implied class legislation; it implied as well a group or class conflict which could only undermine conservative hegemony. For that hegemony was based on a theory of a mass of striving individualists united only as "the people," with equal opportunity for all and special privileges for none. Reformers did not create a new social theory; they rather confronted democratic capitalist theory with an alleged reality of inequality and privilege. A "populistic" ideology defending the interests of the mass of people against the intrusions of organized groups was not a Populist invention but a Lockean precept.

One finds prominent in neither conservative nor reform rhetoric the kind of general defense of group conflict so important to the pluralists. The group approach is hardly alien to American politics. Politics as the clash of group interests has been defended in America at least since *Federalist No. 10.* This defense has been important to observers of the American political scene. In a basic sense, it has been important to participants as well; most groups do not attempt to suppress their opponents but accept the idea of legitimate conflict within a consensus. More specifically, the notion of legitimate conflict has been important for those challenging the status quo since it defends their right to organize. It has been important for established groups since it legitimizes their existence. Nevertheless, the acceptance of group diversity and interest conflict has not been the rallying cry of political debate. In the day-to-day process of winning adherents and discrediting opponents, appeals to the people against "vested interests" or "outside agitators" are more effective.

With the democratic consensus, "populistic" appeals to the people were a pragmatic political weapon. These appeals could attack the status quo; they could also defend it as when Carnegie demonstrated the sacredness of American institutions by the popular support for them. "Populistic" appeals could support broad movements, but also narrow ones. Thus in more recent times, the ideology of "grass roots democracy" defended local Farm Bureau influence in the administration of TVA.[29] And as that example suggests, "populistic" appeals could be made not only by the generally deprived but also by local or national elites that opposed government action. Often, as with TVA, government action poses a threat to the power of locally entrenched elites. Locally powerful groups then call for "decentralization," for decision making by the people in the locality. In its rhetoric of faith in the people, the language is "populistic." But to accept the ideology as a statement of reality is simply to follow the wishes of its propounders. The reality is not democratic participation and popular control. The cry for "grass roots democracy" also does not increase the power of destructive mass movements. It rather functions to protect the power and conservative interests of locally powerful groups. Thus the contemporary conservative cry of returning government to the people takes on meaning within a conservative tradition, the tradition itself configured by the Lockean consensus.[30]

Conservatives and reformers shared a basic "populism," but they did not have identical beliefs. Before the Civil War, Whigs favored federal and state action to aid entrepreneurial effort, and this was the general practice in the states. On the other hand, the Jacksonians developed as pure a version of laissez-faire as the country had yet witnessed.[31] Throughout this period, the agrarian interests defended local sovereignty and were suspicious of a powerful central government. After the war, although they received immense favors from the state, Republicans adopted the agrarian democratic ideology.[32] Their new position led them to a view of limited government. John Forrest Dillon responded to Populist agitation with the commentary that by a written constitution the people had "effectively protected themselves against themselves." He cited Burke's admonition that the people needed a restraint against their passions.[33] Agrarian radicalism did not present such views. One could argue that because conservatives defended established institutions they understood the importance of limited government and constitutional restraints. But at the same time conservatives denied the legitimacy of groups that opposed the status quo and attacked all positive state action in absolutist terms. Is it plausible to find in conservative attacks on "populistic" legislation and mob rule any insight into the virtues of shared power, any tradition of limited government?[34]

In attacking the income tax, Rufus Choate revealed the concrete purpose of the defense of limited government as well as the paradox of conservative anti-"populism." Choate excoriated the income tax as an infringement of "the people's" reliance on constitutional safeguards at the same time that he called income tax principles as ". . . communistic, socialistic — what shall I call them — populistic as ever have been addressed to any political assembly in the world."[35]

"Populism" thus occupies a legitimate if ambiguous place in the conservative tradition. Conservative "populism" is not meant to insure permanent government by the mass of people. It functions rather to stimulate popular support for conservative proposals — support that may involve the direct intervention of the populace in the political process through letter writing, meetings, and similar activities. Often a "populist" ideology specifically serves to disguise the fact that its main promulgators have positions of importance, particularly in local arenas. Conservatives use populistic rhetoric to defend the power of entrenched groups. On the other hand, they use a pluralist-sounding rhetoric of limited government to attack other groups and the legitimacy of their demands. If a confusion between "populist" and pluralist politics is troubling in this analysis, the confusion is in the politics itself.

Conservative Moralism

As conservatism combined "populistic" and pluralistic elements, so also it united moralism and pragmatism. Conservative politics in the agrarian radical period was characterized by considerable shrewdness and extraordinary success. Business obtained from government railroad grants, tariffs, municipal franchises, and a host of other particular and practical benefits. At the same time, it used an abstract social Darwinist ideology to oppose the political demands of other groups. Social Darwinism legitimized the existing order, in which only the unfit had not survived. It explained inequality as the result of individual effort, not differential prestige, power, privilege, wealth, or luck. It demonstrated that changes in the existing order through state action were

52

both impossible and dangerous. If this was an abstract and moralistic ideology, it was nevertheless a practical one indeed.

Conservative moralistic and extremist rhetoric reveals itself best in attacks on reformers and reform legislation. For apocalyptic views of the consequences of opposition success (allegedly a peculiarly Populist trait), consider only the dire warnings of the Supreme Court and its allies about the effects of social legislation. According to the prominent lawyer William D. Guthrie, "Public Policy is the deadly weapon of socialism and communism. . . . If the paternal theory of government is not checked, the worst forms of social legislation will breed under the superstitution so rampant that legislation is a sovereign cure-all for all socials ills."[36] According to Justice Day, if Congress could prohibit the interstate shipment of goods produced by child labor, "all freedom of commerce will be at an end, and the power of the State over local matters may be eliminated and thus our system of government be practically destroyed."[37]

Even if particular conservative political positions were defensible, a general apocalyptic outlook characterized many conservatives. Similarly, without defending the social legislation opposed by conservatism, one can note the deleterious effect of the general conservative view of government. If "populistic" appeals undermine the possibility of a responsible political elite, so also does an ideology which opposes state action. Before the Civil War this antagonism to legislation was more prevalent among agrarian radicals than conservatives. But reformers like the Populists, realizing that individual effort, even aided by local government, was powerless to help them, turned to the national state. Now the antistate position was taken up by conservatives.

Through the use of arguments based on natural law and stringent individualism, conservatives attacked the state. The fact that industrial capitalists were contributing to the bureaucratization of society did not prevent them from attacking state bureaucracy. A tradition running from the post-Civil War conservatives to McCarthyism and contemporary right-wing Republicanism denies that the state is a legitimate agency for social action. This particular tradition is probably far more important than a tradition of direct democracy in undermining popular confidence in state action. After all, the Populist tradition included programs for state action.

The Populist attack on existing politicians was matched by conservative contempt for all politicians. Such an attitude follows naturally from a distrust of state action. As Carnegie put it, "Oh, those grand, immutable all-wise laws of natural forces, how perfectly they would work if human legislators would only let them alone!"[38] According to Carnegie, the best men did not go into politics.

Conservatives were not noticeably less utopian or more imbued with a sense of limits than their radical opponents. The Horatio Alger myth does not reveal a sense of the limits the world places on achievement. An acceptance of the unchangeable is not prominent in it. The triumph of conservatism required an ideology minimizing the obstacles to fantastic success.[39] Nor did this utopianism stop where politics began. Conservatives in America had an antipolitical utopia in which all the supposedly conservative virtues of compromise, acceptance of conflict, and recognition of limits were made unnecessary by the invisible hand. In Carnegie's words,

> When the Democracy obtains sway throughout the earth the nations will become friends and brothers, instead of being as now the prey of the monarchial and aristocratic ruling classes, and always warring with each other; standing armies and warships will be of the past, and men will then begin to destroy custom-houses as relics of a barbarous monarchial age, not altogether from the low plane of economic gain or loss, but strongly impelled thereto from the higher standpoint of the brotherhood of man.[40]

In a speech attacking Populism, businessman William Cornwall told his audience of a "blissful moment" aboard ship.

> Now there is one other thing I think which would produce the
> same feeling of relief and peace in the mind of a businessman,
> and that is to wake up some fine morning and find Congress
> had adjourned for ten years.[41]

If the frustrations of a utopian politics had anything to do
with McCarthyism, the movement does not thereby avoid a
connection with the traditional conservative wing of American
politics.

Conservative attacks on agrarian radicals matched the
conservative rhetoric of antistate extremism. Normal, functioning, integrated members of society greeted the agrarian
radical movements with nativist hysteria. Respectable conservatives, members of the eastern elite, saw in Populism a
foreign conspiracy. After Bryan's defeat in 1896, Henry
Cabot Lodge wrote,

> When this [Democratic] platform was first published, these
> clauses struck the country as merely wild declarations put
> forward without consideration in the hope of catching certain
> bodies of voters. But as the campaign proceeded, it became
> clear to everyone that, instead of being a collection of reckless
> and crazy utterances without cohesion and plan, it was a well-
> drawn and carefully thought out scheme based on socialistic
> and anarchistic theories imported from Europe and involving,
> if successful, nothing short of a revolution in our form of
> government.[42]

In their own states, the agrarian radicals encountered
similar rhetoric. In Kansas the Vincent family, publishers of
a radical newspaper, were called "A Secret Band of Conspirators" through whom "the Henious (*sic*) and Terrible
Monster of Anarchy Rears its Hydra Head."[43] The conservatives attacked the Populists as "outsiders," who were destroying the traditional forms of morality and government.
Populism, the Non-Partisan League, and other agrarian radical movements were the socialistic destroyers of the family,

55

religion, and property. The Non-Partisan League was accused of being a tool of international socialism and the IWW. League leaders were called carpetbaggers. They were charged with advocating free love and desiring to return the saloon to North Dakota. When the League wrote a new North Dakota constitution, it omitted a section extolling "intelligence, patriotism, integrity, and morality." One League opponent saw this as "the malicious cut of a poisoned dagger of treasured licentiousness held in the secret hand of disloyalty and hate; that the hand that penned these lines and deliberately made that change would put poison in the wells in front of the country's armies, or would lead a little sister to the brothel."[44]

One would not wish to imply that all conservatives looked upon agrarian radical movements as foreign conspiracies which, if successful, would destroy the American way of life. But to concentrate a mentality of apocalyptic, conspiratorial, and utopian preoccupations on the agrarian left is to distort history even more. The point here is not to absolve Populism of sins by spreading the guilt, but rather to question interpretations which locate the roots of contemporary provincial extremism specifically in the agrarian radical tradition.

It is not surprising that those in power will seek to damn political opponents by asserting that they violate the moral precepts of the society. Pluralism finds this rhetoric suggestive of the pseudo conservative — the man like McCarthy, who "in the name of upholding traditional American values and institutions and defending them against more or less fictitious dangers, consciously or unconsciously aims at their abolition."[45] Pluralists distinguish the pseudo conservative from the man truly committed to traditional values and institutions — the real conservative. But so-called pseudo conservative rhetoric is also used by real conservatives who feel their power threatened. The pseudo conservative is said to be an extremist, unintegrated into the community. His extremism is said to flow from his isolation. But real conservatives can be functioning, integrated members of their local communities and still interact rarely with those they attack. In this sense they can be as isolated as the pseudo conservatives. The interaction among local businessmen or eastern conservatives did not make them feel any less threatened by movements which attacked their power. Perhaps because of their interaction they felt themselves to be a community, threatened from the outside. Identifying their own positions with the preservation of American institutions, they attacked the "alien," "socialistic" Populists in the name of property, family, and home.

During the agrarian radical period, three factors influenced the character of American conservatism. In the first place, American conservatism had to justify itself with Lockean liberal arguments. The traditions upon which it had to call were abstract and individualistic, not concrete and corporate. Conservatives had to justify their power to a society suspicious of privileged classes and concentrations of power. They had to defend with Lockean arguments the changes they were causing in the older values and the older society. The impulse to utilize an egalitarian, "populistic" ideology was therefore strong.

In the second place, although conservatives were in positions of power, they were also in many cases the bearers of an industrialization that was radically changing the society in which they were strong. Conservatives were not "conservative" in any thoroughgoing sense. In part because of the radical nature of the changes they brought, in part because of their moral commitment to mastery of the world, they were not sympathetic to those cautious souls who pointed to obstacles in the face of action. They lacked the "sense of sin" that makes conservatives attractive to pluralism.

Third, the fact that conservatives were in positions of power did not automatically exclude moralism from their politics. They were often moved to moralistic and extremist rhetoric not only to defend their power but also to obscure the fact that they were powerful.

Conservative ideologies are complicated affairs. One cannot infer moderation from a "moderate" ideology. Practical, pragmatic activity does not exclude moralistic language. Pragmatic support for measures benefiting one constituency join with moralistic opposition to measures in the interests of other constituencies. "Populistic" appeals reinforce defense of the existing order and augment the power of various groups. In sum, American conservatives combine moralism and pragmatism, moderation and extremism, "populism" and pluralism.

Agrarian radical rhetoric has been combed for evidence of "mass" preoccupations — moralism, populism, millennialism, intolerance. Whatever the importance of these preoccupations among the less educated and more isolated members of the society, the more established and integrated elements also employed "mass" rhetoric. This would not be predicted by pluralist theory. It is rather explained by the issues of actual political conflict, by the nature of the liberal tradition in America, and by the use those in power make of that tradition.

WISCONSIN:
McCARTHY AND THE
PROGRESSIVE TRADITION

It is possible in Wisconsin to test two propositions by which the pluralists seek to connect McCarthyism to agrarian radicalism. Both propositions interpret McCarthyism as a mass phenomenon. But the evidence from county voting behavior suggests that McCarthyism was not a radical movement outside of normal American political processes.

The first proposition is that both La Follette and Mc-Carthy mobilized a similar lower-middle-class stratum of the population, particularly sensitive to irrational appeals. Here we must find a relationship between the support obtained by the two political leaders. Pluralists charge that a common ethnic base produced a common concern with status grievances. The evidence points to different ethnic bases and to progressive economic preoccupations contrasting with McCarthy's foreign policy concerns and traditional conservative appeals. Pluralists find McCarthyite roots in the economically dispossessed classes that supported agrarian radicalism. The evidence points to largely contrasting economic bases for La Follette and McCarthy.

The pluralists' second assertion is that both McCarthy and La Follette split apart existing coalitions and upset the group basis of politics. Here we must find that McCarthy and La

Follette mobilized a grass roots support not characteristic of Republican candidates who had run before them. In fact, like La Follette, McCarthy had roots in the traditional Republican vote. Like La Follette, he also mobilized new support. But whereas McCarthy's new support was marginal and short-lived, La Follette's reoriented Wisconsin politics for decades.

Seeking to discover agrarian radical roots for McCarthy, Peter Viereck notes that McCarthy began his career in the Democratic Party and then became a Republican. According to Viereck, this duplicates the experience of Wisconsin's "populist" masses, who were Democratic and authoritarian while they were poor and have become Republican with affluence.[1] Actually, in stressing McCarthy's Democratic beginnings, Viereck fails to support his own interpretation. For the prewar Democratic Party was not the liberal party in Wisconsin but the conservative party, and while the liberal masses became Democratic, McCarthy and his German environment became Republican. Since McCarthy went in one direction while progressivism was moving in the opposite direction, he cannot be the end result of progressivism.

Social Bases

My effort in this chapter and the two following is to uncover the social support for McCarthyism and agrarian radicalism. Toward that end, an analysis was made of the county voting returns in each state in approximately seventy elections between 1886 and 1960. To understand the electoral data it is necessary to know the demographic background of the states. Wisconsin was settled in the nineteenth century by Americans moving west and by Germans and Scandinavians. In 1910, Germans and their children made up 30 percent of the population, while Scandinavians accounted for another 9 percent. The Germans settled mainly in the rich farming country of eastern Wisconsin and in such nascent industrial centers as Milwaukee and Kenosha. Their descendants populate the numerous small cities and prosperous farms in eastern Wisconsin. The Scandinavians, mainly Norwegian, settled in the poorer areas of northwestern Wisconsin (see Figure 3.1). In the twentieth century, a number of Polish and Czechoslovakian immigrants came to the state. They settled on the farms of central Wisconsin; the Poles also joined the working class in Milwaukee and other cities (see Figure 3.2). Because so many of its inhabitants are of German and east-European descent, Wisconsin has a large Catholic population.

The early settlers in Wisconsin grew mainly wheat and other grains. In the north, there was an extensive lumbering industry. By the end of the nineteenth century, the trees and the wheat had largely disappeared, and Wisconsin farmers turned to dairying and diversified farming. More corn was grown in the southwest; there was more subsistence farming in the north. But throughout the state dairying was the major agricultural activity, as it remains today. The principal economic change of the past half century has been the industrialization of the state. By 1930, Wisconsin was in the top quarter of states in the percentage of its population engaged in manufacturing.[2]

Since there have been substantial changes in population and demography in every county in Wisconsin (as in the Dakotas), it is pertinent to ask whether we are justified in comparing county behavior over the course of decades. Indeed, often we will not seek to compare the vote of a single county for two candidates widely separated in time; instead we will relate urbanization, acreage in wheat, the percentage of foreign stock, and so on, to the political behavior of the counties. (The same areas may not be urban in 1890 and 1936, but one can still measure the extent to which urbanism is related to support of Populism and the New Deal.)

Moreover, this study and others indicate the persistence of county and ethnic voting traditions over the space of many

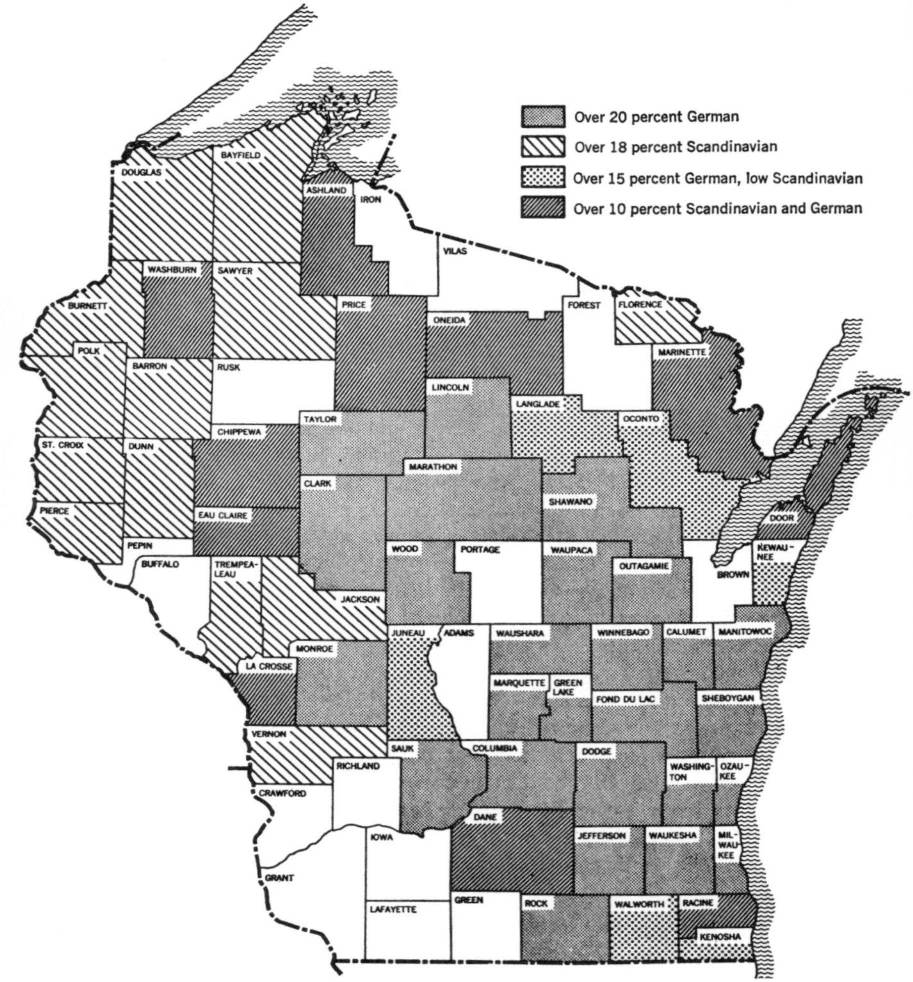

Figure 3.1. The distribution of the Scandinavian and German population in Wisconsin, 1930.

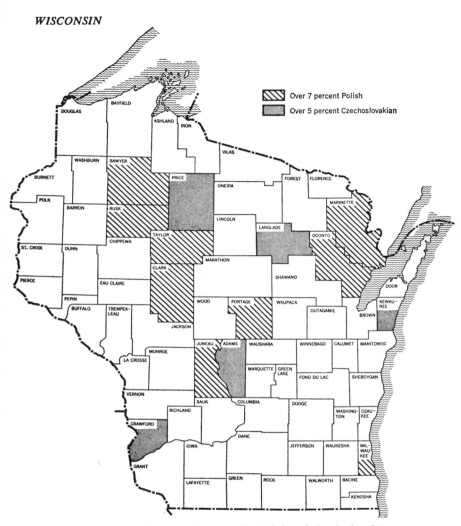

WISCONSIN

Over 7 percent Polish

Over 5 percent Czechoslovakian

*Figure 3.2. The distribution of the Polish and Czechoslovakian
population in Wisconsin, 1930.*

63

years. In most states, party traditions maintain their impact within the counties even while the social characteristics of those counties change significantly. There is evidence that ethnic voting patterns continue to assert themselves even when foreign language newspapers have gone the way of those who speak the foreign language.[3] One would not claim reliability of the highest order for interpretations presented on the basis of county data ranging over half a century. All that is claimed is that historical analysis made with the aid of county statistics is significantly more plausible than analysis that ignores county voting patterns.*

Populism and Progressivism

Both the sources of support for the major parties and the weakness of the Democrats significantly influenced Wisconsin agrarian radicalism. The salient features of Populism and progressivism in the state can be briefly summarized: First,

* There remains the problem of utilizing statistical techniques that will digest and make sense of the mass of quantitative information. The techniques employed here were primarily the correlation coefficient, the partial correlation, the scatter diagram, and the county map.[4]

The correlation coefficient, running on a scale from $+1.00$ to -1.00, measures the relation between two variables such as the state-wide vote by counties in two elections. The higher the numerical value of the correlation, the further one variable will go toward explaining the other. A partial correlation measures the relation between two variables with the influence of a third eliminated — for example the relationship between Truman's and Kennedy's vote with the Catholic population held constant. A scatter diagram represents graphically what is expressed numerically by a correlation. Each county's score on the two variables (e.g., the percentage of Catholics and the percentage for Kennedy) is entered on the graph. The scatter diagram may reveal interesting county variations from the total state picture that are submerged when the relation over the state as a whole is summarized by the correlation. County maps reveal the geographic concentration of particular political movements, ethnic groups, etc. (The statistical techniques are discussed more fully in Appendix A.)

both Populism and progressivism were movements of the poor. Second, as economic movements Populism and progressivism concerned themselves with class demands rather than with status grievances. Third, the La Follette coalition grew out of the traditional Republican vote but differed from the party vote in having an economic base. It also had antecedents in Wisconsin Populism and the Bryan Democracy of 1896 and 1898. Fourth, as Table 3.1 shows, the

TABLE 3.1
LA FOLLETTE'S IMPACT ON WISCONSIN HISTORY

	1904 La Follette	1904 Roosevelt	1910 Republican Governor
1904 T. Roosevelt	83		
1910 Republican Governor	80	91	
1904 Primary	88	70	66
1916 La Follette	60	44	43
1916 Wilson	—24	—49	—38
1924 La Follette	—01	28	00
1934 Progressive Governor	49	37	34
1936 Progressive Governor	54	46	39
1938 Progressive Governor	61	60	52
1940 Progressive Senator	47	38	34
1948 Truman	34	22	17
1952 McCarthy	—10	—03	04

particular support La Follette mobilized at the turn of the century was a cohesive force in Wisconsin politics until World War I, was the major element in the Wisconsin Progressive Party of 1934–1940, and then evolved into Democratic Party support. The support for La Follette in 1904 is closer to the modern Democratic Party than the regular Republican vote of that period. The coalition mobilized by La Follette progressivism thus continued to influence Wisconsin politics through the depression decade and down to the present day.

In his evolution to progressivism after and indeed against

Bryan, La Follette paralleled the careers of Norris in Nebraska, Crawford in South Dakota, Cummins in Iowa, and other progressive leaders. Their opposition to Bryan and Populism raises doubts about the commonly held belief in the continuity of Populism and progressivism. It supports the newer interpretations of such historians as Hofstadter and Mowry, who believe that there was a radical break between Populism and progressivism. But voting patterns in Wisconsin, unlike those in the Dakotas, do not demonstrate this discontinuity.

The Populists were weak in Wisconsin, which had passed beyond the wheat frontier by 1890. In 1894, the Populists, at the peak of their Wisconsin strength, polled only 7 percent of the state vote. Several of the newly settled counties of northern and northwestern Wisconsin, suffering for many years from the collapse of the lumbering boom, gave the Populists more than 10 percent of their vote. The party was also strong in the German urban areas, where it received 20 percent of the vote in Milwaukee, 18 percent in La Crosse and Racine, 12 percent in Sheboygan, and 9 percent in Winnebago (Oshkosh). Much of this German working-class vote was later to become socialist. In its combination of German workers and poor Scandinavian farmers, Wisconsin Populism prefigured the modern Democratic Party. In its northern support, Populism was a prelude to progressivism.

La Follette captured the machinery of the regular Republican Party in 1900, and it is difficult to disentangle his support from the normal Republican vote (see Figures 3.3 and 3.4). It is not simply that La Follette tended to receive a regular Republican vote; his presence on the ticket from 1900 on may have had an important impact on the nature of regular Republicanism. For example, although La Follette opposed Bryan in 1896, he attracted a pro-Bryan, northern Wisconsin following in 1900.[5] La Follette's influence may have returned pro-Bryan Republicans to the Republican Party and sent anti-Bryan Democrats away. But this is

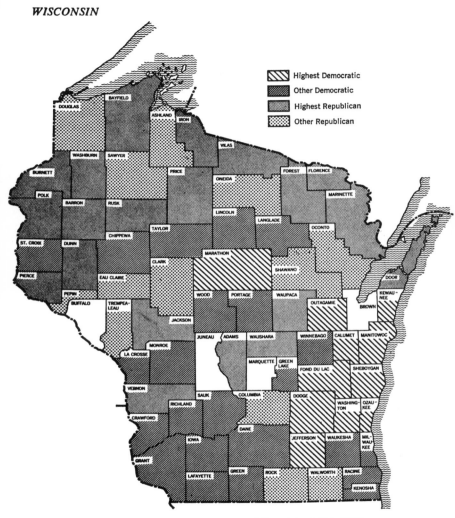

Figure 3.3. The party vote in Wisconsin, 1900–1910.

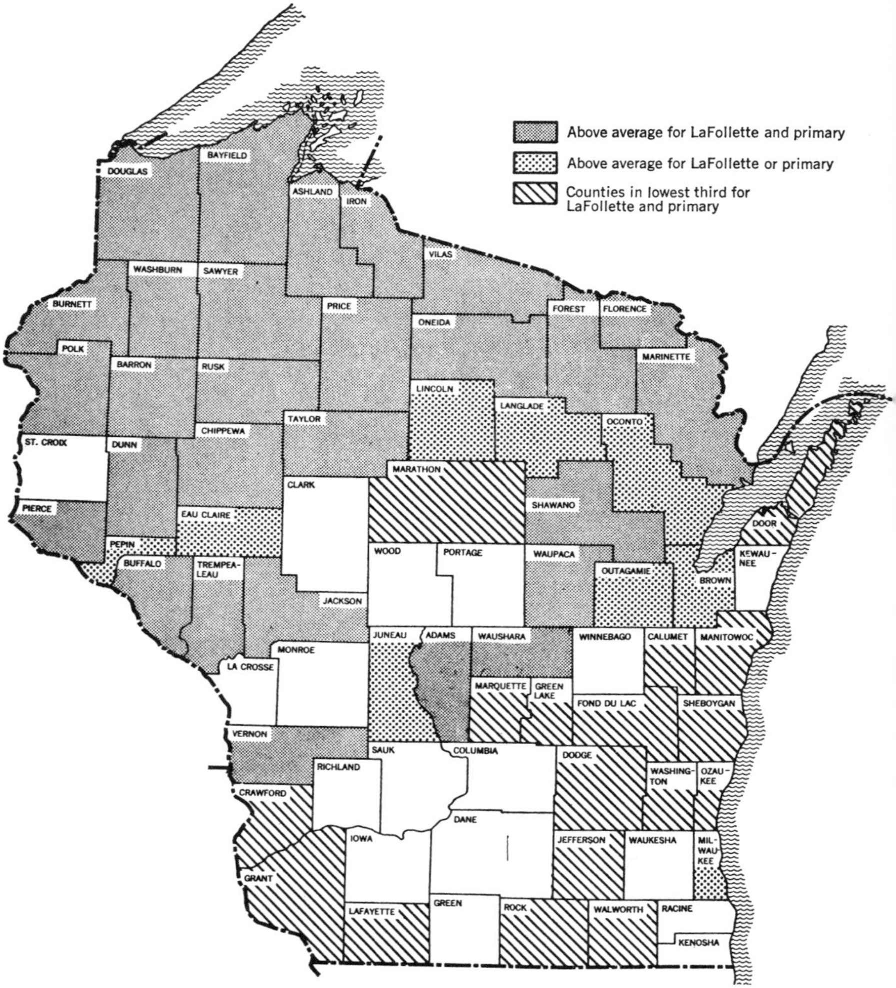

Above average for LaFollette and primary

Above average for LaFollette or primary

Counties in lowest third for
LaFollette and primary

Figure 3.4. La Follette's strength in 1904.

speculative; it is necessary to uncover the uniquely progressive support for La Follette.

In 1904, after voting for La Follette in two general elections, the conservative stalwarts made an all-out attempt to defeat him.*[6] That same year the Progressives sponsored a referendum to obtain voter support for a direct primary law. Support for this referendum correlated .88 with La Follette's 1904 vote, more than twenty points higher than it correlated with other Republican elections. The 1904 elections, then, provide us with an index of progressive support.†

Progressive correlations with the Republican vote between 1900 and 1910 were generally about .6. However, the differences between progressivism and regular Republicanism are important.

The regular Republican and Democratic party votes had a more distinctive ethnic composition than did progressivism. For instance, although German counties opposed progressivism, the German population was a more significant factor in accounting for opposition to regular Republicanism. Scandinavians supported the La Follette movement, but no more than they supported other Republicans. Unlike the regular Republican vote, the progressive vote was not distinctively Protestant, for a number of poor Catholic counties in northern Wisconsin supported La Follette offsetting an anti-La Follette Catholic vote farther south.**

* This differentiated the 1904 election from that of other years, giving it a distinctively progressive coloration. It was correlated ten to twenty points lower with other Republican elections than these elections were with one another.

† There was substantial continuity between progressive strength in 1904 and progressive support ten years later. Both La Follette's 1916 senatorial primary vote and the progressive gubernatorial primary strength of 1914 correlated .5+ with the 1904 progressive elections.

** Regular Republicanism was correlated .6+ with the percentage of Scandinavians and —.6+ with the percentage of Germans. La Follette's Scandinavian correlation was similar; his German correlation was somewhat lower, as several native-stock counties joined German counties in opposing him. Regular Republicanism was cor-

On the other hand, progressive support had a significant economic component. The poorer the county (measured in value of land per acre), the higher the progressive vote (see Figure 3.5).[7] This was in direct contrast to the progressive

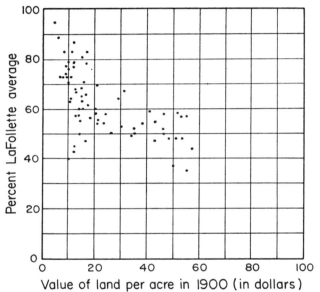

Figure 3.5.   La Follette and agricultural wealth in 1904 (dots represent counties).

vote in South Dakota, which increased with an *increase* in wealth.

Analysis of South Dakota progressivism confirms the Hofstadter-Mowry view that progressivism was a movement of the rich. Whereas the poor Wisconsin counties supported La Follette, the South Dakota progressive vote increased in the richer counties. The differing bases of progressivism in

related about —.5 with the percentage of Catholics, far higher than the La Follette relationship.

South Dakota and Wisconsin are related to the differing natures of the two movements. While La Follette in 1912 tacitly supported Woodrow Wilson for President, the South Dakota progressives, in control of the GOP state organization, united behind Theodore Roosevelt. There was obviously a personal reason for La Follette's decision — anger at Roosevelt for sabotaging his own campaign for the Republican nomination. Yet the different actions of the progressive leaders in the two states are symbolic of the contrast between the two movements.*

Often the difference between La Follette and Wilson on the one hand and Roosevelt on the other is identified with their own catchwords: Wilson's New Freedom versus Roosevelt's New Nationalism. Because of its stress on economic competition among equals, the New Freedom is said to have a reactionary cast. The New Nationalism, with its acceptance of bigness, regulated competition, and monopoly, is said to be more in touch with the modern world and the pragmatic New Deal. Clearly this interpretation of history fits the pluralist picture. Progressives are divided into two groups. One opposed big government and big business, looked backward to a rural world of small entrepreneurs, and was, in short, anti-industrial. The other was willing to accept industrialization and work for reforms within an industrial capitalist order.

The character of La Follette progressivism undermines this interpretation. It is more fruitful to look at American history not in terms of attitudes toward industrialization in the abstract but in terms of the particular demands made by particular groups and classes on the evolving industrial system. The economic classes supporting progressivism in

* The elections to which La Follette's 1904 support was more similar than was regular Republican support include the two Wilson votes but not the Progressive Party campaign of 1912. La Follette supported Wilson tacitly in 1912 and openly in 1916, but more than the personal factor was at work here. Wilson and not Roosevelt received a progressive vote in the Dakotas as well.

Wisconsin differed from these in South Dakota. In part because of his base among the poor farmers, La Follette sponsored more radical social legislation than his counterparts in South Dakota. This radicalism did not make La Follette anti-industrial as the pluralist interpretation implies; on the contrary, it enabled him to press for reforms relevant to the conditions of the poor in an industrializing country. Thus the Wisconsin industrial commissions were precursors of the New Deal; the blue laws of South Dakota's Coe Crawford were not. Moreover, the South Dakota counties that supported progressivism before World War I opposed the New Deal and tend to be Republican today. The more "reactionary" Wisconsin progressive counties supported the New Deal and give disproportionate support to the contemporary Democratic Party. Wisconsin progressives did not react to industrialization in the abstract but to the particular industrial capitalist constellations of power.

From World War I to World War II

During World War I, La Follette progressivism received disproportionate German support. McCarthy, like other post-World War II Republicans, was also to obtain German backing. But to connect progressivism with McCarthyism because of that fact is to misread Wisconsin history. Pluralists relate the progressive's ethnic appeal created by foreign policy to McCarthy's foreign-policy-based ethnic appeal. But one should not overestimate the importance of progressive ethnicity. First, the progressives' German support violated the past economic appeal of the movement; it does not reveal an underlying ethnic or "status" approach to politics. Second, analysis of progressivism from World War I to World War II demonstrates the fleeting character of its ethnic component. Third, the more durable progressive economic base did not provide the underpinnings for McCarthy's electoral victories.

72

By 1916, in part because of his progressive strength, Woodrow Wilson had a base of support that differed markedly from that given to previous Democratic candidates. Northern Wisconsin residents disproportionately supported Wilson and Germans disproportionately opposed him. But the war interrupted any incipient party realignment. The realignment that did occur was in the progressive base. Most Wisconsin progressive leaders followed La Follette in opposing American entry into the war. Germans, who had disproportionately opposed progressivism, now as overwhelmingly supported it. The progressive movement emerged from the war with a following far different from that of previous years.

Thus La Follette received more than 70 percent of the 1922 Republican primary vote because he ran well both in German and in progressive counties.* He had not lost his old base; he had rather gained a new one. But other pro-La Follette progressives were not so fortunate. Running in the 1918 Republican primary, progressive James Thompson narrowly lost his bid for the senate because he could not defeat Irving Lenroot in the old progressive counties.

Lenroot, Thompson's opponent, had been a La Follette protégé and was a prowar congressman from northern Wisconsin. Better known among progressives than Thompson, Lenroot swamped him in the traditionally progressive northern counties. As a result, Thompson polled a vote related .60 to the percentage of Germans. (Thompson's vote was actually negatively related to La Follette's primary vote only two years earlier; see Table 3.2.) In 1920, Thompson ran as an independent for the senate against Lenroot. Compared to 1918, Thompson did better in the old progressive counties and worse in the German counties, but his vote was still

---

* But just as in the Dakotas the Germans by 1922 were deserting the Non-Partisan League, so in Wisconsin some German counties were actually among the lowest for La Follette. However, more German counties were still strongly for him.

TABLE 3.2

PROGRESSIVISM IN WISCONSIN IN THE 1920's*

	1904 La Follette	1904 Direct Primary	1916 La Follette	1918 Thompson	1920 Thompson	1922 La Follette	1924 La Follette	1926 Blaine	1928 B. La Follette, Jr.
1904 La Follette									
1904 Direct Primary	88								
1916 La Follette	60	48							
1918 Thompson	—54	—48	—14						
1920 Thompson	—24	—13	12	77					
1922 La Follette	05	18	16	34	59				
1924 La Follette	19	28	34	36	71	75			
1926 Blaine	—21	—10	06	53	63	57	61		
1928 B. La Follette, Jr.	12	11	28	30	50	72	70	42	
1930 P. La Follette	16	06	36	17	41	47	63	36	61

* All elections reported in this table are primaries except those of 1904 and 1924.

disproportionately German, and he lost another close election.

In the elections between 1918 and 1928, postwar progressivism moved gradually closer to its prewar base (see Table 3.2).[8] Germans were slowly returning to their conservative voting habits.

The progressivism of the 1920's then was a coalition of Germans and poorer Scandinavians. This coalition was split apart by the depression, which realigned progressive support in an economic direction. The progressive movement of the 1930's was in large part a return to pre-World War I progressive politics (see Table 3.3). Progressivism was again strong in the north and west and weak in the richer, German southeast. Gosnell has shown that Progressive Party support was concentrated in the poorer, Scandinavian parts of Wisconsin,[9] a fact clear also from a map of progressive strength in the 1930's (see Figure 3.6).

The cohesive Progressive Party of the 1930's, and with it the modern Democratic Party, began to take shape in Phil La Follette's 1930 gubernatorial victory (compare Tables 3.2 and 3.3). Those who voted for Phil La Follette in November 1930 and for John Blaine in the spring of 1932 went into the Progressive Party of 1934. Progressive Party support itself differed from earlier progressive strength chiefly because it centered more in the urban working class.[10] The major shift came in 1936; the working-class counties of Milwaukee, Kenosha, Racine, and Eau Claire were clearly more progressive from 1936 to 1940 than they had been earlier (see Figure 3.7).*

Progressivism in the 1930's, then, had lost its war-born German support and was economically based. Samuel Lubell, however, asserts that the Progressive Party was a coalition of those voting progressive for economic and ethnic reasons and that World War II split apart the two groups.

---

* The progressive vote was rural in the 1920's, but neither disproportionately rural nor disproportionately urban after 1934.

CHAPTER THREE

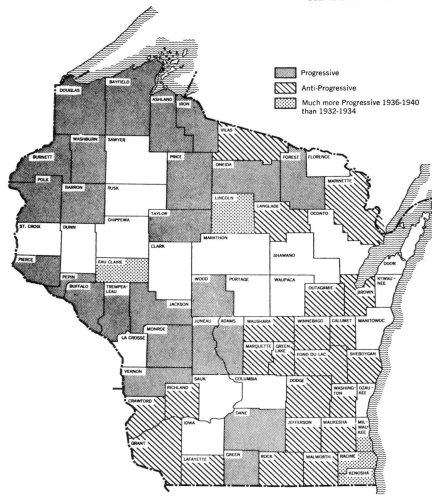

Figure 3.6. Progressivism in Wisconsin, 1932–1940.

TABLE 3.3
COHESIVE PROGRESSIVISM: THE 1930's

	1904 La Follette	1930 P. La Follette Primary	1930 P. La Follette November	1932 Blaine	1934 Prog. Governor	1936 Prog. Governor	1938 Prog. Governor	1940 Prog. Senator	1942 Prog. Governor	1946 La Follette
1904 La Follette										
1930 P. La Follette Primary	16									
1930 P. La Follette November	61	60								
1932 Blaine Primary	48	75	79							
1934 Progressive Governor	49	57	61	80						
1936 Progressive Governor	54	46	65	78	80					
1938 Progressive Governor	61	30	67	70	57	84				
1940 Progressive Senator	47	38	61	71	68	86	86			
1942 Progressive Governor	40	44	54	56	62	68	59	75		
1946 La Follette Primary	27	43	61	67	49	66	72	71	53	
1948 Truman	34	10	32	43	31	61	68	71	36	58

77

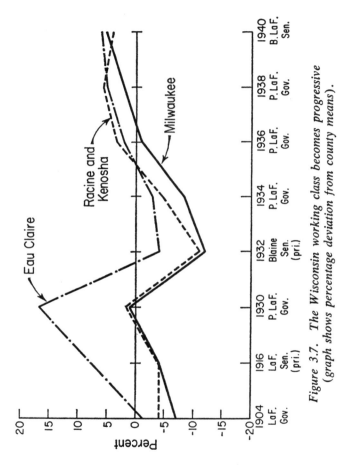

Figure 3.7. The Wisconsin working class becomes progressive (graph shows percentage deviation from county means).

As evidence for his contention, Lubell isolates twenty-two counties in Wisconsin in which Roosevelt's vote dropped 20 percent or more between 1936 and 1940. This drop is alleged to indicate German sensitivity to Roosevelt's interventionist foreign policy. And, Lubell concludes, these German counties similarly deserted Phil La Follette between 1936 and 1938, giving him 45 percent of their vote the first year, 31 percent the second.[11] However, La Follette's vote in the state as a whole dropped almost as much as his vote in these counties — from 48 percent to 36 percent. Note that the Lubell counties were below the state average in *both* elections.

Indeed, since the Progressive Party remained antiwar until after 1940, it would be surprising if the Germans had deserted it disproportionately between 1936 and 1938. Rather the party was to gain German support on the war issue after 1940, support which it had lost on economic grounds ten years earlier.[12] The shift in progressive support seen by Lubell taking place in 1940 for ethnic reasons had actually taken place from 1928 to 1932 for economic reasons.

The dispute with Lubell here is of more than minor historical interest. Lubell made the vital discovery that midwest isolationism had roots in German and other ethnic opposition to the two world wars. He pointed out that since isolationism is ethnically determined, it arises not from indifference to foreign policy but rather from oversensitivity to it. Isolationism is the result not of insularity and lack of concern with Europe but of great attention to the fortunes of one's mother country. Therefore isolationism can turn easily into interventionist jingoism; these are but two sides of the same coin.

In Lubell's analysis, ethnic factors alone explain the isolationist tradition. Progressive isolationism therefore becomes assimilated into the ethnically based, isolationist-jingoist syndrome. Since for Lubell there is only one isolationist tradition, there can be no other explanation for progressive isolationism. Moreover, since McCarthy capitalized on jingoist isolationism, he achieves in this view a connection with agrarian radicalism.

Yet the progressives in Wisconsin were isolationist before attracting German support, and they remained isolationist through the 1930's, after the Germans had left. Moreover, the Germans were progressive for only a short time, configuring the movement much less than Lubell supposed. The evidence thus points to two isolationist traditions, not one.[18] To discover a nonethnic basis for agrarian radical isolationism is to raise questions about the association of radical protest with the ethnic-jingoist syndrome. Agrarian radical notions of foreign policy were essentially the product of disinterest in Europe combined with humanitarian impulses. Without defending the naïve isolationism of the agrarian radicals, one must distinguish it from the foreign policy concerns of the Germans. Both types of isolationism were important during World War I. It was the latter that would contribute so heavily to McCarthy's appeal.

The Pluralists and the Democratic Resurgence

According to Hofstadter and Lubell, the Smith vote of 1928 is important not because of its continuity with the past but because of its radical break with existing political alignments.[14] The Smith election, in this view, contributed to and prefigured the New Deal coalition — a coalition differing sharply from previous reform movements. Pluralist history relies on this view of the 1928 campaign. For the pluralists, Smith's break with the past is a break with progressive moralism. Reform politics would now base itself in the cities instead of the farms. It would now capitalize on practical proposals to alleviate economic distress, not on alienation from the industrial order.

In this view, the difference between the elections of 1924 and 1928 is clear-cut. The La Follette election of 1924 was the last gasp of agrarian radicalism. According to Hofstadter, La Follette progressives returned to the Republican Party after 1924, thus opposing both Smith and the New Deal.[15]

Pluralist history begins here by recognizing an important fact. In many states and in the country as a whole, the Smith vote was both a break with the past and a precursor of the New Deal and the present.[16] However, in just those states where agrarian radicalism was strong, a different picture emerges. In these states, the Smith vote was the product not simply of Catholicism, urbanism, and "wet" sentiments but of agrarian unrest as well. Moreover, in these states the Smith vote did not break with the past and presage the future. In North Dakota, the Smith vote was simply a deviant election. If it had little relation to past North Dakota voting patterns, it bore equally little relation to the future. In South Dakota, the vote was rooted in the progressive past and disappeared in the Democratic present. In Wisconsin, the Smith vote also had a past but no future.

As might be expected, Smith's support was closely related (.80) to the referendum against prohibition the same year. Because Smith brought out a Catholic vote, his highest party correlations (.75 to .8) were with the highly Catholic pre-Bryan Democratic vote. A second source of the Smith vote was the opposition to Coolidge in 1924. Those who voted for Davis or La Follette in 1924 voted for Smith in 1928. His correlation with the Coolidge vote was —.88. This continuity between Smith and La Follette suggests that the roots of the Smith vote in the agrarian unrest of the 1920's should not be ignored.[17] In the Dakotas too, the Smith vote came out of a progressive-German coalition.

Soon after 1928, this German and Catholic coalition with progressivism dissolved. Smith's vote was related .71 and .67 to the Roosevelt elections of 1932 and 1936. It then disappeared as a force in Wisconsin politics until 1960, when its correlation of .43 with the Kennedy vote reflects the Catholic composition of both.[18]

In his first two campaigns, Roosevelt had also been supported by the German counties.[*][19] It was not until 1940 when the Germans made what was to be a permanent shift to the Republicans on the war issue[20] that the modern Democratic Party was born. Democratic elections from 1940 to 1960 form a cohesive cluster with intercorrelations of from .75 to .95.[21]

Indeed, the support given progressive candidates, rather than the Smith and early Roosevelt votes, was the main precursor of the modern Democratic Party. Progressive elections from 1936 to 1940 correlate about .55 with support given the post-World War II Democrats. This progressive vote in turn is related to the pre-World War I Republican vote (.35 to .45) and to the La Follette and primary votes of 1904 (.55). The Progressive Party was the instrument of a reorientation that has resulted in a positive relation between the Republican vote of the La Follette period and the Democratic vote of today. Such a reversal of party lines is most unusual in American history.[†]

The revolution in Wisconsin politics in the 1930's has resulted in two parties unrelated to the two parties that existed before 1936. Thus a map of party strength from 1944 to 1958 shows that the strong Democratic counties of the past have become strongly Republican today, while the Republican Progressive counties have become Democratic (compare Figure 3.3 with Figure 3.8). The German counties in Wisconsin have always been conservative. Before World War II, they could remain in the Democratic

---

[*] Because FDR's support in his first two campaigns remained rooted in the conservative, traditionally Democratic, German counties of the south, these Roosevelt elections were unrelated to the support given progressive candidates. But by 1936, F.D.R.'s base was beginning to change; that election was the first Democratic vote to be highly related to the modern Democratic Party.

[†] Contrast it with the party stability in South Dakota, where the Republican votes before World War I and after World War II correlated about .55.

WISCONSIN

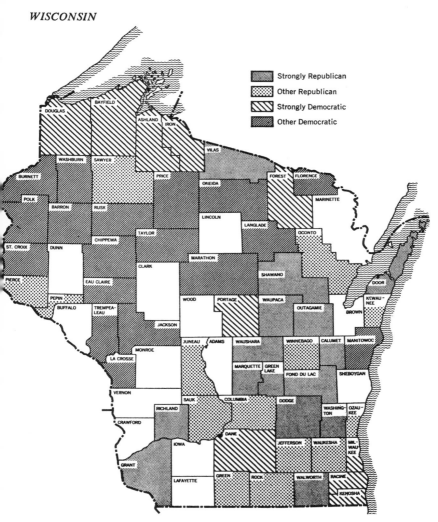

Legend:
- Strongly Republican
- Other Republican
- Strongly Democratic
- Other Democratic

Figure 3.8. The Wisconsin party vote, 1944–1958.

Party, which was the radical party in Wisconsin only in 1896 and 1916. The war drove the Germans from the Democratic Party into the GOP. Since World War II, most non-working-class Germans, for ethnic and economic reasons, have remained in the Republican Party. The GOP is supported as well by the suburban middle class, by those living in Wisconsin's prosperous farming counties to the south, and by the residents of the small cities, towns, and farms of the Fox River Valley to the northeast. The urban working class votes Democratic as do the poor Scandinavian farmers. The modern Wisconsin Democracy is thus a farmer-labor party.[22]

Since 1944, only three elections have deviated from the normal party vote. In the special senatorial election of 1957, Democrat William Proxmire won the seat vacated by McCarthy's death. The second deviant election was the Kennedy election, clearly peculiar because of the Catholic vote. (Normally Catholics do not vote disproportionately Democratic in nonmetropolitan Wisconsin.) The third election was the McCarthy election of 1952 (see Table 3.4).

McCarthy and the Progressive Tradition

McCarthy's electoral relation to the progressive tradition is complex. The distinctive basis of pre-World War I progressivism had been its strength in northern Wisconsin and its weakness in the richer, more German, southeast. Since this constellation of support and opposition influenced the modern Democratic party alignment, there is a relationship in absolute terms between support for progressivism and opposition to regular Republicanism. Since McCarthy received a substantially Republican vote, he received an anti-progressive vote as well. In absolute terms, progressive counties tended to oppose McCarthy more than other counties in the state.[23]

Indeed, those sections of the population supporting the Progressive ticket in the years before the party realignment

TABLE 3.4

THE MODERN WISCONSIN REPUBLICAN VOTE AND THE McCARTHY ELECTION

	1940	1942	1944	1946	1948	1950	1952 Sen.	1952 Pres.	1954	1956	1957 Sen.	1958
1940												
1942	56											
1944	95	54										
1946	88	52	90									
1948	80	54	85	87								
1950	80	61	83	84	93							
1952 Senator	79	46	82	85	81	82						
1952 President	88	50	92	91	91	89	93					
1954	84	56	87	87	91	90	82	92				
1956	73	56	80	79	93	89	76	87	88			
1957	68	56	69	71	77	77	57	70	86	76		
1958	81	59	84	83	90	86	78	89	95	92	86	
1960	76	41	78	76	80	75	70	81	84	75	72	82

85

of 1936–1940 formed the strongest prewar source of opposition to McCarthy.

McCarthy's chief support came from regular Republicans. Nevertheless, he was considerably weaker in the more industrialized and richer counties of the southeast than were other Republicans, and he was stronger in the progressive north.*

When McCarthy ran in the 1946 Republican primary, Bob La Follette, Jr., almost defeated him. Six years later, McCarthy was an easy victor against Len Schmitt, a little-known old progressive. The 1946 primary was clearly in the progressive tradition, with McCarthy on the antiprogressive side. McCarthy's vote correlated at an average of —.64 with the Progressive Party vote (see Table 3.3). McCarthy's 1952 primary vote was also antiprogressive, but the correlations were twenty points lower, and the two primaries correlated only .45. In addition, several counties did not increase their support for McCarthy in proportion to his increases in the rest of the state. These were principally the industrialized southern counties along the shore of Lake Michigan. (For McCarthy's support in the 1952 primary, see Figure 3.9.)

If McCarthy was less opposed by progressives in 1952 than in 1946, this could in large part be explained by the absence of a La Follette on the 1952 ticket against him. But the evidence of McCarthy's progressive support which is suggested by his relation to the Proxmire vote is not so easily dismissed. McCarthy's vote in November 1952 was negatively related to Proxmire's 1957 vote, but the correlation was 25 to 30 points lower than the majority of party correlations in the period. Both Proxmire and McCarthy deviated from the normal party vote in a progressive direction. There are several elections to which McCarthy's vote was

* In the state as a whole, McCarthy mobilized more opposition than support, running last on the state ticket in 1952, 12 percent behind an outspoken Republican foe.

WISCONSIN

Figure 3.9. McCarthy's strength in the 1952 primary.

more positively related than the normal postwar Republican vote and much more positively related than the vote given Proxmire's Republican opponent Steinle. A progressive candidate ran in almost all the elections that meet these con-

TABLE 3.5

MCCARTHY, PROXMIRE, AND THE PROGRESSIVE PAST

	1952 McCarthy	1957 Steinle (Proxmire's opponent)	1950 Republican Governor
1904 La Follette	—10	—33	—28
1904 T. Roosevelt	—03	—21	—18
1904 Direct primary	—23	—42	—31
1914 Philipp (anti-Progressive)	00	18	13
1916 Republican President	30	13	27
1918 Thompson	19	32	37
1922 La Follette	—15	—37	—20
1930 P. La Follette Primary	22	—25	—11
1930 P. La Follette General	—02	—39	—29
1932 Blaine	—09	—45	—41
1932 Hoover	—03	26	01
1934 Progressive Governor	—15	—37	—31
1934 Republican Governor	13	35	23
1936 Progressive Governor	—41	—63	—63
1938 Progressive Governor	—48	—64	—68
1940 Progressive Senator	—58	—64	—74
1950 Schmitt	—07	—53	—29
1957 O'Konski	—15	—54	—27

ditions. In other words, counties which voted progressive in many elections were more likely to support Proxmire than other Democratic candidates of the 1950's and less likely to oppose McCarthy than to oppose other Republicans. For example, McCarthy's correlation with La Follette in 1936 was —.41, Steinle's was —.63. As far back as 1904, McCarthy's correlation with La Follette was —.10, Steinle's was —.39 (see Table 3.5).[24]

How significant was McCarthy's progressive strength, and

how is it to be explained? McCarthy was opposed by urban counties and supported by rural ones all over the state. In order to get a more exact measure of the counties that voted disproportionately for and against McCarthy in 1952, an index was constructed measuring McCarthy's strength with the regular Republican vote held constant (see Figure 3.10).* The correlation between the percentage living on farms and the McCarthy index was .58. McCarthy's losses in urban areas were greater than his gains in rural counties, but he did run better in rural counties than other Republicans of the period. Moreover, McCarthy received substantial regular Republican strength. This, too, was nonurban support; holding German background constant, regular Republicanism correlated —.44 with the percentage in manufacturing.

McCarthy and La Follette had a common agrarian appeal. The index of McCarthy's non-Republican strength and the index of La Follette support in 1904 were correlated .25;† with the percentage living on farms held constant, the correlation dropped to .15.

* First the average difference was computed for each county above or below the state average for three Republican candidates (President 1948 and 1952, governor 1950). Second, the difference for each county from the state average for McCarthy in November 1952 was also computed. Subtracting the regular Republican strength from the McCarthy strength resulted in an index of McCarthy's support with the regular Republican vote held constant.[25]

† The positive correlation is explained by three facts. First, urban counties that had strongly opposed La Follette before the 1930's also strongly opposed McCarthy. Second, of the 26 counties scoring above the state average on the 1904 La Follette index, 19 supported McCarthy more than they supported other Republicans. But McCarthy's over-all differential support averaged only 1.4 per cent. Finally, 8 of the 9 counties that voted for McCarthy as a hometown boy (see discussion later in the chapter) had above-average scores on the 1904 La Follette index. Clearly the friends-and-neighbors effect was more potent than progressivism in their high McCarthy support. As these northeastern counties became wealthier and more developed — in 1914 and particularly by the 1930's — they had ceased to support progressivism.

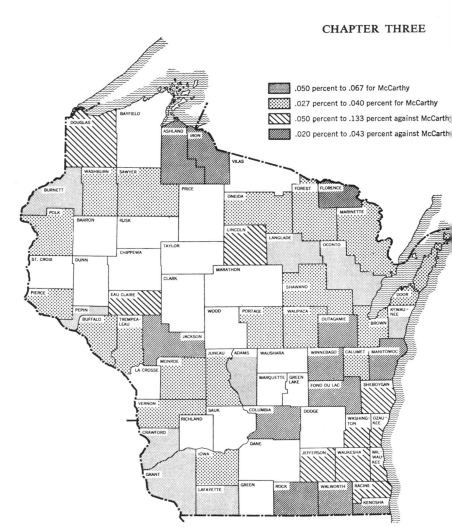

Figure 3.10. McCarthy's strength with the regular
Republican vote held constant.

In explaining rural support for McCarthy, the ideas of the pluralists are helpful. Both McCarthy in particular and midwestern and western Republicanism in general represent a suspicion of the values, groups, and power centers of an urban, industrial society. But McCarthy's version had a particular anger at urban sophistication and respectability that made him marginally stronger in rural areas than orthodox conservative Republicans.

This does not justify locating the source of the anti-industrial tradition in agrarian radicalism. But even only in terms of social support, McCarthy's rural strength does not make him an agrarian radical. McCarthy got support from rural areas generally throughout the state; La Follette had been consistently rejected in the rich, southern countryside. Support for agrarian radicals has usually rested on groups with clear-cut common economic interests. McCarthy in Wisconsin benefited from general rural and small-town discontent. By this fact, the rural supporters of McCarthy were not reacting to the specific economic conditions and constellations of power that produced agrarian radicalism.

More important, McCarthy's rural, progressive strength was only one source of his unique appeal and less important than some others. These are revealed when the McCarthy index is plotted against the percentage engaged in mining, manufacturing, and railroading. The counties on this scatter diagram seem to fall into two clusters, one more pro McCarthy than the other (see Figure 3.11). In both clusters, the lower the percentage employed in industry the greater the support for McCarthy. But the more pro-McCarthy cluster contained three kinds of counties — Czech, Catholic, and those near McCarthy's home.

This cluster included all the Czech counties in the state and 12 of the 15 most Catholic counties.[26] In addition, the more pro-McCarthy group contained all those counties that supported McCarthy on a "friends-and-neighbors" basis (that is, because he was a home-town boy). McCarthy was born in a northeastern Wisconsin county, had lived in two others, and the friends-and-neighbors effect extended to six other northeastern counties. Back in 1944, McCarthy had run against Senator Wiley in the Republican primary. Known

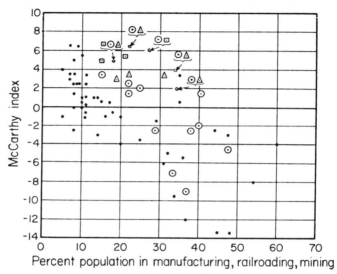

Figure 3.11. McCarthy's strength and the industrial population. Dots represent counties, triangles those NE counties where McCarthy got 40 percent of vote in 1944, circles the 15 highest Catholic counties, squares those over 5 percent Czechoslovakian.

only in his home area, McCarthy polled 31 percent of the vote in the state as a whole. But he received between 41 and 66 percent of the vote in 10 counties. Nine of these form a contiguous bloc in the northeast corner of the state.[27] All were in the more pro-McCarthy group on the scatter diagram (Figure 3.11). Catholicism, ethnicity, and the friends-and-neighbors effect accounted for over 80 percent of the counties in the more pro-McCarthy group, but less than 7 percent of the others.*

* McCarthy's primary strength supports the conclusions arrived at

92

What of McCarthy's general weakness in cities? The evidence, gross as it is, suggests that both the working class and the middle class deserted him. The two congressional districts that existed in Milwaukee in 1952 were drawn roughly on class lines. The Fourth CD was heavily Polish working class and the Fifth was more middle class. The Fourth CD gave Eisenhower in 1952 10 percent more votes than it gave McCarthy, while the Fifth CD gave the President 12 percent more.[29] In both congressional districts, the Senator ran far behind Eisenhower. True, in the more middle-class district he ran further behind, but the difference is small. Moreover, in absolute terms the working-class congressional district gave McCarthy 33 percent of its votes; the more middle-class district gave him 38 percent. If the work-

---

here. In the primary McCarthy ran above his state average in the 5 corn belt counties, some normal Republican counties in the southeast, a bloc of counties near his home territory in the northeast, a few progressive counties in the north and northwest, and a number of counties in central and north-central Wisconsin. These latter counties were mostly those with concentrations of Czechs and Poles. McCarthy ran above his state average in every county more than 5 percent Czech or Polish by the 1930 census except for the 2 Polish counties with by far the largest cities. The Senator ran below his state average in most of the old progressive counties of the north and west, and in the southern industrial counties along the lake front. However, his weakness in the old progressive counties should not be overestimated. He generally received more than 70 percent of the vote in these counties; this figure was below his state average, but very high nevertheless. McCarthy's chief opposition was in the industrial counties (see Figure 3.9).

Similarly, it is possible to locate counties in which Democrats probably voted for McCarthy in the primary. In 5 of the 10 most Democratic counties in the state, the Democratic percentage of the two-party primary vote dropped 10 percent or more between 1950 and 1952. It seems likely that Democrats in these counties had voted in the 1952 Republican primary. In 3 of them, McCarthy ran well below his state average, suggesting Democratic opposition to him. In 2, he ran above his average, apparently attracting Democratic support.[28] The 3 counties where McCarthy did poorly all contain very large cities. The 2 where McCarthy attracted Democratic support were poor counties in central and northeastern Wisconsin—one Polish and Catholic, the other in McCarthy's home territory.

ing class is authoritarian in the abstract, in Milwaukee it was not attracted to an authoritarian figure like McCarthy by abstract considerations.

We have found several different kinds of counties tending to support McCarthy more than other Republicans. Let us compare their average support for McCarthy with the progressive average. These figures will at the same time summarize McCarthy's major sources of non-Republican support. McCarthy averaged above the regular Republican vote as follows: in 5 corn belt counties, 4.3 percent; in 9 friends-and-neighbors counties, 2.2 percent; in 5 Czech counties, 6.7 percent; in 8 Polish counties (omitting the two with large cities), 2.4 percent; in 7 nonindustrial Catholic counties, 3.3 percent;* in the 14 most rural counties, 3.1 percent; in 11 most industrial counties, —6.2 percent; in 26 progressive counties, 1.4 percent.

Apparently, the characteristic of Catholicism, the friends-and-neighbors effect, and Czechoslovakian background reinforced the tendency for rural areas to support McCarthy. They acted *in addition to* ruralness. Progressivism, on the other hand, *is explained by* rural support for McCarthy and contributed no additional support of its own.[30]

Since McCarthy was strong in rural counties whether or not they had been progressive, there was apparently nothing in the particular progressive tradition or base of support that would lead to support for McCarthy. Moreover, judging from the figures, progressive counties were the *least important* source of McCarthy's unique constellation of support in Wisconsin.[31]

McCarthy had more impact in Washington than he did in

* These are the 7 of the 15 most Catholic counties with less than 30 percent of their population engaged in industry. The 8 Catholic counties with large cities or a substantial working class (the presence of nonindustrial cities was not sufficient) averaged 2.2 percent against McCarthy. Note that the nonindustrial Catholic counties were less rural than the progressive counties but supported McCarthy more heavily.

Wisconsin, where he succeeded primarily in driving away urban voters. Martin Trow suggests two reasons for McCarthy's weakness in urban centers. Members of the white-collar, urban middle class were not attracted by appeals to an Americanism attacking the eastern elite, with which they identified. They would not receive status from an assault on the eastern elite and on the bureaucratized industrial structure. Rather they hoped to advance through that structure to places in that elite. Therefore McCarthyism alienated them. As for the workers, according to Trow they had channels through which to express their grievances and hence were not attracted by McCarthy's anomic appeals. Rural voters and small businessmen, he argues, lacking this commitment to modern institutions, could be mobilized by a McCarthy.[32]

Trow's analysis of the urban middle class is persuasive because it focuses on the commitment of professionals, businessmen, and white-collar workers to the existing status hierarchy. His analysis of the working class is incomplete because he does not similarly emphasize working-class attachments to McCarthy's targets. Parsons argues that, as part of the strategy of splitting apart existing political alliances, McCarthy made no attack on the New Deal or on labor unions.[33] In fact, precisely because McCarthy capitalized on existing political alliances, he could not support the New Deal. Had he done so, he would have alienated the most important part of his leadership and rank-and-file support. McCarthy's "radicalism" was in large part an attack on the New Deal, and it was understood as such by his most active supporters. It was not only that workers had unions through which to express their grievances, they also could not be mobilized by an attack on Roosevelt and the New Deal Democratic Party. Parsons may not have agreed, but they apparently thought the Republican senator was hostile to their New Deal gains.

McCarthy could not emancipate himself from his Republican commitments. Nor did he want to, for they pulled him to victory. Far from splitting apart existing political alliances,

McCarthy was elected in Wisconsin by capitalizing on a large Republican following already disturbed about communism and foreign policy. Ethnically, Germans were the main prop of this Republican Party. According to the theory of *The New American Right,* McCarthy made Populist appeals which attracted Germans who wanted to prove their Americanism after two world wars. But McCarthy did not attract Germans who were not already in his party. Were these "Populist" appeals already being made by the Republican right wing? More likely, these were not Populist appeals at all, but appeals which have been general in American politics. Indeed, the attack on Communists, bureaucracy, and the welfare state has traditionally been more an anti-Populist than a Populist appeal. The Germans' overconcern with the Communist issue probably contributes to their recent voting behavior, as Lubell and the authors of *The New American Right* allege. But although Germans were the backbone of McCarthy's support, they were not a group attracted by his unique appeals.

McCarthy did have an appeal beyond that of the regular Republican Party in Wisconsin's nonurban Polish, Czechoslovakian, and Catholic communities. How is this explained? According to *The New American Right,* when people said they liked McCarthy's ends but not his means, they meant the opposite. They did not care about his ends, but liked his tough attacks on the eastern elite and other authorities.[34] In this view, second and third generation immigrants supported McCarthy because in calling the eastern aristocracy un-American he increased the immigrants' social status. But is it not significant that Czechs and Poles rather than Scandinavians and Germans were particularly attracted to the senator? Far from being uninterested in McCarthy's ends, these groups must have been aware of recent Communist seizures of power in their native countries. Czechoslovakia had been the victim of a Communist coup d'état only two years before McCarthy became prominent, and the Czechs were even more clearly pro-McCarthy than the Poles.

It has been argued that the concept of status politics is not a discovery of Lipset and Hofstadter but merely a new name for the ethnic politics always recognized in America.[35] However, ethnic politics has traditionally been conceived in terms of practical conflicts over specific goals. Until Lipset and Hofstadter, few people questioned whether the obvious issues in the struggles were really the important ones. The concept of status politics de-politicizes the ethnic and group conflicts. For that very reason, it fails as an explanation of McCarthyism, since it underestimates the importance of the Communist issue in explaining his appeal.

Similar considerations shed light on Catholic support for the Wisconsin senator. Although aspects of the American Catholic social and family structure and general belief system may be relevant in explaining McCarthy's support among Catholics, the church has traditionally been very sensitive to the Communist question. Catholics probably supported the Senator more from concern for his ends than from delight in his style. Moreover, McCarthy himself was a Catholic. This emphasizes the difficulty of ascribing to political or sociological causes what may be the result of the friends-and-neighbors effect.

McCarthy was also disproportionately supported in the corn belt in the southwest corner of the state. This seems to parallel a finding in South Dakota, where in the 1952 presidential primary Taft ran well in corn belt counties. Wisconsin's corn belt counties, among the most rural in the state, acted like other rural Wisconsin counties in supporting McCarthy more than other Republicans of the period. They then disproportionately voted for the Democrat Proxmire.

Corn belt residents seem to vote simply on the basis of economic self-interest during adversity and ideology during prosperity. (In this sense the area fits into the status-class politics framework of Lipset and Hofstadter.) In South Dakota, the poorer corn belt farmers are Democratic, the richer ones Republican. In a period of agricultural depression, the 1920's, sections of the midwest corn belt supported La Follette. Except when their pocketbooks are involved, corn belt farmers today vote conservative.

Those who have studied life in the corn belt argue that corn belt farmers prize initiative and individualism more than do those engaged in other forms of agriculture.* Perhaps these attitudes lead to a distrust of outside interference, an intolerance for places and events felt to be beyond individual control. There is some evidence that corn belt farmers take matters into their own hands during depression — hence the strength of the Farm Holiday Movement in Iowa in the early 1930's. In times of prosperity, when the corn farmers nevertheless feel confused by outside events, they may be sympathetic to McCarthyite appeals. However, the corn farmers did not support La Follette in the progressive period, or the Populists earlier. Indeed, La Follette and the Populists were in rebellion against the abstract reliance on individual initiative and other characteristics of corn belt Americanism that resulted in opposition to pragmatic social welfare legislation. In this sense, McCarthy's roots in the corn belt were the opposite of his alleged agrarian radical roots.

Corn belt residents, then, may have been attracted to McCarthy because of his general political style. The pluralists emphasize McCarthy's style, his methods, his basic approach to politics both in explaining the character of McCarthyism and in explaining its link with agrarian radicalism. Their

* Traditionally corn farmers were less in touch with outside, more industrialized areas than dairy farmers and less dependent for success on the accidents of weather than wheat farmers. Cooperatives were more common among dairy farmers, while corn farming was more a year-round activity than wheat farming. The typically American values of hard work and self-help, it is argued, therefore found their home in the corn belt.[36]

analysis suffers from three defects. In the first place, the political style that attracted corn belt residents to McCarthy was a conservative not an agrarian radical style. Similarly, McCarthy had his most important roots in the conservative Republican Party. This was a constituency attracted in part by his style but also traditionally antiradical. Second, many of those who voted for McCarthy were attracted not by his style but by the Republican label under which he ran. McCarthy capitalized on the traditional party vote. In the third place, many of those neither traditionally Republican nor attracted specifically to McCarthy by his broad appeals had a particular political concern: The importance of the Communist issue explains much of the support specifically attracted by McCarthy. This fear was the specific product of the cold war; its focus was foreign policy more than the "status politics" preoccupation with the enemy within. And if those attracted to McCarthy by his party or by his style largely came from an antiradical tradition, so too the Communist issue had no particular political appeal within the La Follette movement. Except during and shortly after World War I, foreign policy in general had little saliency to progressives — particularly the ethnic foreign policy which attracted East Europeans to McCarthy. The La Follettes mobilized support not around foreign policy but around economic grievances. Thus neither McCarthy's style nor his political issue place him in the progressive tradition.

Conclusion

Progressivism in Wisconsin mobilized poor Scandinavian farmers against the richer areas of the state. In so doing, it in part sundered existing political alliances and eventually reoriented the traditional party vote. McCarthy, on the other hand, rose to power with the votes of the richer German inhabitants of the farms and small cities in southern and eastern Wisconsin — antiprogressive except when they were

99

victims of McCarthy-type tactics during World War I. McCarthy's unique strength was not as important as this Republican Party strength. In any case, it reflected less a continuity with the progressive past and more the particular issues, preoccupations, and individual attachments of politics in the Korean War decade. Moreover, McCarthy was unable to transfer what progressive support he did obtain to his allies. In 1956, Glenn Davis, a congressman from southern Wisconsin, ran as the McCarthy and regular Republican candidate against incumbent Alexander Wiley in the Republican senatorial primary. Davis, one of the most vociferous McCarthy supporters in the country, came within a few thousand votes of beating Wiley. Yet Davis' vote was not highly related to support for McCarthy.

In 1956, the "friends-and-neighbors" effect so common in state primaries substantially influenced the political picture. Wiley was from northern Wisconsin, and whether for this reason or some other the progressive counties of the north and west clearly opposed Davis (see Figure 3.12).[37] On the other hand, Davis got strong support from the five counties of his own southern congressional district, which had not supported McCarthy. Over-all, Davis' correlation with McCarthy's 1952 primary vote was only .27, and his relation to the McCarthy index is even lower.

McCarthy had been dependent on traditional sources of Republican strength, and Davis too ran best in Republican territory.[38] McCarthy was able to deliver to Davis his own home territory in the northeast.* But it is noteworthy that

---

* Perhaps their common appeal to these conservative German, Polish, and Czechoslovakian counties in the northeast was due to ideology as well as residence. These counties may be similar to the lower-middle-class urban areas that voted against bond issues in the 1950's and were alleged to be sympathetic to McCarthy.[39] Here generalized anger and the status resentments described by *The New American Right* may be operating. The relation between the Davis and McCarthy votes indicates that perhaps the Senator was building a stable basis of support in northeastern Wisconsin.

WISCONSIN

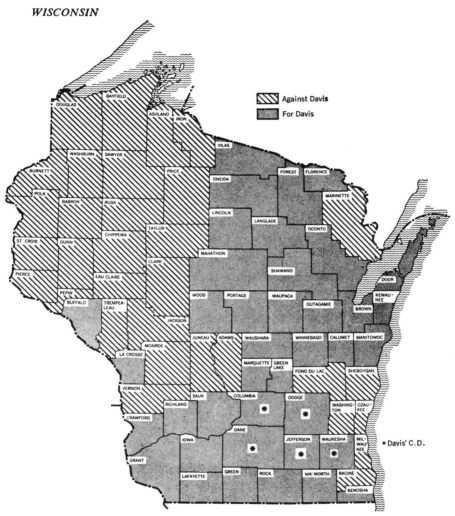

Figure 3.12.   Davis' strength in the 1956 Wisconsin
senatorial primary.

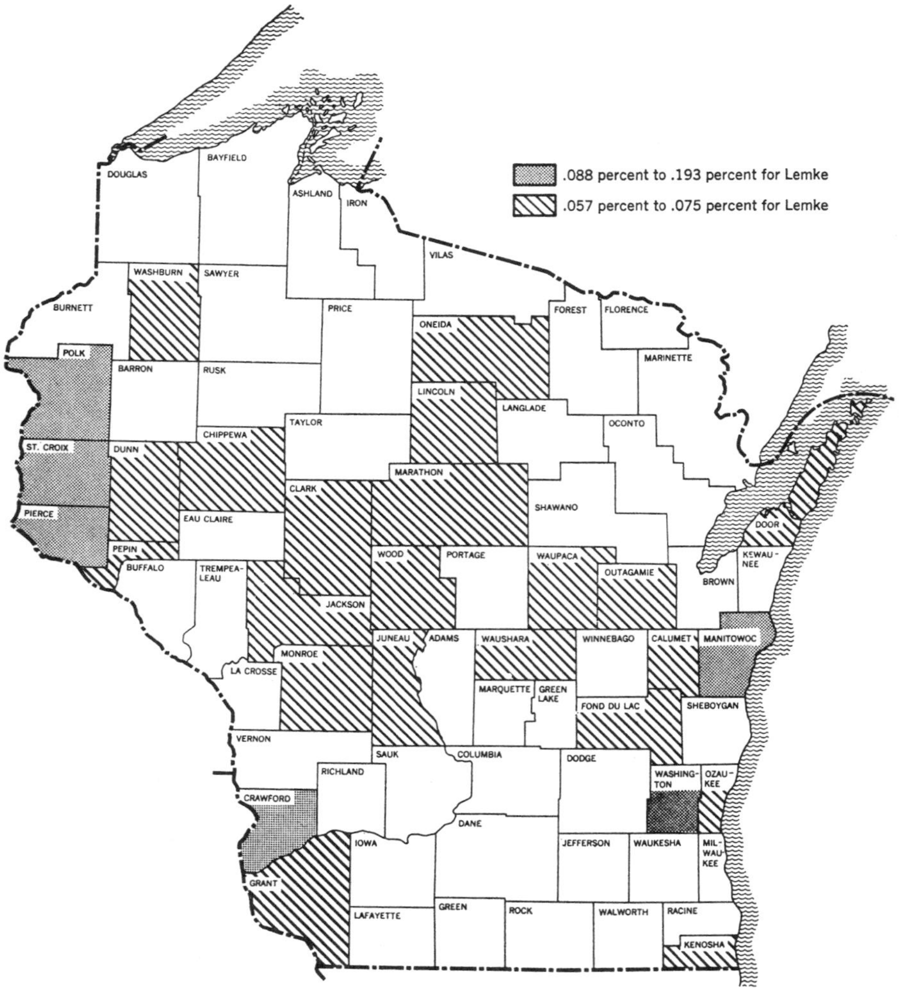

Figure 3.13. Lemke's strength in Wisconsin in 1936.

only two counties in the state could be said to have become consistently more Republican during and after the McCarthy period. One was a corn belt county, the other an urban Catholic county in McCarthy's home territory.

McCarthyism was not a mass protest; it flourished within the normal workings of American politics, not radically outside of them. Perhaps this may be brought home by a brief look at the movement alleged to bridge the gap between La Follette and McCarthy. In 1936, Father Coughlin's Union Party ran William Lemke of North Dakota for President. Lubell writes that the Lemke vote was ethnic rather than economic, Catholic and German rather than progressive.[40] But in Wisconsin Lemke received even less than his state average of 5 percent in the 3 most Catholic counties of the state.[41] He did run well in a number of German counties, but he polled his greatest vote (19 percent) in a Scandinavian progressive county. Other Scandinavian counties were in the top third of Lemke's support. Lemke ran badly in the Polish and Czech counties but did better in several other central Wisconsin counties. These were mostly German but poorer and often less German than the counties to the south and east (see Figure 3.13).

Lemke's vote united ethnic and class elements that were drifting apart during the progressive period. Had Lemke succeeded in developing a new political alliance of poor rural Germans and Scandinavians, he would have created a new American Right. Perhaps someone like McCarthy would have built upon it. But Lemke got significant support from none of the groups in his coalition. The Union party failed because it was a new and radical Right. McCarthy succeeded because of his roots in existing politics. Lemke's 5 percent of the Wisconsin vote was not so much a bridge between progressivism and McCarthyism as the pinnacle of depression-born proto-fascism, irrelevant to later American politics. With its roots in the traditional conservative past, McCarthyism was a more substantial and less radical movement.

NORTH DAKOTA:
AGRARIAN RADICALISM,
ETHNIC AND ECONOMIC

North Dakota has been more consistently radical than any other state in the union. In 1892, Weaver carried it for the Populists. From 1906 to the present, North Dakota has always had either a left-wing governor or a left-wing senator in office. Yet in 1954, both North Dakota senators voted against the censure of McCarthy. More than that, one of them, William Langer, had become prominent as a Non-Partisan Leaguer, had been a radical governor of North Dakota in the 1930's, and in the Senate had voted with the liberal Democrats on domestic issues.

Most of the agrarian radical leaders who evolved in a conservative and McCarthyite political direction had a Non-Partisan League background. Gerald Nye, sent by the League to the Senate in 1926, chaired the "merchants of death" inquiry which blamed munitions makers for American entry into World War I. A liberal hero as late as 1938, Nye had become an arch reactionary by 1944.* Lynn Frazier, first League governor of North Dakota, ended his career after World War II, calling the League "Communist," "anti-

---

* Nationally prominent liberals campaigned for Nye in North Dakota in 1938; in 1944, some of the most reactionary men in America toured the state in his behalf.[1]

Christian," and full of "CIOers." League father A. C. Townley supported Frazier's charges.[2] William Lemke, an early League leader, had been the presidential candidate of Father Coughlin's Union Party in 1936. He then represented North Dakota in Congress for a decade, voting isolationist and erratically conservative. Outside of North Dakota, League products Hendrik Shipstead of Minnesota and Burton Wheeler of Montana ended their careers in the American right wing.

This agrarian radical leadership provided only a fraction of McCarthy's total support. McCarthy received most of his leadership support from traditional conservatives. Nevertheless, the evolution of League leaders in a McCarthyite direction must be explained. Since the Non-Partisan League was strongest in North Dakota, this is the logical state on which to focus for an explanation of the McCarthyite evolution of agrarian radical leadership.

To pluralist theorists the paradox of agrarian radical leaders ending their careers as archconservatives is easily explained. They emphasize the ease of a shift from radical Left to radical Right, the rural and provincial character of the League, and the common eastern enemies of McCarthyism and agrarian radicalism. Locating a single midwestern rural tradition of opposition to the urban and cosmopolitan east, pluralists do not find the switch from agrarian radicalism to McCarthyism surprising. In Viereck's words,

> On the surface, Senators like Wheeler and Nye (originally Progressive and campaigners for La Follette) seemed to reverse themselves completely when they shifted . . . from "liberal" Progressives to "reactionary" America Firsters. But basically they had never changed at all; throughout they remained passionately Anglophobe, Germanophile, isolationist, and anti-eastern seaboard, first under leftist and then under rightist pretexts.[3]

The evidence from North Dakota suggests several reasons why this pluralist notion is incorrect. Most important, Viereck

105

fails to distinguish the Non-Partisan League's preoccupation with foreign policy from domestic agrarian radicalism and fails to perceive that the social base in North Dakota mobilized by the League's foreign policy contrasts with that mobilized by economic appeals. The League was born on the eve of World War I. True to the pacifist-Socialist character of its organizers, it opposed United States entry into the war. The resulting agitation and persecutions of the League elevated foreign policy to an importance that it did not have in the Populist and progressive periods. World War I was the formative and traumatic political experience for the leadership of the Non-Partisan League. Applying their politics of World War I to the international situation of the 1930's, Leaguers led the opposition to collective security. By the end of the decade, this placed them in alliance with the most reactionary elements in American politics, such as those who dominated the America First Committee. Because foreign policy overshadowed all other considerations, many Leaguers became domestic conservatives as well. Their preoccupation with foreign policy rather than domestic agrarian radicalism explains the McCarthyite cast of Shipstead, Nye, and Wheeler.

Many other Leaguers, like Congressman Usher Burdick, modified earlier isolationist attitudes and did not support McCarthy. These men and their descendants currently dominate the liberal North Dakota Democratic Party. Finally, a few Leaguers, like Langer, combined an isolationist foreign policy with domestic agrarian radicalism. Langer's constituency helps explain his politics. He had strong support among North Dakota's Scandinavian and native American farmers, traditionally radical for economic reasons. He had in addition built a base of support in the large Russian-German community of North Dakota. The Russian-Germans, traditionally conservative, were extremely sensitive to foreign policy. Not agrarian radicalism in general but support by the Russian-German constituency in particular is crucial in understanding the isolationist and pro-McCarthy position of Langer.

In the early twentieth century, great numbers of Germans who had settled in Russia emigrated to the United States, a large percentage settling in North Dakota. In 1930, 11 of North Dakota's 53 counties had a population more than 33 percent Russian-German.[4] These counties form a bloc in south-central and southwestern North Dakota (see Figure 4.1). To maintain their cultural identity, the Germans who emigrated to Russia had lived in isolated and tight-knit communities. They maintained these communities in the United States. Unlike the Germans of Wisconsin, who on the whole settled on the more prosperous farmland of the state, these Russian-Germans lived in the poorest areas.

Even before the Russian-German immigration, the North Dakota population had been substantially foreign-born — 44 percent in 1890. Canadians and Norwegians were the dominant ethnic groups then. As late as 1930, there were still more persons of Norwegian than of Russian-German stock in North Dakota.[5] But because the tight-knit German communities voted as a unit, they had an influence in North Dakota politics out of proportion to their numbers. Catholics numbered 17 percent in 1936, higher than in most rural states. This is in part explained by the Catholic composition of North Dakota's Canadian, German and to a lesser extent Russian-German population.

The economic character of North Dakota is of as great political importance as the ethnic composition of the state. North Dakota is the most rural state in the country and has virtually no industry. As late as 1930, 70 percent of the North Dakota population lived on farms. In 1950, the state remained over 40 percent rural-farm. Most of North Dakota's farmers grow wheat. Indeed, in 1930 70 percent of the state's farms were classified as cash-grain farms; these grew wheat almost exclusively. This dependence on one crop is exceptional, even in the relatively undiversified agriculture of the Plains states. Moreover, wheat farming is particularly speculative — dependent on the weather, the international market,

107

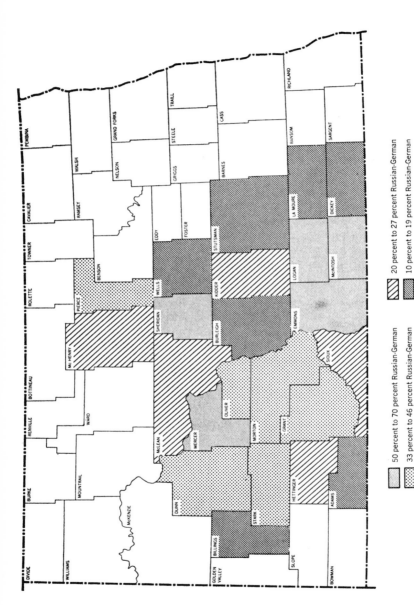

Figure 4.1. *The distribution of the Russian-German population in North Dakota, 1930.*

50 percent to 70 percent Russian-German

33 percent to 46 percent Russian-German

20 percent to 27 percent Russian-German

10 percent to 19 percent Russian-German

and the absence of disease. Given the speculative character of their enterprise, wheat farmers historically have turned to the government for protection. Wheat farming has therefore been associated with agrarian radicalism from the Grangers, to Populism, to the CCF in Saskatchewan, to the Non-Partisan League, to the Farmers Union.

Populism as a Class Movement

The traditional party cleavage in North Dakota was along ethnic lines.* The Democratic Party was a consistent minority party, drawing its chief support from Germans, Catholics, and particularly Canadians (see Table 4.1). Most North Dakotans in the frontier period had migrated from the northeast, from Canada, or directly from Scandinavia. Those from the northeast had traditional Whig-Republican allegiances, augmented by the Civil War. The Scandinavians felt at home in the Republican Party for cultural reasons, such as the party's support for prohibition. This same fact drove Catholics and Germans into the Democratic Party, which was in any case the traditional German and Catholic party in much of America. Canadian Democratic preponderance is difficult to under-

* To enrich the analysis of North Dakota politics, a factor analysis was carried out on the elections from 1889–1928. The concepts and mathematics of factor analysis are explained in Appendix B. For our purposes here, it is necessary to understand only that factor analysis permits the uncovering of "factors" common to several elections. Elections with high loadings (which run from +1.00 to −1.00) on a given factor and low loadings on the remaining factors identify the character of the factor. In North Dakota, there were four factors, representing traditional party, Populist, progressive, and Non-Partisan League strength. (Appendix B contains the table of factor loadings.)

The elections indicating traditional party strength most purely were those of 1889 and 1904. They were averaged together to form an index of traditional party strength. (When correlating the index with demographic data, three southwestern counties included in the original factor analysis were eliminated because of gaps and possible mistakes in the census data.)

TABLE 4.1

ETHNICITY AND THE TRADITIONAL PARTY VOTE IN
NORTH DAKOTA: CORRELATIONS

	Canadian	German	Catholic
Democratic	.62	.30	.30
Democratic holding Canadian constant	—	.58	.21
Democratic holding German constant	.74	—	.23
Democratic holding Catholic constant	.60	.23	—

stand except negatively. The factors propelling most North
Dakotans into the Republican Party were not relevant to the
Canadians, and rivalry between Canadians and "Americans"
may have converted the former to Democratic allegiance.[6]

In contrast to the ethnic base of the major parties, Populism

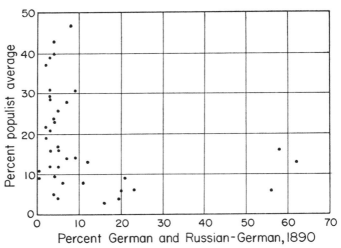

*Figure 4.2. Populism and the German and Russian-German
population in North Dakota (dots represent counties).*

was an economic movement. In order to connect Populism with McCarthyism, pluralists emphasize the ethnic orientations of the Populist movement and underplay its economic character. Certain ethnic patterns do appear in North Dakota Populism. As Figures 4.2 and 4.3 show, the highest Populist

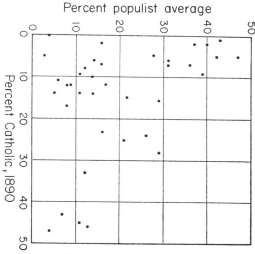

Figure 4.3.   Populism and the Catholic population in North Dakota (dots represent counties).

counties had virtually no Germans, Catholics, or Russian-Germans, while the most Catholic, German, and Russian-German counties were strongly anti-Populist. Scandinavians, on the other hand, supported the Populists (see Figure 4.4; $r = .39$). But there was no tendency for native-stock Americans, allegedly the backbone of "nativist" Populism, to support the movement disproportionately.

The best explanation of the Populist vote is economic. When the value of farm products per farm[7] is plotted against the average of the Populist votes for 1892 and 1894, there is a strong positive relationship between Populism and wealth (see Figure 4.5). The Populist vote increased as the wealth of the counties increased, but then fell off in the six rich counties of the Red River Valley, along the Minnesota border. Omitting those six counties, the richer the county, the greater the Populist vote ($r = .64$).

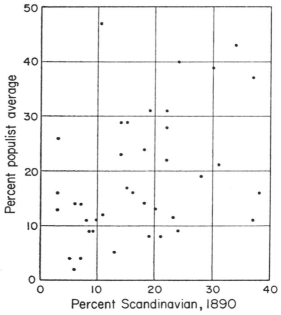

Figure 4.4.   Scandinavians and the North Dakota Populist vote (dots represent counties).

The decrease in the Populist vote in the valley has no explanation but the economic one. These counties were less Catholic and German than the state as a whole. One might hypothesize Populist opposition among nonfarmers and note that the valley counties were less rural than the state as a whole. But they were more Populist than many almost exclu-

112

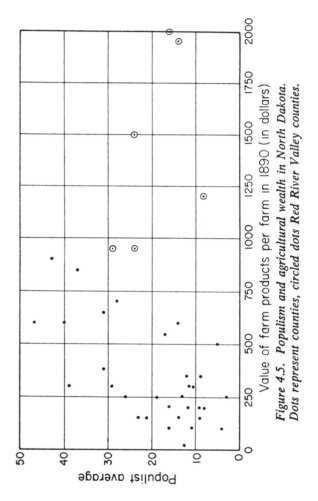

Figure 4.5. Populism and agricultural wealth in North Dakota. Dots represent counties, circled dots Red River Valley counties.

sively rural-farm counties.[8] Finally, the valley counties tended to have somewhat less of their acreage in wheat than was common in North Dakota in the 1890's, but they were still predominantly wheat growing and more Populist than many exclusively wheat counties. Those few counties growing little or no wheat were anti-Populist; they had few settled farmers in any case. After a certain threshold there was no relationship between acreage in wheat and the Populist vote.[9]

Other studies have arrived at analogous results, and the authors have explained rural middle-class Populist strength in terms of mortgage indebtedness, wheat growing, or commitment to the land. None of these explanations holds true throughout the Populist states, however,* and it is necessary to turn to class analysis.

There appear to be both economic and sociological reasons for the strength of Populism in the rural middle class. In the first place, farmers hardest hit by the agricultural depression were those who produced a significant crop for sale. Their fortunes depended on the fluctuations of the international wheat market. The poorest wheat farmers in recently settled areas lived much closer to subsistence level; their fortunes did

* In Kansas, Populism was weakest in the rich east and the poor west and strongest in the central section. Raymond Miller related this to the heavier mortgage burden in the central counties, but his evidence[10] is not conclusive, and he does not consider alternative explanations. Populism was strongest in central Nebraska, but actually negatively related to the degree of mortgaged indebtedness over the state as a whole.[11] In the Dakotas, there was no relation between mortgaged indebtedness and Populism.

Rejecting mortgaged indebtedness as an explanation of the Populist vote, Benton Wilcox and others have seen wheat growing in western Minnesota and central Kansas and Nebraska as the cause of Populist strength there.[12] In Nebraska and South Dakota, however, the correlation with wheat was a necessary but not sufficient cause of Populism.[13] As an alternative to the wheat explanation, Hallie Farmer has suggested that in central Kansas and Nebraska farmers were too committed to their land to leave in the face of the severe depression, and so voted Populist.[14] There was some tendency for the anti-Populist counties in North Dakota to be those which lost voters between 1889 and 1894, but the pattern was inconsistent.

not fluctuate so wildly. On the other hand, the richest farmers had both reserves and a more diversified agriculture on which to fall back.

In the second place, a mass movement such as Populism requires a certain level of consciousness of exploitation. The poorest and most isolated class elements are not likely to be the first to join a mass movement. As Marx pointed out, consciousness requires interaction. The poor, anti-Populist counties were the most sparsely settled. The Populist movement depended on hundreds of schoolhouse meetings, innumerable campaign speeches, the circulation of pamphlets from hand to hand. During the severe depressions of the 1880's and 1890's, the social relations and degree of consciousness in the rural middle class made it the base of the Populist uprising.[15]

In Saskatchewan, Lipset has found that the richer farmers, those with greater experience in cooperative movements, were the original backbone of the Cooperative Commonwealth Federation. He argues that it is more difficult to mobilize the poorer farmers, but once mobilized they retain a greater loyalty to the organization. Thus, by the time the CCF came to power, it was slightly disproportionately supported by the poorer farmers.[16] In a peculiar way, we shall have occasion to observe the same tendency in the evolution of the Non-Partisan League. But the Populist Party was too short-lived. It was born and died a movement of the rural middle class.

The particular ethnic-economic coalition put together by the Populists disappeared quickly from North Dakota politics.[17] The Populist base of social support ceased to be cohesive for two reasons. The first was economic. As the poorer counties reached a minimum level of settlement and diversity, their citizens no longer were opposed to movements of agrarian protest. As the richer counties became more prosperous, their opposition to agrarian radicalism increased. Second, soon after the demise of Populism great numbers of Russian-Germans migrated to North Dakota. For the next half-century their presence dominated the politics of the state.

115

Progressivism and Status Politics

From the election of progressive Democratic governor John Burke in 1906 to the rise of the Non-Partisan League ten years later, progressives were powerful in North Dakota politics. But the overwhelming conservative sentiment in the Russian-German counties prevented progressives from gaining control of the GOP. The index derived from averaging the most purely progressive elections was correlated —.81 with the Russian-German population. Scandinavians, on the other hand, were strongly progressive ($r = .78$).[18]

But progressivism was not simply an ethnic movement; it was also an economic movement of poor farmers.* North Dakota's eastern counties had few Russian-Germans and many Scandinavians. But these counties, particularly those in the Red River Valley, were less progressive than their ethnic composition would predict. Richer and less rural than the counties to the west, they tended to oppose progressivism. The progressives failed to obtain the support of the poorest and most rural areas of North Dakota — those inhabited by Russian-Germans. With the percentage of Russian-Germans held constant, however, there were positive correlations between progressivism and both the percentage of the population living on farms and the poverty of the land.†

* Initially the progressive movement lacked this economic component. It arose when more prosperous easterners opposed GOP machine control, based in the sparsely settled western counties.[19] But North Dakota progressivism gradually came to lose much of its original mugwump flavor.

† Holding constant the percentage Russian-German, the correlations between progressivism and percentage rural-farm and value of land per acre are .43 and —.37. Holding rural-farm constant raises the Russian-German correlation to —.84.

Of the national progressive politicians, Woodrow Wilson like La Follette received strong progressive support. In 1912, Wilson received both a progressive and a traditional Democratic vote. In 1916, his progressive support was particularly striking (see Figure 4.8). But Theodore Roosevelt in 1912 mobilized a distinctive coalition of his own. He tended to be opposed by progressive voters, and supported

North Dakota progressivism had an economic base similar to that of the La Follette movement in Wisconsin. And North Dakota was the one state besides Wisconsin that was carried by La Follette against Teddy Roosevelt in the 1912 presidential primaries. North Dakota's Gronna was the most consistent ally of La Follette in the Senate.

Progressive strength among poor farmers in North Dakota and Wisconsin challenges the "status politics" interpretation that locates progressive strength among the urban and well-to-do. Pluralists argue that the independent middle class was responding to a loss in social status that stemmed from the rise of new industrial elites. From such a standpoint, the "reactionary" character of progressivism becomes clear; it was seeking to halt the triumph of industrialization.

Status politics analysis is offered as an alternative to class analysis, which focuses on concrete economic grievances. But progressive strength among poor farmers is better explained by economic grievances than by concern over loss in social prestige. North Dakota agriculture was undiversified; railroads, bankers, and millers engaged in discriminatory practices; and the state was in economic vassalage to interests in Minneapolis and further east.[21] North Dakota farmers had real economic grievances; the movement they supported had an economic base.

If the economic base of progressivism has an economic explanation, what of progressivism's ethnic support? Status

---

by the traditional Republican electorate. These findings corroborate findings in South Dakota and Wisconsin. In all three states, the 1916 Wilson vote was clearly more progressive than the normal Democratic vote, and Roosevelt's vote was progressive in none of the states. But many analyses of progressivism base their conclusions on the composition of the Progressive Party of 1912. In particular, the urban character of progressivism is deduced largely from Chandler's analysis of Progressive Party leadership,[20] and from the fact that Roosevelt received an urban vote in the 1912 election. The Progressive Party of 1912 did have an urban character. But in the Middle West, at least, general conclusions about progressivism based on the Roosevelt movement cannot stand.

political interpretations focus on ethnic conflicts, ethnic traditions, and ethnic concerns. Indeed, no one can deny the importance of ethnic politics in America. Concern for the social position (status) of one's ethnic group can have powerful political consequences. But it is always necessary to ask what the ethnic politics is about. Sometimes, as with North Dakota's Scandinavian farmers, an ethnic tradition may lead to concern with economic demands.

Moreover, if it is important to ask what ethnic traditions will lead Scandinavians, for example, to support progressivism, it is equally important to ask why Russian-Germans would oppose it. Hofstadter, writing not about Russian-Germans in North Dakota but about European immigrants in American cities, suggests one type of answer. He compares the practical orientation of urban immigrants and urban machine politicians with the moralistic concerns of the progressives. In this view, the immigrant exploited politics for practical favors — jobs, protection against the police, welfare benefits. The progressive, on the other hand, had abstract notions of citizen participation and civic integrity, based on romantic nostalgia for a lost rural utopia. "Often he stood for things that to the immigrant were altogether bizarre, like women's rights and Sunday laws, or downright insulting, like temperance. His abstractions had no appeal within the immigrant's experience."[22]

It is true that in North Dakota the Russian-German immigrants were against prohibition and various blue laws. But in their refusal to support economic change, in their allegiance to their tight-knit communities, they were moralistic in another sense. These communities were fearful of alien influence, rigid and tradition-bound, far less adaptable than the progressives.

Hofstadter uses the notion of status anxieties to explain why certain groups become politically discontented. But status anxieties are only one kind of noneconomic factor that can produce political action. Certain traditions — if not status anxieties — do seem to have predisposed Scandinavians to support agrarian radical movements. Their class position alone does not explain their politics. Nevertheless, among North Dakota and Wisconsin Scandinavians the outcome of nonclass factors was class politics. Thus a status politics interpretation of the ethnic base of progressivism is insufficient. The Russian-German community in North Dakota provides a much more straightforward example of the utility of status politics analysis. The character of the Russian-German communities made them resistant to class appeals. Status anxieties may often explain not the demands of the politically discontented but the failure of groups to support programs for political change. In the agrarian Middle West, status politics better characterizes the opponents of progressivism than progressivism itself.

Although the progressives were tradition-bound in some basic sense, they were able to combine this with practical programs of economic and political reform. As progressive governor of North Dakota from 1906 to 1912, John Burke successfully sponsored a corrupt practices act; antipass and "short-weights" laws to regulate the railroads; pure food, seed, and sanitation laws; laws to control the public utilities; a law regulating child labor; a regulation of lobbying act; and the creation of a public heath laboratory and a state tax commission. The legislation produced by the Non-Partisan League included a state grain-grading system; a state bank deposit guarantee law; a nine-hour day for women; a land title registration law; a money and credits tax; the forbidding of railroad discrimination (for example, on long and short hauls); the reduction of freight rates; heavier railroad and other corporation taxation; state aid for rural education; and constitutional amendment proposals for woman suffrage and for the exemption of farm improvements from taxation. These are hardly the programs of rural reactionaries. The Russian-

German communities, on the other hand, were moralistic and tradition-bound in a simple and obvious sense. They opposed change.[23]

The Non-Partisan League and the Russian-Germans

The Non-Partisan League, which was organized in 1916, followed on the heels of progressivism. The first League elections were correlated with the progressive elections, and load .35 on the progressive factor. But the League even more than progressivism was an economic movement of farmers.* Moreover, in its farm-by-farm organization for strictly economic ends, the League was beginning to overcome the resistance of many Russian-German farmers to political radicalism. Although Russian-Germans as a whole remained more prominent among League opponents, the correlation went down to —.4. (For a comparison of the impact of progressivism and the League, see Figure 4.6.)

World War I shook the Russian-Germans even more forcefully from their traditional voting habits. In the 1918 North Dakota Republican gubernatorial primary, Lynn Frazier retained his rural support of two years previous. He received in addition a significant German vote. Eliminating the influence of the 1916 League vote, Frazier's relation to the Russian-German population was .68. This was a tremendous shift from the Russian-German opposition to the League of only two years previous. As in other states, the Russian-Germans voted for La Follette for President in 1924,[24] although the League elections of the 1920's were actually slightly negatively correlated with the percentage Russian-German. Still, the war and the League had brought significant numbers of Russian-Germans into the agrarian

---

* Frazier's correlation with the percentage rural-farm went up to .4; holding percentage Russian-German constant, the correlation was .59.

radical camp; the Russian-German population was for the first time fairly evenly split between radicalism and conservatism.

Russian-Germans did not give the League an ethnic coloration in the 1920's, but other groups did. The perennially pro-

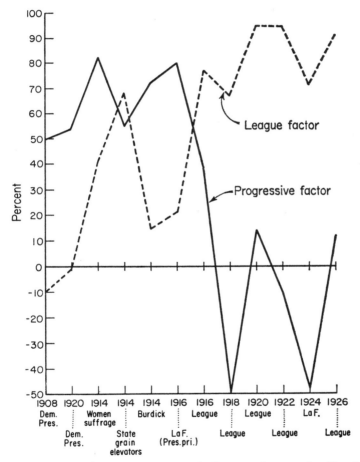

Figure 4.6. The progressive and League factors in North Dakota elections, 1908–1926.

121

gressive Scandinavians were slightly pro-League ($r = .36$ with rural-farm held constant). Catholics in the eastern part of the state were strongly anti-League.*

The problem of explaining the ethnic and religious basis of the predepression League is analogous to the problem of ethnic support for progressivism. Just as the Scandinavian conflict with Russian-Germans was most important in progressivism, the League mobilized Protestants against Catholics. We have noticed this lack of affinity between Catholicism and agrarian radicalism before. One explanation traces it to the moralistic and anti-Catholic attitudes of the agrarian radicals.[25] In this view, Catholics represented an alien threat to the rural homogeneity desired by the radicals. This is the kind of status anxiety alleged to produce progressivism as well. We earlier suggested, however, that status analysis be applied to the opponents of agrarian radicalism as well as to its supporters. Clearly Catholics are subject to status anxieties and moralistic intolerance — as the pluralists argue when they analyze Catholic support for McCarthy. It is at least plausible that Catholic support for McCarthy and opposition to the Non-Partisan League had similar roots. Both the Communist conspiracy and Non-Partisan League could be looked at as atheistic, immoral intrusions into a stable, homogeneous moral environment. Clearly, the Catholic leadership in North Dakota opposed the League because of its felt immorality. Both the Bishop of Bismarck and an official of the North

* Over the state as a whole, the correlation was only $-.34$, but it was markedly reduced by League strength in three highly Catholic western counties, where economic factors discussed later produced a high League vote. An earlier study (George A. Lundberg, "The Demographic and Economic Basis of Political Radicalism and Conservatism," *American Journal of Sociology,* Vol. 32 [March 1927]) mistakenly attributed particular League sympathy to the foreign-born. This study suffers from the small number of counties used as indicators of League and anti-League support. More than that, Lundberg's index of League strength includes one prewar, one war, and one postwar election, thus averaging out the relationship between Russian-German background and the League.

Dakota German-Catholic Union attacked the League. Catholics charged one Leaguer with being a free-lover.[26]

In addition to League support among Scandinavians and opposition from Catholics, the League was more likely to be supported by farmers than nonfarmers.[27] But this tendency was limited in the state as a whole by the striking division along geographic lines between supporters and opponents of the League. League strength came from western and north-central North Dakota. The League was weakest in the eastern third of the state and in a bloc of counties in south-central and southwestern Dakota (see Figure 4.7). In part, this demonstrates the appeal of the League in the newly settled, poorer western counties and its weakness in the more stable, richer, and agriculturally diversified counties of the east. Like the midwest Populists and like La Follette progressivism in Wisconsin, the League was strongest along the settled frontier.[28]

The frontier explanation fails to account for League weakness in the bloc of poor, rural, recently settled southern counties. League weakness in these counties also lowers the relationship between League support and such economic indexes as the value of land per acre and the percentage of wheat farms.[29] With one exception, the anti-League southern counties contained significant concentrations of Russian-Germans, yet other poor, Russian-German counties were pro-League (compare Figures 4.1 and 4.7). Perhaps particular economic conditions or particular organizational factors in the southern counties militated against the League. For example, Langer, then a League opponent, was from Morton County in the southern bloc. A decade and a half later, the southern counties would be the backbone of the League.*

* The League was the most disciplined political force in 1920's North Dakota. Intercorrelations among League elections approximated .9. Even before the appearance of the League, major party intercorrelations had rarely reached .8; in the 1920's, major party allegiances were dominated by loyalty and opposition to the League.

Figure 4.7. Non-Partisan League strength in North Dakota, 1921–1926.

Highest for League

Others for League

Most anti-League

Others anti-League

Senator Langer and the Non-Partisan League: The Ethnic Component of McCarthyism

At the depths of the depression in 1932, William Langer revived the declining Non-Partisan League and led it to victory in the Republican gubernatorial primary. Langer had been a Republican politician from southwestern Dakota who had split with the League after temporarily joining forces with it at its inception. After the 1928 League defeat, Langer took over the organization and catapulted himself to twenty-five years of political power in North Dakota.

The concern here is not to relate the vagaries of Langer's political career.[30] Suffice it to say that Langer found no contradiction in radical and illegal action to raise the price of wheat in North Dakota in the 1930's, support for welfare legislation, civil rights, and civil liberties in Washington in the 1940's and 1950's, and attacks on the U.N., the British, and the censure of McCarthy after World War II. What was the relation of this political career to Langer's social support at the electoral level?

North and South Dakota suffered perhaps more seriously than any other states during the depression. A series of droughts in the middle 1930's compounded already severe economic hardship. In 1936, the two states had higher proportions of their population on relief than any other states in the Union. The south-central and western portions of North Dakota, Langer's home territory, and the center of Russian-German settlement, were hit particularly hard. As a result, the Russian-Germans voted somewhat disproportionately for Langer in 1932. In addition, Langer's support was more exclusively farm-based ($r = .64$) than that of previous League candidates, and this farm support was more important than his Russian-German support.[31]

Langer got an even more disproportionate Russian-German and farm vote in 1934.* In 1936, with the Republican Party

* Actually Langer was in jail at the time and his wife was the

125

briefly in hostile hands, Langer ran for governor as an independent. The base he had built in the Russian-German community paid off in a close victory for him. This was the first election in which his Russian-German correlation was higher than his rural-farm correlation; the latter continued to be above .6 even with the Russian-German percentage held constant, but the former rose to .76. In 1940, thanks to the war issue and Langer's isolationism, his correlation with the percentage of Russian-Germans rose to .84. The intercorrelations of the four League elections from 1936–1940 average about .87 with each other, less than .6 with the 1932 vote, and .3 or below with the League vote of the 1920's.

The coalition of the German and the farm vote sent Langer to the Senate in 1946.[32] In order to understand subsequent developments, it is necessary to examine the regular party vote in the 1930's and 1940's.

Before the rise of the Non-Partisan League, the Democratic Party vote had combined a traditional factor and a progressive factor (see Figure 4.8). The most typical Democratic election had been the presidential campaign of 1908. Although it loads high on the progressive factor, its progressive component was due solely to its non-Russian-German character and not to any agrarian radical support.[33] This election continued to be positively related to the modern Democratic vote, but only moderately ($r = .3$ to .6). A far more significant presursor of the modern Democratic vote was the progressive vote. Thus La Follette's 1916 election was correlated .6 to .7 with the post-1938 Democratic vote. This is because as the Non-Partisan League became Russian-German the Democratic Party became as strongly non-Russian-German.

In this process, the Smith and first Roosevelt elections were exceptions. The Smith vote was Catholic, of course ($r = .54$), but equally Russian-German. Crucial here was Russian-German opposition to prohibition.[34] In 1932 Russian-Ger-

official candidate. Her vote was correlated .62 with the percentage Russian-German, .71 with the percentage rural-farm.

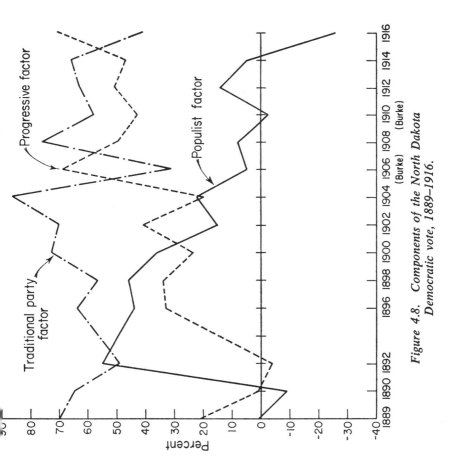

Figure 4.8. Components of the North Dakota
Democratic vote, 1889–1916.

127

mans responded to the depression by voting for F.D.R. as well as Langer.* The Roosevelt and Smith votes were actually negatively correlated with the Democratic elections that preceded and followed them. By 1936, the Roosevelt vote was non-Russian-German.† In the wake of World War II, the negative correlations between percentage Russian-German and percentage Democratic became extremely high. After a flirtation with Smith and Roosevelt, Russian-Germans were back in the Republican Party more exclusively than ever before.

Indeed, the key to the Russian-German vote lies in the fact that it maintained its adherence to the Republican Party longer than its support of the League. As prosperity returned to North Dakota and as foreign policy became salient, the Russian-Germans became generally Republican rather than specifically League in behavior. The 1944 election reveals this development. In that year, Langer's candidate, Usher Burdick, ran against Nye — a radical turned conservative isolationist — for the Senate in the Republican primary. (Orthodox conservatives had their own candidate, who hailed from the Red River Valley.) In 1938, Langer himself had opposed Nye for the Senate. To national liberals, Nye was then the progressive candidate; Langer's support among the Russian-Germans came close to beating him. Nye's correlation with the percentage Russian-German in 1938 was — .69. In 1944, Burdick was clearly the progressive candidate and received a rural vote.³⁵ But Burdick was beaten in the Russian-German counties by Nye's isolationism. In spite of the Langer ma-

* One should not overlook the agrarian radical component of the Smith vote; like La Follette's, it loaded positively on the League factor. Smith's vote was actually rural, not urban; Roosevelt's was highly rural ($r = .58$), suggesting the economic basis of his support. As in other states, Roosevelt's 1932 vote was more rural, his 1936 vote more urban, but the shift was far more striking in North Dakota.

† F.D.R.'s correlation with the Russian-German population went from +.55 in 1932 to —.41 in 1936.

128

chine, Nye's correlation with the percentage of Russian-Germans was .52.

In 1946, Langer was able to maintain significant support for himself in the Russian-German communities. But in 1952, a well-organized conservative group was becoming powerful in the GOP. Running against a conservative isolationist in the Republican primary, Langer's relation to the Russian-German population dropped to .37. Holding constant his strength among farmers, Langer's relation to the percentage Russian-German was only .27.*

While Langer's Russian-German support declined after World War II, the Republican presidential vote maintained its striking base in the Russian-German community,[36] where, after 1938, sensitivity to foreign policy was clearly precedent to domestic agrarian radicalism. The Russian-Germans were voting their opposition to World War II and the Korean War, supplemented by their increased prosperity.

Langer's Russian-German support, like Roosevelt's, had been called forth by the depression. But helped by his isolationist foreign policy, Langer was able to retain the allegiance of this essentially conservative group, while Roosevelt and Burdick were not.

Asserting that one of McCarthy's supporters was an agrarian radical without stressing Langer's ethnic base gives a misleading impression of the McCarthy movement. Langer and McCarthy shared foreign policy concerns in particular, not rural radicalism in general. Langer's agrarian radical rhetoric and program were the product of economic hardship and economic concerns, while McCarthyism was a movement that emerged in prosperity because of a concern over foreign policy. The economic roots of Langer's agrarian radicalism seem less important in his support for McCarthy than does his base in an ethnic community that was *anti-agrarian radical*

---

* Indeed, Langer's opposition tried to capitalize on voter suspicion of communism and foreigners. They called Langer a Communist-sympathizer in an "alien racket" (the League).[37]

in the Populist and progressive periods. Certainly, support for McCarthy by politicians with a Russian-German base reveals a significant amount about the character of McCarthyism.

It is risky, nevertheless, to attribute the behavior of a man like Langer to a single factor. There were elements in his agrarian radical ideology apart from the ethnic base that could also have led him to oppose McCarthy's censure. Two factors seem significant but both actually differentiate Langer from McCarthy. First, many supporters of McCarthy saw his crusade not as an attack upon free speech but as an exercise of free speech.[38] For an agrarian radical leadership forged in the persecutions accompanying World War I, this was especially true. A perversion of the agrarian radical sensitivity to individual rights could have led to Langer's support for McCarthy. But this very peculiarity gave Langer's pro-McCarthyism a different character from that typical of the period. Unlike McCarthy, Langer always strongly supported civil rights, civil liberties, and minority group interests. He and Lehman were the only two senators to object to three contempt citations issued by McCarthy's Senate investigating committee. Langer charged that the committee had treated Corliss Lamont unfairly.[39] Did the same sensitivity to individual rights lead him to vote against the censure of McCarthy — this time to defend McCarthy's rights?

The agrarian radical roots of Langer's isolationism also contrast with McCarthy's nationalism. Langer attacked Russia, but reserved most of his fire for the British aristocracy and the British empire.* The one favorable speech in six years that Langer made about Britain was to endorse the Socialist-supported Beveridge Plan for a welfare state.[40] McCarthy did not emphasize British imperialism at the expense of Russian, as he virtually always vilified the Socialists in his attacks on Britain and rarely attacked British imperialism without mentioning its Socialist character. Langer's anti-

---

* Soon after World War II, Langer claimed that Britain, not Russia, was the imperialist threat.[41]

British rhetoric had a Populist flavor; the suspicion was of aristocracy. McCarthy's attacks on Britain had Irish and German roots; socialism and the Korean and world wars were the crucial issues.

Still, thanks to World War I and his Russian-German constituency, Langer was preoccupied with foreign policy in a way that could lead in McCarthyite directions. This was not true of the nonethnic agrarian radicals.

McCarthyism and Orthodox Agrarian Radicals

The Scandinavian and native American farmers, who supported agrarian radicals for reasons of economics rather than foreign policy, were not immune from political extremism. But the movement they supported had an economic and pseudo-Populist appeal, very different from McCarthy's.

In 1936, William Lemke, an ex-Leaguer, ran for the presidency on Father Coughlin's Union Party ticket. According to Lubell, Lemke got a Catholic and German vote, reflecting the isolationist rather than the economic side of agrarian radicalism.[42] This was perhaps true in the cities, but not in the Dakotas or Wisconsin. In North Dakota, Lemke failed to appeal to the Russian-Germans, who were attracted by direct economic benefits and specifically ethnic appeals, not by soured Populism. Lemke ran best in northwestern North Dakota, the most undiversified wheat-farming region of the state (see Figure 4.9).*

This was the same sort of area where Populism had been strong.† Both Lemke and the Populists ran best in one-crop wheat areas hard-hit by depression and drought. These areas

---

* Lemke's highest correlation with a demographic variable was .45 with the percentage of cash-grain (wheat) farms. Holding constant Lemke's *negative* relation with Catholicism, the correlation rises to .51.

† Lemke's counties grew no wheat at all in the 1890's, so a correlation coefficient relating support for Lemke to the Populists would be meaningless.

131

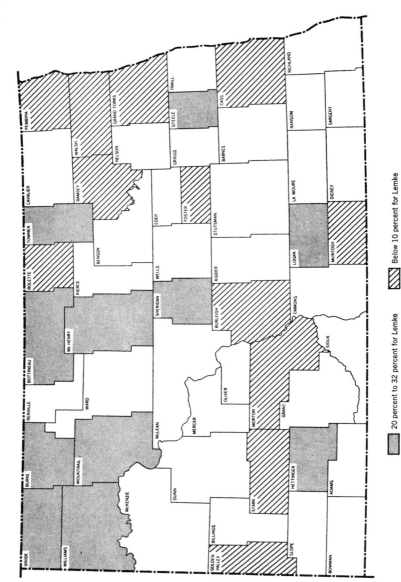

Figure 4.9. *The Lemke vote in North Dakota, 1936.*

20 percent to 32 percent for Lemke

Below 10 percent for Lemke

had been settled recently, but not so recently that they were in too primitive a stage to support movements of agrarian protest. This is not to say that the similar bases of support make the two movements similar — that the authoritarian character of the Union Party is proof of the authoritarian character of Populism. The similarity is in social support, not necessarily in political character.

Langer, by remaining a domestic radical, had retained his agrarian support. But Lemke soon became a more orthodox conservative; like Nye, he lost his agrarian constituency and gained strength among the Russian-Germans.[43] The non-German agrarian radical constituency turned elsewhere. It supported Usher Burdick for Senator against Nye in the 1944 senatorial primary,* and was mobilized by the Farmers Union when it became politically active after World War II.

By 1947, the Farmers Union had 37,000 members in North Dakota — between 55 percent and 65 percent of the farmers of the state.[44] In its willingness to work within the Democratic Party and in its more liberal positions on domestic and international questions, the Farmers Union came into conflict with old-guard Non-Partisan Leaguers. It also encountered the opposition of elements within the Democratic Party. However, in 1956 the Farmers Union succeeded in capturing the Democratic primary nominations, and in 1958 it elected Quentin Burdick Congressman for North Dakota.[45] The resurgence of the Democratic Party under the aegis of the Farmers Union came in a period of relative agricultural hardship. In a special election in 1960 to fill the senate seat vacated by Langer's death, Burdick was narrowly elected.

Both in his congressional victory in 1958 and in his senatorial victory in 1960, Burdick attracted many of the Russian-German farmers who had previously voted Republican. But

* Lemke's 1936 vote had its second highest correlation (.5) with the Burdick vote. (Its highest, —.57, was with Lemke's opponent, F.D.R.)

the Russian-German community as a whole remained strongly anti-Democratic. Burdick's correlation with the percentage Russian-German was — .55 in 1960, while in the general election two years earlier Langer's support, because it was Republican, had been correlated +.67.[46]

Quentin Burdick is the son of Usher Burdick, a man whose career spans the years from progressivism through the Non-Partisan League to the Farmers Union. Indeed, Quentin Burdick had been elected to the congressional seat of his retiring father. Both father and son were anti-McCarthy. The Burdicks came from an agrarian radical tradition which because it was not preoccupied with questions of foreign policy did not degenerate in a McCarthyite direction during or after World War II.* It rather found expression in the Farmers Union. The Farmers Union was anti-McCarthy. Before McCarthy came on the scene its national leadership had been guilty less of Red-baiting than of fellow traveling. The Union opposed aid to Greece and Turkey in 1947, and much of its leadership was sympathetic to Henry Wallace in 1948.[47] Unlike McCarthy, the Farmers Union was economically radical and tended to project its economic radicalism onto foreign policy. Its "isolationism," as that of progressives like Bob La Follette, Jr. and Congressman Merlin Hull of Wisconsin, was of a pacifist-humanitarian character, very different from McCarthy's. The danger was not so much Communist-phobia as Communist-philia, although La Follette and Hull were immune from this disease, and the Farmers Union suffered from it for only a brief period.†

* Usher Burdick was one of two congressmen to vote against outlawing the Communist Party in the House, while Langer voted for it in the Senate. George McGovern, the South Dakota counterpart to Quentin Burdick, was for a time the director of the Food for Peace program in the Kennedy administration. Like Burdick, McGovern was elected Democratic Congressman in 1958. He followed Burdick into the Senate in 1962. Both Burdick and McGovern criticized Lyndon Johnson's Vietnam policies from a point of view similar to Fulbright's.

† The difference over foreign policy between Langer and the

The orthodox agrarian radical constituency could, under severe economic hardship, support a Lemke. Its leaders might be briefly guilty of humanitarian naïveté in foreign policy. But it was not drawn to the very different appeals of McCarthy. McCarthy drew sustenance from leaders of a Republican Party based in the conservative Red River Valley and in the Russian-German counties. True, the GOP gained strength in North Dakota after 1948. In part, the return of prosperity was to blame. In part, there was also no doubt general dissatisfaction over "Communism, Corruption, and Korea." In dramatizing these issues, McCarthy may have contributed to Republican resurgence. But this resurgence came across the state. Far from realigning the sources of support for the Republican Party, McCarthy flourished during the greatest party stability North Dakota has ever known. When the nonethnic agrarian radical constituency again became important in North Dakota in the late 1950's, it supported the antinativist, liberal Quentin Burdick, not a McCarthy or even a Langer.

North Dakota produced three agrarian radical movements — Populism, progressivism, and the Non-Partisan League. At first it appears that these three movements mobilized differing bases of political support and were independent of each other. One must ask whether there is an agrarian radical tradition at all, much less one related to McCarthyism. The changing ethnic and economic composition of North Dakota made the particular county-by-county base of support for Populism irrelevant to later agrarian radical movements. The failure of progressivism to recruit Russian-German support made its base very different from the later Non-Partisan League base. Nevertheless, on closer inspection all three movements exhibited similar preoccupations and analogous

---

Union was revealed in the 1952 Republican primary election. In that campaign, Langer, whom the Union supported, stressed domestic issues. He had tried isolationist appeals early in the campaign, but dropped them after a conference with the Union.[48]

bases of social support. Agrarian radicalism tended to be strongest in the poorer, agriculturally less diversified, more recently settled areas of the state — except, as in the Populist case, where the most recently settled areas were still in a very primitive stage of development, or, as in the progressive case, where particular ethnic traditions prevented many poor farmers from becoming agrarian radical. A common thread runs through the three movements — not a thread of status anxieties and generalized resentments against industrialization but of common concern with concrete economic grievances.

An additional kind of agrarian radical support appeared briefly during World War I and then again during the depression and the Second World War. This was support from a Russian-German constituency which could only be shaken from its traditional conservatism by tremendous shocks — the Great Depression and the two wars against Germany.

William Langer built a political career out of combining the two agrarian radical constituencies. By the 1950's, he shared the Russian-German constituency with conservative Republicans — and like them he opposed the censure of McCarthy. Also during the 1950's, the economic constituency of agrarian radicalism, under the impact of the Farmers Union and an agricultural recession, began to move into the Democratic Party. Both the power and the liberal political stance of the North Dakota Democratic Party depend on the support of these agrarian radicals. Langer had his agrarian radicalism in common with opponents of McCarthy and his McCarthyism in common with opponents of agrarian radicalism.

SOUTH DAKOTA:
FROM LEFT TO RIGHT

Writing in 1946, John Gunther described South Dakota as a model of political conservatism.[1] This was indeed a short perspective. In the 1890's the state had been a Populist stronghold. Scorning fusion with the Democrats before 1896, the Populists polled between 30 percent and 40 percent of the vote. In 1896 and 1898, Fusion candidates were victorious. Only six years later, a progressive captured the Republican nomination for governor; and from then until the 1930's South Dakota was a banner progressive state. Teddy Roosevelt carried it in 1912, and it gave strong support to the Non-Partisan League and to the La Follette campaign of 1924. However, the transformation of the Republican Party during the New Deal led to a period of conservative control which was the longest in South Dakota history. In the late 1950's, there was a Democratic resurgence.

South Dakota thus supported the left wing of the Republican Party before the New Deal and the right wing after it. Its electorate contributed to Populist strength in the 1890's, its political leadership to McCarthyite strength in the 1950's. Yet South Dakota agrarian radicalism did not become conservative; rather it declined as a viable alternative to traditional conservatism. There were several reasons for this. Politically, with the New Deal liberal state politicians no longer found a home in the Republican Party. But the GOP continued to dominate South Dakota politics. Before the New Deal the Republican Party had contained many liberal progressives who held state office in South Dakota by winning Republican primaries. Now liberal leaders did not enter the GOP, but ex-progressive voters, dominated by traditional party loyalty, remained Republican. Nevertheless, to some extent former agrarian radicals did move into the Democratic Party. Those whose politics had been primarily economic — Populists and 1920's progressives — were more likely to do so than those like the prewar South Dakota progressives whose political demands had been more moralistic.

Perhaps the most important factor in the decline of agrarian radicalism was the reduction in the percentage of farm families in South Dakota by almost one half between 1890 and 1950. Economically radical movements had generally pitted farmers against their conservative, small-town rural neighbors. As the relative proportions of farmers in the Middle West declined drastically, the conservative, nonfarm vote increased in importance. Hence, conservative strength in South Dakota and other former agrarian radical territory indicated in large part the disappearance of the agrarian radical social base. Moreover, the farm prosperity brought by World War II muted the appeal of economic slogans to those farmers who remained.

Populism and Its Impact on the Major Parties

For five elections from 1890 to 1894, the Populist Party polled between one quarter and one third of the South Dakota vote. The Fusion tickets of 1896 and 1898 narrowly carried the state for President and governor. Those elections in which the Populists ran without Democratic allies are all highly intercorrelated;[2] voting patterns in the state would not be so stable again for almost half a century.

The economic character of North Dakota Populism challenged the view that Populism appealed primarily to ethnic-

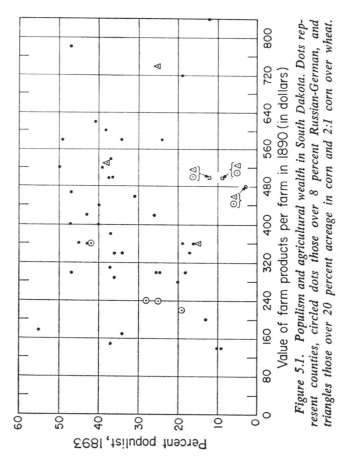

Figure 5.1. Populism and agricultural wealth in South Dakota. Dots represent counties, circled dots those over 8 percent Russian-German, and triangles those over 20 percent acreage in corn and 2:1 corn over wheat.

based status resentments. The best explanation of the Populist vote in South Dakota is also the wealth of the counties.[3] Although this tendency was not so clear-cut as in North Dakota, the Populist vote tended to increase in the richer counties and fall off in the very richest. Yet it remained high in one of the four richest counties, and there were four counties of middling wealth that were much less Populist than the other middle-class counties. The three least Populist were the only three corn belt counties whose population was more than 8 percent Russian-German (see Figure 5.1). North Dakota Russian-German residents were also anti-Populist. The fourth county contained the only real city in the state, suggesting an urban vote against Populism.[4]

Crop patterns also influenced the Populist vote. Populist counties were concentrated in the wheat belt, anti-Populist counties in the corn belt (see Figures 5.2 and 5.3). But the relationship between the percentage of land planted in wheat and the Populist vote was not high ($r = .33$).

Ethnic influences lowered the association between Populism and wheat. Seven of the eight counties more than 15 percent Scandinavian were more Populist than their acreage in wheat would predict.[5] Eight of the nine counties more than 12 percent German and Russian-German were less Populist than their acreage in wheat would predict (see Figure 5.4). Thus, taking into account the influence of wheat, there was an ethnic vote for and against Populism. Moreover, the low Populist vote in the poorest and in two of the three richest wheat counties in the state substantially lowered the over-all relationship between wheat and Populism.*

* Other ethnic data bear on the Populist vote. The two Czech counties were anti-Populist. The one Populist wheat county among the three richest wheat counties was far more Scandinavian than the other two.

As in other states, the Populist vote was related to Republicanism and prohibitionism, probably for ethnic reasons. The prohibition referendum averaged about .55 with the Populist elections. The Populist elections were far more negatively related to the Democratic

140

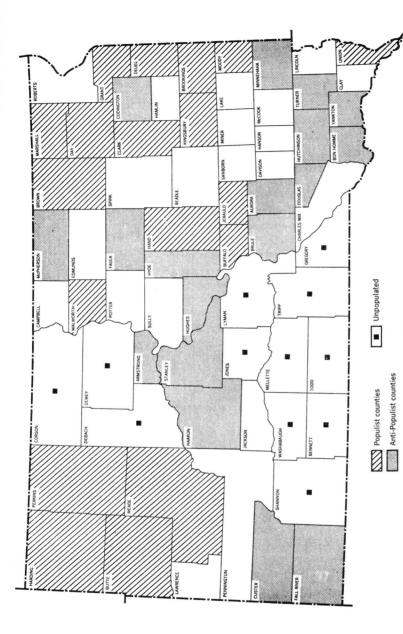

Figure 5.2. *Populist strength in South Dakota, 1890–1894.*

Populist counties

Anti-Populist counties

Unpopulated

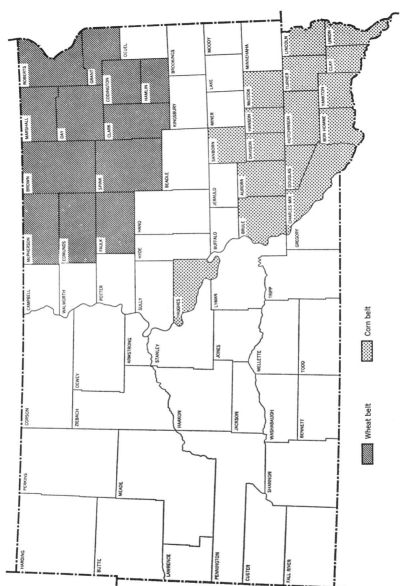

Figure 5.3. *Wheat and corn belts in South Dakota, 1890.*

Wheat belt

Corn belt

Did farmers support Populism more than nonfarmers? Over the state as a whole, there was no such tendency. This was because many other factors — ethnicity, crop, wealth — produced considerable farmer opposition to the Populists. However, it is likely that within counties predisposed by these other factors to support Populism, farmers voted for

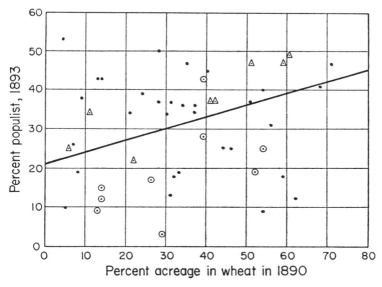

Figure 5.4. Populism, wheat, and ethnicity in South Dakota. Dots represent counties, circled dots those over 12 percent Russian and Russian-German, and triangles over 15 percent Scandinavian.

the movement far more than nonfarmers. In states where precinct patterns have been examined, this was indeed the case.[6] In any event, farmers were a clear majority of the South Dakota population, and provided most of the Populist votes.

The Populist Party and the Fusion campaigns of 1896-1900 reoriented the major party vote in South Dakota. The

vote of 1889 than to the Republican vote of that year, except in 1892, when many Democrats voted for Weaver for President.

Democratic vote in the first decade of the twentieth century remained far closer to the Populist-Democratic fusion base than the traditional Democratic vote had been (see Table 5.1). However, it would be a mistake to exaggerate the extent of this reorientation. Many ex-Republican Populists entering the Democratic Party in 1896 returned to the GOP after 1898.*

The major party vote in South Dakota was less cohesive than it was in the more settled states farther east, but one consequence of the party reorientation was a growing stability in the major party vote from election to election. Since the Republican Party consistently carried the state by large majorities, the conflict within the GOP between progressives and stalwarts determined South Dakota's stance in state and national politics.

Progressivism and the Non-Partisan League

Pre-World War I progressivism in South Dakota differed in two respects from the Populist Party, the Non-Partisan League, and the progressive movements in North Dakota and Wisconsin.

First, in those states progressivism was a movement of the poor; in South Dakota, it was supported by the rich. The vote for Thorson in 1910, which had the highest intercorrelations with other progressive elections, was correlated .66 with the value of land per acre.

The progressive counties included five of the richest corn belt counties. The stalwart counties included three of the four

---

* Democratic counties remained opposed to prohibition, but the average correlation was —.49, compared to —.58 for the pre-Populist Democratic vote. There was in both periods a low relationship between Catholicism and the Democratic vote. The over-all relationship between German background and the Democratic vote, low in 1889, disappeared after Fusion. Nevertheless, German counties remained somewhat Democratic, as were western, native-stock, and Austrian counties. Russian-German and wheat-belt counties were Republican.

TABLE 5.1

POPULISM AND THE PARTY VOTE IN SOUTH DAKOTA

	1889 Dem. Gov.	1893 Pop. Judge	1893 Dem. Judge	1896 Fus. Pres.	1898 Fus. Gov.	1900 Fus. Pres.	1902 Dem. Gov.	1904 Dem. Pres.	1906 Dem. Gov.	1908 Dem. Pres.	1910 Dem. Gov.	1912 Dem. Pres.
1889 Democratic Governor												
1893 Populist Judge	−36											
1893 Democratic Judge	51	−57										
1896 Fusion President	−01	61	11									
1898 Fusion Governor	−12	51	06	73								
1900 Fusion President	14	36	24	77	83							
1902 Democratic Governor	42	−05	55	53	48	74						
1904 Democratic President	57	−20	63	37	34	58	84					
1906 Democratic Governor	43	−07	54	43	38	63	81	85				
1908 Democratic President	47	02	49	50	57	77	80	75	82			
1910 Democratic Governor	55	−28	56	19	29	52	60	62	70	76		
1912 Democratic President	40	00	34	42	34	55	56	55	52	70	51	
1916 Democratic President	10	17	19	48	56	73	52	41	54	65	39	65

Russian-German counties, a bloc of counties in the south-west, and no corn belt counties but the Russian-German Hutchinson (see Figure 5.5).*

The strong support for progressivism in the rich, corn belt counties suggests an analysis of the South Dakota movement in terms of status politics rather than economic grievances. The tone of South Dakota progressivism, rooted in corn belt individualism, was more economically moderate and moralistic than the movements in North Dakota and Wisconsin. On the other hand, status politics interpretations have presented progressivism as an urban movement of native-born Protestants. In South Dakota, there was no relation between the proportions of farmers, Catholics, or native-born and the progressive vote.†

The ethnic component of progressivism lay in disproportionate Scandinavian support for the movement and large-scale Russian-German opposition to it.[7] These were the only characteristics of progressivism common to the Dakotas and Wisconsin; they relate progressivism to Populism as well.

South Dakota progressivism differed in a second respect from progressivism in North Dakota and Wisconsin. It was politically diffuse. Whereas other agrarian radical movements exhibited considerable stability, the progressive base of support in South Dakota shifted from election to election. Although Coe Crawford became the progressive Republican

* Progressive and stalwart counties were those consistently progressive or stalwart in four progressive elections. (Sterling's vote was omitted because of its extremely low correlations with the other progressive elections.)

† Evidence about the ethnic and class composition of the progressive movement has come from the Roosevelt campaign of 1912, which did not attract typical progressive electoral support. But even the evidence about the Progressive Party is dubious. In Massachusetts, state Progressive Party leaders resembled Republicans. The latter were even more likely to be native-born, Protestant, and of British heritage. Lawyers were equally prominent in both parties. Cf. Richard B. Sherman, "The Status Revolution and Massachusetts Progressive Leadership," *Political Science Quarterly*, Vol. 78 (March 1963), pp. 59–63.

Figure 5.5. *Progressivism in South Dakota, 1908–1914.*

Progressive

Anti-Progressive

Unpopulated

governor of South Dakota in 1904, only ten years after the height of Populism, his election, his later primary votes, and the votes given other progressives were related neither to Populism nor to any other electoral configurations in South Dakota's history.[8] Progressive elections showed little connection not only with the past but with each other (see Table 5.2). This is a striking difference from Populism. As a more moderate political movement, progressivism created neither the organizational nor the ideological commitments necessary to make a distinct impression on the South Dakota electorate.

TABLE 5.2
SHIFT IN BASE OF SOUTH DAKOTA PROGRESSIVISM, 1908–1916

	1908 Crawford	1910 Thorson	1912 Sterling	1912 Taft	1914 Crawford
1908 Crawford					
1910 Thorson	56				
1912 Sterling	26	38			
1912 Taft	−01	−46	−09		
1914 Crawford	33	47	16	−53	
1916 Norbeck	08	20	29	04	05

The progressive faction was so powerful in South Dakota that it succeeded in making Teddy Roosevelt the regular Republican candidate on the November ballot in 1912. However, Coe Crawford was defeated in the 1914 Republican senatorial primary, and the gubernatorial primary victory of progressive Peter Norbeck in 1916 marked another shift in progressive support. Norbeck's vote was even less related to earlier progressive elections than they had been to each other and was positively related to the Fusion Democratic vote of 1896. Most important, Norbeck did not get disproportionate support from the rich areas of the state.[9] But any chance Norbeck had of building a stable base of support was thwarted by the Non-Partisan League and the war.

The Non-Partisan League, which was organized in 1916 in North Dakota, contested its first South Dakota election in

1918. In North Dakota, the League had been organized around the grievances of wheat farmers. While its base of support shifted from non-German to German in 1918, it had already made an economic impact that limited its antiwar

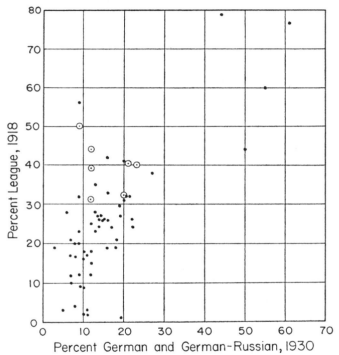

Figure 5.6. German support for the Non-Partisan League in South Dakota, 1918. Dots represent counties, circled dots those counties strongly for League 1918–1922.

appeal to the Germans. By the time the League participated in its first South Dakota election, the United States was at war. The League's 1918 vote in South Dakota correlated .71 with the German and Russian-German population. Progressive governor Norbeck, on the other hand, favored the war and lost what earlier German support he had had. Norbeck's pre- and postwar votes were unrelated to each other.[10] After 1924, when La Follette received strong antiwar support, Germans stopped supporting or opposing progressives on the basis of the war issue.[11]

Wheat and corn-and-wheat counties that had supported the League in 1918 remained with it in 1920 and 1922 as its German support evaporated (see Figure 5.6).[12] The opposition to the League, as to La Follette in 1924, was concentrated in the cattle counties west of the Missouri.

TABLE 5.3
CORRELATIONS OF VOTE FOR PROGRESSIVE CANDIDATES IN SOUTH DAKOTA, 1924–1932

	1924 McMaster	1926 Norbeck	1926 Bank Guarantee Act	1930 McMaster
1924 McMaster				
1926 Norbeck	25			
1926 Bank Guarantee Act	22	20		
1930 McMaster	35	53	47	
1932 Norbeck	12	41	20	56

Unlike its North Dakota counterpart, the South Dakota League disappeared after only a few years of activity. In North Dakota, progressivism disintegrated under the onslaught of the League; in South Dakota, the League failed to unseat progressive governor Norbeck. South Dakota progressivism was as vital in the 1920's as it had been before.

A depression in agriculture had succeeded the prewar agricultural prosperity, and progressivism in the second half of the 1920's and in the early years of the Great Depression was primarily a movement of economic protest. The 1930 senatorial primary vote for McMaster, which was fairly closely related to other progressive elections (Table 5.3), provides evidence for the economic character of postwar progressivism. South Dakota was divided into four agricultural regions in 1930 — corn, wheat, transitional from wheat to corn, and cattle. McMaster did not receive the support of the poorest farmers throughout the state as a whole. But within the corn and transitional regions the poor counties supported McMaster and the rich counties opposed him.[13] Whereas the rich corn belt counties had been progressive before the war, the poor corn belt counties were the most progressive in the state during the late 1920's and early 1930's. In addition, farmers had invaded some southern cattle counties west of the Missouri River in the 1910's and 1920's. Farmers in these counties had suffered considerable hardship from drought, and they tended to support progressivism. The antiprogressive vote was scattered in this period; only a few counties were consistently antiprogressive. (Compare the delineation of South Dakota's economic areas in Figure 5.7 with the map of progressive strength, Figure 5.8.) This progressive pattern had no antecedents in South Dakota political history. It did, however, have consequences.

The Major Party Reorientation, 1928–1936

In many states, the Smith election of 1928 ushered in a voting pattern that broke radically with the past. South Dakota, however, tells a different story. True, the Smith vote bore little relation to previous Democratic elections. In part, the cause of the new party cleavage was Smith's Catholic support, but the correlation between Catholicism and the Smith vote was only .45. Similarly, Smith's support correlated only .4 with the vote to repeal prohibition. In other states Smith got a much more Catholic, wet vote. But in South Dakota, Smith's vote was in large part progressive. This was true also of F.D.R.'s 1932 vote, which was related .83 to Smith's support but only barely related to Catholicism and prohibition. Both Smith and Roosevelt were strong in progressive counties; their votes were correlated .57 and .61 with McMaster's 1930 primary vote. Their correlations with La Follette's 1924 vote were lower but still significant ($r = .37$

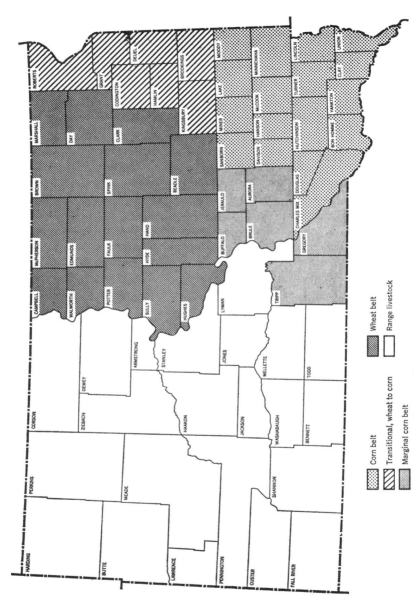

Figure 5.7. South Dakota state economic areas.

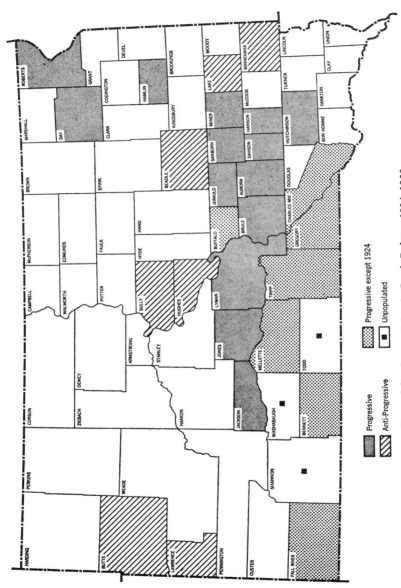

Figure 5.8. *Progressivism in South Dakota, 1924–1930.*

Progressive except 1924

Unpopulated

Progressive

Anti-Progressive

and .44).[14] The Smith-Roosevelt and progressive votes were united by their economic similarity. Like the McMaster vote, the Roosevelt vote was greatest in the poor corn counties ($r = .57$). In the northeast transitional counties, the relationship between poverty and the Roosevelt vote was .8. In the western counties, the relationship was .63.[15] Only in the wheat belt was there no differentiation along economic lines.

Nevertheless, the poorest counties in the state, in the far west, were the strongest anti-Democratic counties in 1928 and 1932. These same counties had opposed pre- and post-war progressivism. They had been disproportionately Democratic since statehood. But as the progressives moved into the Democratic Party, they moved into the Republican Party.

The party vote reoriented itself in 1928. But this reorientation did not increase Democratic support among the urban and foreign-born as much as it did among the poor rural supporters of agrarian radicalism. The Smith and Roosevelt votes had roots in the pre-New Deal reform past.

The Smith election departed from traditional Democratic voting patterns.[16] But the new party politics did not come fully into existence until the Roosevelt elections of 1936 and 1940 (see Table 5.4). Party stability finally reasserted itself after two decades of instability going back to World War I and the postwar ferment. The contemporary party stability is no more a child of the Smith revolution than it is a return to pre-World War I party lines.[17] The votes for President in 1908 and 1948, for example, are correlated .54. This must be contrasted with the reversal of pre-World War I party allegiances in contemporary Wisconsin. We turn now to the modern party vote in South Dakota — its continuities with the past and its differences.

The Modern Party Vote

McCarthy is alleged to have won Catholic and German voters from their Democratic allegiances. But the Democratic

TABLE 5.4

CORRELATIONS OF VOTE FOR SOUTH DAKOTA REPUBLICAN PRESIDENTIAL CANDIDATES, 1920–1960

	1920	1924	1928	1932	1936	1940	1944	1948	1952	1956
1920										
1924	20									
1928	37	45								
1932	45	49	83							
1936	59	04	52	55						
1940	44	—20	30	28	80					
1944	48	—12	33	32	85	89				
1948	52	—02	44	44	81	82	94			
1952	61	07	52	48	80	83	89	93		
1956	55	15	49	46	72	74	79	86	91	
1960	50	08	50	35	67	72	76	82	87	90

155

Party in South Dakota had lost the distinctively Catholic composition of the Smith campaign well before McCarthy came on the scene. In addition, Russian-German voters had deserted the party in large numbers (see Figure 5.9). The

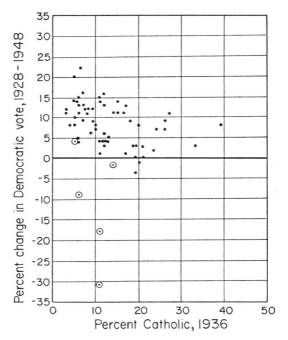

Figure 5.9. The change in the South Dakota Democratic vote, 1928–1948. Dots represent counties, circled dots those that are Russian-German.

pre-McCarthy Democratic Party differed not only from the party of Al Smith but also from the pre-World War I Democracy. It had gained strength in some eastern wheat counties, and significantly less of its support came from German and western cattle counties.[18]

The relative position of the Democratic Party in the corn belt has remained the same since the days of Smith. The poorer corn belt farmers still support the Democratic Party. Including the seven northeastern counties, which are now part of the corn belt proper, the relation between the percentage of poor farmers and the Stevenson vote in 1952 was .56.[19] Since Smith was the classic urban candidate, it is ironic that this should be one of the lasting changes in the Democratic base associated with the 1928 reorientation. In so far as the Democratic vote has reoriented itself, the economic base of the Non-Partisan League and 1920's progressivism played an important role. These were movements based in the wheat and poorer corn counties and opposed in the west. In this specific sense, the modern Democratic Party has a heritage in post-World War I agrarian radicalism.

Perhaps more significant than the reorientation of the party vote is the current stability in party lines. The intercorrelations of the Democratic vote from 1936 to 1960 fall below .66 only in the relationship between the 1938 and 1940 votes. While the correlations are perhaps lower than in an urban state with two-party equality, there is no period in South Dakota history that rivals the modern period either in the length or in the degree of party stability.[20]

By the 1950's, then, regularized competition between the two parties relatively undisturbed by the intrusions of agrarian radical movements characterized South Dakota politics. Mc-Carthyism grew out of this environment. Its sources of support may be examined in two ways. There is first the support for the traditional right wing of the Republican Party, whose leadership supported McCarthy. We can examine this in the light of the Taft-Eisenhower presidential primary campaign of 1952. There is, second, the support McCarthy is alleged to have mobilized outside this traditional right wing and outside of the Republican Party altogether. We can examine the elections of the McCarthy years for evidence of McCarthy's "mass" appeal.

Right-Wing Republicanism, Isolationism, and the German Vote

The isolationist predispositions of Americans of German ancestry are by now familiar. In 1952, Germans supported

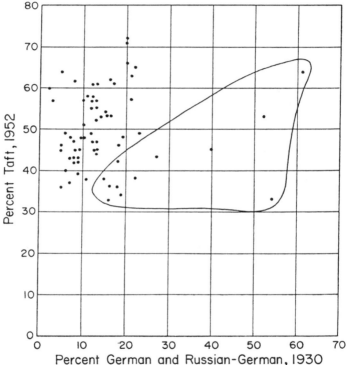

Figure 5.10. *The German population and the Taft vote in South Dakota, 1952 (dots represent counties).*

Taft in his Wisconsin and South Dakota primary campaigns.[21] However, German residents in the South Dakota corn belt were much more likely to support Taft than those in the wheat belt as shown by the encircled dots in Figure 5.10. An analo-

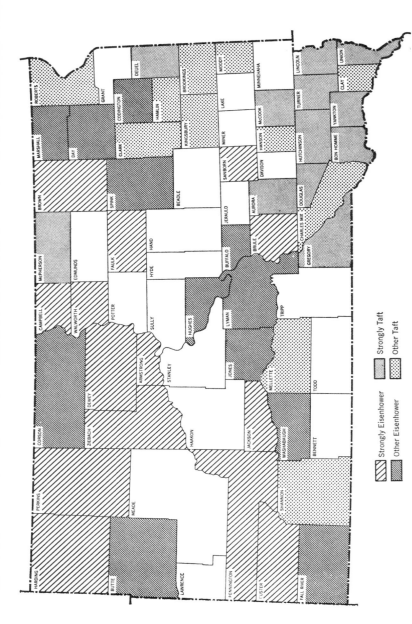

Figure 5.11. *Distribution of the vote in the South Dakota presidential primary, 1952.*

Strongly Eisenhower

Other Eisenhower

Strongly Taft

Other Taft

gous development had occurred in 1940, when German corn belt counties deserted the Democratic Party over the war far more significantly than German wheat belt counties. Moreover, Taft in 1952 received strong support in corn belt counties whether or not they were highly German (see Figure 5.11). By their behavior in 1940 and 1952, corn belt Germans and other corn belt residents have indicated their sensitivity to isolationist appeals.

The Republican Party as a whole in South Dakota was disproportionately German[22] and strong in the corn belt. This combination of an ethnic and economic base for the Republican Party and its right wing is analogous to the support for Republican Parties in North Dakota and Wisconsin. In Wisconsin, the rich and the German areas vote Republican. In the party battle in North Dakota, the poor German and rich eastern areas oppose the resurgent Democratic Party. In these states, if McCarthy disturbed traditional party allegiances at all, his impact was short-lived. Does South Dakota present a different picture?

McCarthyism

The Populist Party mobilized one third of the South Dakota electorate and influenced the development of the major parties. Politicians who called themselves progressive dominated South Dakota politics for thirty years. In this period, party lines were continually shifting, and the support that a particular leader could generate was evident. Thus in 1926, a progressive Republican ran for the Senate while a conservative Republican ran for governor. The former's vote was correlated thirty points higher with Franklin Roosevelt's vote in 1932. Unlike agrarian radicalism, McCarthyism arose in a period of great party stability and made no obvious impact, temporary or permanent, on party lines.

The alleged ground swell for McCarthy is not evident at the electoral level. In Wisconsin, McCarthy's strength was a regular Republican strength first and foremost. In South Dakota, the Republican officeholders who supported McCarthy did not significantly differ from other Republicans in their electoral support. The contemporary lines of party conflict in South Dakota had formed by 1940. The elections of the McCarthy period did not show up as either deviant or critical elections — they neither deviated from normal party lines nor reoriented the party vote on new lines. The significance of McCarthyism, unlike that of the agrarian radical movements, does not lie at the mass level.

Recognizing the limited impact of McCarthy's electoral appeal, it may still be possible, as it was in Wisconsin, to locate electoral sources of support for the Senator. However, in South Dakota McCarthy himself was not a candidate. If his impact on the Wisconsin electorate was slight, one would expect his impact in a state where he was not a candidate to be even more elusive.

Both South Dakota senators were supporters of McCarthy. Mundt had been elected to the Senate in 1948 following prominence in the House Un-American Activities Committee. He was reelected in 1954, McCarthy making a campaign speech for him. Case had beaten the internationalist Republican incumbent in the 1950 primary on a program of isolationism and economy.[23] In the Senate, he supported McCarthy, but unlike Mundt he voted for the censure resolution. This was because, as a member of the Watkins committee which recommended censure, he was subject to severe pressure. Nevertheless, he was the only member of the committee to waver prior to the final censure vote and was instrumental in having the section referring to General Zwicker removed from the final resolution.

Case was first elected in 1950, the year in which the defeat of senators Tydings, Lucas, and Myers established McCarthy's electoral reputation. Mundt was reelected in 1954, at the height of the controversy over the censure of McCarthy. Either or both of these elections should provide evidence of

161

pro-McCarthy sentiment among the South Dakota electorate.

In order to hold constant the regular party vote but minimize factors irrelevant to McCarthyism associated with the various postwar South Dakota elections,[24] four indexes of McCarthyism were constructed. In each case, county percentages above or below the state average on the measure of McCarthyism were subtracted from county percentages above or below the state average on the measure of regular Republicanism. This gave each county a score on each of the four McCarthy indices.*

The differences in the four indexes underscore the fact that on the whole McCarthyism in the 1950's did not supplant the normal political patterns of off-year elections, ethnicity, and economics. Nevertheless, a broadly consistent trend emerges. McCarthy Republicans picked up strength west of the Missouri and in the western corn belt and lost strength in the wheat belt and among the rich counties of the corn belt. The geographic consistency of the gains and losses is noteworthy. (For a map showing the average scores on the McCarthy indices, see Figure 5.12.)

One can only speculate about the meaning of this pattern. The absence of any political tradition from Populism to McCarthyism is immediately evident. The Populist counties were among the strongest anti-McCarthy counties. They did not support Taft against Eisenhower in 1952; McCarthy and Taft were both weak in the wheat belt.

Pre-World War I progressivism was also not related to McCarthyism. The rich corn belt counties that voted progressive before World War I were anti-McCarthy. Scandinavians, who had been progressive, tended to oppose

* The four indices were (1) the deviation by counties of the Michelson vote from the state average for Michelson (1946 Republican gubernatorial candidate) minus the deviation by counties of the Case vote from the state average for Case; (2) the average of the Michelson and Dewey deviations minus the Case deviations; (3) Michelson minus the average of Case and Mundt; (4) Michelson and Dewey minus Case and Mundt.

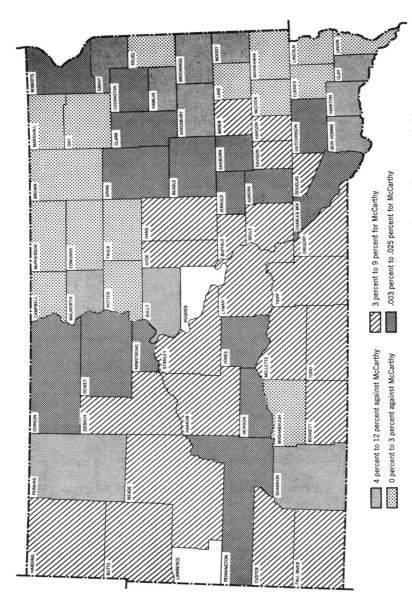

Figure 5.12. McCarthy's strength in South Dakota with the regular Republican vote held constant.

4 percent to 12 percent against McCarthy.

0 percent to 3 percent against McCarthy

3 percent to 9 percent for McCarthy.

.003 percent to .025 percent for McCarthy

McCarthy.[25] Germans already tended to be Republican and right wing before 1950, and they did not become more Republican after. There was, on the other hand, a slight tendency for the Catholic vote for Mundt and Case to increase over the vote for Dewey and Michelson ($r = .26$). This parallels the increased Catholic vote for McCarthy found by Bean in several states in 1950.[26]

There was a clear connection between the economic progressivism of the 1920's and the support for Mundt and Case. The two tiers of counties in southern South Dakota extending from the Missouri River almost to the eastern border were banner progressive counties, and they also supported McCarthy Republicans. There was, in other words, a tendency for poorer corn-growing areas to support progressivism during times of economic distress and pro-McCarthy Republicans during prosperity. Three factors may have contributed to the behavior of these counties. Perhaps McCarthy was irrelevant to their growing Republicanism, a response instead to corn belt prosperity in the early 1950's.* Alternatively, their support for McCarthy may have been analogous to his strength in the poor, ex-progressive counties of northern Wisconsin. Finally, like the McCarthy support in the Wisconsin corn belt, it may reflect particular corn belt political characteristics. In the 1930's the depressed corn areas produced the Farm Holiday Movement and the radical wing of the Farmers Union. One might hypothesize that the corn belt is sensitive to economics during hard times and may take extreme action then and is sensitive to McCarthy-type ideological appeals during good times. But the evidence is far too meager to do more than speculate.[27]

Finally, the western part of South Dakota became more

* The measures of the party vote are from 1946 and 1948, elections previous to those which measure the impact of McCarthy. But to choose an election in the 1950's to measure the regular vote would be to run the risk of overlooking a general shift in the nature of party support brought about by McCarthyism.

Republican during the McCarthy period. This reflects the shift of these conservative counties to the Republican Party as the Democratic Party became more progressive. The shift of the southern counties just west of the Missouri River was perhaps due to recovery from the serious drought and over-utilization of land that plagued this area until World War II. Except for the late 1920's and early 1930's, this southern area had not been progressive. The west as a whole was anti-progressive. If poor corn belt support for McCarthy is seen as the fruition of agrarian radicalism in any sense, then western support for McCarthy must equally be seen as the fruition of conservatism.

The point that must be stressed is that there were no great upheavals in the party vote during the McCarthy period. The McCarthy indexes register shifts of only a few percentage points. Certainly there was no resurgence of Populism — either in the sense of the demographic traits characteristic of Populism, or in the sense of specific Populist counties supporting McCarthy. We began by asking what effect McCarthyism had on the existing party base; we found that McCarthyism was itself dominated by the existing party base.

Conclusion

Evidence and speculation about the history of party politics in America has led many historians to believe both that the New Deal represented a sharp break with past voting patterns and that the progressive Republicans of the pre-New Deal period vote Republican and conservative today. There is no necessary contradiction between these two views, but they point in different directions. In the agrarian midwest before the New Deal, the progressive-stalwart conflict was carried out within the dominant Republican Party. Since the coming of the New Deal the Republican Party has become the conservative party. If the New Deal changed the electoral basis of party politics in these states, it is possible that those who

165

would have been Republican progressives are now Democrats. The ideological change in the parties in the New Deal period would reflect and anticipate a change in their constituencies. If it is true that pre-New Deal Republican progressives vote Republican today, then the New Deal did not radically shift the bases of the major parties.

In Wisconsin, progressive Republicans did in large part become Democrats with the New Deal. In South Dakota, the story is more complicated. In part, progressives and conservatives changed parties. Western ranching counties changed parties because they remained conservative. Poor corn belt counties switched parties in 1928-1932 because they remained progressive. There was a tendency for wheat farmers, more favorable to governmental action, to move into the Democratic Party. But the party realignment during the Smith-Roosevelt era was hardly total. The reassertion of traditional party loyalty after 1932 means that in South Dakota the kind of people who were voting Republican — and progressive — before World War I are voting Republican — and conservative — now.

In two senses, then, the New Deal Democratic Party in South Dakota was not a complete break with the past. In part, it was the outcome of the progressivism of the 1920's; in part, after 1932 it returned to its pre-New Deal, pre-World War I base. But if the base of the South Dakota parties has remained relatively stable in the last half-century, their ideologies have not. Progressives controlled the Republican Party before World War I; conservatives control it now. Many of the same types of people vote for leaderships which seem at opposite ends of the political spectrum.

This continuity of support should not be overdone. The direct support for progressivism — expressed in the primaries — shows little relation to the party vote, either Democratic or Republican. But there is evidence that those who voted specifically progressive prior to World War I vote disproportionately conservative today. Taft was strong in old pro-

166

gressive territory. There is no similar evidence of continuity from Populism to reaction. In part this was because Populism created no permanent organizational loyalties upon which later movements were able to capitalize. Not the Populist mass movement but the established traditions of the Republican Party permitted a continuity of support despite a change in program. Moreover, the absence of Populist continuity with reaction reflects the fact that the Populist constituency had particular political-economic goals. Pre-World War I progressivism in South Dakota was a more diffuse movement, stressing moral reform as much as political change. The Populist program was more alien than the progressive platform to contemporary Republicanism.

The most clearly agrarian radical movements in South Dakota — Populism, the Non-Partisan League, and 1920's progressivism — did not evolve into contemporary conservatism. But the weakness of agrarian radicalism after World War II left no significant challenge to conservative Republicanism. McCarthyism rose to power in the Middle West in the context of conservative dominance. While he had marginal agrarian radical support, the overwhelming majority of those who sent McCarthy-supporters to the Senate was part of the regular Republican constituency. In the eastern Middle West, a Republican Party that had rarely been progressive gave McCarthy his support. In the Plains states, McCarthy became strong with the conservative defeat of agrarian radicalism.

POPULISM

Political movements in a crisis period encompass both ideology and economic demands. Their proposals look to changes in the wider society and are in this sense broader than the proposals of interest groups. Their constituents, in deprived positions in society, require more large-scale changes. Moreover, in the disrupted position in which people find themselves during a crisis, they require some general explanation of the relation between narrow economic demands and their general welfare. Deprived of power, they are not likely to be motivated to act to change their situation by appeals to practical self-interest alone. Because the obstacles to surmount are so great, such appeals seem illusory and in fact often are. Therefore, some emotional appeals are essential; protest movements have crusade characteristics. The movements of farmers in the 1890's, workers in the 1930's, and Negroes in the 1960's have all been crusades. The emotional appeals of these movements transcend rationality defined in terms of Benthamite narrow self-interest. But narrow groups are specifically irrational in a crisis period because their methods can succeed neither in achieving results nor in attracting adherents.

To treat mass movements in pluralist terms is to make them a priori irrational. When they are viewed as responses to social crises, a different picture emerges. Populism must be understood not as a foolish departure from interest group politics but as the product of the widespread and severe stresses of rapid industrialization and a serious depression.

The economic and cultural dislocation brought by industrialization has produced mass movements all over the world. These movements can take several forms. They can reject industrialization entirely and favor direct action and sabotage. This approach often dominated anarchist movements. They can reject any sort of liberal society, and seek to resolve economic and cultural problems with totalitarian control. This was the approach of fascism. They can seek to utilize industrialization to solve the problems it itself has created. This was the character of Marxism in Western Europe and Populism in America.

Adam Ulam has suggested that Marxism in Europe, in diverting resentment from the industrial process itself and onto the capitalist, socialized the working class to an acceptance of industrialization. Whereas the Luddites and anarchists fought the industrial work process itself, Marxist workers organized to fight the capitalists. In so doing they took the crucial step of accepting the industrial situation and working to improve their situation within it. Placing anti-industrial feeling in the service of industrial logic, revolutionary Marxism led to reformist trade unionism.[1]

In *The Paradox of Progressive Thought,* David Noble has made a parallel analysis of American progressivism. Hofstadter suggested that the progressives and Populists feared industrialization. But according to Noble, they reinterpreted it as a mechanism for freeing man from the burden of traditions and institutions and for reintroducing agrarian innocence into an advanced civilization.[2] In Ulam's terms, American reformers channeled a potential anti-industrial emotion in the direction of an acceptance of industrialization for the benefits it could bring if properly controlled. The parallel is exact, for the reformers focused their attacks not on the industrial process itself but on the particular bearers of industrialization — in their terms, the plutocrats and the interests.

Populist rhetoric and the Populist program were anti-industrial capitalist not anti-industrial. In the words of one Populist paper, "The people do not want to tear down the railroads nor pull down the factories . . . They want to build up and make better everything." Another explained that the Populists "shall make of this nation an industrial democracy in which each citizen shall have an equal interest." Technology, the Populists argued, could be used to enslave man but also to liberate him.[3] *

True, the Populists opposed capitalists who were industrializing America. Does this make the capitalists progressive, the Populists reactionary? An analogous approach makes Stalinism in Russia into a progressive force because it, too, industrialized. Such overviews ignore the particular issues upon which conflict was joined. Conflict between Populists and conservatives was not about industrialization in the abstract, but about the control of railroads, the power of monopolies, the falling prices of crops, the benefits and dangers of inflation, big business control of politics, and other

---

* Many Populists, although not anti-industrial, were loath to admit that basic and irreversible changes in American society had caused the problems the farmer faced. Kansas Senator William Peffer began *The Farmer's Side* with a long, realistic description of the effect of industrialization and technology on the self-sufficient farmer. The farm situation, he wrote, had been produced not by the machinations or conspiracies of a few men but by the general development of the society. This evolution could not be reversed; rather the farmers should seek to benefit from it. But Peffer followed this section with another in which he blamed usury for all the farmers' troubles.[4] Here Peffer drew back from the real problems brought by industrialization. Money panaceas became a substitute for the more radical program implied by the earlier analysis. Clearly the two aspects of Peffer's argument are mutually contradictory. If industrialization is the cause of agrarian unhappiness, there is no possibility of going back to an earlier utopia. If usury and the evil actions of a few men explain everything, there is no need to deal with the basic problems brought by industrialization.

issues which could all have been met as the Populists desired without undermining industrialization.*

Had Populism attempted to escape from the problems brought by industrialization it would have relied on finding scapegoats, attacking freedom, and appealing to prejudice. Such a politics could rely — as McCarthyism relied — on the support of local elites. The democratic character of Populism flowed from its willingness to seek concrete, economic solutions to farmer grievances and to challenge local elites in the process.

Because they challenged those in power, Populists could appreciate freedom. They came to see the importance of social relationships rather than individual morality in explaining political attitudes. If conservatives could stress the individual corruption and evil conspiracies of a few men, reformers learned to look deeper.[7] They concentrated on specific economic grievances rather than vague, unfocused resentments. The very existence of agrarian radicals increased the alternatives in rural society, thereby promoting diversity.

Certainly there were aspects of Populism which make the modern observer uncomfortable. Populist leaders appealed to rural suspicion of the city and were unable to suppress their belief in rural superiority. The rural, fundamentalist Populist rhetoric made it difficult to attract urban allies, without which the movement was doomed. Many in the Populist crusade were cranky and narrow-minded. But a total assessment of Populism cannot be made so easily. Let us evaluate the movement in light of the specific pluralist attacks.

---

* Populists demanded a graduated income tax, government ownership or regulation of the railroads and the telegraph, control over monopoly, a lower tariff, increased education, direct election of senators, the secret ballot, the initiative and the referendum, an eight-hour day on government work, support for the labor movement, the free coinage of silver, a plan for government loans to farmers at low interest rates, and restriction on alien and corporate landholding.[5] If the Populists longed for a "rural utopia,"[6] this longing was not operational.

Some of these charges have to do with the general Populist ideology. Hofstadter has criticized the movement for its naïve belief in a natural harmony of society and a two-sided struggle between the people and the interests. These charges need not long detain us. The Populist rhetoric here derives from Lockean liberalism and was shared by conservatives as well as Populists. Conservatives and Populists attacked each other for interfering with the natural harmony of the world; each saw the other as a special interest. That reality is more complex than political slogans should surprise no one.[8]

More serious is the alleged Populist commitment to a conspiracy theory of history. As a rural movement with religious roots, Populism was especially prone to dramatize experience. It existed at a time when politics as a whole was played at this level. Where Populists saw conspiracies of bankers, conservatives feared anarchist conspiracies. There is little question that many Populist writers exhibited a conspiracy mentality. It is harder to come to an assessment of the importance of that mentality in the movement. Hofstadter argues that Populism was preoccupied with conspiracies. On the other hand, a recent study of Kansas Populism concludes that those who went to "international conspiracy" extremes were a small lunatic fringe of Populism.[9]

More than that, the Populists had been left behind by industrialization, left out of politics by the east and by their own local elites. There were, for example, virtually no farmers in local positions of party leadership in pre-Populist Kansas and Nebraska. But most of the local Populist leaders were farmers. Their perception of courthouse "rings" making political decisions was close to the truth.[10] Similarly, on the national level agreements and conspiracies between capitalists were an important part of industrialization. In the legal world, the American Bar Association played an important role in cementing close ties and informal contacts between judges and conservative lawyers.[11] Perhaps Henry Demarest Lloyd paid insufficient attention in *Wealth Against Commonwealth*

172

to the general laws of capitalist development in the creation of Standard Oil. Certainly Sumner and Spencer paid insufficient attention to the illegal acts and conspiracies of particular men.

In part, Hofstadter recognizes this and suggests a distinction between the perception of particular conspiracies and the perception of history as a conspiracy. This is an intellectually impeccable distinction, but one should not overestimate the ease of drawing it in the political practice of the late-nineteenth century.

Perhaps the most serious concrete charges laid against Populist ideology are the charges of nativism and anti-Semitism. According to Hofstadter, Populism activated most of American popular anti-Semitism. Viereck, Bell, Lipset, and Handlin all give currency to the allegation of Populist anti-Semitism.[12] It is particularly important to our argument here because in so far as Populists focused on Jews rather than economic targets they were failing to come to grips with the real problems of industrialization. This failure would have given an authoritarian cast to the movement. Thus Oscar Handlin specifically related Populist anti-Semitism to the movement's fear of the forces brought into play by industrialization — specifically, the Haymarket Affair, the Pullman Boycott, and the western mining strikes.[13]

The fact is, however, that the Populists sympathized with the Haymarket anarchists and were for the Pullman Boycott. The Populist governor of Colorado intervened for the workers in the Cripple Creek strike.[14] It is true that anti-Semitism would have been an alternative to an alliance with a rising labor movement. But while the evidence of Populist support for labor stands out,[15] the evidence of Populist anti-Semitism is very meager. A few Populists like Mary Ellen Lease seem to have been anti-Semitic. Moreover, one can find stereotyping of Jews in some Populist allegorical writing, like Donnelly's *Caesar's Column.*[16] The Jewish theme does not dominate *Caesar's Column,* and stereotyping of immigrant groups was common practice in the late nineteenth century.[17] Donnelly is even sympathetic to the plight of the Jews, but his sympathy is part of an over-all animosity and distrust. Perhaps not unusual in the tawdry romantic novel of the period, Donnelly's portrayal of the Jewish characters is anti-Semitic by modern standards. One Jew heads the plutocracy and another is the evil genius of the revolution. The Jews had survived for hundreds of years under Christian tyranny, writes Donnelly, and now the Christians are paying "for the sufferings inflicted by their bigoted and ignorant ancestors on a noble race."[18]

The anti-Semitism in Donnelly's fantasy can be exaggerated, but if Populist rhetoric in general had been as anti-Semitic as *Caesar's Column,* the case for Populist verbal anti-Semitism would be made. However, the picture of Populist anti-Semitism has been created from slender evidence. Careful examination of tens of thousands of Populist newspapers, pamphlets, and books in Kansas and the other centers of midwestern Populism has uncovered no anti-Semitism in the collections of the state historical societies and only two or three references in the immense production of the Populist press.[19] As for the frequent references in Populist literature to the power of Shylock and the House of Rothschild, it is doubtful if these symbols had specific anti-Semitic connotations. In Kansas Populist literature, the House of Morgan was as frequent a Populist target as the House of Rothschild. The remaining examples of Populist anti-Semitism, such as the charge that Bryan's cross of gold peroration had anti-Semitic intent,[20] are extremely far-fetched. Comparing Populist "anti-Semitism" with the verbal anti-Semitism then common throughout the United States, the restrictions against Jews in respectable eastern society and the riots against Jews in the cities, it is possible to argue that the Populist movement was less anti-Semitic than late-nineteenth century America as a whole.

Although much is made of alleged Populist anti-Semitism,

little attention is paid to the resistance of southern Populism to anti-Negro rhetoric and activity. Racism was a tool of the conservatives, who sought to discredit and defeat the Populists by arousing the specter of Negro supremacy. Populist supporters in the south may have been anti-Negro, but during the Populist period it was more important to them to ally with Negro farmers along economic lines. In Georgia, Tom Watson attacked Democratic outrages against the Negro. At one point, a number of white Populist farmers rode all night to prevent the lynching of a Negro Populist. Moreover, agrarian reformers like Tillman who remained Democrats were as anti-Negro as their conservative opponents. It was the more radical, ideological, third-party Populists who defended Negro rights.[21]

What of alleged Populist hostility to foreigners? Populism is often interpreted as a revolt of native-born farmers, but outside the South there is virtually no basis for this impression. In the South, Populism tended to be strongest in the hill country of independent, Protestant, native-born farmers and weakest in the black belt. Populists received significant Negro support in some areas but did poorly among Mexicans and others of foreign stock.[22] In Iowa in 1892, the Populists also ran relatively best in the predominantly native-born counties and worse in the German and Scandinavian counties; but Populism generally was weak in Iowa. In Nebraska and the Dakotas, there was no relation between the proportion of native-born and Populism. In Kansas, the Populists scored successes in both native and foreign-born counties. Indeed, a higher percentage of immigrants ran for public office under the Kansas Populist banner than in either of the major parties.[23] Thus to relate the movement to Anglo-Saxon fear of immigration or old-American longing for a distant past is at best questionable.

The support of foreign ethnic groups for Populism varied somewhat from state to state. In Kansas, the Populists ran best in Irish, Bohemian, Welsh, and Danish precincts, and

worst in German, Russian-German, and particularly Men-
nonite and Swedish precincts. In Nebraska, the Populists did
poorly in German, Bohemian, and Catholic areas. Over the
Plains states as a whole, Norwegians and Danes seem consistently to have given disproportionate support to Populism
and Catholics, Germans, and Russian-Germans to have provided a source of opposition.

Populism could have blamed the changes taking place in
America on foreigners[24] and sponsored nativist legislation.
Indeed, there was some antiforeign sentiment among local
Populists in some areas,[25] although research has failed to
uncover significant Populist nativism on the Great Plains.
That unfriendliness toward immigrants existed in the Populist movement conflicted with the belief that America was and
should be the home of the oppressed.[26] Thus Weaver, running
for President in 1892, repudiated a restrictionist plank in the
1892 Populist platform. The plank was only there at the
request of the Knights of Labor. The Knights feared competition from cheap foreign labor, a fear that led the AFL also
to favor immigration restriction. Similarly, in Kansas the
Populists only accepted immigration restriction at the behest
of the Knights of Labor. Eastern Republicans were much
more unambiguously for immigration restriction than were the
Populists.[27] The Populist platforms did always include planks
calling for a prohibition on alien ownership of land. These
planks were not nativist in motivation, but were directed
against the ownership of land by large foreign corporations
and by nonresidents who held the land for speculative purposes.

Britain was the one country toward which the Populists
were hostile. In part, this was antiaristocratic prejudice
(which also motivated someone like Carnegie); in part, it
was caused by the ties of Wall Street and Grover Cleveland
to British bankers.[28] The significance of Irish influence within
Populism on this score also should not be discounted.

There is no significant evidence of jingoism in Populist
foreign policy. The Populists on the whole favored Cuban

liberation but opposed the Spanish American War and the annexation of Cuba and the Philippines.[29] As was the case with nativism, the more moderate progressives were more often jingoist in foreign policy than the "extremist" Populists. Much of the evidence cited of Populist jingoism is perverse indeed. The assertion of an anti-Populist Congressman that McKinley's foreign policy was hurting the Populists (because they opposed it) clearly suggests that the Populists lost support because they were *not* jingoist. Similarly, to derive Populist jingoism from jingoist attitudes in "Populist areas" is not only to confuse the party with its social base but also to overlook a conservative opposition to Populism that was always either dominant or extremely powerful in "Populist areas." That there is a jingoist tradition in the Middle West is not at issue; the question is the relation of the Populist movement to that tradition.[30]

As for Populist attitudes toward Catholics, Catholics did tend to vote against the Populist party, but this seems as likely to have been due to Catholic characteristics as Populist ones. The Populists often sought fusion with the Catholic party, the Democrats. Moreover, the American Protective Association reached its height in the Populist period. This was an anti-Catholic organization, but it was not involved with the Populists. The APA was strongest in the old Middle West, where Populism was virtually nonexistent. Aside from being anti-Catholic, the APA was strongly anti-Populist. It attacked the Populists with the kind of moralistic language attributed so often to the Populists.[31] The Populists made moralistic attacks on the APA in the name of individual freedom. They accused Republicans in many states of being tools of the APA, and in fact the Republican parties often did have APA connections.[32]

The Populist Crusade

If specific charges of jingoism and anti-Semitism fail, what of the general view of Populism as a moral crusade, destruc-

177

tive of individual differences and privacy? One should not underestimate the elements of a crusade in Populism.

Populism was a Protestant revival in an already intolerant rural setting. There was in rural society little attention paid to the freedom of individuals as individuals. Individual freedom was enforced, if at all, by group power rather than by neutral societal institutions concerned with the protection of individual rights. In practice, the individual Hatfield might be protected by his family against the individual McCoy, the individual Congregationalist by his church against the Anglicans. In theory, there were few institutionalized protections for minority rights. For John Locke, the theorist of rural liberalism, homogeneity seemed to obviate the need for minority safeguards. The major protections entirely altered the relationship between the individual and the society — the right to leave and the right of revolution.[33] With the growth of an urban society, anonymity and individual freedom grew too. Bureaucratic structures concerned with restraints on government arose. Supreme Court interpretations of the Bill of Rights and the Fourteenth Amendment to guarantee individual liberties are strikingly a twentieth-century phenomenon, as is the growth of the American Civil Liberties Union.[34]

Frederic Howe captured the flavor of rural society well when he described his boyhood in Meadville, Pennsylvania:

> One could be sharp in business, possibly corrupt in politics, but one should not forget that life was a serious business, that duty should be always before one's eyes, that one should be diligent in things distasteful, and that self-fulfillment meant getting on in the world, being assiduous to church-going, rather exhibitive in attendance on revivals, the holding to one's particular church denomination, and the avoidance of even the appearance of careless morals, drinking or association with men of questionable opinions.
>
> The other important thing was to live as other men lived, do as other men did, avoid any departure from what other men thought. Not to conform was dangerous to one's reputation.

178

Men who had strange ideas, who protested, who thought for themselves, were quietly ostracized.[35]

As Howe recognized, much of the evangelicalism and intolerance of this rural environment went into the reform movements. Indeed, the roots of Populism in a grass roots, evangelical Protestant mentality cannot be exaggerated. The Populist revolt called forth perhaps the most intense and widespread political involvement in American history. As the historian of the Texas People's Party puts it,

> Populism sprang from the soil. It came into being in many sections of the state within the space of a brief period almost as if by pre-arrangement, yet there was no relation between the various local phases of the movement aside from that provided by the common conditions from which all grew. It was, then, in its incipient stages a spontaneous, almost explosive force.[36]

Progressivism was primarily an elite phenomenon. Populism was a mass uprising. Farmers traveled miles with their families to large camp meetings. They read the immense outpouring of the Populist press, passing the pamphlets and newspapers from hand to hand. They filled local schoolhouses in the evenings, and participated in politics in hundreds of counties throughout the Great Plains and the South. The major parties could count on traditional loyalties, and their local organizations were often moribund. The Populists would have been lost without the remarkable activity of their grass roots supporters.[37]

The revivalist character of this mass uprising is striking. Ministers and ex-ministers were active in the movement; the camp meetings resembled nothing so much as religious revivals. Populist gatherings were sober affairs, suspicious of luxury and full of religious paraphernalia. The party was known as the party of righteousness, and such groups as the Germans feared for their Sunday cards and beer.[38]

Surely this supports the perception of the movement as a

dangerous, mass fundamentalist crusade, particularly in light of the Scopes trial, the 1920's Ku Klux Klan, and the more recent manifestations of fundamentalist extremism.

The rural, Protestant Populist environment hardly seems fertile soil for a tolerant, democratic, forward-looking politics. But analyzing the Populist crusade as a product of the intolerance of rural respectability misses a fundamental point. To be an agrarian radical was to challenge respectability. The dominant institutions of nineteenth century rural America — church, press, politicians, local business elites — were all opposed to agrarian radicalism. The established elites owed their political power in part to the cultivation of intolerance; to moralistic appeals to patriotism, Americanism and the like; to religious fundamentalism; and to the power of conformity. Agrarian radicalism in part participated in this style of politics but in a more basic sense had to combat these methods of political control.

Certain kinds of crusades under certain circumstances destroy privacy and individual differences. But the circumstances in which Populism found itself are important. Because it was a minority movement against powerful elites, because it was in an American tradition of individualism and freedom, the movement could see many of the advantages of free speech and privacy. Thus Populists pushed for the introduction of a secret ballot. Nor did Populist "Americanism" cause them to persecute the opposition. Like agrarian radicals during World War I, Populists were the victims of superpatriotism rather than its perpetrators.

There are three specific areas in which the Populist crusade is alleged to have interfered with freedom. The first of these is in the university. In the Populist and progressive periods there was considerable interference with academic freedom, for academic tenure was not firmly institutionalized as it is today. Although many writers cite Populist interferences with academic freedom,[39] in point of fact there is only one example. In Kansas, the Populists ignored academic tenure in reorganizing the Kansas State Agricultural College. This was not, it should be pointed out, because they were suspicious of "overeducation"; they rather had a somewhat naïve faith in what education could accomplish. In Kansas, they desired to introduce a liberal arts curriculum into an exclusively agricultural college.[40] In this case the interference with academic freedom resulted not from anti-intellectualism but from enthusiasm for education. This is not the sort of mentality traditionally associated with attacks on academic freedom. Moreover, the view that the populist attitudes of the American masses make them anti-intellectual ignores the crucial question of which particular elites (if any) are going to lead anti-intellectual crusades or give in to them. On the whole, in America these functions have been performed by conservative elites, and radical intellectuals like Thorstein Veblen have been the victims. The Populists were not the fathers of modern witch-hunts.

Populist support for prohibition is also cited as evidence for the dangerous effects of the Populist crusade. It is true that Populist voters tended to support prohibition referenda and that prohibition was one of the progressive reforms associated with the initiative, the referendum, and female suffrage.[41] In part, this was because liquor interests played a corrupt role in state politics. In part, it was because temperance, like economic reform, was seen as a necessary precondition for individual advancement. In part, it was out of simple intolerance for the habits of particular ethnic groups and urban classes. However, a proviso should be entered here. In the early days of the prohibition movement, the Prohibition Party platform was generally radical. In the 1890's Prohibition platforms resembled Populist platforms. However, the real cultivation of rural ignorance and prejudice came not in this period, but with the rise of the practical, single-interest, conservative Anti-Saloon League.

Moreover, our concern is not only with the attitude of Populist constituents toward prohibition but the attitude of the movement itself. At the county level, Populists and Pro-hibitionists often had close relationships. Some state Populist parties, as in North Dakota, endorsed prohibition. It was more common, however, for the movement to steer away from that controversial issue, as it did in South Dakota, Iowa, Texas, and generally in Kansas.[42]

Another charge leveled against the Populist crusade is that it sought to destroy representative democracy. Here again one must measure Populist practice against the claims of its opponents. While many Populists favored the initiative and the referendum, the political reforms most stressed by the Populists were the secret ballot and the direct election of senators. Certainly the Populists sought to challenge the po-litical and economic power of those who dominated Ameri-can society at the turn of the twentieth century. Certainly the direct election of senators increased the power of the people vis-à-vis the elites. But it is highly dubious that such a Popu-list reform was a threat to representative democracy. Finally, the Populist attacks on the courts indicate disregard for law and order not so much by the Populists as by the courts themselves. In 1895 alone, the Supreme Court invalidated the income tax and refused to apply the Sherman Act to the sugar monopoly while upholding Debs' conviction under it.[43] This consistent, narrow partiality in interpreting the laws and the constitution explains Populist attitudes better than deduc-tions concerning "plebiscitory democracy."

That Populism was in significant measure a Protestant crusade is impossible to deny. It is also true that the conditions permitting a movement of this sort to focus on concrete eco-nomic reforms were fast disappearing. Nevertheless, charges that the Populists were authoritarian are not supported by the evidence. Particularly in contrast to the politics it opposed, Populism was clearly a democratic phenomenon.

Are we required, then, to call Populism an example of class rather than status politics? In the categories of class and status politics, we meet the issue of moralism and pragmatism in another form. For the Beardians, Populism was a pragmatic class movement, representing the special interests of farmers as other groups represented the special interests of their constituencies.[44] The pluralists have seen that Beardian analysis cannot describe the Populist movement successfully. However, in their distinction between "class" and "status" politics they have not transcended Beardian categories. Accepting the narrow Beardian definition of an economic movement and finding that Populism was more than this, they have underplayed its economic character. Rather than transcending the Beardian analysis, they have stood it on its head.

Hofstadter, for example, implicitly interprets Populism as an example of status politics. Distinguishing between the hard and the soft side of the agrarian spirit, he writes,

> The farmer's commercial position pointed to the usual strategies of the business world: combination, cooperation, pressure politics, lobbying, piecemeal activity directed toward specific goals. But the bathos of the agrarian rhetoric pointed in a different direction: broad political goals, ideological mass politics, third parties, the conquest of the "money power," the united action of all labor, rural and urban.

Relating this to Populism, Hofstadter explains that in bad times the farmer rejected his role as a capitalist and "withdrew into the role of the injured little yeoman." The Farmers Alliance and the Populist Party had their hard side (business methods, pressure politics), he says, but as the depression deepened the soft Populist rhetoric triumphed and all issues were dropped for the silver panacea.[45]

In order to make the progressive movement an example of status politics, Hofstadter argues that status politics is born of prosperity. This will not do for the Populists; since they flourished during a depression, they would become a class political phenomenon. But Hofstadter reserves class politics for narrow interest groups. The term would place the Populists in an incorrect and — for him — too favorable light. He therefore first treats the Populist party as an irrational response to crisis; it appears to be an example of status politics. He then turns to the achievements of practical farm organizations with narrow economic goals. According to him these were associated with agricultural prosperity. This was the same period of prosperity that produced progressive status politics.[46]

Hofstadter could overcome the contradiction here explicitly by excepting rural politics from the normal class-status cycle. But this would hardly render his treatment of Populism itself more convincing. For while Populism was certainly more than a narrow pressure group, it was still an economic movement making practical demands. As C. Vann Woodward has pointed out, the Populist demands did not ignore economics but rather were "obsessively economic."[47] The business ventures of the Farmers Alliance were in part examples of farmer unwillingness to come to terms with industrial capitalism. In shifting to politics, the farmers recognized the insufficiency of purely business methods. The politicizing of the Alliance was not simply the result of self-pity; the depression rendered nonpolitical solutions futile. In fact, Hofstadter himself later attributes a measure of success to the third party.[48] Finally, if "the bathos of agrarian rhetoric" produced the free silver panacea as well as the third party, why did free silver destroy both the third party and the general third-party demands? The answer is that free silver did not dominate third-party Populism. It was rather the panacea of the more conservative (and practical?) Democrats like Bryan who were too conservative to make demands for basic changes in American society; they preferred panaceas. Indeed, free silver did not dominate the Populist movement until, in its practical desire to win power, it sought fusion with the Democrats. Here is the ultimate irony; Hofstadter damns Populism for the practical, opportunistic concern for power at the expense of broad, ideological principles — the very politics that wins his praise when practiced by the major parties.

Hofstadter's treatment makes of Populism an irrational,

unnecessary movement. This is also the consequence of other pluralist arguments. In Kornhauser's scheme, mass movements arise when the masses are available for mobilization and the elites are accessible to influence from below. In his analysis, the only societies where the masses are available but the elites inaccessible are totalitarian.[49] Surely some finer distinctions are in order. One would like to know which elites are accessible and which inaccessible. To which constituencies are elites accessible, to which inaccessible? By what methods are elites accessible, and what methods will they resist or ignore?

In a basic sense, the elites in America are accessible to popular influence, but mass movements generally arise because of the inaccessibility of elites to the interests of the members of mass movements and in this sense their inaccessibility to the pressure group politics of pluralism. Thus in Populist states, politics was often controlled from outside and the elites that made political decisions were not accessible to the bulk of people. On the national level, the elites were also inaccessible. Particularly important here was the role of the Supreme Court in rejecting legislation that reformers were able to pass. Because the Supreme Court was not accessible to reform influence, it played the role of radicalizing political discontent.[50]

Other factors besides the inaccessibility of elites obviously contribute to the rise of mass movements and determine their character. But whether the movements are democratic or totalitarian, their appearance is related to the inaccessibility of elites.[51] By basing mass movements on the accessibility of elites, Kornhauser denies them the possibility of being a rational response to social crises. For if the elites are accessible, mass movements are unnecessary.

Similarly, when Kornhauser writes that the "objects" of mass movements are "remote" and do not "directly concern the individual,"[52] he again makes mass movements irrational by definition. Interest rates, railroads, corporations, and the

185

money supply certainly concerned the Populist farmers directly. And the Populists were perfectly reasonable in believing that control over railroads, interest rates, corporations, and the money supply was exercised in places remote from the Great Plains. Would they have been more rational to focus their anger on neighboring shopkeepers?

Just as the distinction between moralism and pragmatism cannot contain the Lockean ideology, so the distinctions between proximate and remote concerns, class and status politics, cannot contain agrarian radicalism. As conceived of by the pluralists, class (proximate) politics are concerned with immediate economic group self-interest, status (remote) politics with position in the social structure. Class politics seek gains for the value of the gains themselves (more money, better working conditions, tax benefits, and so forth). Status politics seeks gains because of what they signify (conspicuous consumption, keeping up with the Jones, demonstrating Americanism vis-à-vis the Anglo-Saxons, etc.). Contrary to the pluralist view, periods of prosperity and satisfaction seem to produce both status and class politics in America. As de Tocqueville recognized, in America these are not so different. The group scramble that dominates politics during prosperity involves both "status" concerns and direct, narrow, economic advancement. In a crisis period, however, neither interest-group nor status politics can succeed. In the Populist period, "business methods" were doomed to failure. Similarly, in Wisconsin during the 1930's depression a precursor of McCarthy attempted to win office on the ("status") issue of communism.[53] Ignoring the economic grievances of the people, he was soundly beaten.

Populism, like Marxism, sought to combine a general program for the political control of industrialization with the concrete demands of a significant social force. But the Populist movement was hardly revolutionary. For better or worse, neither the movement nor the farmers it represented wanted to free themselves from the Lockean inheritance.

186

Rural Insurgency

Marxism was revolutionary; Populism was not. But this was hardly the only difference between them. If agrarian radicalism played a role in America analogous to the role of Marxism in Europe, then in a sense American farmers took the place of European workers.[54] In Europe industrialization uprooted the peasants from the land and brought them to the cities, where they became revolutionary workers. But the uprooted European peasants who settled in American cities remained conservative. In America the farmers who stayed on the land played the role of European workers as the major force challenging industrial capitalism.

How is this to be explained? The absence of feudalism on the one hand hindered the development of working-class consciousness. On the other hand it provided a yeoman farming class instead of a tradition-bound peasantry. The commitment to individual mobility obstructed the rise of socialist consciousness among workers, but it fostered agrarian radicalism. Farmer mobility, farmer experience in self-help, farmer cooperation along the frontier, all enabled farmers to organize politically. They did not require a Napoleonic leader to represent them. Moreover, fascism, feudal in its corporateness and in its attack on individualism, was less likely to appeal to American farmers. And as the class most committed to self-help and individual success, they reacted bitterly against the neofeudal society they saw being created around them.

For three-quarters of a century after the Civil War, there were continual movements of rural protest in the western Middle West. Movements like Populism and 1920's progressivism arose in response to specific agricultural depressions. But depressions alone cannot explain the continual strength of agrarian radicalism in this period. Both farmers and progressives prospered in the decade before World War I. The Non-Partisan League was organized in North Dakota during prosperity and declined during depression. One must look beyond depressions to the long-term structural situation of the American farmer.

The greater exposure of agriculture to international market conditions after the Civil War increased the instability of agricultural life. To compound dependence on the market, newly settled farmers usually produced a single crop; this exposed the farmers not only to market conditions in general but to the widespread fluctuations in the price of a single commodity. Moreover, farming methods had not yet made much impact on the hazards of weather on the Great Plains. Agrarian radicalism has always been stronger in the wheat than in the corn-hog areas. Wheat farming depends more on the weather and on other events over which the farmer has no control. The wheat farmer is traditionally inclined to take the help he can get from outside sources like the government. Corn-hog farming, on the other hand, depends far more on the day-to-day activities of the individual farmer. The conservative, antigovernment commitment to rugged individualism is more meaningful in the corn belt.

The Populist-progressive era was close to the period of settlement. One cannot speak with certainty about the influence of the frontier, but it seems reasonable to suppose that the frontier unsettled tradition and increased the effort to meet problems through political self-help.[55] As the frontier influence declined, these areas became more conservative.

Ethnic traditions also contributed to political protest. The West North Central states plus Wisconsin had far higher percentages of foreign-born in their populations than the states of any other region in the country. This concentration of the foreign-born was particularly striking compared to other rural areas. Early studies showed a tendency for the foreign-born to support protest movements more than native-stock Americans. The research here provides no similar evidence within the progressive states. But if the foreign-born as a whole did not disproportionately support agrarian radicalism at the same time, different groups of foreign-born perpetuated it at different times. Scandinavians and Germans were concentrated in the western Middle West. The Scandinavians consistently supported Populism and progressivism. The Germans, usually resistent to agrarian radicalism, kept it alive during and after World War I.

One might argue, moreover, that ethnic conflict provided a challenge to the political systems in the West North Central states. In the eastern cities, this challenge was met by the machine. In the countryside such a solution was impractical for several reasons — the different character of the ethnic groups, the contrasts in urban and rural political styles, the visibility of economic targets for resentment, the conditions of agriculture, the strength of a tradition of agrarian revolt, the greater isolation within rural areas. Therefore, ethnic dissatisfaction focused on broader class and political goals.[56]

Political conditions added their weight to economic and cultural factors. Politically, the farmers of the Middle West were isolated from the centers of power in the society. This did not mean that they were ignorant of the problems of the larger society so much as it meant that the larger society did not understand their problems. The midwest rural world lacked the power to make the outside political elites sensitive to agrarian demands and moderate on agrarian issues. Political control in the trans-Mississippi West was more nakedly in the hands of railroads and other businesses than was the case in states with a longer political tradition. In many instances, the western states were controlled by outside railroads and corporations. This elite inaccessibility provoked radical demands and radical movements.

Agrarian society, however, was not static. The changes that had produced agrarian radical movements finally undermined them. Consider for the moment only the decline in farm population. In 1860, 59.7 percent of all workers in the country worked on farms. By 1900, the figure was down to 35.7 percent.[57] Farmers were no longer a majority of the population. The decline in the relative number of farmers

189

continued in the twentieth century. From 1920 to 1944, there was a large net migration from the farms. In the West North Central states, where agrarian radical movements had flourished, this decline was especially pronounced. Between 1920 and 1944, the net migration from farms in the West North Central states averaged about 2 percent for each four-year period.[58] By 1950 less than 15 percent of the total United States population lived on farms.* Thus, if farmers in America played the role of workers in Europe, workers were the wave of the industrial future on both continents. A farmer-labor alliance in the 1890's might have altered the course of American development, but labor was turning in a different direction. Workers voted against Bryan in 1896, and Gompers had earlier refused to ally the AFL with the Populist Party. As he interpreted working class mentality, it was through with the middle-class radicalism that had permeated the labor movement since Jacksonian days. Before the rise of the AFL, the aim of working-class organizations had been to keep the class structure fluid, to provide for social mobility. This led to alliance with "the people" (farmers and others of the small middle class) rather than to specific class action and specific job-oriented demands. In joining purely class-oriented craft unions, workers accepted the permanency of the wage-earning status for themselves if not for their children. When European workers organized on a class basis, they recognized their wage-earning status only in order to challenge the permanency of a system which had wage-earning statuses in it. But in America, class action was a substitute for a general challenge to the industrial capitalist system.

The class organizations of American workers, then, tended

* Moreover, those who have left the farms have been primarily young people. The older rural residents, traditionally more conservative, have therefore become a greater political force.[59] This exodus from the farms to the cities has provided an urban safety valve for rural discontent.[60]

not to participate in broad movements of social change from the Populist period through the 1920's. (However, at certain times and in selected areas some American workers allied themselves with socialism and progressivism.) After the defeat of Populism, agrarian radicalism continued to flourish to the First World War and beyond. But the New Deal and the rise of the CIO reoriented American politics. Workers came to supply the main base of reform, not in alliance with rural areas but against them. Farmer leadership in American radicalism had come to an end.

THE TRANSFORMATION
OF THE REFORM IMPULSE

The Progressive Heritage

The decline of the Knights of Labor in the 1880's and the defeat of the Populist Party ten years later initiated a new era in American politics. Narrow interest groups — the American Federation of Labor and the American Farm Bureau Federation — rose to take the place of protest movements which had attempted to organize all farmers, all workers, or all common men.[1] During the same period, the urban machine, product in large part of the growth in city size and the influx of immigrants, came to dominate America's cities. Just as the AFL organized workers on narrow craft lines — carpenters, plumbers, printers — so the machine organized its constituents on narrow ethnic lines — Irish, Italians, Jews. Like the Farm Bureau and the AFL, the urban machine sought to supply narrow tangible favors. The jobs, contracts, food baskets, and police protection which the machine provided corresponded to the AFL's concentration on wages, hours, and working conditions and the Farm Bureau's concern with demonstration farms, marketing coops, and parity.[2] Each of these narrowly based organizations followed the line of least resistance; they satisfied the immediate demands of their constituents and challenged the power structure and business values of the larger society as little as possible.

Progressivism arose as a response to the growing power of these urban machines, private interests, and giant corporations. Developments in American society were calling into question the relevance of the Lockean ethic, which had sustained the reform impulse. Reformers could no longer take for granted the existence of a world of competing individuals, who had bargaining power in the economic and political marketplaces. They could no longer assume that individuals controlled the disposition of their own property, independent of the whims of others. Heretofore, Americans had believed that self-reliance and success were synonymous. There was little need to control society politically, since the decentralized economy and the power of the individual permitted him to succeed by his own efforts. In the new world, individual self-help appeared increasingly unrelated to success. The identity of self-help and efficiency had depended on the rural, small entrepreneurial character of pre-Civil War America. But the rural homogeneity that had produced the Lockean consensus splintered as the country urbanized and industrialized, as it filled with new immigrants and new bureaucracies.

Progressives were preoccupied with the loss of homogeneity.[3] They feared the society would fragment, that basic conflict between the new poor and the new rich would split it apart. Too easily, therefore, the progressives can be dismissed as "reactionaries," whose longing for a bygone, harmonious world was irrelevant to urban, industrialized America. But the progressives did not believe that return to the preindustrial world was possible. Instead they sought to make the experience of that world relevant in the new circumstances.[4]

The spontaneous workings of society would no longer produce harmony. But harmony could be created from above, by a neutral, administrative state. The state could eliminate

193

conflict, or at least limit it to the petty inessentials of narrow group squabbling — even Croly had room for that. In their moral clothes, the progressives feared the disintegration of society, the irrelevance of Lockean precepts. As pragmatic experts, they then developed a host of proposals to solve the moral crisis. Many of these proposals were salutary, but they are not the only progressive heritage. For while the progressives may have been fearful of organizations and bureaucracies, they bureaucratized the reform impulse.* Society left to itself could not be trusted to preserve the consensus; reform must be removed from the concrete social struggles of deprived groups. Thus is the desire for the lost harmony of preindustrial America made contemporary. Reform was seen as the outcome not of conflict but of consensus management. American liberals and the pluralists themselves owe too much to this progressive legacy. The progressives were quite relevant to the future of America; unfortunately, relevance is not the only virtue.

Combining moral intensity with a practical boast was second nature to the progressives. Charles McCarthy's *The Wisconsin Idea* begins by attacking impractical reformers. It then provides admirable detail on the Wisconsin reforms, justifying them by their specific operations and consequences. McCarthy concludes,

> What is the need of a philosophy or an "ism" when there is obvious wrong to be righted? Whatever has been accomplished in Wisconsin seems to have been based upon this idea of making practice conform to the ideals of justice and right which have been inherited. . . . If certain social classes are forming among us, can we not destroy them by means of education and through hope and encouragement make every man

---

* I speak, as throughout the discussion, of the mainstream of the progressive movement. Progressivism was appallingly diverse, containing a rural and an urban wing, and laying claim to all three presidential candidates in 1912. La Follette and others of the more radical progressives stand partially outside the mood developed here.

more efficient so that the doors of opportunity may always be open before him?

If you were responsible for the business of government, would you not apply the common rules of efficiency, Mr. Business Man? Do you not believe that it would pay well to make a heavy investment in hope, health, happiness, and justice? . . . Isn't there something worthwhile, something which will pay in the strong ideal of this New Individualism of Wisconsin?[5]

Could any two paragraphs more confound an attempt to distinguish moralism from pragmatism? McCarthy appeals in moral terms to equality of opportunity (self-help) and to efficiency. He argues that making men efficient will help them to help themselves. He calls upon business principles to justify state action. He defends unemployment insurance, workmen's compensation, and other Wisconsin reforms by calling upon "inherited" values. This appeal to the past does not make progressivism into a rural, reactionary movement any more than the appeals to "Mr. Business Man" make progressivism pro business.*

But to say that the progressives combined moral concerns with pragmatic solutions only begins the story. Every threat to social cohesion and individual rights required a specific solution. In each case, the question was how the harmonious

---

* Thus the perennial question of whether the progressives were too moralistic or too pragmatic is beside the point. Eric Goldman, arguing that their revolt against the moral standards of post-Civil War America left the progressives with no guides to positive action, quotes J. Allen Smith: "The real trouble with us reformers is that we made reform a crusade against standards. Well we smashed them all, and now neither we nor anybody else have anything left."[6] Hofstadter, however, writes, "My criticism of the Progressivism of that period is the opposite of Smith's — not that the Progressives most typically undermined or smashed standards, but that they set impossible standards, that they were victimized, in brief, by a form of moral absolutism."[7] Goldman explains the failures of progressivism in practice by the absence of standards, Hofstadter by the absence of concern with practical results. When one considers the nature of liberal moralism, these are simply two sides of the same coin.

pre-Civil War society was relevant, since in each case the problem was new. Even at their most defensive, progressives rarely sought simply to recreate the old society. Those who wanted to keep out the immigrants, for example, were introducing new principles of exclusion and control to retain the ethnic mix of the eighteenth century. Racism and immigration restriction were perhaps more prominent among regular Republicans than progressives.* But progressive intellectuals like E. A. Ross brought with them a set of "facts" about immigrant inferiority, which, like the "facts" on child labor, were quite in keeping with progressive pragmatism.

The progressive attitude toward democracy reveals even better their reinterpretation of the preindustrial experience. On the surface, it appears that proposals for the initiative, referendum, recall, and direct primary manifest a naïve and even dangerous faith in the people, the other side of a destructive distrust of elite autonomy. Here one sees, it is argued, the plebiscitarian strain in agrarian radicalism. Seeking to return to the lost town-meeting world, direct democracy challenges the legitimacy of elected representatives and established institutions.

Such a view is seriously in error. It overlooks, first, particular political motives for and against the direct democracy proposals. In the Middle West, the direct primary and the direct election of senators were necessary to combat machine control of the states. Electing judges by popular vote seemed one way of removing the judiciary from business control. Those who opposed these reforms, on the other hand, were not necessarily more sophisticated about, and less frustrated by, remote and impersonal government. In states like Wisconsin, the major opposition to direct democracy came from

* Racism was common among progressives, rare among Populists. But Hofstadter makes progressive racism a "populist" legacy, incorrectly finding it most prominent among the radical progressives. Cf. Richard Hofstadter, *The Age of Reform, op. cit.*, pp. 133–134, 286.

the Germans. They were not supporting general elite autonomy; they rather hoped to preserve the traditions and autonomy of their own communities. They valued their own cultural unity and wanted to protect it from alien influences.[8] This opposition to direct democracy did not insulate them from later support for such right-wing "plebiscitarians" as McCarthy.

More important, many progressives did not support direct democracy proposals from a simple desire to return government to the people. There was nostalgia for citizen participation in an idealized rural world, but progressives were not naïve enough to believe modern conditions permitted simple application of town meeting democracy. The function of direct democracy was rather to aid strata that had difficulty organizing groups to strive for government power themselves. These strata included the "amateur" middle-class business and professional men and the experts. Direct democracy reforms, it was felt, would eliminate the power of special interest groups and political parties and thus permit the people to elect prominent and knowledgeable individuals to office. In an atomized population, thought the progressives, the experts and the unorganized middle class could rule.* Direct democracy reforms were not meant to introduce direct democracy at all; they did not rely on the power of the people to help themselves. The people were required only to recognize and select expert and efficient leaders and to follow their lead on legislation.[9]

Direct democracy was an alternative to organization at the grass roots; yet it was an alternative from the point of view of elite autonomy, not "populism." Theodore Roosevelt was not the only progressive who feared mass democracy and sought to create political institutions insulated from mass pressure. Indeed, similar pluralist fears and desires are rooted

---

* Croly and his allies on *The New Republic* sponsored direct democracy, whereas Brandeis, more fearful of concentrated power, opposed it.

in these progressive preoccupations. That interest groups or large corporations might be more "prominent" than independent professional men or local economic notables was one unforeseen consequence. That politically successful local notables might not be progressive was another.* But most progressives never anticipated direct popular control of government.

Few progressives, nevertheless, were consciously antidemocratic. Some, like Croly, meant by democracy a popular nationalist spirit "represented" by the heroic man of talent. But most did not go this far. Instead they saw no contradiction between faith in the experts and faith in the people. Both progressive "populism" and progressive elitism were founded on a confidence in harmony of interests. Believing in commonly shared ends, the progressives blurred the distinction between the people acting for themselves and the experts acting in their name. Given underlying harmony, the people could be trusted through discussion and communication to arrive at decisions that expert knowledge would sanction.[12] And if the people were not yet ready to appreciate expertise and know their own interests, education could prepare them.

---

* Since their inception in the progressive era, the initiative and referendum have been used by special interest groups rather than by the mass of the people. Concluding their study of the operation of the initiative and referendum in California, Key and Crouch write, "Groups advocating initiatives which seriously affect the interests of powerful and well-organized financial, industrial, or commercial groups have little chance of success." They explain that well-financed groups, not spontaneously formed reform organizations, generally sponsor initiative propositions. Similarly, conservatives have utilized the referendum to defeat bills that the state legislature has passed. In sum, the initiative and referendum have made no important alterations in the composition, methods, or objectives of California's powerful groups.[10] Nonpartisan local government, another progressive reform, has also not furthered popular control but has rather made that control more difficult. Lacking a party label to identify their allies, the lower classes — even in a city like Detroit — have voted for prominent businessmen, newspaper-supported candidates, or other local notables with access to money and publicity.[11]

Far from being rural fundamentalists suspicious of education, the progressives found education vital to their consensual dream.

As the progressives saw politics, social reform raised questions of fact that could be objectively resolved, not conflicts between opposing values. In the Eastern Rate Case of 1910–1911, Louis Brandeis introduced the efficiency doctrines of scientific management into progressive prominence. He argued that there was no necessary conflict between the railroad and the shippers. The railroad, by applying the principles of scientific management, could save so much money that it would not have to raise rates. Reform, in this view, became a technical question. Good and evil corresponded to knowledge and ignorance, not to the struggle of one class or group against another.[13] The progressives interpreted the distinction between politics and administration not to restrict administration to questions of means but to subordinate politics to those competent in "social engineering." The educated and influential could be politically important in making "administrative" decisions defined in the broadest possible terms.*

The neutral state, administered by experts, was thus the main intended beneficiary when the progressives applied

* Even those progressives preoccupied with corruption cannot be dismissed as moral utopians; they were pragmatic utopians as well. Large sections of the progressive movement believed that personal corruption had caused the evils afflicting American life. With their focus on individual sin, such groups as the Los Angeles progressives were generally antilabor and opposed to significant social legislation. Laws of moral reform — against divorce, gambling, drinking, smoking — which many progressives advocated, were dominant here.[14] Those preoccupied with corruption, although moral absolutists, were politically moderate where questions of social reform were concerned. In addition, they spoke continuously of business principles in government and of organizing city governments as if they were corporations.[15] These were the progressives concerned with civil service and municipal reform. Their moralism came not from an uncritical reliance on self-help but from a belief that efficiency would solve social problems.

tenets of expertise and efficiency to industrial America. The state benefited as well from a reinterpretation of the self-help strand of Lockeanism, particularly prominent in the La Follette wing of the movement.

With the rise of a laissez-faire ideology after the Civil War, Social Darwinists counterposed paternalistic government to self-reliant individuals. But the reformers argued that with the growth of private power and the restrictions on individual economic opportunity private self-help injunctions were losing their meaning. Where existing opportunities were already restricted, the state provided new opportunities; far from restricting liberty, it enhanced it.* Quoting John Stuart Mill, Charles McCarthy explained, "Energy and self-dependence are, however, liable to be impaired by the absence of help, as well as by its excess. It is even more fatal to exertion to have no hope of succeeding by it than to be assured of succeeding without it."[17] Unemployment insurance, wage-and-hour laws, and other positive social legislation helped individuals to help themselves. Defending unemployment insurance, trade unionist Max Zaritsky said,

> I am not ready to propose that we sell the independence, the boast of our working men and women to some government agency, but I am ready to ask myself the question . . . if the worker in Great Britain who has to register for unemployment insurance is not an outstanding and self-respecting worker, what about the worker in America who is today the subject of the most miserable system of charity? What is a worker in America when he is starving and seeing his wife and children

* Progressives, friendlier to the state than to private centers of power, defended social legislation with self-help arguments more than they defended unions. Voluntarism — the philosophy of the AFL — stressed the right and the power of free, organized workers to achieve their goals. Some progressives, like La Follette and Francis Heney, also justified unions in these terms. Others were doubtful, seeing unions less as attempts at collective self-help and more as private centers of power destructive of self-help. Many progressives, such as those in Los Angeles, were clearly antagonistic to organized labor.[16]

starving every minute of the day? Can he retain his manhood as an independent worker? Can he satisfy himself with the proud phrase of "Rugged Individualism?"[18]

Surely this was a valuable insight. Moreover, their confidence in state action made the progressives responsible for a host of worthwhile, practical reforms — pure food and drug laws; factory inspection and sanitation laws; child labor, wage and hour, and workmen's compensation statutes; conservation measures; laws regulating and taxing railroads and other corporations; and constitutional amendments for an income tax, the direct election of senators, and woman suffrage.

Progressive faith in a neutral state was meant to preserve self-help in the face of ever-increasing decisions by bureaucratic authorities in government and in the economy outside the apparent control of the individual. Was individual freedom not restricted if an impartial state made collective decisions that were identical with the individual decisions he would have made? Could not the individual permit state action and "still remain as free as before"?[19] Clearly, however, there is a difference between making decisions oneself and supporting decisions in one's alleged interest that someone else has made. Faith in neutral and efficient decisions was in effect turned against self-help, with the implicit assumption that no one could want anything inefficient.

Progressive pragmatism, then, had anti-individualistic consequences. The problem was not, however, that progressive rural values led to the attempt of the state to enforce social reforms and codes of conduct on the individual. Rather the progressive mentality could justify acquiescence in bureaucratic decisions by a variety of large institutions, public and private. Even the public agencies that made decisions were hardly characterized by their millennial preoccupations. They concerned themselves with particular problems and particular constituencies and had been given no standards beyond "efficiency" to guide them. Seeking standards and seeking

201

support, the "experts" looked to the groups with the most expertise and the most power. The ICC established friendly relations with the railroads, the Forestry Service with the lumber interests, the Bureau of Land Management with the cattlemen.[20]

Of course, progressive preoccupation with efficiency does not alone explain the capturing of administrative agencies by the groups meant to be regulated. The most direct cause was the continuing political power of these groups. But progressive doctrine was in part to blame. Not realizing the permanence both of value conflict and of social conflict, progressives failed to spell out "public interest" values and find specific social support for them. They did not fully comprehend that one had to counterpose more than honest and scientific administration to business power and business values. Their faith in harmony made them innocent of the fact that norms of efficiency and expertise could not supply values. This problem was endemic to Lockean liberalism. Its pragmatic character gave the progressives great flexibility. But in seeming to justify everything that worked, liberalism provided too few operational standards. Assuming the identity of ends, it allowed means to run rampant. Progressive faith in a scientific public interest did not produce a "populistic" democracy that threatened private groups and private interests. It rather aided in the adjustment to private hegemony.[21]

It may appear paradoxical that progressivism, hostile to organized groups, aided the acceptance of their power. This was, indeed, an unanticipated consequence of progressive doctrine; yet there was an important strain of corporate thinking among progressives. They were, of course, suspicious of private centers of power. Special interest groups, they thought, corrupted efforts by altruistic, reasonable men to reach solutions in the interests of all. Nevertheless, the private groups which often dominate administrative decisions today were encouraged during the progressive period. Leading businessmen encouraged movements for self- and even state regulation of industry, with which progressives sympathized. Important progressive regulatory legislation — meat inspection and banking regulation, for example — owed much to big businessmen's desires to rationalize their industries.* Even progressive enthusiasm for trust busting had few operational consequences, serving mainly to reconcile men who had demonstrated their moral purity to the now less threatening corporate world. Here World War I played an important role, as business seemed to cleanse itself by cooperating voluntarily in the national interest. Hopefully, the spirit of cooperation could be extended beyond the wartime emergency.†

Progressives were not opposed to organized interests; they rather sought to locate groups which would "represent" the people in a semicorporate society. They were hostile not so much to groups as to competing, independent groups. The progressives did fear conflict between organized interests and rule by private power. And, in fact, organized conflict

* Smaller provincial businessmen opposed state intervention, but the significant point is that the allegedly provincial progressives were closer to the eastern giants than to western and midwestern entrepreneurs. Gabriel Kolko argues that the national progressives were quite close to the corporate giants and sought, like them, to rationalize and bring order into the chaos of capitalist competition. Cf. Gabriel Kolko, *The Triumph of Conservatism* (New York: Free Press, 1963), pp. 12–112, 190–204, 280–285. For a somewhat different emphasis, cf. Robert Wiebe, *Businessmen and Reform* (Cambridge, Mass.: Harvard University Press, 1962).

† Herbert Hoover, briefly supported for President by *The New Republic* in 1920, encouraged trade associations to form and make rules for the regulation of their industries. This "new individualism" was an alternative, in Hoover's eyes, both to governmental coercion and to destructive competition. It was what he meant in calling for national guidance, national planning, and national efficiency. Brandeis, too, had supported the trade association movement, favoring such schemes as resale price maintenance to preserve business against unregulated competition. Croly at times supported schemes for functional representation along economic lines.[22] His proposal, in *The Promise of American Life,* for compulsory membership in government-controlled unions was antiunion but hardly antiorganizational.

has not been the main consequence of the trade association movement or of the proliferation of centralized interest groups. The result has rather been the parceling out of government to organized groups, which do not compete with each other but rather divide pieces of power. What would have surprised and dismayed the progressives is not the pervasiveness of conflict but rather the current locus of power. They did not foresee that power would reside in the organized groups more than in the state.

In terms of actual achievements, the New Deal made a far greater impact on American society than the progressive movement. But doctrinal contrasts cannot explain this difference. Franklin Roosevelt was forced to deal with the severest cataclysm in the history of American capitalism; no similar crisis impelled action in the progressive period. In addition, the New Deal depended on and reacted to a mass working-class base. In its demands for concrete reforms this base was more analogous to the Populist farmers than to the progressive middle-class professionals, not driven by economic necessity.

Doctrinally, the New Deal owed much to the progressive movement. Its vaunted manipulative, experimental approach had a progressive flavor; indeed much doctrinal clearing of the underbrush by progressives permitted the New Deal its anti-ideological luxuries.[23] More concretely, agencies like the AAA and the NRA had roots in progressive wartime experience. These were not New Deal departures; as genuine reform measures, moreover, their pedigree is dubious.

New Deal social legislation also derived from progressive experience; it was brought to Washington by Wisconsin reformers.[24] Seeking to redistribute power and income, the "second New Deal" was closer to La Follette than to more moderate progressives. Here that wing of the movement with a largely rural economic base had its impact. Pragmatic social welfare laws sprang from the more Jeffersonian, anti-bigness (reactionary?) progressives, not the middle-class reformers.

Progressivism disappointed many of its intellectual adherents, who had hoped for a transformation of American society. The movement's roots in the past have often been blamed. But a more important focus is the well-to-do, middle-class base of much of the movement. Most progressives sought to deal with the problems of capitalist chaos and mass deprivation without disturbing the basic social and power relationships in America. Therefore, it was quite natural for progressives to stress moral reform and the public interest, while often working closely with existing powerful social groups. This was one kind of progressive symbiosis between moralism and practicality. It arose less because progressives were prisoners of the past and more because they were enmeshed in the present.

The consequences for the future of American reform were great. Progressivism introduced administrative liberalism into American politics. A politics of the public interest was meant to prevent the rise of social classes and to thwart popular uprisings as well as big business control of politics. And this approach did have concrete advantages. In relying on "facts" rather than disputing over ultimate values, the progressives helped win acceptance for reform proposals. Some progressives were able to learn the lesson that the AFL, the Farm Bureau, and the urban machine had also learned — that concrete rewards were more important than efforts to create a middle-classless society. In part, this was the consequence of progressive insistence that politics deal with reality, not with formalisms.

But a concrete approach was not sufficient in itself. Administrative progressives often spoke the language of pragmatism without engaging in activity beneficial to the poor and deprived. Narrow groups, on the other hand, were active enough; but they focused only on the most immediate needs of their constituents, filtered through the organizational interests of their leaders. The urban machine provided patronage jobs but showed little interest in large-scale efforts at job creation by the state. The AFL fought for high wages in its shops but opposed unemployment insurance for those not working. The Farm Bureau favored public power in the Tennessee Valley but sabotaged programs there to aid the rural poor.

The progressives who pushed concrete reforms the hardest were impelled not only by doctrine but by their economic base. A politician like La Follette saw that the larger goals opposed by narrow groups were no less practical for his constituents. He utilized moral appeals in the service of large-scale, tangible reforms, thus maintaining the broad, agrarian radical approach to political change that the narrower groups had given up. La Follette progressivism combined moral appeals with social reform in part because it represented a constituency with real economic grievances — the poor midwestern farmer. Where progressive moralism focused instead on political management, it drained the agrarian radical heritage of its relevance and foreshadowed the administrative character of later liberal politics.

Progressives and Rural Radicals in Decline

The progressive movement itself was shattered by the First World War. Prowar progressives redirected their reforming zeal from changing American society to making the world safe for democracy. In their efforts to unite America behind the war effort, many became more tolerant of conservatives and more conservative themselves. This was particularly true for those prowar progressives who, like Lenroot in Wisconsin, confronted powerful antiwar progressive leaders and were forced to seek conservative allies.[25] As the actual consequences of the war did not live up to progressive expectations, many became disillusioned with reform altogether. Having placed all their hope for reform on the war, they universalized their disappointment as well.[26]

The war also damaged the reform impulse of the antiwar progressives. Antiwar progressives suffered most immediately from the hysteria of the war years and the red scare that followed. In addition, progressives like Hiram Johnson became more conservative after the war, embittered by what they perceived as the hypocrisy of Wilsonian progressivism.[27] And the conflicts among progressives, first over the war and then over ratification of the Versailles Treaty, further sapped the strength of the movement.

With progressivism increasingly fragmented, with antiwar progressives tarred by the brush of disloyalty, with prowar progressives more interested in foreign policy than in domestic change, mass concern for progressive politics could only suffer. At the popular level, World War I killed progressivism in two stages. There was first the relief of finding in the war a shared national substitute for the tensions and ambiguities of making political choices. At the same time, the war was a public symbol; the political enthusiasm of the progressive period reached a climax over the war. After the war, political enthusiasm went the way of political judgment; one senses the relief with which the 1920's settled down to normalcy, jazz, or anything else private and personal. This political exhaustion following World War I paralleled the Great Barbecue after the Civil War and the political apathy and private indulgence following World War II.[28]

Other factors besides the war weakened progressivism in the 1920's. The strikes and radical activity of the first postwar years and the Red scare lost for reform much of its urban, middle-class base. A generally conservative political leadership often strong in progressive states rallied popular support for the prohibition amendment and for immigration restriction.[29] Rural progressivism did remain significant, as the Middle West suffered from an agricultural depression throughout much of the decade.[30]* But the twenties saw a significant shift in agrarian tactics. The McNary-Haugen bill, with its equivalent of a tariff for agriculture, was the first important instance in which progressives supported a special interest measure for the relief of agriculture.[31] Farmers were becoming, after all, numerically only another partial interest.

It is difficult to measure the effect on the minds of American farmers of the change from majority to minority status. Certainly this change has influenced farm leadership and farm organization. In Populist days, farm leaders could still see America as a rural society and make agrarian demands in the name of all the people. The growth of farm organizations to deal with particular agricultural problems was a recognition that farmers were a special interest group.[33] Moreover, as the society changed from rural to urban, farmers and their leaders became generally more uncomfortable. Labor organized itself into a strong movement, and the national government became increasingly ubiquitous — this apart from the more cosmopolitan tone of the country as a whole. Farm movements were ill equipped to deal with the problems of the new society. The rural vision of America was simply too irrelevant to provide a rational basis for broad social reform, as it still had in the Populist period. As farmers achieved narrow ends, the larger society drifted further and further from its rural moorings. Hence the rise of farm pressure groups went hand in hand with the rise of a politics of rural irrationality — Ku Klux Klan, the most ugly sides of prohibition, jingoism, and the like. It is not that former Populists became Klansmen. Groups such as the Anti-Saloon League and the Klan were not disproportionately strong in Populist and progressive areas; the Klan, for exam-

* Progressive Republicans like Norris, Norbeck, and Bob La Follette, Jr., and their Democratic allies from the West and Middle West provided crucial support for the more radical aspects of the New Deal and opposed its more conservative manifestations.[32] But as progressive senators in such states as Nebraska and South Dakota died, new ones did not come to take their places.

ple, was weak on the Populist Great Plains and strong farther east.[34] But changes in American society had brought new types of rural activists and new rural preoccupations to the fore.

American agriculture was as much affected by changes within it as by changes without. The revolution in agricultural technology made farming more prosperous and drove many marginal farmers off the land, a process that continues today. As agriculture became commercial, class differences on the farm sharpened. Farm tenancy increased and the corporation farm depending on hired labor and mechanization became more important.[35] Class differentiation on the farm also distinguished the farm owner from the nonfarm worker. An ideology that united all farmers, or all commen men, became more difficult.

As agriculture became more specialized and more diversified, farming became less of a gamble and more of a science. Diversification insulated the farmer against sharp changes in the price or conditions of a single crop. The fortunate farmer found economic solutions for what had heretofore been political problems. Moreover, political developments augmented economic well-being on the farms. World War II ushered in an unprecedented period of agricultural prosperity, sustained subsequently by parity and the cold war. Agricultural recessions have occurred, but they have not matched in length or in severity the depressions of the 1890's, 1920's, and 1930's. When farmers feel threatened by depression, they vote their pocketbook.[36] In the prosperous times, more common since 1940, midwest farmers support the Republican Party. It is their village and small-town neighbors who provided the GOP with its electoral backbone.

As the farmers have lost in numbers, they have gained in political power. Federal and state legislatures were until recently apportioned to favor rural voters. More than that, agrarian organizations have made effective use of political power and of alliance with business interests. This increased political power has been bought at the price of attention to the needs of agricultural laborers and of poor, marginal farmers.

The changes brought by industrialization have transformed rural politics. These changes did not turn agrarian radicalism into McCarthyism; they rather sapped the vitality of the agrarian radical approach. As long as it seemed possible to reconcile industrialization with agrarian virtue, agrarian radical movements proposed concrete programs to deal with specific problems. Agrarian ideology in part served to reconcile farmers and their leaders to the changes that were occurring in American society. But the very changes that had made midwestern farmers more prosperous than ever removed them even further from the moral world with which they had been taught to deal. Farm prosperity depended on the successful functioning of an industrial society. This society challenged the values of moral integrity and individualistic self-help so central to the rural world. The consequence has been the strengthening of rural conservatism.

In understanding where agrarian radicalism went and where McCarthyism came from, the nature of this conservatism must be understood. I have earlier suggested that traditional conservatism is both economically self-concerned and extremely ideological. In addition, it combines economic with political conservatism. Social scientists have distinguished "position" issues from "style" issues. Position issues refer to the traditional Left–Right cleavage on economic demands. Style issues are noneconomic: civil liberties, civil rights, foreign policy. Position and style issues are said to tap two different dimensions of political cleavage.[37] But rural conservatism is not only more right wing than agrarian radicalism on such issues as rural electrification, public power, social welfare, and support for trade unions. It also tends to be less tolerant, more jingoist, more anti-intellectual, and more provincial. In so far as farmers make left-wing economic demands, they place themselves behind a generally liberal leadership. In so far as rural economic demands are conservative, the leadership supported is generally conservative.[38] The political and economic dimensions in American rural society have generally been collapsed into one.

There is nothing inevitable about this combination. Logically, political liberalism and welfare-state economics need not go together. But the pluralists make more than a logical point in connecting McCarthy's witch-hunts with an agrarian radicalism that was allegedly only liberal on economic issues. In the background of their analysis is European politics, where anticonstitutional movements with a small middle-class and rural base have grown strong by making "left-wing" economic demands. In France, Louis Napoleon had a peasant base but was more than a traditional conservative politician.[39] In Germany, as the liberal peasant parties of the Weimar Republic declined, their rural supporters switched to the National Socialists.[40] These fascist movements mobilized discontented elements with a combination of vague "left-wing" economic demands and attacks on civilized institutions and democratic processes. They developed as a more traditional agrarian politics was on the decline. Had the same evolution occurred in America, it would vitiate the argument that political and economic liberalism have gone together in rural politics. Had agrarian politics remained left-wing on economic issues but become authoritarian, agrarian radicalism could be linked to McCarthyism. What then is the evidence bearing on the development of "neo-fascist" movements in America and their links to McCarthyism and agrarian radicalism?

Rural Extremism

The current literature connects agrarian radicalism with fascism as well as with McCarthyism. Indeed, there is more evidence of a Populist link to neofascist movements in America than there is of a Populist link to McCarthyism. But

Populism in America did not lead to fascism because neo-fascist movements in this country have been outstanding in their weakness. By the same token, Populism did not lead through fascism to McCarthyism. If fascism was a possible although not actual outcome of Populism, McCarthyism was an actual outcome of conservative politics.

Much of the effort to connect Populism with fascism is ludicrous. Ferkiss, for example, finds Populist roots in fascism because both movements favored government intervention in the economy to preserve capitalism. By this token, the New Deal was also fascist. He finds Populism tending toward fascism because it attacked control of the press by the special interests, which "even if true" undermines a free press. One wonders what the special interest control does to press freedom. He sees opposition to organized labor emerging from Populism in spite of the fact that the movement was clearly pro labor.[41]

But Ferkiss' general arguments have more merit. He suggests, first, that the "plebiscitary" ideology of fascism has Populist roots and second that the fascist appeal to small merchants and farmers squeezed between big capital, big labor, and big government particularly attracts the Populist base. Rural fundamentalism and rural suspicion of the cosmopolitan city link the Populist base to fascism.[42]

This argument has roots in Marxist suspicions of the rural petite bourgeoisie, a "reactionary" class in industrial society.[43] European developments provide evidence supporting it. In America there are few examples of a link between Populist and fascist bases because American fascism has never been a significant political movement. However, there is some marginal evidence. In the 1930's, Lemke and Huey Long mobilized voters on programs which combined economic and authoritarian appeals. We have pointed out Lemke's strong 1936 showing among the wheat farmers of northwest North Dakota. In Louisiana, Huey Long was strongest in his first elections in the old Populist hill country.

The correlation between the Populist vote in 1896 and Long's primary victory in 1928 was .62.[44] The progressive counties in northern Wisconsin which once supported La Follette have sent a nativist agrarian radical to congress for many years.

The main evidence of rural support for neofascist movements derives from agrarian radical attitudes toward the Union Party of 1936. The product of Father Coughlin's hysterical preaching against Roosevelt, the Union Party was on that familiar borderline between social reform and fascism. With knowledge of the later activities of Lemke and Father Coughlin and with a perspective that the depression-bred atmosphere did not provide, it is easier to see the authoritarian elements in the Union Party today than it was thirty years ago. Moreover, like Long, Lemke in 1936 concentrated his fire on the centers of power in the society rather than on the Jews and other scapegoats. This distinguished the movement in a crucial way from German fascism. Still, there were more than the beginnings of Coughlinite anti-Semitism in 1936, and the Union Party was not distinguished by its concern for constitutional norms.

Thus even in 1936 the careful liberal observer rejected the Union Party. The Wisconsin Progressives refused to support it, and at the national Farmer-Labor Progressive convention the party's program was described as "a pot-pourri of political clap-trap." On the other hand, the Union Party was also described as "an opening wedge so we can win national victory in 1940." Both Governor Olson of Minnesota and Bob La Follette, Jr., "voiced respect" for the Union Party, although they opposed splitting the vote for Roosevelt.[45]

The radical wing of the Farmers Union actually supported the Union Party, although it lost power in its own organization on this issue. This wing of the Union combined a stress on legislative remedies for the farmer with a hatred of government action. E. E. Kennedy, the secretary-treasurer, supported Coughlin even after the anti-Semitism started. Milo Reno, leader of the radical Farm Holiday strikes in Iowa, spoke of Roosevelt's brain trust in these terms:

> In the old days they became preachers, but now whenever a boy is entirely effeminated they send him to college and make him a professor. When he isn't any good at that they put him in the Cabinet as one of the Braintrusters.

This radical wing favored direct farmer action such as strikes and the prevention of foreclosure sales; often these activities were successful.[46]

Like Langer's efforts to raise the price of wheat in depression-ridden North Dakota, the practical actions of the radical wing of the Farmers Union were often illegal but successful. Given the terrific economic hardship of the depression, one should not condemn these actions out of hand. Nevertheless, the anti-intellectualism and nascent anti-Semitism of some of the radical leaders, plus the combination of economic panaceas with hatred of the government, pointed in a neo-fascist direction. The radical wing of the Farmers Union was weak in the old Populist wheat areas where the Union was strongest, and strong in very depressed corn and hog areas like southern Iowa. But this does not eliminate the organizational connection between agrarian radicalism and incipient authoritarianism.

The Great Depression produced unsavory politics in Progressive Wisconsin as well. In 1937, Governor Phil La Follette called a special session of the state legislature and abrogated parliamentary procedures to pass his legislation.[47] The Governor's action, denounced by prominent progressives, was the first indication of the road La Follette was to travel — through America First and ending with a prominent role in the MacArthur for President boom of 1948.

Agrarian radicalism in the 1930's was thus not free from authoritarian entanglements. In a situation of prolonged rural depression, one might look for these tendencies to reassert themselves.* But our main concern here is with the relationship between agrarian radicalism and McCarthyism. This is not out of some calculated desire to ignore fascism, but out of the strength of McCarthyism and the weakness of American fascism.

McCarthyism was significantly not a fascist movement.[48] It lacked an economic program, was free of anti-Semitism, did not challenge local elites, and provided no physical violence. Nor was it a revolt of the masses. McCarthyism grew out of conservative rural politics. And conservative rural politics is a mass politics in no meaningful sense; it is rather the politics of local elites. Its leadership is based in the conservative small towns and small cities of the Middle West. Far more striking than the relationship of Populism to fascism is the strength of conservative politics in formerly Populist states. Conservatives had always been strong in these states; as agrarian radicalism declined conservative politics were all that remained. This politics, which differs from both Populism and fascism in being antistatist, provided the organization and electoral backing for McCarthy.

The weakness of Lemke and American neofascism contrasts with the power McCarthy wielded during his career. The Union Party was a mass movement — it sought to split apart existing coalitions, it arose from severe hardship, and its power rested on the attempt to mobilize mass support. It failed miserably. And indeed, with all the mass strength the Populists were able to command, they met firm resistance from the conservative centers of power in society. Elites resisted mass pressure in agrarian radical days; yet they are seen as yielding to Populist mass pressure during McCarthyism. It is necessary to look more closely at the sources of McCarthy's strength and the nature of his support.

* But even in hard times farmers have supported authoritarian leaders far less prominently than Populism, Debs, La Follette, Roosevelt, and the Farmers Union.

McCARTHYISM
AS MASS POLITICS

From 1950 through 1954, Joseph McCarthy disrupted the normal routine of American politics. But McCarthyism can best be understood as a product of that normal routine. McCarthy capitalized on popular concern over foreign policy, communism, and the Korean War, but the animus of McCarthyism had little to do with any less political or more developed *popular* anxieties. Instead it reflected the specific traumas of conservative Republican activists — internal Communist subversion, the New Deal, centralized government, left-wing intellectuals, and the corrupting influences of a cosmopolitan society. The resentments of these Republicans and the Senator's own talents were the driving forces behind the McCarthy movement.

Equally important, McCarthy gained the protection of politicians and other authorities uninvolved in or opposed to the politics motivating his ardent supporters. Leaders of the GOP saw in McCarthy a way back to national power after twenty years in the political wilderness. Aside from desiring political power, moderate Republicans feared that an attack on McCarthy would split their party. Eisenhower sought for long months to compromise with the Senator, as one would with any other politician. Senators, jealous of their prerogative, were loath to interfere with a fellow senator. Newspapers,

216

looking for good copy, publicized McCarthy's activities. When the political institutions that had fostered McCarthy turned against him, and when, with the end of the Korean War his political issue became less salient, McCarthy was reduced to insignificance.

Politics alone does not explain McCarthyism; but the relevant sociopsychology is that which underpins normal American politics, not that of radicals and outsiders. Psychological insights are not relevant alone to the peculiar politics of the American Right. Equally important, the ease with which McCarthy harnessed himself to the everyday workings of mainstream politics illuminates the weaknesses of America's respectable politicians.

Attention to sociology and psychology must be concentrated within the political stratum, not among the populace as a whole. It is tempting to explain the hysteria with which McCarthy infected the country by the hysterical preoccupations of masses of people. But the masses did not levy an attack on their political leaders; the attack was made by a section of the political elite against another and was nurtured by the very elites under attack. The populace contributed to McCarthy's power primarily because it was worried about communism, Korea, and the cold war.

The analysis of McCarthyism presented here focuses on political issues, political activists, and the political structure. As an alternative to this interpretation of McCarthyism, the pluralists have suggested an analysis that goes further beneath the surface of American politics. To be sure, unlike La Follette and Hitler, McCarthy mobilized no cohesive, organized popular following. Nevertheless, for the pluralists the concept of mass politics captures both the flavor of McCarthy's appeals and the essence of his threat to American institutions.

In the first place, they argue, McCarthyism drew sustenance from the American "populist" tradition. "Populists," suspicious of leadership, seek to register the unadulterated popular

217

will at every level of government. Giving McCarthyism as his example, Lipset writes,

> American and Australian egalitarianism is perhaps most clearly reflected in the relative strength of "populist" movements through which popular passions wreak their aggression against the structure of the polity. . . . Conversely, in Canada as in Britain such problems have been handled in a much more discrete fashion, reflecting in some part the ability of a more unified and powerful political elite to control the system. . . .
> The values of elitism and ascription may protect an operating democracy from the excesses of populism . . . whereas emphasis on self-orientation and anti-elitism may be conducive to right-wing populism.[1]

In this view, McCarthy had to go outside the "political stratum"[2] to obtain support; his power came from his ability to exploit mass resentments.

The alleged mass character of McCarthyism flows, in the second place, from the character of the popular resentments he exploited. He is said to have mobilized feelings of uneasiness over a sophisticated, cosmopolitan, urban, industrial society. He focused these vague discontents, the argument continues, on such specific symbols as intellectuals, striped-pants diplomats, homosexuals, and effete eastern aristocrats. McCarthyite status politics was thus radical in its rejection of industrial society as well as in its suspicion of responsible political leadership.

The third perceived mass characteristic of McCarthyism flows from the first two. McCarthyite appeals, it is argued, were not rooted in the traditional cleavages between the major political parties and groups in America. Like other mass phenomena, McCarthyism split apart existing political coalitions. Talcott Parsons sees it as

> . . . not simply a cloak for the "vested interests" but rather a movement that profoundly splits apart the previously dominant groups. This is evident in the split, particularly conspicuous since about 1952, within the Republican Party. . . .

218

But at the same time the McCarthy following is by no means confined to the vested-interest groups. There has been an important popular following of very miscellaneous composition. . . . The elements of continuity between western agrarian populism and McCarthyism are by no means purely fortuitous. At the levels of both leadership and popular following, the division of American political opinion over this issue *cuts clean across the traditional lines of distinction between conservatives and progressives. . . .*[3]

For the pluralists, then, McCarthy disrupted the traditional group basis of politics by exploiting popular resentments over changes in American society. In the view adopted here, McCarthy exploited popular concern over foreign policy, structured by existing political institutions and political cleavages. Four subjects provide evidence relevant to these alternative contentions. The first is the political and social background from which McCarthy rose to power. Did the Wisconsin Senator disrupt political alliances? Did he transform traditional conservative politics? If McCarthy was merely a traditional conservative, why did he achieve so much more notoriety than other conservatives?

Second, we will look at McCarthy's ideology. Was this ideology new for a conservative Republican? Did it exploit populistic resentments and moral indignation? Whom was it likely to attract?

Third, we will investigate the evidence bearing on McCarthy's popular support. What social groups supported the Wisconsin Senator? What psychological characteristics and political attitudes led to sympathy for him? What was the relationship between approving of McCarthy in a public opinion poll and voting for him in the election booth? Was McCarthy's popular support sufficient to explain his influence?

The final inquiry will be directed at the response to McCarthy by political institutions and elites. Did the "political stratum" defend the "rules of the game" against this outsider? Did the education and political sophistication of elites insulate them from suspectibility to McCarthy? Were there important differences among elites in this respect? Do the varying fortunes in the war between elite pluralism and mass populism successfully account for the rise and fall of Joe McCarthy?

The Context

The entry of the Senator from Wisconsin onto the political stage did not split apart a previously united Republican Party. The split in the GOP between the East and the western Middle West goes back decades before McCarthyism. In Populist and progressive days, the West North Central states were the center of liberal opposition to an eastern-dominated Republican Party. During the New Deal and World War II, the two wings of the Republican Party switched places. On "traditional economic issues"[4] as well as on foreign policy, midwest Republicans had been more conservative than their eastern counterparts for a decade before McCarthyism. The midwest wing of the party had been more isolationist for perhaps half a century.[5]

It was this wing that mobilized itself behind McCarthy. It supported him on the censure resolution in the Senate,[6] and Republican businessmen in the Middle West were more sympathetic to McCarthyism than those in the East.[7] McCarthy did not split apart an elite, the parts of which had been equally conservative before him. He rather capitalized on an existing liberal-conservative split within the existing Republican elite.

Former centers of agrarian radicalism, like the plains states, sent right-wing Republicans who supported McCarthy to the Senate. But McCarthy was not the agent who disrupted the traditional agrarian radical base. Before these states supported McCarthy, they had already undergone an evolution from agrarian radicalism to extreme conservatism. (Of the states analyzed here, South Dakota was typical of the trans-Mississippi West and North Dakota the exception.)

The decline of agrarian radicalism increased conservative power in the trans-Mississippi West, but there have been important continuities in the conservative outlook. An ambiguity about the state of the country continues to plague these conservatives; in some ways they are satisfied and in others they are not. The right wing of the Republican Party reveals an uneasiness about cosmopolitan values and styles of life, about large cities and big bureaucracies. In this sense it seeks to change American institutions, not to conserve them. At the same time, it profoundly wishes to preserve the status quo in its own areas — not simply in terms of rural virtues but in terms of the local prestige and economic power of the elites that have since the decline of agrarian radicalism controlled the Republican Parties of the rural and small-town Middle West. This ambiguity — complacency at home and fear of the outside world — is nothing new for midwest conservatism. Half a century ago, it motivated midwestern conservative opposition to agrarian radical movements, which were perceived as alien imports from the bureaucratized and hostile outside world. McCarthy sprang from this conservative background.

For Leslie Fiedler, McCarthy's support among local newspapers indicated his populist roots. Anyone could get the support of a millionaire or two, Fiedler explained, but the

resolutely anti-intellectual small-town weeklies and . . . the professionally reactionary press . . . continue to say in [McCarthy's] name precisely what they have been saying now for thirty-five years. To realize this is to understand that McCarthyism, generally speaking, is the extension of the ambiguous American impulse toward "direct democracy," with its distrust of authority, institutions, and expert knowledge; and that more precisely it is the form which populist theory takes when forced to define itself against such a competing "European" radicalism as Communism.[8]

221

The "resolutely anti-intellectual" small-town newspapers, however, led the opposition to every agrarian radical movement from Populism to La Follette to the contemporary Farmers Union. The Populists and the Non-Partisan League, for example, had to start their own newspapers because the existing local press would not give them a fair hearing in their news columns, much less support them on the editorial page.[9] The small-town press may be suspicious of certain authorities and institutions, but it is supported by others — particularly local business interests. The role of this press provides evidence for McCarthy's conservative inheritance, not his "populist" roots.

There are important continuities between nineteenth century conservatism and the contemporary variety, but several new developments have had their impact. There has, first, been a change in the character of eastern conservatism. As the industrial giants of the East become more established and bureaucratized, they become less militantly conservative. Taft blamed Eisenhower's victory over him in 1952 on eastern financial interests.[10] This Populist-sounding charge hardly reflects Taft's Populist roots; the Taft family has always opposed agrarian radicalism. It reflects rather a change in the politics of "Wall Street."

The New Deal created a balance of forces more opposed to midwest conservatism than this country had seen since the Civil War. Social legislation and trade unions became prominent, and the power of the national government increased. It is quite true, as Parsons argues, that McCarthy directed little fire against trade unions and the New Deal. Indeed, much of McCarthy's genius lay in his ability to concentrate on the single issue of communism — so pressing and popular an issue in the early 1950's — and not raise other, more divisive appeals. But the activists around the Senator supported him so enthusiastically just because they knew he was attacking their enemies. McCarthy's attacks on foreign policy were often framed as attacks on Roosevelt and the New Deal, and his attacks on Britain were generally tied to its Socialist leadership.[11] A writer for *Fortune* who conducted a survey of business opinion about McCarthy wrote, "Among business-men who approve of McCarthy's war on subversion there is a satisfaction, subconscious perhaps but very strong, over his incidental licks at all longhairs, eggheads, professors and bright young men of the 1930's and 1940's."[12]

This support, so important to McCarthy, explains why he did not develop an overtly statist appeal. The activists around McCarthy were traditional conservatives, rejoicing in McCarthy's attack on the party of Roosevelt. Like the busi-nessmen in the *Fortune* study, they would have deserted the Senator had he developed a demagogic "liberal" economic program.[13]

Democratic control of national politics added to Republi-can discontent. By 1952, the GOP had been out of power for twenty consecutive years. And Republicans were not accus-tomed to opposition; between 1856 and 1932 they failed to control the presidency for a total of only twenty years.

The international situation brought the frustrations of midwest conservatism to a head and at the same time seemed to offer a political issue and a way out. The new long-term importance of foreign policy reinforced an already power-fully moralistic political approach. Much as some progres-sives at the turn of the century had reacted with defensive moralism to the waves of immigrants, so conservatives now reacted to the Communist threat. There had not yet been time to become accustomed to the new situation.

Traditionally, the Middle West has been isolationist for both ethnic and geographic reasons. Many of the region's political leaders thought Roosevelt had forced the country into a war against Germany; now Truman seemed afraid to fight a much worse enemy. Communism represented to them the epitome of an alien world — atheism, immorality, de-struction of the family, and socialism. But far from defeating this enemy or withdrawing from the outside world that it contaminated, the Democratic Party dealt in an ambiguous atmosphere of international involvement, limited war, and compromise with evil.

Communism in the abstract was threatening enough. The danger became concretized and symbolized by two traumatic events. The first of these was the "loss of China." The right wing insisted with a stridency born of inner doubt that only a failure to apply traditional American values and tactics could have caused this defeat. The loss of China was a loss of American potency; it could only cease to be frightening if those responsible were identified.

Following hard upon the loss of China came the Korean War. Wars in America often produce superpatriotism, and this in turn claims victims. Those suspected of opposing wars have often been the victims of 100 percent Americanism. But during the Korean War the superpatriots perceived the very prosecutors of the war as the ambivalent ones. This again was something new and reinforced right-wing Republican fears that the centers of power in the society were working against them. If Woodrow Wilson had not approved of all the excesses of the superpatriots during and following World War I, he at least approved of the war. In the Korean War, the powers that be seemed unenthusiastic; one had to seek support for superpatriotism elsewhere. This was fertile ground for McCarthy.

If China preoccupied conservative elites, the Korean War attracted the attention of the population as a whole. Here real fighting brought to a head amorphous cold war anxieties and intensified concern over communism. McCarthy's prominence coincides with the years of the Korean War. He made his famous Wheeling speech in February 1950, and as its impact appeared to be ending the Korean War began in June. Three years later a truce was signed, and a year after that the Senate censured McCarthy.[14]

Less than 1 percent of a national sample interviewed in the early 1950's volunteered communism as something they worried about. Many more, however — 34 percent — checked it off a checklist of things they had recently talked about.[15] In addition, almost all families knew someone fighting in Korea. The poll data did not suggest a mass political uprising over the question of communism, but no more did it suggest the issue's political irrelevance.

Of the authors of *The New American Right,* only Parsons placed foreign policy at the center of his analysis, and even he did not mention the Korean War. But Parsons, although he saw the importance of foreign policy, seriously underestimated the role of elites in shaping McCarthyism. Parsons knew that at the popular level "liberal" attitudes about domestic and foreign policy did not go together. He therefore concluded that since the focus of McCarthyism was foreign policy, it cut across the Left–Right cleavage on domestic politics. This analysis failed to comprehend that McCarthyism was the product less of attitude syndromes at the mass level than of the character of political leaders whom the people supported. Parsons failed to see that fear of communism was generally most salient among those who already voted conservative. He overlooked the fact that McCarthy and anticommunism were far more salient to the conservative elite — from precinct workers to national politicians — than to the mass of voters. If the attitude structure at the popular level was not coherent, those whom the people supported did have a coherent set of attitudes. McCarthyism fed into an existing conservative tradition at the elite level, very conservative on both domestic and foreign questions. (Similarly, Parsons found evidence for the "mass" character of McCarthyism in its strength in former agrarian radical territory because he missed the intervention of conservative elites in the political evolution of those states.)[16] This underestimation of the role of political elites in structuring McCarthyism recurs in pluralist analysis, and we will return to it.

Those who did not stress foreign policy in explaining McCarthyism had additional difficulties. They rightly saw that their analysis had to explain why some people supported McCarthy and others did not; presumably everyone was anti-Communist. Therefore they examined the American social structure to find groups particularly prone to status political appeals of the type McCarthy employed. In this view, McCarthy's concern with communism and foreign policy was only the immediate condition which enabled status seeking and populist groups to act out their frustrations. For example, Lipset wrote, "On the national scene, McCarthy's attacks are probably more important in terms of their appeal to status frustrations than to resentful isolationism."[17]

Those who took this approach still had to explain why McCarthyism should be so powerful in the early 1950's and not at some other time. They had to explain why those with personal and status concerns were seeking a political outlet. Bell wrote, "A peculiar change, in fact, seems to be coming over American life. While we are becoming more relaxed in the area of traditional morals . . . we are becoming moralistic and extreme in politics." Bell explained the growing ideological character of American politics by such factors as the prominence of large, symbolic groups like labor, business, and government.[18]

Whatever the plausibility of this interpretation, Bell himself implicitly rejected it a few years later. Entitling a collection of his essays "The End of Ideology," he argued that ideological politics was on the way out in America. He now viewed McCarthyism as an exception to this general trend.[19] In thus contradicting his earlier effort to explain why McCarthyism flourished in the early 1950's, Bell had nothing else to offer. But the aim here is more basic than simply to catch Bell in a contradiction. Pluralist analyses failed to explain the appearance and meaning of McCarthyism because they overlooked the political context in which McCarthy appeared. They underestimated his roots in an already-existing conservative faction inside the GOP — a faction even more concerned about communism, the cold war, and

Korea than was the country as a whole. McCarthy came out of an old American Right. What was in part new was the intensity and hysteria he provoked. This in turn is largely explained by changes in American society and politics that agitated the conservatives and by the new importance of foreign policy. Analysis of McCarthy's ideology and of his popular following reveals the role foreign policy and conservative Republicanism played in his power.

The Ideology

When they first became prominent in the middle 1950's, pluralist interpretations of McCarthyism relied very little on empirical evidence.[20] They focused instead on McCarthy's ideological appeals, where the evidence for McCarthy's anticosmopolitan "populism" was strongest. But even McCarthy's ideology was rooted in traditional conservative rhetoric.

In their analysis of McCarthy's rhetoric, the pluralists have accepted the evaluation of McCarthyism presented by its proponents. Both the pluralists and the supporters of McCarthy agreed that McCarthyism was a democratic movement against the elite, that it was opposed to social pretension, that it represented a movement of morality in politics.[21] If liberals have taken Populist rhetoric at face value and analyzed the movement in its own terms, the authors of *The New American Right* have done the same with McCarthyism. But I have argued that moralism was found as much on the Right as on the Left in pre-New Deal American politics and that appeals to the people have been a conservative weapon as well as a liberal one.

A further point is relevant here. In examining the ideology of a movement, one must look beyond the attitudes of the masses. The syndrome of attitudes said to characterize the radical Right does not exist together at the mass level. Trow found in Bennington that authoritarianism, isolationism, political intolerance, ethnocentrism, and a "get-tough" foreign policy were not found in the same people.[22] In the poll data Polsby analyzed, various pro-McCarthy attitudes were not highly associated in the public mind.[23] Similar evidence about liberal ideology also exists.[24] This does not mean that liberalism and the radical Right ideology are unimportant. Rather it points to the importance of elites and activists in structuring disorganized attitudes into a relatively cohesive ideology. An ideology usually reveals more about the pre-occupations of elites than of masses.

To his most devoted followers McCarthy was fighting more than the Communists; in this the pluralists are certainly right. Speaking in eulogy of the Senator from Wisconsin, Congressman Smith of Kansas said, "In a world which has lost its understanding of the concepts of right and wrong, truth and error, good and evil, and seeks only to adjust itself to what is expedient, a man like Senator McCarthy is a living contradiction of such Machiavellianism."[25] This sentiment was reiterated in newspaper obituaries.[26] A study of McCarthyism in a Wisconsin county found the same emotion among McCarthy supporters at the grass roots.[27]

That McCarthy should be so widely viewed as a moral figure is no paradox to the pluralists. It is just in his cultivation of a political concern with good and evil that they find his relation to agrarian radicalism. But McCarthy attacked the traditional devils of the conservatives. Just as traditional conservatives had feared the intrusion of alien bureaucrats, alien social legislation, and alien agrarian radicals into their stable world, so McCarthy attacked communism. Godless radicals, intellectuals, and bureaucrats were targets of American conservatism many decades before McCarthyism. If he was more extreme than many conservatives, he was extreme within that tradition.

Moreover, one cannot counterpose McCarthy's moralism to a healthier American pragmatism. For one thing, by McCarthy's use of the document-filled briefcase and the elaborated and detailed untruth, he was able to play upon the devotion of Americans to concrete detail. He promised always to "name names"; he always knew of a specific number of Communists; he had lists, affidavits, reports, right in his hand. McCarthy's "fact-fetishism" played upon our attention to the "real world." Had McCarthy not capitalized on the American weakness in the face of the practical and concrete, he would have been far less effective.[28]

Nor was McCarthy's appeal an alternative to the corrupt but safer image of the ordinary politician. In many ways, such as his insistent friendliness with men he had just pilloried, McCarthy was a caricature of the ordinary politician. He was deliberately crude and liked to be thought of as a "guts fighter," a tough guy. There was something quite prurient in his atmosphere. As a punishing figure, he could immerse himself in the evil around him — loving both the immersion and the punishing in good sadistic fashion. Perhaps his supporters, turning their guilt at their own illicit desires into anger at the corruption of the outside world, could permit themselves to experience McCarthy's lasciviousness vicariously, since he was wreaking vengeance against their external enemies. In any case, dichotomies between a politics of purity and one tolerant of human corruption hardly do justice to the seaminess of McCarthy's appeal.

McCarthy's rhetoric was hardly principled; what principles there were had traditional conservative antecedents. Yet did not McCarthy attack traditional conservative institutions and defend the virtues of the plain people? How is this part of a traditional conservative approach?

In his Wheeling speech McCarthy attacked

> the traitorous actions of those men who have been treated so well by this Nation . . . who have had all the benefits that the wealthiest nation on earth has to offer — the finest homes, the finest college educations, and the finest jobs in Government we can give. . . . The bright young men [in the State Department] who are born with silver spoons in their mouths are the ones who have been most traitorous. . . . [Acheson is a] pompous diplomat in striped pants with a phony British accent.[29]

229

Demonstrating his disdain for established institutions, McCarthy appealed for classified information from State Department employees. When Senator McClellan charged, "Then you are advocating government by individual conscience as against government by law," McCarthy replied, "The issue is whether the people are entitled to the facts."[30]

A gigantic rally called in honor of McCarthy sang "Nobody Loves Joe But the People," suggesting that if political leaders and institutions could not be relied on, the people could. Other alleged examples of McCarthy's "populism," such as his calling for telegrams against Eisenhower, are examples less of "populism" than of traditional American political practice.[31] Nevertheless, the antielitist flavor of McCarthy's rhetoric is clear.

This fact alone, however, does not remove McCarthy from the conservative tradition. Since the decline of the Federalists, American conservatives have used "populist" rhetoric; in American politics this rhetoric is essential. "Populist" rhetoric does not necessarily reflect a reality of popular enthusiasm and power; often it disguises the power resting in the hands of local and national elites. "Populism" is often an ideological formula used to gain legitimacy, not a factual description of reality.[32]

Moreover, nothing in McCarthy's rhetoric would have frightened several conservative elite groups away. In so far as McCarthy's appeal transcended anticommunism, its roots were in groups disturbed about cosmopolitanism and about the prestige given to the educated and the established families and businesses of the East. Success in their own bailiwick did not insulate the political and economic elites of the Middle West from these concerns any more than prosperity per se insulated the population at large. The nouveaux riches, however wealthy, could still be upset about those born with silver spoons in their mouths. The midwest political elite, however long established, was still upset about striped-pants diplomacy, intellectuals in the State Department, Harvard intellectuals, and British "pinkos." These were McCarthy's targets, and in the Middle West attacks on such targets did not frighten the elite. Furthermore, McCarthy and other midwestern conservatives never went beyond rhetorical attacks on eastern corporate patricians. They never proposed to injure the vital interests of eastern businessmen, who were, like their midwestern business counterparts, members of the moneyed classes.

Nevertheless, there was in McCarthy's rhetoric a heightened sense of betrayal by the rich and well-born. In part this reflected the growing anxiety of midwestern conservatism in the face of the New Deal and the "liberalism" of Wall Street. Equally important, McCarthy himself was personally very different from other midwestern conservatives. Far from being a man of dangerous principles, McCarthy was a thoroughgoing nihilist. Other conservatives — Goldwater is the prime example — believe in something; he believed in nothing. Whatever the psychological roots of McCarthy's political approach, its sociological roots lay in his one-man struggle for power and prestige, handicapped by a background of relative poverty most unusual in a successful American politician.

McCarthy's personal and social makeup fitted him for the role of destroyer. Perhaps his destructiveness found a sympathy denied his more righteous conservative colleagues. Certainly his outrageous gall catapulted him to a position of power he could exploit.

But McCarthyism is alleged to be more than the exploits of a single man; it is said to reveal the stresses and strains of the American social structure. Analysis of the Senator and of the ideology he employed tells us little about his reception. Did McCarthy's rhetoric in fact embolden the masses to an attack on modern industrial society? Did his "populist" rhetoric in fact attract ex-radicals, or even ex-Democrats? Did the danger from McCarthyism in fact flow from popular passions?

231

The Popular Following

In January 1954, a majority of the American population approved of Senator McCarthy. For the next eleven months, one third of the total population consistently supported him; eliminate those with no opinion, and the figure rises to 40 percent (see Table 8.1). This man, terribly dangerous in the

TABLE 8.1

McCARTHY'S POPULARITY IN THE GALLUP POLLS*

Date	Favorable	Unfavorable	No Opinion
8/51	15%	22%	63%
4/53	19	22	59
6/53	35	30	35
8/53	34	42	24
1/54	50	29	21
3/54	46	36	18
4/54	38	46	16
5/54	35	49	16
6/54	34	45	21
8/54	36	51	13
11/54	35	46	19

* Data reported in Nelson W. Polsby, "Towards an Explanation of McCarthyism," *Political Studies,* Vol. 8 (October 1962), p. 252, and Frank J. Kendrick, "McCarthy and the Senate," unpublished Ph.D. dissertation, Department of Political Science, University of Chicago, 1962), p. 331.

eyes of sophisticated observers of American politics, had obtained the backing of millions of American people.

McCarthy's popularity in the polls reenforced a growing belief among intellectuals that the mass of people could not be relied on to defend civil liberties and democratic rights. The Stouffer study of popular attitudes toward communism and civil liberties, published the year following the censure of McCarthy, seemed to demonstrate the willingness of the mass of people to deny civil liberties to socialists and atheists, much less Communists. Community leaders, on the other hand, were much more tolerant of divergent and unpopular points of view.[33] Leaving issues of democratic rights up to the people was apparently a dangerous business; better if they could be decided among political leaders without resort to popular passions. McCarthy had apparently achieved his successes by taking questions of communism and civil liberties out of the hands of the political elite.

In a simplified form, this theory of McCarthy's power ran into trouble. There is evidence to suggest that mass attitudes are not so different in other countries, such as Britain, without producing anything like McCarthyism.[34] Therefore Lipset has suggested that one must look beyond popular attitudes to the political structure that mobilizes and channels those attitudes.[35] This is an important argument, which could have led the pluralists to question the association between popular attitudes and McCarthy's power. But the pluralists contented themselves with pointing to two elements in the American political structure that *fostered* the translation of popular attitudes into political programs. First, it is alleged that McCarthy supporters lacked group ties to the institutions of modern industrial society. Second, Americans are said to lack deference for political leaders; they are not willing to permit a sufficient amount of elite autonomy.[36] With this "populist" outlook, they will be more willing to trust their own (anti-civil libertarian) views than the views of their elected representatives.

Pluralist explanations focused on the "mass" character of McCarthy's appeal, challenging political leaders and cutting across party lines. But perhaps the single most important characteristic of supporters of McCarthy in the national opinion polls was their party affiliation; Democrats opposed McCarthy, and Republicans supported him. In April 1954, Democrats outnumbered Republicans more than two to one among those having an unfavorable opinion of McCarthy; 16 percent more Republicans than Democrats had a favorable opinion of the Senator.[37] Totaling support for McCarthy in a series of Gallup Polls in the early 1950's reveals that

36 percent of the Democrats favored McCarthy while 44 percent opposed him. The comparable Republican figures were 61 percent for and 25 percent against. Democrats were 8 percentage points more against McCarthy than for him, Republicans 36 points more for him than against him. The total percentage point spread by party was 44 points. In these polls, as in the data reported by Polsby, no other single division of the population (by religion, class, education, and so forth) even approached the party split.[38]

Similarly, in October 1954 respondents were asked whether they would be more or less likely to vote for a candidate endorsed by McCarthy. The strong Republicans split evenly, the strong Democrats were five to one against the senator, and the weak and independent Democrats divided four to one against McCarthy. By that date, only hard-core Republicans were actively sympathetic to the Wisconsin senator; even the weak and independent Republicans strongly opposed him.[39]

As Lipset suggests, there is evidence that pro-McCarthy sentiment influenced party preference as well as vice versa.[40] Nevertheless, the great disproportion in support for McCarthy along the lines of previous party commitment was not predicted by the pluralist approach. Pluralism stressed McCarthy's roots in the social structure but not his roots in the existing political structure.

Support for McCarthy was also reasonably close to attitudes on political and economic questions of the day. On a whole range of foreign policy issues, McCarthy adherents had right-wing preferences (see Table 8.2).[41]

Perhaps more surprising, "McCarthy also drew disproportionately from economic conservatives. Measures of such attitudes as position on liberalism in general, laws to prevent strikes, a federal health program, and support of private development of national resources all indicate that the conservative position on these issues was associated with greater support for McCarthy."[42]

234

On the other hand, Trow found in Bennington that those with a hostile attitude toward big business as well as big labor were most likely to support McCarthy. This suggested

TABLE 8.2

Opinions on Foreign Policy Issues and Attitude Toward McCarthy*

Issues		Attitudes Toward McCarthy		
		Pro	Con	N
Break off diplomatic	Yes	21%	32%	(3641)
relations with Russia	No	14	43	(2550)
Withdraw from	Yes	28	26	(870)
the United Nations	No	14	38	(6291)
Peaceful coexistence	Favor	32	55	(694)
policy	Oppose	46	46	(399)
United States should	Favor	33	55	(1042)
support the	Oppose	47	34	(231)
United Nations				
How to handle	Offensive war	37	28	(274)
the Russians	Keep strong	32	34	(1923)
	Peaceful settlement	26	42	(343)
Korean War policy	Do as we did	23	40	(577)
for United States	Keep trying			
(asked 1952)	for peace	21	43	(665)
	Go further militarily	37	34	(1284)
	Be tough	45	32	(1585)
	Pull out of Korea	31	26	(378)
Give economic aid to	Yes	16	37	(5343)
underdeveloped countries	No	20	32	(1620)
Blocking the coast of	Favor	43	43	(495)
Communist China	Oppose	31	60	(550)
Withdraw foreign aid	Favor	37	46	(1059)
from nations which refuse to cooperate with the United States	Oppose	29	58	(258)

* Data reprinted, with permission, from S. M. Lipset, "Three Decades of the Radical Right: Coughlinites, McCarthyites, and Birchers," in Daniel Bell (ed.), *The Radical Right* (Garden City, N.Y.: Doubleday Anchor, 1964), p. 409.

McCarthy's roots in a small business, nineteenth-century mentality.[43] But in a national sample such a relationship did not hold. The antibusiness, prolabor group was more anti McCarthy than any other group, and the "nineteenth-century liberals" were no more pro McCarthy than those who were antilabor and pro big business or those favoring both big business and big labor.[44] This evidence further locates McCarthy's roots in existing political cleavages.

Clearly McCarthy drew support from the traditional constituency and traditional attitudes of the Republican right wing. However, he also received considerable backing in the polls from traditional Democratic ethnic and social groups. The relevant survey data comes from a variety of different sources, and although the pattern of support for the Senator is consistent, the degree of cleavage varies. Without holding the influence of party constant, religion and occupation best distinguish opponents of McCarthy from supporters. (For the most striking occupational data, see Table 8.3.) Professional people were more anti-McCarthy than any other occupational group. On five of six reported polls they were the most anti-McCarthy group, and on four of these polls they were far more anti-McCarthy than any other group.[45] Wealthy businessmen were also apparently anti-McCarthy, although there is less evidence about them. Unskilled workers and small businessmen were the most consistently pro-McCarthy groups.[46] However, union membership significantly increased the opposition to McCarthy among laborers. Apparently the liberal impact of the union leadership reached significant numbers of workers who would otherwise have been neutral or ignorant about McCarthy.[47]

Farmers also tended to be pro McCarthy, but their degree of support varied sharply from poll to poll. Perhaps this provides further evidence of farmer political volatility. In one combined group of polls, farmers were clearly the most pro-McCarthy group; in other polls they were no more for McCarthy than were unskilled workers and small businessmen.[48]

The occupational impact on support for McCarthy is clear. In several polls, occupational differences at the extremes

TABLE 8.3

OCCUPATION AND ATTITUDE TOWARD MCCARTHY,* PERCENT DIFFERENCES BETWEEN APPROVERS AND DISAPPROVERS[a]

I.N.R.A. 1954[b]			Roper 1952[c]		
Professional	—35	(731)	Professional and Executive	—17	(219)
Executive and Manager	—24	(511)	Small Business	0	(123)
White Collar	—19	(1144)	Clerical and Sales	—11	(387)
Independent Business	—14	(583)	Factory Labor	—3	(317)
Supervisor and Foreman	—16	(405)	Nonfactory Labor	—6	(235)
Skilled	—14	(2323)	Services	—4	(178)
Unskilled	—14	(1019)	Farm Owner Manager	—6	(184)
Personal Service	—10	(677)	*Gallup Dec. 1954[d]*		
Farmers	—21	(824)			
Retired	— 3	(709)	Professional	—44	(163)
Students	—34	(59)	Executive	—24	(154)
Michigan 1954[d]			Clerical and Sales	—23	(188)
Professional and Business	—40	(246)	Skilled	—10	(237)
			Unskilled	8	(286)
Clerical and Sales	—44	(102)	Labor	7	(68)
Skilled	—30	(337)	Service	—10	(103)
Unskilled	—16	(144)	Farm Owner	— 9	(165)
Farmers	—17	(104)			

* Table reprinted, with permission, from S. M. Lipset, "Three Decades of the Radical Right: Coughlinites, McCarthyites, and Birchers," in Daniel Bell (ed.), *The Radical Right* (Garden City, N.Y.: Doubleday Anchor, 1964), p. 400.

a Cell entries represent percentage difference between approval and disapproval of McCarthy. The more negative the entry, the greater the predominance of anti-McCarthy sentiment.

b Occupation of respondent recorded, or of chief wage earner if respondent is a housewife.

c Occupation of respondent recorded; housewives omitted from table.

d Occupation of head of household recorded.

237

equaled or exceeded the party differences. The size of both party and occupational differences is particularly striking since these usually worked against each other. Professionals tended to belong to the pro-McCarthy party, workers to the anti-McCarthy party.

Like occupation, the impact of religion also cut across party loyalties, with the exception of the heavily anti-McCarthy, pro-Democratic Jews. Lipset does not report re-

TABLE 8.4

RELIGION AND ATTITUDE TOWARD MCCARTHY*

Religion	Gallup, August 1951–March 1954 Attitude Toward McCarthy			SRC, October 1954 Attitude Toward McCarthy-Supported Candidate			
	Pro	Con	No Opinion	Pro	Con	Neutral	Other
Protestant	45%	36%	19%	9%	39%	43%	9%
Catholic	56	29	15	21	24	48	7
Jew	12	83	3	6	53	29	12

* Data reported in Frank J. Kendrick, "McCarthy and the Senate," unpublished Ph.D. dissertation, Department of Political Science, University of Chicago, 1962), p. 330, and Angus Campbell and Homer C. Cooper, *Group Differences in Attitudes and Votes* (Survey Research Center, University of Michigan, 1956), p. 146.

ligious data except within the political parties. Other studies demonstrate that in spite of Catholic and Protestant party affiliations, Catholics were significantly more pro McCarthy than Protestants (see Table 8.4). In these polls, the religious differences were greater than the occupational differences,[49] but they were not greater than the occupational differences reported by Lipset, whose occupational measures were more discriminating.

Within the parties the influence of religion was even more apparent. The percentage point spread in attitudes toward McCarthy between strong Democratic Protestants and Catholics was 33. The difference between strong Republican Catholics and Protestants was 21. On the other hand, for strong party identifiers party seems to have been even more important than religion. Strong Democratic Protestants differed in their attitudes from strong Republican Protestants even more than they did from strong Democratic Catholics. And Republican Catholics were closer to Republican Protestants than to Democratic Catholics.[50] Since workers tend to be Catholics, religion and class reinforced each other. Either factor might have declined in importance if the other had been held constant.

Ethnic data also cut across party lines to some extent. Irish and Italian Catholics, traditionally Democratic, were highly pro McCarthy. However, the influence of party may explain the greater support McCarthy received from German than Polish Catholics, as the latter are strongly Democratic. Among Protestants, differences by ethnic background were small and inconsistent, although Germans were clearly more pro McCarthy than British.[51]

Finally, level of education was of great significance in explaining support for McCarthy. Without holding party constant, differences are apparent, but they are less significant than occupational influences.[52] However, when party is held constant the effect of education upon support for McCarthy is truly pronounced. The percentage point spread between graduate-school Democrats and grade-school Republicans was 65, the largest spread in all the poll data. However, college-educated Republicans were no more anti-McCarthy than grammar-school Democrats.[53]

The polls provide us with considerable evidence about support for McCarthy, and reveal a broadly consistent pattern. When the influence of party is eliminated and often even when it is not, the lower socioeconomic groups, the more poorly educated, and the Catholics tended to support McCarthy, the big business and professional classes, the better educated, and the Protestants to oppose him. These differences cannot be dismissed as small or insignificant.

There is also clear evidence linking support for McCarthy to the "authoritarian personality." The evidence does not suggest a very strong relationship, however, particularly compared to the impact of party, political issues, and demographic variables. In Bennington, holding education constant, the relationship held only among those who had graduated from high school and not among the grade-school or college educated.[54] In a national sample, there was a slight relationship at all three levels, but it reached substantial proportions only among the college educated. As Lipset writes, "Among the less educated, a high authoritarian score reflects in some part attitudes common to the group, which are also subject to modification by more education. If someone is well educated and still gives authoritarian responses, then the chances are that he really has a basic tendency to react in an authoritarian fashion."[55] Where authoritarianism is simply an artifact of low education, it may reflect broad cultural values that lack psychological or political relevance.

An Alabama study sheds additional light on the relationship between psychological authoritarianism and support for McCarthy. High scorers on authoritarianism not only supported McCarthy; they also supported agrarian radical Jim Folsom for governor. But Folsom's support among authoritarians was in part an artifact of his strong support in the lower class. If Folsom's relation to authoritarianism had an economic explanation, McCarthy's had a political meaning. McCarthy supporters were less likely to express faith in the viability of the political system. This political factor was more important to McCarthy's support than psychological authoritarianism; when it was held constant, authoritarianism ceased to be significant.[56]

Hofstadter attempts to relate psychological characteristics to pro-McCarthy attitudes by introducing the factor of social mobility. He writes,

> Social studies have shown that there is a close relation between social mobility and ethnic prejudice. Persons moving down-

ward, and even upward under many circumstances, in the social scale tend to show greater prejudice against ethnic minorities . . . I believe that the typical prejudiced person and the typical pseudo-conservative are usually the same persons, that the mechanisms at work in both complexes are quite the same, and that it is merely the expediencies and the strategy of the situation today that cause groups that once stressed racial discrimination to find other scapegoats.[57]

Martin Trow, examining the limited evidence cited by Hofstadter, concludes that it does not support a connection between mobility, prejudice, and allegiance to pseudoconservative movements. In Bennington, with education held constant, Trow found no relationship between either political intolerance or ethnocentrism and support for McCarthy.[58] At the national level, there was also no relationship between ethnocentrism and pro-McCarthy sentiments.[59] Nor has it been possible to establish any relationship between social mobility and support for McCarthy. However, one community study has demonstrated that those with felt status incongruities (that is, those who felt they got less money than their education entitled them to) did support the Senator.[60] This is perhaps the best evidence that McCarthy's appeals tapped generalized discontent.

The data, in sum, do not suggest intense, active, mass involvement in a McCarthyite movement. Efforts to relate status frustrations and psychological malformations to McCarthyism have not proved very successful. Party and political issue cleavages structured McCarthy's support far more than pluralist hypotheses predicted. But the ignorant, the deprived, and the lower classes did support McCarthy disproportionately. Were they expressing their animus against respectable groups and institutions?

To answer this question, we must ask two others: Why did McCarthyism attract a large popular following of this character, and what impact did support for the Senator have on political behavior?

241

Most people supported McCarthy because he was identified in the public mind with the fight against communism. In June 1952, a national sample was asked whether, taking all things into consideration, they thought committees of Congress investigating communism, like Senator McCarthy's, were doing more good than harm. In a period when less than 20 percent of the population had a favorable personal opinion of the Senator, 60 percent were for the committees and only 19 percent against them.[61] The more McCarthy's name was identified with anticommunism, the more support he got from the population. Perhaps because they themselves feared the Communist menace, the pluralists underplayed the anti-Communist component of McCarthy's appeal.[62]

In the Stouffer study, respondents were asked to name someone whose opinions about how to handle communism they especially trusted. Most votes went to J. Edgar Hoover and Eisenhower — 27 percent and 24 percent respectively. McCarthy was third with 8 percent. Respondents were then asked whether they trusted this person because they knew his opinions pretty well or because of the kind of person he was. The results were[63]

	Opinions	Person
Hoover	33%	55%
Eisenhower	19	65
McCarthy	58	31

McCarthy's appeal was the functionally specific appeal of a single-issue promoter, not the diffuse appeal which mobilizes the "mass man." McCarthy's stress on communism may have suggested "the weakness of a single issue"[64] for building a right-wing mass movement, but by the same token it explained the strength of McCarthyism.

Popular concern over communism could have symbolized a basic uneasiness about the health of American institutions. So it did for McCarthy and his most vociferous supporters, who saw a government overrun with dupes and traitors. For them, the Communist issue was the issue of Communists in government; internal subversion was the danger. For the American people, however, communism was essentially a foreign policy issue. In the 1952 election, less than 3 percent expressed concern over Communists in government — fewer than referred to the Point Four program. Foreign policy, on the other hand, was an extremely salient issue, and those concerned over foreign policy were more likely to vote Republican. The external Communist threat and the fear of war benefited the GOP at the polls in the 1950's: the internal Communist danger, salient to committed Republicans alone, did not. Moreover, mass concern about foreign policy did not appear over the loss of China, which the right-wing invested with such peculiar moral significance. It was only when American soldiers went to Korea that foreign policy became salient at the mass level. And the desire there — as expressed in the election of Eisenhower — was for peace not for war.[65]

Why then, if McCarthy's appeal had specifically to do with foreign policy and the Korean War, did he receive greater support among the poorer and less-educated groups? Had the working class been actively concerned about McCarthy, we might expect this support to overcome the relative lack of political knowledge among those of low socioeconomic status. But asked to name the man who had done the best job of fighting communism, the less-educated and poorer strata volunteered McCarthy's name no more than did the better-educated and rich. Highly conscious pro-McCarthy sentiments were as prevalent among the upper as the lower classes. (Those of higher socioeconomic status, with more political information and sophistication, were more likely to name McCarthy as someone who had done a particularly bad job.)[66] Disproportionate working-class support for McCarthy thus only manifested itself when his name was actually mentioned in the polls; it was not powerful enough to

243

emerge when workers had to volunteer his name on their own.

The evidence does not suggest that the Communist issue preoccupied the lower classes, or that they were using that issue to vent general grievances about their position in society. More likely, they simply had less information about McCarthy's methods, a less sophisticated understanding of their nature and less concern in the abstract about possible victims of the Senator's techniques. Therefore, when the pollsters specifically mentioned McCarthy's name, it tapped among the middle-class revulsion over McCarthy's crudities and opposition to his infringements of individual rights. Among the working class, it tapped an anticommunism relatively less restrained by these concerns.

Still, lack of sophistication on matters of civil liberties can have as dangerous consequences as the political mobilization of status anxieties and anti-industrial hostilities. It can, that is, if it becomes politically mobilized. But sympathy for McCarthy among the less politically sophisticated was not translated into action. To many Americans, especially those in the lower classes who were not actively in touch with events in the political world, McCarthy was simply fighting communism. Support for McCarthy meant opposition to Communists. This was a long way from being willing to break traditional voting patterns, or vote against other interests, in order to support the Wisconsin Senator. In fact, the issue of McCarthyism was more salient to its opponents than to its sympathizers — precisely because McCarthy's opponents were more concerned with political events. In January 1954, when a majority of the total American population favored McCarthy, only 21 percent said they would be more likely to vote for a candidate he sponsored, while 26 percent said they would be less likely to. Three months later 46 percent of the population had an unfavorable opinion of the Senator and 43 percent claimed they would be less likely to vote for a candidate he supported. Thirty-eight percent of the population favored McCarthy; only 17 percent would let this influence their vote intention. The results in October were similar.[67]

With this relation between opinion and behavior, apparent paradoxes such as occurred in the Maine senatorial primary are easily understandable. Half of a Maine newspaper sample favored McCarthy, but virtually no one supported the candidate he had put up to oppose Margaret Chase Smith. There was no relation in the election between the areas which had supported McCarthy in the poll and those which voted against Mrs. Smith.[68] It was one thing to be against communism, quite another to accept McCarthy's insinuations that Margaret Chase Smith supported communism — or even to have heard of that charge.

Analysis of electoral data confirms both the minimal impact McCarthy had on actual political behavior and his greater salience to opponents than supporters. In Connecticut in 1952, McCarthy made a particular effort to unseat William Benton, but Benton's support was virtually identical to that given the rest of the Democratic ticket. The Eisenhower landslide defeated Benton; McCarthy did not. In Wisconsin and particularly in the Dakotas, McCarthy's impact on the regular party vote was also minimal. There is some evidence that he hurt Republican senators in states where he campaigned for them.[69]

Of the groups that supported McCarthy in the public opinion polls, farmers in Wisconsin voted for him but workers voted against him.[70] Impressionistic evidence from eastern working-class centers like Boston and Brooklyn does suggest strongly felt working-class support for the Senator. Like other impressionistic evidence of McCarthy's popularity, this strength was probably real but exaggerated. Perhaps it would have affected voting behavior more if union leaders and urban liberals had taken a more outspoken anti-McCarthy line (so that workers would have felt forced to choose between pro-McCarthy and pro-Democratic or pro-union sentiments). In

245

any case, whatever intense feelings existed here were probably caused more by religion than by class; these were predominantly Catholic workers, living in cities where church newspapers and the hierarchy were outspokenly pro McCarthy.

Catholics did vote for McCarthy in South Dakota, Wisconsin, and other states.[71] This may have been little different from the favorite son effect which caused Catholics to vote for Kennedy in 1960. In particular, this would explain McCarthy's strong Irish Catholic following in the polls. Also important is the fact that Catholics generally voted more Republican from 1950 to 1956. In 1956 a majority of the Catholic population voted for Eisenhower.[72] This may have been because of the preaching of the church against communism or simply because increased prosperity weakened traditional Catholic ties to the Democratic Party. In fact, all the "status politics" reasons advanced to explain Catholic support for McCarthy also explain Catholic support for Eisenhower. Eisenhower, no less than McCarthy, permitted Catholics to stop voting Democratic without becoming committed to the Republican Party. Upward social mobility could produce support for Eisenhower no less than for McCarthy. Support for Eisenhower no less than for McCarthy could express conformity to "Americanism." There is, however, one crucial difference between the two figures: Eisenhower was a political moderate.

One need not assume the worst about the motivations for conformity, or about its consequences, or about the aspects of the American tradition that inspire conformity. Compulsive Americanism may have produced Catholic support for Eisenhower. That hardly makes it look like a dangerous source of political extremism. In our society, those with severe personal problems are likely to turn their back on politics. Status anxieties may find an outlet in political moderation. One must not too readily identify personal anxieties or status politics with political extremism.[73] No particular political consequences follow from nonpolitical attitudes such as status anxieties. The intervening political and organizational structures and attitudes are crucial.

The McCarthy years were also the Eisenhower years. Far from demonstrating their discontent with respectable political leadership, the mass of Americans responded to the political anxieties of the cold and Korean wars and whatever social and personal anxieties may also have been relevant by electing Eisenhower. Eisenhower's personal and political appeal depended on the belief that he could be trusted to take care of things without disrupting the society.[74] Eisenhower politics was the politics of deference to responsible leadership, of apolitical moderation. Support for Eisenhower indicates more about the mood of the populace in the America of the 1950's than does support for McCarthy. And McCarthy became prominent in the vacuum of popular apathy and moderation, not on a wave of radical mass mobilization.

What are we to conclude, then, about McCarthy's "mass" appeal? McCarthy's popular following apparently came from two distinct sources. There was first the traditional right wing of the midwestern Republican Party. Here was a group to whom McCarthy was a hero. He seemed to embody all their hopes and frustrations. These were the militants in the McCarthy movement. They worked hardest for him and were preoccupied with his general targets. To them, communism was not the whole story; their enemies were also the symbols of welfare capitalism and cosmopolitanism. These militants were mobilized by McCarthy's "mass" appeal. Yet this appeal had its greatest impact upon activists and elites, not upon the rank-and-file voters. And while McCarthy mobilized the Republican right wing, he did not change its traditional alliances. This was not a "new" American Right, but rather an old one with new enthusiasm and new power.

McCarthy's second source of popular support were those citizens mobilized because of communism and the Korean war. Concern over these issues throughout the society increased Republican strength, although this increase in popular support accrued not so much to McCarthy as to Eisenhower. McCarthy's strength here was not so much due to "mass," "populist," or "status" concerns as it was to the issues of communism, Korea, and the cold war. At the electoral level, there was little evidence that those allegedly more vulnerable to "mass" appeals were mobilized by McCarthy to change their traditional voting patterns.[75]

McCarthy had real support at the grass roots, but his was hardly a "movement in which popular passions wreaked their aggression against the structure of the polity."[76] In a period in which the populace gave overwhelming support to Eisenhower, it can hardly be accused of failing to show deference to responsible political leadership. In so arguing, I by no means wish to minimize the danger of McCarthyism. But the pluralists, writing in a context of fear of the masses, have misunderstood both the source and the nature of that danger. They see a rebellious populace threatening the fabric of society. In fact, McCarthy did immense damage to the lives and careers of countless individuals. He exercised an inordinate influence over policy making. But popular enthusiasm for his assault on political institutions simply cannot explain the power he wielded. In so far as McCarthy challenged political decisions, political individuals, and the political fabric, he was sustained not by a revolt of the masses so much as by the actions and inactions of various elites.

The Elites

Conservative Republican activists provided McCarthy with the core of his enthusiastic support. In addition, groups ranging from Catholic Democratic workers to conservative southern senators contributed to McCarthy's power — the workers by verbal approval in the polls, the senators by their actions and silences in Washington. Having examined the contribution of the masses to McCarthyism, we turn now to the elites.

The pluralists argue that McCarthy was not simply attacking Communists, but also had as his targets the eastern, educated, financial, political, and intellectual elite. There is merit in this view; nevertheless, McCarthy enjoyed the support of some wealthy and influential political elites, and even some of those he attacked played a role in augmenting his power. The existence of a powerful Republican right wing, the new appeal of the issues of communism and foreign policy, and McCarthy's own tactical brilliance raised McCarthyism to a place of national prominence. But there was more to McCarthy's success than this. The response of a variety of political elites — by no means simply allies of the Wisconsin senator — enabled him to harness himself to the everyday workings of American politics. Those already part of this machinery often did not approve of McCarthy. Some, like moderate Republicans in their battle with the Democrats, congressmen in their battle with the executive, newspapers in their search for news, thought they could use him. Others, like southern Democrats, saw no need to treat McCarthy differently than they treated other senators. Still others, moderate Republicans in their desire for party unity, liberal Democrats in their desire for reelection, were afraid of him. Political and psychological reasons made a variety of political elites anxious to avoid a confrontation with McCarthy. Until it became clear to them that McCarthyism was more than politics as usual, they failed effectively to challenge it.

We have already pointed to the importance of the political structure in influencing McCarthy's mass support. Regardless of attitudes toward civil liberties and even toward McCarthy in the abstract, traditional political allegiances kept the workers in the Democratic Party in the 1950's and business and professional men in the GOP. McCarthy's "mass" appeal did not register directly in politics because many who supported him cared more about the Democratic Party, the New Deal, their trade unions, or their wives and families than they cared about McCarthy. They therefore did not break their traditional political habits.

Just as the political structure limited the sustenance Mc-Carthy could derive from the grass roots, so it influenced the behavior of political elites. We look now at conservative Republicans and GOP moderates, at the Senate and the southern Democrats, at the press and at the liberals.

Most of those who mobilized behind McCarthy at the national level were conservative politicians and publicists, businessmen, and retired military leaders discontented with the New Deal, with bureaucracy, and with military policy. Of nineteen businessmen in the leadership of the Ten Million Americans mobilizing for McCarthy, only one had inherited wealth.[77] These men had been part of the Republican right wing before McCarthy; they were joined by an occasional ex-agrarian radical like Burton Wheeler. Numbers of former Marxist intellectuals such as Louis Bundenz, James Burnham, and John Chamberlain became McCarthy publicists, but they lacked political influence or popular support. The political conservatism of the elite supporters of McCarthy ran the gamut of domestic and international policy.

We have already discussed the historical reasons for Mc-Carthy's conservative support. The evolution of politics in the Middle West and the nation had had two political consequences for conservatives. They were in heretofore unprecedented positions of political power at the state level and political weakness at the national level. Their desperation is suggested by Taft's famous advice to McCarthy, "If one case doesn't work, then bring up another."[78] This political elite sustained McCarthy. It helped dramatize his issues and fight his fights. Conservative Republican activists provided money and enthusiasm for the Senator's cause. In Wisconsin, for example, McCarthy did not mobilize the mass of voters. But he did mobilize the local elites of the Republican Party. The near-hysterical enthusiasm with which they identified with the Senator gave the movement its emotional intensity. The regular Wisconsin Republican organization — in an action almost unprecedented in American politics — put up a candidate to oppose Wisconsin's other incumbent Republican senator because he had not voted against McCarthy's censure.

How to explain the mentality of these McCarthy supporters? Lipset, analyzing American politics as a conflict between values of achievement and egalitarian populism, argues that political excesses such as McCarthyism derive from America's egalitarian strain.[79] Thus it is argued that Britain was spared a McCarthyite episode because the populace had deference for its established leaders. But a more important difference between Britain and the United States on this score is the character of conservative politics of the two countries. The British example suggests by comparison what American conservatives were willing to do.[80] Certainly these conservatives were unrestrained by aristocratic traditions, but to ascribe this to populist values rather than to the capitalist-achievement ethic is perverse. In a Protestant, competitive society, an individual can blame only himself for failure, and the fear of failure appears at all levels of the social structure. The attendant insecurities and frustrations will often produce conspiracy theories, scapegoat hunting, and terrible resentments. McCarthy was supported by the activists of a party that emphasizes free enterprise, achievement, and individual responsibility. The politics of these people seems more sensibly explained by their preoccupations with achievement and failure than by their populistic concerns.

McCarthy, however, was not simply another conservative Republican. Mundt, Wherry, and a host of other right-wing Republicans had sought to dramatize the communism issue, but only McCarthy succeeded. And McCarthy succeeded while the others did not in part because of his thoroughgoing contempt for the rules of political controversy. This contempt stemmed partly from his career pattern. McCarthy came from relatively low social origins, and was elected to the Senate without either the inherited status position of some senators or the record of political or professional accomplishment of

251

others. In the period from 1947 to 1956, this was true of only 4 percent of America's senators. Moreover, McCarthy did not conform to Senate folkways; thus he voted with small minorities against large majorities more than most of his colleagues. Clearly, McCarthy had less commitment to established norms than other conservative Republicans; in fact, his career pattern and behavior in the Senate resembled Langer's.[81]

It is important to stress McCarthy's uniqueness, but the pluralists stress it for the wrong reasons. McCarthy's significance as an individual did not derive from new alliances he personally mobilized to assault the social fabric. It lay rather in the fact that he personally, not the masses or even elites behind him, did tremendous damage and wielded great power. And this personal power in large part derived from his willingness not to play by the rules — he was, after all, an extremist. But without the issue of communism and without the enthusiasm he evoked from right-wing Republicans who did conform to Senate folkways and orthodox career patterns, he would have been merely what Langer was — a maverick without influence.

Moderate Republicans were clearly less enthusiastic about McCarthy than the conservative wing of the party, yet without their support as well McCarthy would have been far less powerful. Eastern and moderate Republicans and their allies desired political power, and were also genuinely concerned about the Communist question. For a long time, they acquiesced in McCarthy's power. Viereck writes that McCarthy's targets were not the Communists, but those who had always stood for the rule of law and moderation, like Senator Watkins.[82] By the time Watkins headed the committee which recommended McCarthy's censure, he was an anti-McCarthy pillar of strength. Earlier, however, he had been one of many Republican signers of a statement attacking the Truman administration and the Gillette committee investigation of McCarthy. The official Republican leadership did not sign

252

this pro-McCarthy statement, but Watkins and other future McCarthy critics did.[83]

There are other examples of support for McCarthy by moderate Republicans. Senator Carlson, an Eisenhower Republican, hammered hard at the Communist issue during the early 1950's. He called McCarthy's 1952 primary victory a "great victory."[84] Later that year, Eisenhower deleted a favorable reference to General Marshall from a Wisconsin campaign speech under McCarthy's pressure. After his victory, the President decided that the use of his office to attack McCarthy would split the Republican Party and aid the Democrats. A timid chief executive, Eisenhower also wanted to avoid making enemies, particularly in Congress. Orders went out telling members of the administration not to criticize McCarthy — and those like Stassen who did were publicly humiliated. In appointing a McCarthy man as Personnel Officer, Eisenhower gave the Senator an effective veto over appointments to the State Department. He made every effort to avoid a fight with him over the army. "Among the opponents of McCarthy in the administration (and he also had friends)," reports one chronicler, "the view was that McCarthy should be handled behind closed doors." If McCarthy benefited from airing his charges to the public, he benefited also from moderate unwillingness to combat him openly.[85] By 1954 moderate Republicans were appeasing McCarthy because they feared splitting the party more than because they hoped they could use him. But in both cases McCarthy was able to capitalize on existing political alliances. He had succeeded in harnessing respectable elites and respectable institutions, to which the populace paid deference.

McCarthy's popularity itself in large part depended on his moderate Republican support. Before the 1952 elections gave the GOP control of the Senate, most Americans had not heard of McCarthy and only 15 percent had a favorable opinion of him. By the middle of 1953, McCarthy had sent Cohn and Schine to Europe, had control of a Senate committee, and had been legitimized by the Republican Party; 35 percent of the population approved of him. Having achieved the instruments of Senate power and publicity, McCarthy could keep his name before the public day after day.[86]

In this achievement, he was aided not only by the moderate Republicans but also by the Senate and by the press. Seniority gave McCarthy his committee chairmanship, and Senate traditions permitted him virtually unchecked power. Individual senators were unwilling to interfere with committee prerogatives or with the power of McCarthy as chairman, since their own personal influence depended in large part upon their own committee positions. Many senators also feared that interferences with McCarthy's activities as an individual senator could later rebound to their disadvantage; they feared creating unpleasant precedents. The famed individualism encouraged by the Senate thus worked to McCarthy's advantage.[87]

Moreover, McCarthy capitalized on congressional-executive rivalry. Always a factor in American politics, this institutional conflict was at its height in the McCarthy period. The growing power of the executive, attributable to the New Deal and to the importance of foreign policy, produced congressional concern over the decline in congressional prerogatives and prestige. Relations were further strained by the presence in Washington of New Deal administrators, so different in outlook from the more particularistic, locally oriented congressmen. McCarthy tried to make himself the champion of congressional power and at least succeeded in exploiting the executive-congressional rift.[88]

The Senate in the McCarthy period was dominated by conservative Republicans and southern Democrats. About the former enough has already been said. The southern Democrats, embodying the institutional traditions of the Senate, were unwilling to jeopardize the prerogatives of an individual senator or of the Senate as a whole. As McClellan of Arkansas remarked, "I do not want to do unto one of my colleagues what I would not want him to do unto me under the same circumstances."[89] Southern senators were not pro McCarthy. But they were perhaps not unhappy to see their northern liberal colleagues and the Fair Deal administration embarrassed. (Reprisals from the populist masses hardly worried these safe-seat senators, particularly since southerners opposed this Catholic Republican in the polls.)

Without the newspaper treatment he received, McCarthy's impact would have been far milder. Large numbers of newspapers, particularly outside the major metropolitan centers, actively supported him.

The respectable press opposed the Wisconsin senator, which suggests to the pluralists McCarthy's absence of elite backing.[90] But McCarthy benefited from their treatment of him in the news columns. Desiring to dramatize the news, the wire services featured McCarthy's activities without regard to their importance. Stories and headlines gave the impression that charges were facts.[91] Even *The New York Times* fostered the myth that McCarthy's investigations had some connection with demonstrated espionage. The coverage of the other anti-McCarthy press was no better. McCarthy's popularity in the polls reached its all-time high during the well-publicized Fort Monmouth investigations.

Eventually *The Times* realized that McCarthy had taken them in. Columnist Peter Kihss concluded a series of articles setting the record straight (lacking the prominence of the earlier stories) with the observation,

> For the newspapers Fort Monmouth has been a lesson that will not be quickly forgotten, but the reading public should understand that it is difficult if not impossible to ignore charges by Senator McCarthy just because they are usually proved exaggerated or false. The remedy lies with the reader.[92]

Thus newsmen like politicians sought to lay the blame for McCarthy's prominence on the public and argue that their own hands were tied. Newsmen like Kihss often justify their activities by saying that they print the news and the news is what happens. To understand the role of the press in the McCarthy period one must realize that a figure who gains notoriety sells more papers, and that to ignore such a figure is to risk losing sales to competing publishers.[93]

Finally, many prominent liberals failed actively to oppose McCarthy. Here McCarthy could feed upon feelings of guilt and insecurity pervading the nation's capital. Democratic politicians and government bureaucrats had to adjust to replacing the Popular Front, the New Deal, and the wartime Soviet alliance with the new cold war attitudes. This change weakened the will of the elites to resist McCarthy, since they felt vaguely guilty of his accusations.[94] In addition, liberal politicians were simply afraid of McCarthy's power to retaliate at the polls. They saw Millard Tydings oppose McCarthy and go down to defeat in 1950, William Benton attack him and lose his Senate seat in 1952. The evidence suggests that although McCarthy may have contributed to Tydings' defeat he had no impact on Benton's. Certainly his power at the polls was greatly exaggerated.

Nevertheless, Lippman and others argued at the time that liberals had lost the confidence of the country over the issues of communism and foreign policy which sustained McCarthy and that only the moderates and conservatives could stop him. If this argument is true, it cuts both ways. For if the moderate Republicans and southern Democrats had this power, why did they not exercise it earlier? McCarthy's influence and his popularity reached their heights during the Eisenhower administration. If moderates and conservatives can take credit for McCarthy's defeat, they must share a large portion of the blame for his successes.

The failure of American elites to confront McCarthy immeasurably enhanced his power. This unwillingness cannot be explained as a response to mass pressures. But if these existed in the minds of observers of McCarthyism, surely they were also in the minds of the political actors themselves. If the populist attitudes of the masses did not enhance McCarthy's power, what of leadership fear of popular pressure? Shils, for example, argues that a "populist" system of authority weakens the will of elites in America. Political leaders lack confidence in themselves, it is alleged, because the value system promotes suspicion of independent leadership. The environment of the legislator makes him too willing to accede to real or imagined popular whims. In this view, the people may not seek to wreak their passions against the body politic, but the politicians, victims of populist rhetoric, will accede to demands which seem to speak for popular passions. Where the politician can look to other sources of authority besides the people — institutions, established procedures, groups, values — he can be more autonomous.[95]

About the desire for elite autonomy more will be said subsequently.[96] We can agree now, however, that one would have preferred elites whose will to resist McCarthy had been firmer. But to blame this weakness on a populist system of authority, holding out pluralist values as alternatives, is too simple a view. An urge to give in to real or imagined popular passions is not a democratic virtue. But the question is not the attitudes of the people in the abstract or the attitudes of the leaders about the people in the abstract. The question is what one wants protection against. Groups often use "populist" rhetoric to insulate themselves from popular control. They may speak of the grass roots to protect their bailiwicks against outside, popularly supported political leaders. A wider political constituency, often sustained by "populist" rhetoric and appeals to principle, can strengthen political leadership against group pressure. It can help political elites confront such figures as McCarthy. The relation between populism and pluralism is more complex than is suggested by the image of practical and procedure-conscious organizations opposed to ideological and authoritarian masses. The "masses" did not produce McCarthyism in America, and groups and their leaders alone did not save us from him.

Consider first the specific reasons for elite tractability, called forth by the nature of McCarthy's issue. Other movements — agrarian radical ones for example — have played on a populist system of authority without achieving anything like the inroads and the power of McCarthy. Racist Governor George Wallace captured the support of masses of northern, urban whites during the 1964 presidential primaries without hindering the passage of a pending civil rights bill. But McCarthy's situation was uniquely favorable. On the one hand, he benefited from the nondivisiveness of his issue: many groups, elites, and institutions were for "Wall Street," the railroads, or "the interests," but no one was for communism. But at the same time, McCarthy could capitalize on divisions and insecurities within the elite structure. Wallace was up against a northern elite consensus on civil rights (created, paradoxically enough, by mass Negro pressure). But McCarthy fed upon Republican suspicion of Democrats, Democratic anxieties about their past policies, and a mood of temporization and passivity in Washington.

Second, here as elsewhere the symbiosis between "populism" and pragmatism cannot go unnoticed. One might blame elite weakness on the instrumentalism and pragmatism of political leaders, which made them less willing to stand up for principle and more willing to give in to the line of least resistance. It was easier to remain silent than to oppose McCarthy, so many remained silent. Individuals did not want to risk their personal gains by opposing the Wisconsin senator. Perhaps the business orientation and narrow self-concern in the society make politicians unwilling to stand up for the commonweal. The principled politics feared by the pluralists might have been an asset here.

Third, institutional restraints and traditional allegiances may be alternatives to populist values, but they augmented

McCarthy's power. The Senator capitalized on the routine politics of the political stratum — Senate traditions, executive-legislative rivalry, Republican party loyalty, anxiety to keep disputes out of the limelight. The general unwillingness of American politicians to assume responsibility for controversial actions became increasingly bizarre during the years of McCarthy's hegemony. This monumental insistence that politics continue as usual is surely a classic example of the banality of evil.

One would have hoped for a greater presidential appreciation of the dignity of the executive branch. One would have welcomed greater respect for the rule of law and for individual rights. Yet when Eisenhower finally fought for executive dignity and the rule of law, he had to resort to the instruments of publicity and open confrontation. Only with the publicity of the Army-McCarthy hearings did American politicians gain the confidence and integrity openly to oppose and then to ignore McCarthy.

Temporization and surrender having failed, the Eisenhower administration finally challenged McCarthy directly. Big businessmen who had heretofore supported the Senator began to back away, as he attacked their administration and an institution (the army) with which they identified.[97] After the censure, the Senate "club" would have even less than usual to do with him.[98] The respectable press, allegedly forced to publicize McCarthy's charges because they were news, stopped giving him coverage. Meanwhile, the Korean War had ended, and the tensions of the cold war eased. Observers agree that McCarthy's influence then reached a low point from which it never recovered. All McCarthy had left was the support of those in the populace basically hostile to American society. Undaunted, perhaps even encouraged by his attacks on the institutions in American life from which they were alienated, these anomic "masses" continued to support the Wisconsin Senator. They had no more influence on his power than they had ever had. When McCarthy became a real antagonist of the institutions which conservatives respected — the Republican Party, the Senate, and the Army — he lost influence both among moderately conservative political leaders and among the population at large. As McCarthy became "radical," he lost his hold on American politics.

PROTEST POLITICS
AND THE PLURALIST VISION

I

A theory may distort our understanding of historical phenomena for two reasons. Perhaps a perfectly sound theory has been misapplied in the particular instances. Alternatively, the failure of those who use the theory may reveal weaknesses in the theoretical structure itself. Pluralism has failed to explain McCarthyism, agrarian radicalism, and the relation between them. We will first review the evidence that refutes pluralist interpretations of these movements. We will then examine the defects in the general theory of pluralism that have contributed to its specific failures here.

Pluralist interpretations of McCarthyism and agrarian radicalism suffer from four misconceptions. First, the pluralists see a continuity in support that does not exist and misunderstand the evolution of American politics. Second, they exaggerate the "mass" character of McCarthyism and misinterpret the "mass" character of the agrarian radical movements. Third, they minimize the importance of the specific issues with which McCarthy and the agrarian radicals sought to deal. And fourth, they fail to understand the role of moralism in the American political tradition.

The difference in electoral support between McCarthyism and agrarian radicalism is easiest to demonstrate objectively.

Both McCarthy and the agrarian radical movements did receive their strongest electoral support in rural states. Within those states, however, the groups upon which they drew were very different. Populism based itself on Scandinavian, wheat-growing, middle-class farmers. Progressivism in North Dakota and Wisconsin drew support from the poor, Scandinavian areas. Germans and Catholics tended to oppose these movements. But Germans were the chief ethnic group in McCarthy's electoral base, while significant numbers of Democratic Catholics were won over by his appeals. Where an agrarian radical supported McCarthy, as in North Dakota, this was because of a German support unusual for peacetime agrarian radicalism.

The lack of continuity in social support means that much of McCarthy's constituency had opposed agrarian radicalism. If the agrarian radical movements had the same concerns as McCarthyism, why were McCarthy's supporters not disproportionately agrarian radical? That so much of McCarthy's support came from traditional conservative constituencies suggests that many of McCarthy's underlying concerns were those that had traditionally activated the opposition to agrarian radicalism.

At the same time, the electoral evidence gives little comfort to those who have seen direct continuity from Populism or progressivism to modern liberalism and anti-McCarthyism. Where agrarian radicalism had an economic base among the poor and where it maintained a cohesive following over the years, its supporters tended to become part of the modern Democratic constituency. This placed them in opposition to McCarthy. Bob La Follette, Jr.'s 1940 Senate vote was correlated —.7 with McCarthy's Senate vote twelve years later. But where agrarian radical movements rose and fell without continuity, they made little disproportionate contribution either to the modern Democratic vote or to the opposition to McCarthy.

Moreover, holding the party vote constant there was a tendency for rural areas disproportionately to support McCarthy. Many of these rural counties, in South Dakota and Wisconsin, had earlier been progressive. The amount of support for McCarthy contributed by these former progressive counties was small; but pluralists could argue that it symbolizes the core of common concerns uniting McCarthyism and agrarian radicalism.

There is little question that farmers no longer dominate the Left in American politics as they did in the days of Jefferson, Jackson, and the Populists. Agrarian radicalism virtually disappeared in the decade of the New Deal and World War II. Class politics replaced sectional politics, and workers replaced farmers as the mass bulwark of the Left.

As the number of farmers declined drastically, as agriculture became more of a business on stable foundations, and as World War II and the cold war ushered in an unprecedented agricultural prosperity, the base for agrarian radicalism declined. The farmers that remained had little enthusiasm for movements of economic protest. As the larger society became more bureaucratized, as the strange forces of big labor and big government arose in the urban world, as a cosmopolitan outlook encroached on rural values, the programs of agrarian radicalism seemed unable to solve the problems that continued to agitate rural society. Finally, the increased importance of foreign policy and the Communist menace brought to a head the rural concern with moral questions. The trans-Mississippi West became the center of ideological conservatism instead of agrarian radicalism.

But simply because a group plays a different role in one period of history than another is no reason to read back its later conservative politics into the earlier radical period. Marx, writing about French farmers, distinguished the role they played at the time of the first Napoleon with their role at the time of the second, fifty years later.[1] One can make an analogous interpretation of the role of America's rural inhabitants. Not to make such distinctions is to ignore the importance of history.

The pluralists justify their ahistorical view of rural politics because they detect a moralistic thread running through its progressive and conservative phase. Populism, progressivism, and McCarthyism were all in the pluralist view mass moralistic protests against industrialization.

The first difficulty with this view arises when the "mass" character of the movements is examined. A close look at the "mass" nature of McCarthyism and agrarian radicalism suggests the gulf that separates these phenomena rather than the bonds that unite them. The difference between McCarthyism and agrarian radicalism at the grass roots is striking. McCarthy mobilized little specific organizational support outside the grass roots Republican Party organizations. He encountered little opposition from local elites. He gave little evidence of exerting a mass appeal that uprooted voters from their traditional loyalties. Agrarian radical movements, on the other hand, held hundreds of meetings, organized at the grass roots for innumerable electoral campaigns, and created new voting patterns that often influenced events after the movements themselves had disappeared. Although these mass movements had a salutary effect on American politics, they exhibited many of the effects of mass activity that the pluralists fear. McCarthyism exhibited few of these effects. It neither split apart existing coalitions nor created an organized, active mass following. If Populism was a mass movement in the sense of its grass roots appeal and McCarthyism was not, McCarthyism had "mass" characteristics, such as contempt for the rule of law and generalized hostility to cosmopolitan values, that were lacking in agrarian radicalism. But such anomic characteristics were found more among political leaders and local elites than among masses. Since McCarthyism cannot be explained by the "mass" preoccupations of the masses, one must examine the support for

McCarthy among certain elite groups and the tolerance or fear of him among others. The pluralists' preoccupation with mass movements as threats to a stable, democratic group life prevents them from analyzing McCarthyism in this fashion.

When the relevant political issues are closely examined, the anti-industrial character of McCarthyism and agrarian radicalism — and therefore the alleged connection between them — also evaporates.

Like the agrarian protest movements, McCarthy drew sustenance from concrete political issues; but his issues were not the agrarian radical issues. Populism, La Follette progressivism, and the Non-Partisan League attacked industrial capitalists, not industrialization. They proposed concrete and practical economic reforms. McCarthy focused on the political not the economic order. While many McCarthy activists were in rebellion against modern industrial society, this society included — and was in their eyes dominated by — New Deal reforms of the type agrarian radicals had favored. This was a very different society from that of the "trusts" and the "robber barons" at the turn of the twentieth century, against which agrarian radicals directed their fire. Moreover, most of McCarthy's supporters on public opinion polls cared more about communism, Korea, and the cold war than they did about modern industrial society. McCarthyism could not have flourished in the absence of these foreign policy concerns.

If no direct links are sustained by the evidence, the pluralists may still retreat to the general argument that McCarthy utilized a peculiarly moralistic, agrarian radical, political style. They point to an alleged agrarian radical tendency to seek moral solutions to practical problems. As Hofstadter explains, "We are forever restlessly pitting ourselves against [the evils of life], demanding changes, improvements, remedies, but not often with sufficient sense of the limits that the human condition will in the end insistently impose upon us."[2] The pluralists argue that as the agrarian radical world of moral certainty disappeared, this progressive optimism became frustrated. Former agrarian radicals sought scapegoats to explain their defeats. It was an easy step, for example, from the progressive belief that only special interests stood in the way of reforms to the McCarthy certainty that only treason could explain the failures of American foreign policy.[3]

Consider, as evidence for this interpretation, the career of Tom Watson. Watson, the leading southern Populist of the 1890's, supported the political organization and economic demands of the southern Negro farmer. He made a reasoned analysis of the causes of rural misery and opposed economic panaceas. But out of frustration generated by the defeat of Populism, Watson became an anti-Negro, anti-Catholic, anti-Semitic, southern demagogue.[4] For the pluralists, Watson's career symbolizes the development of McCarthyism. Hofstadter writes, "While its special association with agrarian reforms has now become attenuated, I believe that Populist thinking has survived in our own time, partly as an undercurrent of provincial resentments, popular and 'democratic' rebelliousness and suspiciousness, and nativism."[5]

But here the pluralists substitute the sin of noncomparative analysis for the sin of static analysis. Examination of the moralistic character of American politics discloses that (a) prior to the New Deal political moralism was by no means confined to agrarian radicals; (b) American political moralism asserts the reality of a public interest and denies the need for basic irreconcilable conflict, and thus much of the moralistic flavor of American politics is a condition of pragmatism rather than an alternative to it; (c) McCarthy's particular moralistic preoccupations were typical of traditional conservatism more than of left-wing progressivism.

The Populist tradition could produce antidemocratic and even neofascist figures, but given the nature of American society and the absence of strong elite backing for these figures, they had little success in national politics. Tom Watson, who combined anti-Semitism with sympathy for the Soviet Union, was clearly a product of Populism gone sour; McCarthy was not.

McCarthy and the agrarian radicals came from two contrasting political traditions. Both traditions stressed self-help, but the Populists did not attack bureaucracies indiscriminately. Agrarian radicals sought to meet the threat of private bureaucracies by increasing the role of the state. The agrarian radical tradition was anti-Wall Street, anti-vested interests, anti-industrial capitalist. This tradition has been dying out as the role of left-wing protest politics has passed to the cities. Its evolution has produced Tom Watsons and Burton Wheelers, but sophisticated, humanitarian liberals like Quentin Burdick and George McGovern have been equally prominent. Perhaps their independence from Johnson on the Vietnamese war owed something to the agrarian radical heritage. McCarthy's ideological conservative tradition was anti-intellectual, antistatist, antibureaucratic, and antiforeign.[6] Locally prestigious and wealthy elites have dominated this politics, generally attracting widespread popular support as well. McCarthy, the son of a poor farmer, was marginally outside this conservative tradition. He effectively exploited this marginality, but without the support of the conservative tradition he would have made little impact.

Behind the pluralist misinterpretation of McCarthyism and fear of agrarian radicalism lies a legitimate suspicion of mass movements. But this fear, fed by the triumph of totalitarianism in Russia, Italy, and Germany, obscures the differences among mass movements. To find radical roots for McCarthy's support is to underestimate the middle-class diversity of the American populace. For the pluralists, McCarthyism and agrarian radicalism were united by their *petit bourgeois* character. But in America the *petit bourgeois* class is both enormous and diverse. Different political movements can call on support from different segments of that class; their support

267

can be *petit bourgeois* without being significantly related. It is a mistake to identify mass movements with authoritarianism and pressure groups with democracy. Rather there are authoritarian and democratic mass movements, just as there are authoritarian and democratic pressure groups. The Populist mass movement operated within the established constitutional framework of the republic; it was not a threat to democracy.

The danger of McCarthyism, on the other hand, while real, was not the danger of a mass movement. McCarthy had powerful group and elite support. He did not mobilize the masses at the polls or break through existing group cleavages. McCarthy's power was sustained only in part by the vague discontents of frustrated groups. Communism and the Korean War played crucial roles. The real danger posed by McCarthy should not distort our understanding of agrarian radical movements in America, nor should the pluralist criticisms of mass movements blind us to the real nature of McCarthyism.

II

"Pluralism" has become a term of praise in the academic political vocabulary, just as "democracy" and "freedom" are in the language of the population at large. "Pluralism" tells social scientists to look for a multiplicity of causes and not be satisfied with monistic explanations. It points to the importance of competing groups and diverse values in sustaining a stable democracy. It suggests the virtues of compromise and pragmatic activity. Complexity becomes a virtue both in scientific investigation and in democratic life. Now compromise, civilized values, competing groups, and an outlook that appreciates complexity are certainly praiseworthy in the abstract. The question we must ask, however, is whether these orientations, when brought to bear on particular historical events, aid or hinder our understanding of them.

Pluralism is both a method of investigation and a description of reality. As to methodology, perhaps the easiest criticism to make of a theory that stresses complexity is that it does not take us very far. We can all agree that historical events have more than one cause and that societies are affected by more than a single group or orientation. (Who would similarly deny that a monolithic political structure is inferior to one that encourages diversity?) But to say that a phenomenon has more than one cause is hardly to make an analysis. Unless pluralist theory can tell us which causes are the most important ones, its stress on complexity becomes a substitute for explanation, not an explanation itself.

Pluralist analysis of McCarthyism and agrarian radicalism, however, does not stop by asserting that the phenomena were complex. The most striking difficulty with pluralist methodology lies in the opposite direction. Having told us to look for complexity, the pluralists rely too heavily on a single factor. Pluralism focuses on a perceived conflict over industrialization and favors pro-industrial (instrumental) groups and attitudes over anti-industrial ones.

The consequence of this limitation of focus is that pluralism misses the actual complexity of American history. It makes the Populists into reactionaries because they opposed big business and had rural support. Dichotomizing rural and urban orientations, it misses the agrarian support for Al Smith. It collapses two isolationist traditions into one, and overlooks the contrasts between German and non-German support for agrarian radicalism. Each of these specific historical oversimplifications flows from inattention to the variety of groups, values, and forces that have contributed to American political conflict. In each case, a framework stressing general attitudes toward industrialization distorts the actual, concrete, specific conflicts over the nature of industrial society.

But pluralism is supposed to emphasize the variety of

269

groups, values, and forces that influence American politics. Have the pluralists here simply failed to follow their own methodological injunction to look for complexity? Have they simply ignored their own substantive hypotheses? The trouble, I would argue, lies deeper. The very "pluralism" they perceive leads directly to their oversimplified view of American society and social change.

Pluralism perceives a multitude of groups — farmers, businessmen, workers, political party activists, and more of the same. It thus apparently stresses the vertical divisions within society. The pluralist society seems at first blush exceedingly complex, but this would be a hasty conclusion. Consider the society pictured by the classical economists and the classical liberal political theorists. That society also contained tremendous movement and competition. Yet the classical liberals had in fact homogenized society in the sense of ignoring important distinctions among social phenomena. They had homogenized society first in fragmenting it into discrete, individual particles, second in assuming that each of these particles had more or less equal power, and third in postulating a basically similar outlook (rational maximization) among the particles.[7] That the classical liberal assumptions did in fact homogenize society is by now familiar doctrine. Yet each of these three homogenizing assumptions has its analogue in the modern pluralist vision.

First, although the group is a larger unit than the individual, it is still smaller than the class. A Marxist would argue that to substitute groups for individuals in analyzing society is still to miss the larger and more important social divisions. A society viewed in terms of innumerable competing groups, he would say, is still unduly fragmented. Without making a simple "class" interpretation of American political conflict, we shall see that this criticism of the group approach has validity.

Second, the pluralist vision makes no distinction in kind among the power of different groups in an industrial society.

Some groups have more power than others, in the pluralist view, but no groups are without power or the ability to acquire it if their members so desire. If the market solved the problem of power in classical liberal society, the countervailing power of groups serves the same function in modern industrial society.[8]

Third, the pluralist view makes no basic distinctions among the kinds of groups that exist in the pluralist society. Group theorists like Bentley and Truman are often charged with missing the role played by social consensus. But the real difficulty with pluralist analysis is precisely the opposite. Social consensus plays an overwhelming role in the pluralist vision. For the pluralists, group tactics and goals may vary, but since all groups accept pragmatic, democratic values and seek only piecemeal change, there is no essential difference among them.

Each of these three pluralist tenets is in some sense "true." Groups are more important actors in everyday American politics than classes, American political power is dispersed, and American political actors do share important similarities in values, tactics, and goals. But these three pluralist principles lead to three kinds of oversimplification. Pluralists oversimplify the character of mass movements, the relations between leaders and followers, and the role of political issues.

Consider first the pluralist view of mass movements. Complexity is reserved for the treatment of pluralist society; mass phenomena that fall outside that society are all lumped together as anomic, irrational, and anti-industrial. Group conflict and the satisfaction of concrete, group grievances, seen as a normal part of pluralist politics, are excluded from the analysis of mass movements: Populism, its specific targets minimized, becomes broadly anti-industrial. Political institutions mediating between individual attitudes and political behavior, stressed in pluralist politics, are ignored in analyzing "mass" behavior: party and congress have little impact

271

on McCarthyism. The role of elites in structuring and creating ideologies, vital to pluralist politics, does not enter the treatment of "mass" ideologies: McCarthy's rhetoric reflects the preoccupations of masses rather than of elites or of McCarthy himself.

Each of the three pluralist homogenizing tenets outlined above distorts the pluralist treatment of mass movements. First, all groups which do not accept a narrowly instrumental orientation and fail to rely mainly on pressure group tactics become "mass" phenomena. Such an outlook cannot perceive the essential differences between McCarthyism and Populism, for example. Not all mass movements are anomic, irrational, and anti-industrial; and not all phenomena that reject instrumental orientations are mass movements.*

Having denied the importance of a problem of power, pluralists do not treat mass movements as rational forms of organization by constituencies that lack power. Just because power is dispersed does not mean that all strata have a significant share of it. Extraordinary direct-action techniques like marches and demonstrations may be the only way in which deprived constituencies can exert influence; normal pressure group tactics may not be effective for them. Indeed, these extraordinary techniques may be particularly necessary to force action on a lethargic, decentralized ("pluralist") political system. But since the pluralists stress that power is shared in a pluralist democracy, movements that do not accept the normal political techniques of that society must be

* The concept of mass politics includes movements that mobilize masses of people, movements that cut across previous alliances, movements that exhibit millennial preoccupations, political actors who do not accept the rules of the game, and groups that utilize direct-action techniques, legal as well as illegal. There have been movements, like fascism, that combined these characteristics, but preoccupation with the dangers of fascism does not illuminate our understanding of American politics, where fascist movements have never flourished. Yet it is out of this preoccupation that "mass" phenomena are all seen as endangering pluralist stability and therefore all treated in similar terms.

dangerous and irrational. Their activities can only be ascribed to "the bathos of agrarian rhetoric" or to a basic hostility to modern industrial society.

Finally, the pluralists assimilate class politics to narrow interest group demands, reserving the concept of mass politics for broader political activity.[9] Such terminology denies legitimacy to what was in an older view the meaning of class action — namely, broad activity transcending narrow group lines. So-called mass phenomena in American history have been in this older sense class phenomena — uniting or attempting to unite groups of people along common, broad, economic lines. The Populists attempted to unite farmers in the 1890's; the earlier Knights of Labor and the later sit-down strikes partly succeeded in uniting workers. A "class" view of American politics gives meaning to these movements and to the obstacles they faced without needing to fit them into the pejorative straightjacket of mass theory.

The pluralist view of the complexities of group politics is only one side of the coin; the other side is a monolithic treatment of mass movements. It would be a mistake to conclude, moreover, that group politics itself is treated with sufficient complexity. That is certainly the intention, but the results are far different. I have suggested that the pluralists make three "homogenizing" assumptions about pluralist society. Consider the consequences of these assumptions for pluralist analysis regarding first the relations between leaders and followers and second the role of political issues.

The pluralists' stress on the vertical divisions in society — among groups and political actors in general — is meant to be an alternative to Marxist theory, which carried over the horizontal stratification of socioeconomic classes into the political arena. It also contrasts to Marxism in multiplying the number of important political actors. This in itself may be praiseworthy, but it has a further, unfortunate, consequence. As the number of groups increases, the divisions between them become less and less obvious. Society in effect becomes a blur; it is homogenized. In this blur one division does stand out — that between leaders and everyone else. Having stressed the similarities in outlook and power among political actors, pluralism underplays the vertical divisions at the expense of this single horizontal division.[10] Its significance, in pluralist eyes, lies in the special role played by the leadership stratum in maintaining democratic stability.

This reliance on leadership may not seem to be required by pluralist thinking. Is not pluralism simply a matter of group conflict; do not the threats of membership withdrawal and of the formation of new groups keep leaders on their toes and preserve democracy? I have suggested earlier[11] how the pluralist reliance on groups and on civilized values leads to a reliance on leaders. In pluralist eyes, groups and group leaders control their members rather than vice versa. Group leaders are the force for moderation and compromise. Political leaders, whether formal group leaders or not, have a greater commitment to democratic values and a greater knowledge of political issues than does the population at large; survey evidence demonstrates this.

The pluralists therefore conclude that these political activists play the game of democratic politics and preserve the democratic rules. The less educated and less sophisticated the members of a stratum, the more important it is for that stratum to have formal group leaders. Workers, farmers, and Negroes, for example, play the democratic game best through the leaders of their organizations. Educated people do not require such organizational restraints; it is indeed fortunate, as the pluralists see it, that the educated are the main political activists.

From an appreciation of the virtues of the leadership stratum, it seems but a short and straightforward step to the conclusion that the rapid entrance of new masses into politics — which is what mass movements are all about — can only be destructive of a stable democracy. Thus populistic faith in the common man and his political wisdom, leading to efforts to involve him in politics, seems directly to conflict with pluralism. As the pluralists see it, the political actors in a stable democracy are elites not masses, and it is deference to these elites rather than faith in the people that permits effective and democratic government. Behind pluralist analysis is the hope that if only responsible elites could be left alone, if only political issues could be kept from the people, the elites would make wise decisions.[12]

But for earlier writers on American politics, such as de Tocqueville, populism and pluralism were symbiotic. Nineteenth-century America, preindustrial and "populist" as it was, was overrun with groups. De Tocqueville argued that the American's belief that he could successfully take things into his own hands and successfully influence political elites led him incessantly to form and join organizations. As part of his populistic pluralism, de Tocqueville observed and favored widespread democratic participation within groups. Eliminate the populism, in this view, and the pluralism goes too.

The modern pluralists, however, are less concerned with forming new organizations than with preserving old ones. They are less interested in creating new group leaders than in creating respect for established ones. Their elite pluralism contrasts to de Tocqueville's grass-roots pluralism. Can it successfully emancipate itself from the populist heritage of American pluralism?

There are two difficulties in this effort, one involving the nature of deferential and "populist" attitudes in America, the other the character of political leaders. A syndrome of "populistic" attitudes among the masses may be dangerous in the abstract. But there is evidence that such a syndrome does not exist in America. The same people who support the Populist economic approach are not the ones who adhere to the authoritarian values allegedly found in Populism. In addition, those who express faith in the common man do not exhibit excessive hostility to all constituted authority. On the contrary, that hostility tends to be found in the same people who also have the deferential attitudes the pluralists applaud. The authoritarian pattern is one of hostility and submission, not hostility alone.

One recent national survey included a "populism" scale, derived from the literature of and about the Populist movement. The scale contained a series of economic items — such as antagonism toward monopoly, hostility to Wall Street, support for a worker-farmer alliance — and a series of noneconomic items — anti-intellectualism, antiexpertise, anti-eastern power, the view that decisions are made in secret, adherence to Bible Belt puritanism. Those scoring high on economic populism tended to have prolabor attitudes. High scores on noneconomic populism were associated with pro-business attitudes.[13] These data suggest (1) that the economic program of Populism is not associated in the public mind with a syndrome of "populist" authoritarianism, (2) that a generalized suspicion of economic and noneconomic authorities (which is alleged to give McCarthy Populist roots) does not exist at the mass level, (3) that what the pluralists see as populist-authoritarianism is found with conservative rather than with left-wing attitudes.

This so-called populist authoritarianism does not appear to be associated with faith in the people. It may very well be that generalized deference and generalized "populism" are not alternatives but rather that the same people who are excessively suspicious of some authorities are excessively deferential to others. Consider those who express deferential attitudes toward authority. They reveal the least faith in the common man and tend to be the most authoritarian, least-educated, most rigid, most hostile, and most ethnocentric members of the society. They also tend to be, like the plura-lists, most worried about stability and fearful of change.[14] If a naïve faith in the people and in progress is required to sustain tolerance and elite autonomy, this may be a paradox with which it would be dangerous to tamper.

But is the aim of protecting elite autonomy itself praiseworthy? Clearly leaders are better educated, better informed, and more politically skillful than the mass of Americans; clearly they are more verbally committed to preserving democratic rights. But they also have other characteristics. At least since World War II, leaders of the Republican Party have been far more conservative than their own party supporters — who are on many issues closer to Democratic leaders than to Republican ones.[15] Here, then, is a pressure to the Right in American politics from a powerful elite group. Deference to these leaders would increase conservatism in particular, not democratic stability in general.

And more than economic conservatism is at work here. The activists who supported McCarthy were drawn from Republican Party workers. Those whom Goldwater emboldened, if they were not Republican activists already, came from the well-educated and wealthy segments of the population. In a country that produces such political elites, increasing elite autonomy is not an entirely salutary prescription.

There are also problems with increasing the autonomy even of more moderate and democratic leaders. Leaders as a whole develop organizational interests that make them unwilling to take risks. They tend to overestimate opposition and to confine themselves to the realization of goals as noncontroversial as possible. They develop friendly relations with other leaders and fear to endanger their own prestige, the stability of their organizations, or the achievements that have been won.[16] Powerful organized groups may fragment government so that each group seeks hegemony within its sphere of special concern. Under such conditions, public policy emerges from the decisions of narrow groups, each relatively unchecked within its own sphere. Social change becomes extremely difficult, as even the impetus provided by narrow group conflict is minimized.

Moreover, the ideology of organized groups, which usually favors cooperation and opposes force, is deceptive. Consider the moderate and democratic language of Samuel Gompers, founder of the American Federation of Labor. Gompers insisted that "no lasting gain can ever come from compulsion" and urged "sincere democratic deliberation until a unanimous decision is reached."[17] But the function of this language, for Gompers as for other group leaders, contrasts with the spirit. To argue that discussion can resolve all differences, in an apparent spirit of tolerance and democracy, implies that no legitimate conflict of interest or opinion exists. Those who seek to organize and exert pressure in opposition to those with power then become illegitimate. Often their efforts are met with the coercion frowned upon and disguised by the ideology.[18] The rhetoric of reasonableness, whether employed by group leaders, national politicians, or liberal intellectuals, can too easily be turned against thoroughgoing political opposition. Conflict-inhibiting anxiety about the propriety of their ends and the fragility of their institutions often makes leaders more suspicious of democracy than they will admit in the abstract.

For all these reasons, the case for relying upon leadership autonomy is not convincing. Leaders may have "good" attitudes on civil rights, for example, but the way to get those attitudes transformed into action is not simply to make the leaders more autonomous. In a pluralist society, leaders will always be under pressure, and the solution (for civil rights goals) is not independent leaders but leaders dependent on the "proper" sources of support. This has been the function performed by the civil rights movement in recent years. In the absence of this mass activity, the "enlightened" leaders have acted slowly or not at all.

One function of mass movements, then, is to overcome the political conservatism of sections of the leadership stratum and the organizational conservatism of that stratum in general. Even the existing leaders most directly concerned may develop organizational interests that insulate them from responding to constituency pressure. The Populist Party of the 1890's organized independently of the existing parties, and the sit-down strikes and the organization of the CIO in the 1930's took place mainly outside the established trade union bureaucracy. And the civil rights movement of the 1960's began outside such established Negro organizations as the ghetto political machine and the NAACP. Each of these mass movements thrusts masses from below — first farmers, then workers, now Negroes — into political life. Each was necessitated in part by the resistance to change among better-educated, better-informed leadership elements in the society. How is it, given pluralist analysis, that these movements have not been authoritarian threats to a pluralist democracy?

Pluralist theory has presented us with a society in which (1) the positions of groups on issues, given a social consensus, are not decisive for democratic stability, and (2) the general differences between leaders and followers are more important for stability than the issue differences that divide leaders among themselves and unite a leader with his group of followers. There is truth in both these propositions, but their effect as a tool of analysis is to minimize the importance of political issues in political controversy. The focus of pluralism has been on groups in the abstract, "populism" in the abstract, deference in the abstract, and popular and elite attitudes in the abstract. Pluralist theory has paid insufficient attention to the differential effects of mobilizing masses on the basis of different political issues. It is these political issues — economic and political reform in the Populist case, communism for McCarthy — that decisively influence the way in which masses will be mobilized, if at all, and the directions that mass activity will take.

Let us assume, with the pluralists, a high incidence of antidemocratic attitudes among the relatively apathetic mass of people. This does not mean that when people are mobilized from among this mass, antidemocratic attitudes will be relevant. Mass activity is goal directed; and the nature of the goals is decisive in determining who will be mobilized, how they will be mobilized, and what their relation to other groups in political life will be.

Mass movements, in the first place, activate only a tiny minority of the previously uninvolved citizens. The March on Washington for civil rights in August 1963, largest demonstration of its kind in American history, mobilized no more than 2 percent of the adult Negro population. Once it is realized that only a small minority of the populace becomes involved in mass activity at any one time, it becomes important to know who those people will be. The picture of a homogeneous mass of potentially mobilizable citizens (united, for example, by hostility to industrial society) has little connection with reality. Different issues will draw upon different mass constituencies. The new political activists will vary in their commitment to democratic values, depending on whom the issue has made active. The issue of the Communist menace will involve different people and create different activists than the issue of the "trusts"; the issue of discrimination will involve still a third set of activists.

Second, the political issues determine which segment of an individual's total bundle of attitudes will become relevant. White workers may be prejudiced against Negroes in the abstract and if mobilized on the issue of neighborhood housing may take anti-Negro positions. But if they are mobilized on the basis of common economic grievances, as happened in the organization of the CIO in the 1930's, the activity of white workers may be pro-Negro. Even the white farmers of the south when mobilized on an economic basis by southern Populism engaged in pro-Negro activity.

There is no reason to assume that the antidemocratic attitudes of masses mobilized by depression or discrimination will affect their actual political activity. Indeed, their activity may change their attitudes. Members of elite groups, with "better" attitudes in the abstract, may engage in antidemocratic activity out of fear of the mass movements. Behavior cannot be predicted from attitudes alone. Our concern should be not with analyzing the people or popular attitudes as a whole but with locating the relevant attitudes of the relevant people.

Third, the pluralists portray American politics in terms of conflict among discrete, narrowly focused, nonideological political actors. This picture underestimates the extent to which ideological commitments and the requirements of political alliance amalgamate discrete interests and discrete groups. Positions on political issues decisively influence who will ally with whom. In the real political world alternatives are structured; some issues are tied to others.

The mass of Americans do not have developed political ideologies,[19] but the consequences of their actions may be influenced by leadership ideologies. Workers, because of their economic interests, support union and political party leaders committed to civil liberties and civil rights. That this consequence may not be intended does not make it less important or more "accidental." Similarly, in order to support McCarthy, workers would have had to vote Republican. McCarthyism was thus tied to a party and an economic outlook repugnant to most workers. Feeling for the Wisconsin Senator would have had to be fairly intense before workers would actively support him. On the other hand, for Republican leaders, a better informed and more tolerant group than workers, support for McCarthy was tied to their interest in maintaining party harmony, to their anti-New Deal attitudes, and to their foreign policy concerns. This tying together of issues influences the direction that political activity can take; it helps explain why McCarthyism did not become a mass, lower-class movement and why northern Democrats from white constituencies supported Negro political demands for many years more than did northern Republicans as a whole.

Because it minimizes the significance of issue content, then, pluralism fails to explain how (1) certain issues can activate masses without antidemocratic consequences while (2) other issues, more antidemocratic in character, can receive elite

281

support and not significantly agitate the populace at all. Pluralism, instead, must praise all elites and interpret all political phenomena it fears in "mass" terms. The consequence is far from a scientific theory of politics.

Pluralist thinkers have focused attention on a wide range of important subjects. Pluralism has attacked several traditional left-wing shibboleths. It has exploded myths about popular virtue and revealed the dangers in thoughtlessly democratic thinking. It has pointed out the risks to constitutionalism inherent in millennial preoccupations. Pluralism has stressed the value of groups, of diversity, and of the rule of law. It has directed attention to the role of political leadership. It has sought to go beneath the apparent aims of political movements and to discuss general social developments.

Pluralist thinking has not produced scientific propositions so much as useful insight. And for this it deserves credit. At the same time, because of its underlying preoccupations, the pluralist vision is a distorted one. The fear of radicalism and the concern for stability, however legitimate as values, have interfered with accurate perception. Thanks to its allegiance to modern America, pluralism analyzes efforts by masses to improve their condition as threats to stability. It turns all threats to stability into threats to constitutional democracy. This is a profoundly conservative endeavor. Torn between its half-expressed fears and its desire to face reality, pluralist theory is a peculiar mixture of analysis and prescription, insight and illusion, special pleading and dispassionate inquiry. Perhaps pluralism may best be judged not as the product of science but as a liberal American venture into conservative political theory.

CORRELATION
COEFFICIENTS

A correlation coefficient measures the relation between two variables. The correlation coefficients in this study measured either the relation between elections or between votes in elections and background variables such as Catholicism. The basic unit of measurement was the percentage vote in a county for a given candidate. For example, if the relation between support for Roosevelt in 1936 and Stevenson in 1952 was being analyzed, each county would be assigned two scores — the percentage of votes cast for the Democratic presidential nominee in the two elections. The highest correlation coefficient possible is 1.00, which would be obtained if there was a parallel rate of increase in the percentages given the candidates in the two elections. For example, if the vote in County A was 45 percent for Roosevelt and 40 percent for Stevenson, in County B 50 percent and 45 percent, respectively, in County C 55 percent and 50 percent, County D 60 percent and 55 percent, and this pattern of one-to-one increase persisted in all the counties in the state, then a 1.00 correlation would be obtained. If, however, for County E the Roosevelt vote was 61 percent and the Stevenson vote was 85 percent, the parallel rate of increase would be disturbed. Even though for each county the higher the support for Roosevelt, the higher the support for Stevenson, the magnitude of the correlation coefficient would be below 1.00.

If there was no relation between the percentage vote cast in two elections, the correlation would be 0.00. The maximum negative correlation of 1.00 is obtained when the county vote for one candidate decreases as the county vote for the other candidate increases.

Partial correlation coefficients were also calculated, to show the relation between two variables with the influence of a third eliminated. Sometimes two elections were compared with a social background factor eliminated (for example, the similarity between voting support for Smith and Kennedy with the impact of Catholicism removed). At other times a background factor and an election were compared with the influence of a second background variable eliminated (for example, the relationship between German ethnicity and the Populist vote with the influence of rural residence removed).[1]

Analysis of county voting returns and census data provides only indirect evidence of individual behavior within the counties. For example, this study demonstrates a correlation between the percentage living on farms and the percentage voting for McCarthy (with the influence of the regular party vote eliminated). However, because counties with large farm populations also have large small-town populations, it might be that small-town residents and not farmers were supporting McCarthy. The technique of partial correlation helps to eliminate "accidental" correlations, but final certainty about individual behavior can rarely be inferred from aggregate data such as election returns. Checking the logic of the theory used to explain the data, applying the same research techniques on other data in different states or the same state at different times, and developing an informed sensitivity to possible sources of the misinterpretation of statistics mitigate the dangers of using aggregate data.

Greater certainty about individual behavior is obtained through the analysis of other research material (particularly survey data). However, survey data are not always available, particularly in analyzing past voting behavior. Often surveys contain incomplete information: There may be no question on religion or on past voting behavior. Finally, election returns have the advantage of indicating behavior rather than statements about behavior.

FACTOR ANALYSIS

Factor analysis aims at discovering underlying relationships that exist in any table of numbers. Consider Table B.1:

TABLE B.1
HYPOTHETICAL DATA TABLE

2	4	6	8	10	12
1	2	3	4	5	6
1	1	1	1	1	1

It is clear that the first two rows are proportional to each other; multiply the second row by the constant 2 and you reproduce the first row. We can say that this matrix of three rows can be reduced to two rows that are independent of each other — that is to say, no operation that can be performed on either of the two independent rows can make them identical. Factor analysis aims at reducing all the rows of a data table to the number that are independent of each other. By performing mathematical operations on the rows of a factor matrix, it is possible to reproduce the original data matrix to a given degree of approximation.[1]

There is a mathematically precise method of calculating optimal values for a given number of rows (or factors) from the original data table. This is known as the principal axis solution. The first principal axis is that row of numbers that accounts for the largest sum of squares of the entries in each row of the original matrix. Once the correlations corresponding to the principal axis have been subtracted from the original matrix, a residual matrix remains. The second principal axis is extracted from this residual matrix.

Some judgment is required as to when a sufficient number of principal axes have been extracted, but the criterion used to determine the number of principal axes is unambiguous. Each row of the original matrix has a loading on each principal axis. The sum of squares of the loadings of the original rows on the principal axes becomes smaller for each new axis extracted. This is because the first principal axis accounts for the maximum possible sum of squares in the correlation matrix, the second principal axis for the maximum remaining sum of squares in the first residual matrix, and so on. The sum of squares of the loadings of the original rows on each factor is set equal to the latent root.

In the present factor analysis, the latent roots of the correlation matrix corresponding to the principal axes were 14.75, 8.74, 3.17, 2.59, .5, and .4. It is clear that there was a sharp drop in the latent roots after the fourth principal axis was extracted. Therefore, it was determined to utilize only the first four principal axes. These were considered sufficient to reproduce the original matrix to a satisfactory approximation.[2]

The principal axis solution is mathematically precise, but it is not a good one with which to interpret the data. For interpretation one desires a factor matrix that approximates a simple structure. A simple structure solution is one in which the factors isolate groups of rows in the original matrix with the least in common with each other. At the same time, a simple structure solution maximizes the number of zero entries in the factor matrix, so that there is one factor on which rows *a, b,* and *f* are pure, another on which rows *c,* and *j* are pure, and so forth.[3]

Let us assume that we have determined by the principal axis method that two factors are sufficient to approximate the original data table. However, unlike a principal axis solution, a simple structure solution may or may not exist clearly

TABLE B.2
FACTOR LOADINGS OF NORTH DAKOTA ELECTIONS

Num-ber		Factors			
		Tradi-tional Party	Popu-list	Progres-sive	Non-Partisan League
1	1889 Democratic Governor	70	01	21	21
2	1890 Democratic Congress	65	—09	01	—10
3	1892 Fusion President	49	55	—04	13
4	1892 Populist Congress	—19	77	15	02
5	1894 Populist Governor	—15	69	17	12
6	1896 Fusion President	64	44	33	16
7	1898 Fusion Governor	57	46	34	—03
8	1900 Democratic President	73	36	24	02
9	1902 Democratic Governor	70	15	41	—16
10	1904 Democratic President	86	22	20	—13
11	1906 Democratic Governor	32	05	69	—13
12	1908 Twitchell (Progressive)	27	24	46	—18
13	1908 Democratic Governor	59	—05	59	—08
14	1908 Democratic President	76	08	50	—10
15	1910 Engerud	—26	—05	—16	—41
16	1910 Democratic Governor	59	—02	43	—03
17	1912 T. Roosevelt	—39	—07	—28	19
18	1912 Democratic President	63	14	51	—18
19	1914 Woman Suffrage	04	—10	82	40
20	1914 Initiative	—07	—49	36	56

TABLE B.2 (continued)

		Factors			
Num-ber		Tradi-tional Party	Popu-list	Progres-sive	Non-Partisan League
21	1914 Grain Elevators	—05	—34	55	68
22	1914 Burdick (Progressive)	—10	—13	72	14
23	1914 Dem. Secretary of State	66	05	47	—01
24	1916 La Follette	—01	09	80	21
25	1916 Frazier (League)	08	18	38	77
26	1916 League Judge (Dem.)	02	12	31	86
27	1916 Democratic President	41	—26	71	25
28	1916 Democratic Senator (Prog.)	58	—26	70	02
29	1916 Democratic Treasurer (League)	47	11	47	55
30	1918 Frazier	—28	22	—50	67
31	1920 Ladd (League)	05	—05	14	96
32	1920 Democratic President	47	13	54	—01
33	1920 Sunday Theaters	13	—31	—37	12
34	1921 League Governor	—12	—14	—31	88
35	1922 League Governor	—08	—09	—11	96
36	1922 Frazier	—03	04	—08	97
37	1924 La Follette	—20	31	—48	71
38	1924 Dem. Secretary of State	55	24	22	—31
39	1926 Nye (League)	—04	07	12	91
40	1928 Democratic President	25	—01	—57	29

in a given set of data. There is in fact rarely a data table that fits as neatly into a simple structure. The present factor analysis achieved a fairly good approximation to a simple structure. See Table B.2.

In the ideal simple structure, the first principal axis would be on a 45-degree line passing between the two clumps of data. This is because it is based on what all the data rows have in common — in a sense, the first principal axis is the average of the data rows. Simple structure factors, on the other hand, are based on the difference between the data rows. Therefore, one desires to rotate from a principal axis solution to an approximation to a simple structure solution. There are several different methods of rotation. The one used in this analysis follows Butler. The rows of the principal axis matrix were normalized. Those rows loading highest positive and negative on the second, third, and fourth principal axes were selected as trial rows for a new matrix. This gave six rows. The intercorrelations between each of these rows were computed according to the method in footnote 2. The four rows with the lowest intercorrelations were selected to form the new factor matrix.[4] We then rotated from the four factors of the original principal axis matrix to the four factors of this new factor matrix.[5]

In order to determine whether our new matrix was the best approximation to a simple structure, the loadings on each factor were plotted.[6] From examining the graphs we discovered a new rotation that would improve the structure of the factor matrix. This was an oblique rotation; that is, after the rotation the two factors involved were no longer orthogonal to each other.[7] The set of factors that resulted from the new rotation were plotted against each other. An inspection of the new graphs did not reveal a rotation that would improve the approximation to a simple structure. Therefore, the interpretation was made from the loadings on this factor matrix. (For the loadings of each election on the four factors, see Table B.2.)

NOTES

Introduction

1. Richard Rovere, *Senator Joe McCarthy* (New York: Meridian Books, 1960), pp. 5-6.
2. Cf., for example, Thomas A. Bailey, "The West and Radical Legislation 1890–1930," *American Journal of Sociology*, Vol. 38 (January 1933), pp. 603–611; Edgar Eugene Robinson, "Recent Manifestations of Sectionalism," *American Journal of Sociology*, Vol. 19 (January 1914), pp. 446–467.
3. Cf. Richard Hofstadter, *The Age of Reform* (New York: Knopf, 1955); Seymour Martin Lipset, *Political Man* (Garden City, N.Y.: Doubleday, 1960); Edward Shils, *The Torment of Secrecy* (Glencoe, Ill.: Free Press, 1956); Peter Viereck, *The Unadjusted Man* (Boston: Beacon Press, 1956); William Kornhauser, *The Politics of Mass Society* (Glencoe, Ill.: Free Press, 1959); Daniel Bell, *The End of Ideology* (Glencoe, Ill.: Free Press, 1959); Daniel Bell (ed.), *The New American Right* (New York: Criterion Books, 1955). *The New American Right* contains essays by Bell, Hofstadter, Lipset, Viereck, Talcott Parsons, David Riesman, and Nathan Glazer. It has been republished with some new material as Daniel Bell (ed.), *The Radical Right* (Garden City, N.Y.: Doubleday, 1963). Cf. also Will Herberg, "Government by Rabble-Rousing," *The New Leader*, Vol. 37 (January 18, 1954), pp. 13–16; Oscar Handlin, "American Views of the Jews at the Opening of the Twentieth Century," *Publications of the American Jewish Historical Society*, Vol. 40 (June 1951), pp. 323–344; Edward Shils, "Authoritarianism: Right and Left," in Richard Christie and Marie Jahoda (eds.), *Studies in the Scope and Method of the Authoritarian Personality* (Glencoe, Ill.: Free Press, 1954).
4. David Riesman and Nathan Glazer, "The Intellectuals and the Discontented Classes," Daniel Bell, "Interpretations of American Politics," and Peter Viereck, "The Revolt Against the Elite," in Daniel Bell (ed.), *The New American Right, op. cit.*, pp. 68,

27, and 95; Peter Viereck, *The Unadjusted Man, op. cit.,* p. 201; Seymour Martin Lipset, *Political Man, op. cit.,* p. 168; and Edward Shils, *The Torment of Secrecy, op. cit.,* pp. 98–99.

Chapter One

1. Many pluralists published books in the late 1940's sharply at variance with their views of a few years later. Hofstadter, for example, ended his introduction to *The American Political Tradition* (New York: Knopf, 1948) by defending himself against "pietistic biographers" of our national heroes. "A democratic society, in any case," he wrote (p. xi), "can more safely be overcritical than overindulgent in its attitude toward public leadership." Seven years later, Hofstadter focused on the dangerous American tendency to be suspicious of power and overcritical of political leadership. Similarly, Lipset's first book, *Agrarian Socialism* (Berkeley, Calif.: University of California Press, 1950), like Philip Selznick's first book, *TVA and the Grass Roots* (Berkeley, Calif.: University of California Press, 1949), is not concerned with the threat to stability posed by mass movements. Lipset and Selznick rather focus on the power that narrow groups have to erode the influence of mass movements and prevent the realization of broad goals.
2. Compare Hofstadter's treatment of Bryan in *The American Political Tradition, op. cit.,* pp. 186–205, with his analysis of Populism seven years later.
3. Edward Shils, *The Torment of Secrecy* (Glencoe, Ill.: Free Press, 1956), pp. 38–41, 46, 98–108, 169–184; William Kornhauser, *The Politics of Mass Society* (Glencoe, Ill.: Free Press, 1959), pp. 59–60, 102–103, 131–134.
4. Others not concerned with McCarthyism and agrarian radicalism have also called themselves pluralists. Most notable are those political scientists whose pluralism derives primarily from their attention to local politics. Although their pluralism has some points of contact with the doctrine developed here, they are not the main focus of attention: Cf. Robert Dahl, *Who Governs* (New Haven, Conn.: Yale University Press, 1961); Nelson Polsby, "How to Study Community Power: The Pluralist Alternative," *Journal of Politics,* Vol. 22 (August 1960); Edward Banfield, *Political Influence* (New York: Free Press of Glencoe, 1961); James Q. Wilson, *The Amateur Democrat* (Chicago: University of Chicago Press, 1962).
5. For a list of pluralist writings, see the Introduction, note 3. Cf. also Gabriel Almond, "Comparative Political Systems," *Journal of Politics,* Vol. 18 (August 1956), pp. 391–409; Emil Lederer, *The State of the Masses* (New York: Norton, 1940). Let me stress that the pluralist writers have a variety of different emphases. Shils, for example, is relatively less interested in groups

and more interested in broad traditions. Lipset has a Marxist heritage and retains an interest in class analysis. Viereck, although his objections to mass movements are pluralist, relies for an alternative not on groups but on a substantively conservative and elitist tradition.

6. I would be the last to deny that modern pluralists value liberty. Their very concern with stability is to safeguard individual freedom. But their interest in the freedom of the nongroup member and in the problem of freedom within the group is minimal. Because the pluralists are so quick to see dangers to stability, their concern for liberty in practice can become secondary. Thus for the authors of *The New American Right,* the great danger of McCarthyism was its attack on social stability. The damage done to innocent individuals received much less notice.

7. José Ortega y Gasset, *The Revolt of the Masses* (New York: New American Library, Mentor Book).

8. Cf. Edward Shils, "Daydreams and Nightmares: Reflections on the Criticism of Mass Culture," *The Sewanee Review,* Vol. 54 (1957), pp. 587–608; Daniel Bell, "The Theory of the Mass Society," *Commentary,* Vol. 22 (July 1956), pp. 75–83.

9. José Ortega y Gasset, *The Revolt of the Masses, op. cit.,* p. 35.

10. Ortega, *ibid.* (p. 84) wrote, "America is the paradise of the masses." On the relation between the two theories of mass society, cf. William Kornhauser, *The Politics of Mass Society, op. cit.,* pp. 15–37. For pluralist defenses of industrialization, cf. William Kornhauser, *ibid.,* p. 231; S. M. Lipset, *Political Man* (Garden City, N.Y.: Doubleday, 1960), pp. 45–76; and Daniel Bell, *The End of Ideology* (Glencoe, Ill.: Free Press, 1959), pp. 372–375. An excellent discussion of the relation between pluralism and industrialization is Ludwig Mahler, "Ideology and History in America," *New Politics,* Vol. 1 (Fall 1961). Many pluralists are friendly to Britain because of its preindustrial (aristocratic) elements. But they tend to believe that increased industrialization will dissolve the problems exacerbated on the continent by the early stages of industrialization. They believe that, in the protection of constitutional stability, mature industrialism is the functional equivalent of the British aristocratic tradition.

11. I have selected from Weber's total view those aspects most congenial to pluralism. Weber himself was by no means completely happy about the demystification of the world. See, for example, "Politics as a Vocation," in H. H. Gerth and C. Wright Mills (eds.), *From Max Weber: Essays in Sociology* (New York: Galaxy Books, 1958).

12. Cf. Joseph Talmon, *The Origins of Totalitarian Democracy* (London: Secker and Warburg, 1952).

13. Emile Durkheim, *The Division of Labor in Society* (Glencoe, Ill.: Free Press, 1947). See especially, "The Anomic Division of Labor," pp. 343–373.
14. David B. Truman, *The Governmental Process* (New York: Knopf, 1951). Adam Smith's political views are far more complex than the brief references in the text imply.
15. William Kornhauser, *The Politics of Mass Society, op. cit.*, pp. 43–49.
16. Daniel Bell, "Interpretations of American Politics," in Daniel Bell (ed.), *The New American Right* (New York: Criterion Books, 1955), pp. 25–28.
17. S. M. Lipset, "The Sources of the Radical Right," and Richard Hofstadter, "The Pseudo-Conservative Revolt," in Daniel Bell (ed.), *The New American Right, op. cit.*, p. 168 and pp. 43–45.
18. T. W. Adorno *et al.*, *The Authoritarian Personality* (New York: Harper, 1950).
19. S. M. Lipset, *Political Man* (Garden City, N.Y.: Doubleday, 1960), pp. 97–130. Lipset does recognize the importance of nonpsychological variables (see later). Note also Bell's friendly treatment of psychological explanations of Soviet behavior in *End of Ideology, op. cit.*, pp. 310–320. In *The Age of Reform* (New York: Knopf, 1955), pp. 23–93, Richard Hofstadter analyzes farmer psychology to explain the meaning of Populist political activity. In all three cases, the influence of social conditions is crucially mediated through psychological malformations.
20. Edward Shils, "Authoritarianism: Right and Left," in Richard Christie and Marie Jahoda (eds.), *Studies in the Scope and Method of Authoritarian Personality* (Glencoe, Ill.: Free Press, 1954), pp. 43–45.
21. Richard Hofstadter, *Age of Reform* (New York: Knopf, 1955), pp. 137, 144–153, 215–216; David Riesman and Nathan Glazer, "The Intellectuals and the Discontented Classes," in Daniel Bell (ed.), *The New American Right, op. cit.*, pp. 58–63. For a pluralist critique of policy made out of the jumble of special interests, cf. Daniel Bell, "The Three Faces of New York," in *Dissent,* Vol. 8 (Spring 1961), pp. 230–232.
22. Cf. Richard Hofstadter, "The Pseudo-Conservative Revolt" and Talcott Parsons, "Social Strains in America" in *The New American Right, op. cit.*, p. 53 and p. 139; Edward Shils, *The Torment of Secrecy* (Glencoe, Ill.: Free Press, 1956), pp. 48–49.
23. William Kornhauser, *The Politics of Mass Society, op. cit.*, p. 44.
24. *Ibid.*, pp. 43–44.
25. *Ibid.*, pp. 43–49.
26. Emil Lederer, *The State of the Masses, op. cit.*, pp. 17–31.
27. Cf. Bernard R. Berelson *et al.*, *Voting* (Chicago: University of Chicago Press, 1954), pp. 19–20, 27, 129–132, 283–285; Angus

Campbell, *The Voter Decides* (Evanston, Ill.: Row, Peterson, 1954), pp. 130–132, 157–164, 202–203.

28. Angus Campbell, *ibid.*, pp. 130–132, 157–164, 202–203.

29. Stanley Rothman, "Systematic Political Theory: Observations on the Group Approach," *American Political Science Review*, Vol. 54 (March 1960), p. 22.

30. Robert Michels, *Political Parties* (Glencoe, Ill.: Free Press, 1949 [First published 1915]).

31. The influence of the study by Samuel Stouffer, *Communism, Conformity, and Civil Liberties* (Garden City, N.Y.: Doubleday, 1955) has been crucial. It should be noted, however, that Lipset and Glazer have written a critique of this study. They point out that many factors intervene between the expression of an attitude and its translation into action. Cf. Nathan Glazer and S. M. Lipset, "The Polls on Communism and Conformity," in Daniel Bell (ed.), *The New American Right, op. cit.*

32. For example, cf. S. M. Lipset, "The Political Process in Trade Unions: A Theoretical Statement," in Walter Galenson and S. M. Lipset (eds.), *Labor and Trade Unionism* (New York: Wiley, 1960), pp. 238–239; S. M. Lipset, *New Politics*, Vol. 2 (Fall 1962), pp. 148–149.

Union Democracy, by Lipset, Martin Trow, and James Coleman, applies pluralist analysis to the internal structure of a voluntary association and defends a stable system of elite competition (democracy) within the International Typographical Union. But the authors conclude that the factors producing democracy within the I.T.U. are not duplicated in most other voluntary associations, that complex unions could not survive and be effective without an oligarchy controlling membership conflicts, and that the members would abridge minority rights more than the leadership. Cf. Seymour Martin Lipset, Martin Trow, and James Coleman, *Union Democracy* (Garden City, N.Y.: Doubleday, 1962), pp. 15, 89–90, 338–339, 346–347.

33. Stanley Rothman, *loc. cit;* Joseph R. Gusfield, "Mass Society and Extremist Politics," *American Sociological Review*, Vol. 27 (February 1962), p. 29.

34. Hofstadter, *Age of Reform, op. cit.*, pp. 10–21, 303–324, especially pp. 315–316.

35. Writing in 1963, Bell noted that McCarthyism had not been an organized movement but an "atmosphere of fear." From the pluralist point of view, if McCarthyism was not a mass movement it nevertheless generated mass appeals. Cf. Daniel Bell, "The Dispossessed," in Daniel Bell (ed.), *The Radical Right* (Garden City, N.Y.: Doubleday, 1963), p. 4.

36. Cf. C. Vann Woodward, "The Populist Heritage and the Intellectual," *American Scholar*, Vol. 29 (Winter 1959), p. 61.

37. Daniel Bell, "The Dispossessed," in Daniel Bell (ed.), *The Radical Right, op. cit.*, pp. 2–3, 22.

38. In addition to the works cited in note 3 of the "Introduction," cf. Angus Campbell *et al.*, *The American Voter* (New York: Wiley, 1960), pp. 425–440; Leslie A. Fiedler, "McCarthy," *Encounter*, Vol. 3 (August 1954), pp. 10–21; Victor C. Ferkiss, "The Populist Influences on American Fascism," *Western Political Quarterly*, Vol. 10 (June 1957), pp. 350–373: Victor C. Ferkiss, "Populism: Myth, Reality, Current Danger," *Western Political Quarterly*, Vol. 14 (September 1961), pp. 737–740.

39. In a limited sense, this interpretation can be used to relate agrarian radicalism to McCarthy's strength among urban workers. This support showed up in nationwide survey data and in Trow's study of support for McCarthy in Bennington, Vermont. Workers are not farmers, but their support for McCarthy could have been analogous to rural support for agrarian radicalism. Trow suggested that pro-McCarthy workers, motivated by status envy, found sustenance in McCarthy's attack on prestigious persons and institutions. At the bottom of the industrial hierarchy, many workers resented the whole structure. This is an urban form of "status politics," of which agrarian radicalism could be a rural counterpart. Cf. Martin A. Trow, "Right-Wing Radicalism and Political Intolerance: A Study of Support for McCarthy in a New England Town," unpublished Ph.D. dissertation, Department of Political Science, Columbia University, 1957, p. 212.

40. S. M. Lipset, *Political Man, op. cit.*, pp. 131–133.

41. *Ibid.*, p. 140.

42. Martin Trow, pp. 23–29. Trow summarizes his important findings in "Small Business, Political Tolerance, and Support for McCarthy," *American Journal of Sociology*, Vol. 44 (November 1958), pp. 270–281. Lipset used Trow's data alone to justify his assertion that opinion surveys supported the fact "that McCarthy appealed to the same social groups as did 'left-wing' populism." Lipset, *Political Man, op. cit.*, pp. 168–169. However, more recent data reported by Lipset for a nationwide sample found no association between "nineteenth century liberalism" and support for McCarthy. The data did provide further evidence of small business support for the Wisconsin senator. Cf., Seymour Martin Lipset, "Three Decades of the Radical Right: Coughlinites, McCarthyites, and Birchers," in Daniel Bell (ed.), *The Radical Right, op. cit.*, pp. 333–336, 340–341.

43. See the works cited in note 38 of this chapter and note 3 of the "Introduction."

Chapter Two

1. Cf. David E. Apter, "The Role of Traditionalism in the Political Modernization of Ghana and Uganda," *World Politics*, Vol. 13 (October 1960), pp. 45–68.

2. Here should be noted the pervasive influence of Daniel J. Boorstin, *The Genius of American Politics* (Chicago: University of Chicago Press, 1953). Starting from Boorstin's analysis of the pragmatic character of the American consensus, one can either interpret the reform movements as ideological exceptions or absorb them into American politics alongside the various interest groups.

3. Cf. Talcott Parsons, *Structure and Process in Modern Societies* (Glencoe, Ill.: Free Press, 1960), pp. 173–174; Seymour Martin Lipset, "A Changing American Character," in Seymour Martin Lipset and Leo Lowenthal (eds.), *Culture and Social Character* (Glencoe, Ill.: Free Press, 1961). Lipset quotes Hofstadter in support of his point of view, p. 161.

4. Cf. Norman Pollack, "Hofstadter on Populism: A Critique of the Age of Reform," *Journal of Southern History*, Vol. 26 (November 1960).

5. Alexis de Tocqueville, *Democracy in America*, Vol. 1 (New York: Vintage Books, 1960), p. 266.

6. Louis Hartz, *The Liberal Tradition in America* (New York: Harcourt, Brace, 1955).

7. A politics of narrow self-interest is certainly possible without a consensus and can even flourish in the absence of one. The politics of *interesse* in southern Italy is a good example. But a society with such politics cannot begin to solve its problems and is only kept from entirely flying apart by externally imposed force. Cf. Edward Banfield, *The Moral Basis of a Backward Society* (Glencoe, Ill.: Free Press, 1958). Again in France, the politics of narrow favors (*incivisme*) is only the other side of the coin of fundamental social conflict. Since politics cannot solve problems, individuals seek only narrow favors from the state. American politics is distinguished from French not by its pragmatism but by the agreement on ends which makes that pragmatism workable.

8. Take the following example: I have been suggesting that the politics of American reform came out of the same American consensus that produced the economic actions of capitalists. It is currently fashionable to stress the guilt-ridden character of reformers as evidence that they were not concerned with reform but with expiation of their guilt. But guilt and concern with results are not mutually exclusive. Capitalists, too, were motivated by guilt. As their spokesman Elbert Hubbard put it, "Life without industry is guilt." But capitalist guilt meant a frenetic concern with results. One should not assume that, in the shift to politics, concern with results disappeared. The important question is not so much whether reformers were guilt-ridden as what changes were required to assuage their guilt.

9. Cf. Max Weber, *The Protestant Ethic and the Spirit of Capitalism* (New York: Scribner's, 1958), p. 105.

10. Cf. Sven Ranulf, *Moral Indignation and Middle Class Psychol-*

ogy (Copenhagen: Levin and Munkegaard, 1938), pp. 60–95. There is limited survey evidence supporting the authoritarianism of those with a commitment to puritan ideology. Gwynn Nettler reasoned that the belief in individual responsibility for actions was a Puritan notion that indicated punitive attitudes. On a questionnaire administered to social workers, belief in individual responsibility was related to the measures of authoritarianism utilized in *The Authoritarian Personality* and related studies. Cf. Gwynn Nettler, "Cruelty, Dignity, and Determinism," *American Sociological Review*, Vol. 24 (June 1959), pp. 375–384. The special nature of the population sampled may, however, vitiate the significance of this finding.

11. In the *Second Treatise*, Locke seems to justify private property by the fact that great inequality will not exist, since no one is entitled to more than he can use before it spoils. But a few pages later, by the characteristically Lockean democratic myth of tacit consent, he introduces the use of money. This destroys his own limit on wealth. Cf. John Locke, *Of Civil Government* (New York: Dutton, Everyman's Library), pp. 131, 139–140.

12. Daniel J. Boorstin, *The Lost World of Thomas Jefferson* (New York: Henry Holt, 1948), pp. 43, 139.

13. C. Wright Mills makes a similar point, namely that the freedom and rationality which had been united in eighteenth and nineteenth century thought split apart under the impact of a bureaucratic society. Rationality became located in large institutions, from where it challenged both the freedom and the rationality of the individual. Cf. C. Wright Mills, *White Collar* (New York: Oxford, 1956), p. xvii.

14. Cf. Joseph A. Schumpeter, *Capitalism, Socialism, and Democracy* (New York: Harper, 1950), pp. 81–106.

15. Antiauthoritarian attitudes on survey questionnaires always express the optimistic side of the equation. Often, indeed, the optimism is unwarranted (Does the average man really have a lot to say about what goes on in Washington?). But it is nevertheless antiauthoritarian. The Stouffer study is instructive here. The greater the fear of an internal Communist threat, the lower the political tolerance. Cf. Samuel A. Stouffer, *Communism, Conformity and Civil Liberties* (Garden City, N.Y.: Doubleday, 1955), pp. 188–210. For a discussion of the consequences of "realistic" attitudes, considering the character of the American consensus, see Chapter 9.

16. Cf. Marvin Meyers, *The Jacksonian Persuasion* (New York: Vintage Books, 1960); David W. Noble, *The Paradox of Progressive Thought* (Minneapolis, Minn.: University of Minnesota Press, 1958).

17. Cf. Sidney Fine, *Laissez-Faire and the General Welfare State* (Ann Arbor, Mich.: University of Michigan Press, 1956); Robert Green McCloskey, *American Conservatism in an Age*

of Enterprise (Cambridge, Mass.: Harvard University Press, 1951); Benjamin R. Twiss, *Lawyers and the Constitution* (Princeton, N.J.: Princeton University Press, 1942); Richard Hofstadter, *Social Darwinism in American Thought* (Boston: Beacon Press, 1955).

18. On the latter question, cf. Reinhard Bendix, *Work and Authority in Industry* (New York: Wiley, 1956), pp. 254–340.

19. On this last point, Adams, for example, wrote, "There is no special providence for Americans, and their nature is the same with that of others." Cf. *Works of John Adams* (Boston: Little, Brown, 6 vols., 1851–1865), Vol. 4, p. 401. Indeed, it is instructive to compare Adams on this point with Jefferson. Later in the *Defense* (at p. 487), Adams continued, "In the present state of society and manners in America, with a people living chiefly by agriculture, in small numbers, sprinkled over large tracts of land, they are not subject to those panics and transports, those contagions of madness and folly, which are seen in countries where large numbers live in small places in daily fear of perishing for want. We know, therefore, that the people can live and increase under almost any kind of government, or without any government at all. But it is of great importance to begin well; misarrangements now made will have great, extensive, and distant consequences; and we are now employed, how little so ever we may think it, in making establishments which will affect the happiness of a hundred millions of inhabitants at a time in a period not very distant."

For Adams, Americans must create a government that would have to work when America became like Europe. In letters to Madison and Adams twenty-five years apart, Jefferson expressed a consistently different view. Indeed, in the second letter he looked forward to a time when Europe, becoming like America, could enjoy the advantages of our uniquely American form of government: "Educate and inform the whole mass of the people . . . they are the only sure reliance for the preservation of our liberty. . . . This reliance cannot deceive us, as long as we remain virtuous; and I think we shall be so, as long as agriculture is our principal object, which will be the case, while there remain vacant lands in any part of America. When we get piled together upon one another in large cities, as in Europe, we shall become corrupt as in Europe, and go to eating one another as they do there." And again: "Before the establishment of the American states, nothing was known to history but the men of the old world crowded within limits either small or overcharged, and steeped in the vices which that situation generates. A government adapted to such men would be one thing; but a very different one, that for the man of these states. . . . Everyone by his property, or by his satisfactory situation, is interested in the support of law and order. And such men may

299

safely and advantageously reserve to themselves a wholesome control over their public affairs, and a degree of freedom, which, in the hands of the *canaille* of the cities of Europe, would be instantly perverted to the demolition and destruction of everything public and private. . . . But even in Europe a change has sensibly taken place in the mind of man." (Cf. *The Life and Selected Writings of Thomas Jefferson*, Adrienne Koch and William Pedan (eds.) (New York: Random House, 1944), pp. 440–441, 633.)

The view of the Federalists adopted here follows Louis Hartz, *The Liberal Tradition in America, op. cit.,* pp. 70–86. For confirmation from Adams' writings of the specific points made, cf. *Works of John Adams, op. cit.,* "A Dissertation on the Canon and Feudal Law," Vol. 3, pp. 449, 450–451, 454, 463–464; "Thoughts on Government," Vol. 4, pp. 193–196; "The Report of a Constitution or Form of Government for the Commonwealth of Massachusetts," Vol. 4, pp. 219–225; "A Defense . . . ," Vol. 4, pp. 283–286, 292–293, 297–298, Vol. 6, pp. 50–62, 218; "Discourses on Davila," Vol. 6, pp. 232–237; "Letters to John Taylor," Vol. 6, pp. 457–458.

20. The natural harmony Jefferson saw in society and the artificial harmony Madison thought to create through politics are not very different. For the European analogue cf. Elie Halevy, *The Growth of Philosophic Radicalism* (Boston: Beacon Press, 1955), pp. 15–19.

21. On Adams and lions, cf. *Works of John Adams, op. cit.,* Vol. 4, p. 287. Consider also Madison's famous refusal, in *Federalist No. 10,* to assign to every citizen "the same opinions, the same passions and the same interests." Since Madison believed the causes of faction were inevitable, he relied on size and diversity to mitigate its effects. In fact, Americans had more homogeneous opinions, passions, and interests than he realized. Had Madison not ignored the Lockean consensus and exaggerated the majoritarian threat to property rights, his solution to the problem of faction would have been precarious indeed. In perceiving the unique character of America, Jefferson the idealist was more realistic than Madison (see note 19 of this chapter).

22. Cf. Seymour Martin Lipset and Paul Seabury, "The Lesson of Berkeley" and Nathan Glazer, "What Happened at Berkeley," in Seymour Martin Lipset and Sheldon S. Wolin (eds.), *The Berkeley Student Revolt* (Garden City, N.Y.: Doubleday Anchor, 1965), pp. 285–303 and 340–349; James F. Petras and Michael Shute, "Berkeley '65," *Partisan Review,* Vol. 32 (Spring 1965), pp. 314–323.

23. Particularly interesting sources here are Marvin Meyers, *The Jacksonian Persuasion* (New York: Vintage Books, 1960), pp.

234–275; and Stanley Elkins, *Slavery* (Chicago: University of Chicago Press, 1959).

24. America does have a patrician-in-politics tradition, but the patricians have had to couch their political appeal in democratic terms. Moreover, at the turn of the century the big business elite was not yet sufficiently established to produce its own patricians. One need only compare Nelson Rockefeller with John, Henry Ford II with Henry Ford I, and the Carnegie foundation with Andrew Carnegie. Influential Republican patricians at the turn of the century tended, like Henry Cabot Lodge, to be similar to other conservative Republicans — or else they were themselves progressives.

25. Cf. Louis Hartz, *The Liberal Tradition in America, op. cit.,* pp. 89–113.

26. Lee Benson, *The Concept of Jacksonian Democracy* (Princeton, N.J.: Princeton University Press, 1961), p. 10. Cf. in addition pp. 11–54, 86–106, and Louis Hartz, *Economic Policy and Democratic Thought: Pennsylvania, 1776–1860* (Cambridge, Mass.: Harvard University Press, 1948).

27. Andrew Carnegie, *Triumphant Democracy* (New York: Scribner's, 1887), pp. 5–6.

28. Louis Hartz, *The Liberal Tradition in America, op. cit.,* pp. 203–227. The whole treatment of conservatism here owes much to Hartz.

29. Philip Selznick, *T.V.A. and the Grass Roots* (Berkeley, Calif.: University of California Press, 1949).

30. When one notes the brilliant use conservatives have made of an apparently democratic rhetoric, it is most difficult to argue that these "leftist values" have placed American conservatives on the defensive. The ideology of democratic capitalism has been at least as friendly to conservative as to liberal ends. But cf. Seymour Martin Lipset, *Political Man* (Garden City, N.Y.: Doubleday Anchor, 1963), pp. xxi, xxv.

31. Cf. Lee Benson, *The Concept of Jacksonian Democracy, op. cit.;* Louis Hartz, *Economic Policy and Democratic Thought, op. cit.,* p. 309 and *passim.*

32. Cf. Sidney Fine, *Laissez-Faire and the General Welfare State, op. cit.,* pp. 3–29, 96–125; Louis Hartz, *Economic Policy and Democratic Thought, op. cit.,* pp. 3–33, 289–320.

33. B. R. Twiss, *Lawyers and the Constitution, op. cit.,* p. 158.

34. There is no intent to accuse all conservatives of failing to appreciate the importance of shared power. But the tenor of the ideology is not as moderate as might first appear.

35. B. R. Twiss, *Lawyers and the Constitution, op. cit.,* p. 114.

36. *Ibid.,* pp. 197–198. Note that lawyers have often been referred to since de Tocqueville as the aristocracy of America. Moreover, modern critiques of Populism emphasize antagonism to lawyers as a revealingly irrational aspect of Populist ideology.

301

37. *Hammer* v. *Dagenhard;* 247 U.S. 251.
38. Andrew Carnegie, *Triumphant Democracy, op. cit.,* p. 48.
39. This has often been noted. For an excellent analysis of the industrializing ideology of Britain, cf. Reinhard Bendix, *Work and Authority in Industry, op. cit.,* pp. 22–116.
40. Andrew Carnegie, *Triumphant Democracy, op. cit.,* pp. 281–282.
41. William G. Cornwall, *Free Coinage from the Businessman's Standpoint* (Buffalo, N.Y.: Matthews-Northrup Co., 1891), pp. 7–8.
42. Henry Cabot Lodge, "The Meaning of the Votes," *North American Review,* Vol. 164 (January 1897), p. 2. Fear of the anarchist "conspiracy" dominated conservative thinking. Recall conservative reaction to the trial of the Haymarket anarchists and also the attitude toward the Pullman boycott and other labor union activity.
43. Walter R. Nugent, "Populism and Nativism in Kansas, 1888–1900" (unpublished Ph.D. dissertation, Department of History, University of Chicago, 1961), p. 37n (now published as *The Tolerant Populists* [Chicago: University of Chicago Press, 1963]). For further evidence of anti-Populist conservative hysteria, cf. Norman Pollack, *The Populist Response to Industrial America* (Cambridge, Mass.: Harvard University Press, 1962), pp. 129 ff.
44. Robert L. Morlan, *Political Prairie Fire* (Minneapolis, Minn.: University of Minnesota Press, 1955), pp. 61, 68, 103.
45. *The Authoritarian Personality,* quoted by Richard Hofstadter, "The Pseudo-Conservative Revolt," in Daniel Bell (ed.), *The New American Right* (New York: Criterion Books, 1955), p. 35.

Chapter Three

1. Peter Viereck, "The Revolt Against the Elite," in Daniel Bell (ed.), *The New American Right* (New York: Criterion Books, 1955), pp. 93–95, 112.
2. Cf. Leon D. Epstein, *Politics in Wisconsin* (Madison, Wis.: University of Wisconsin Press, 1958), Chapter 1.
3. The seminal works here are Samuel Lubell, *The Future of American Politics* (New York: Harper, 1952), pp. 129–157; V. O. Key, Jr., and Frank Munger, "Social Determinism and Electoral Decision, The Case of Indiana," in Eugene Burdick and Arthur J. Brodbeck (eds.), *American Voting Behavior* (Glencoe, Ill.: Free Press, 1955).
4. A factor analysis was also carried out for a table of correlation coefficients of North Dakota elections from 1889 to 1928. This method is explained in Chapter 4 and Appendix B.
5. State Representative Hall and the remnants of Populist leadership in northern Wisconsin were closely associated with La Follette after 1900. Cf. Robert S. Maxwell, *La Follette and the*

Rise of the Progressives in Wisconsin (Madison, Wis.: State Historical Society of Wisconsin, 1956), p. 58.

6. Donald R. McCoy, "The Development and Dissolution of the Wisconsin Progressive Party of 1934–1946" (unpublished Master's thesis, Department of Political Science, University of Chicago, 1949), p. 19.

7. In this period, the progressive vote correlated only .22 with the percentage rural-farm, as the economics of sectional politics overcame rural-urban divisions in the state as a whole.

8. The major exception is 1926, when progressive Blaine attracted German support with a probeer platform.

9. Harold F. Gosnell, *Grass Roots Politics* (Washington, D. C.: American Council on Public Affairs, 1942), pp. 55–56.

10. Nevertheless, one should not ignore working-class support for progressivism before the depression both in Wisconsin and other states. As early as 1920 Wisconsin progressive Blaine ran best in farm villages and working-class wards, although the German factor may explain the working-class vote. In Minnesota, Farmer-Labor candidate Shipstead got farm and labor support in 1920 and his major opposition came from the small towns. In the years after 1920, the Minnesota Farmer-Labor Party was strongest in the cities. Finally, workers in Iowa supported insurgent Smith Brookhart in 1920. Cf. Stuart A. Rice, *Farmers and Workers in American Politics* (New York: Columbia University Press, 1924), pp. 153–163; Murray S. Stedman and Susan W. Stedman, *Discontent at the Polls* (New York: Columbia University Press, 1950), p. 138; Jerry Alvin Neprash, *The Brookhart Campaigns in Iowa, 1920–26* (New York: Columbia University Press, 1932), pp. 76–78.

11. Samuel Lubell, *The Future of American Politics* (New York: Harper, 1952), pp. 144–145.

12. The 1942 Progressive vote for governor was a deviant election. It has a closer relation to the warborn progressive vote of 1918–1930 than to the progressive vote of the depression. Like that earlier progressivism, it was unrelated to the modern Democratic vote.

13. For other evidence of a nonethnic isolationist tradition, cf. Ralph M. Smuckler, "The Region of Isolation," *American Political Science Review,* Vol. 47 (June 1953), and the reply in Samuel Lubell, *The Revolt of the Moderates* (New York: Harper, 1956).

14. Richard Hofstadter, *The Age of Reform* (New York: Knopf, 1955), pp. 298–299; Samuel Lubell, *The Future of American Politics, op. cit.,* pp. 3, 34–39.

15. Richard Hofstadter, *The Age of Reform, op. cit.,* p. 298. In fact, the German components of the two votes made them fairly similar. Indeed, Hofstadter recognized the German support for both candidates. The implication is that when the Germans voted for La Follette in 1924 they were voting their reaction to

the war rather than "genuine" liberalism, but when they voted for Smith in 1928 they were pragmatic precursors of the New Deal (cf. pp. 281, 296–299).

16. Samuel Lubell, *The Future of American Politics, op. cit.,* pp. 34–39 and *passim;* V. O. Key, Jr., "A Theory of Critical Elections," *Journal of Politics,* Vol. 17 (February 1955), pp. 4–11; Duncan MacRae, Jr., and James A. Meldrum, "Critical Elections in Illinois: 1888–1958," *American Political Science Review,* Vol. 54 (September 1960), pp. 678–681.

17. Lipset has pointed out to me that La Follette, as the most outspoken anti-Klan candidate, also received substantial Catholic backing.

18. Baggaley has shown that the Catholic and anti-Catholic votes were bigger factors in the Smith election than in the Kennedy vote but that the religious issue was still very important in 1960. Cf. Andrew R. Baggaley, "Religious Influence on Wisconsin Voting, 1928–1960," *American Political Science Review,* Vol. 56 (March 1962), pp. 66–70.

19. H. F. Gosnell, *Grass Roots Politics, op. cit.,* pp. 54–56.

20. Progressive James Thompson's 1918 vote, which had revealed German sensitivity to the war, was highly related to Roosevelt's 1936 vote and Wilkie's 1940 vote. Note that the 1948 Republican vote was actually slightly more German than the vote in 1940 (.52 to .48), indicating no tendency for Germans to return to the Democratic Party after the war.

21. The first Democratic election to be positively related to the modern Democratic vote was the Wilson election of 1916. Wilson is supposed to reflect the old party politics and Smith the new, but Wilson's vote was more clearly a precursor of the modern Democratic vote than Smith's.

   The Wilson election aside, the modern party vote is closer to the pre- than to the post-Bryan party vote. Again, this pattern began not with Smith but with the vote for Coolidge in 1924.

22. Since the German counties in Wisconsin tend also to be the most highly industrialized, the relationship between class, ethnicity, and the party vote is not a simple one. The percentage of Germans in 1930 and the percentage Republican in 1948 were related .52 and the percentage Republican and the percentage in manufacturing —.17. But with German background held constant, this relationship jumped to —.44. The relationship between German background and the Republican vote with manufacturing held constant was .63 — as high as 1906 but with the sign reversed. Baggaley found a correlation of .95 between the percentage of white-collar workers and the 1954 Republican vote in Milwaukee's wards.

   Epstein has shown that the Democratic Party is strongest in cities with more than 50,000 people and weakest in cities and villages below 10,000. Showing that workers in large cities are more likely to vote Democratic than workers in small cities, he argues that size itself creates a diversity that permits a break with a Republican past. This seems plausible; ethnic analysis might help explain the data. Cf. Andrew R. Baggaley, "White Collar Employment and the Republican Vote," *Public Opinion Quarterly,* Vol. 20 (Summer 1956), pp. 471–473; Leon Epstein, *Politics in Wisconsin, op. cit.,* pp. 58–70.

23. The average county vote for McCarthy was 62.6 percent. The twenty-six counties high on the 1904 La Follette index gave McCarthy 60.4 percent of their votes.

24. In 1950, Len Schmitt, an old Progressive, ran against Walter Kohler in the Republican gubernatorial primary. Seven years later, northern Wisconsin Congressman O'Konski, a demagogic and illiberal agrarian radical, ran in the Republican primary which was to choose a successor to McCarthy. Both these men got virtually all their support from northern Wisconsin. Proxmire's vote correlated .5 with both, but these primary votes were unrelated to the vote in the 1952 senatorial election (see Table 3.5).

25. The formula for these computations is $(M - R) - (m - \bar{r})$. A numerical example may make the process clearer. Let us say county Z was 4 percent above the state average for Republican governor in 1950, 8 percent above for Eisenhower, and 3 percent below for Dewey. Its average Republican strength would then be $+3$. If county Z was 6 percent above the state average for McCarthy, its score on the McCarthy index would be $6 - 3$, or 3.

In his analysis of McCarthy's strength in 1952, Louis Bean compares McCarthy's strength with his showing in 1946. However, three regular Republican elections in which McCarthy was not involved give a better indication of the regular Republican vote than one election in which the Senator was involved. Bean's findings in part support and in no case successfully contradict the findings reported here. Cf. Louis Bean, *Influences in the 1954 Mid-Term Elections* (Washington, D. C.: Public Affairs Institute, 1954), pp. 10–16, 37–41.

26. The other three Catholic counties contained cities of more than 10,000 population, while less than half of the twelve did.

27. The tenth county was Dane county in the south, home of La Follette and of the University of Wisconsin. Dane county supported McCarthy in 1944 not on a "friends-and-neighbors" basis but because McCarthy's opponent was an antiprogressive. It voted strongly against McCarthy in 1952, opposing him slightly more than it opposed other Republicans. Thus, the one county that supported McCarthy in 1944 but not in 1952 was the home of the La Follette movement.

28. James G. March, "McCarthy Can Still Be Beaten," *Reporter,* Vol. 7 (October 22, 1952), pp. 17–19.

29. The percentages are the averages of ward totals in each CD and

are not the same as the direct popular vote. Unfortunately, ward lines in Milwaukee were not redrawn to conform to the 1950 census until after 1952, so it is difficult to identify working- and middle-class wards.

30. Note that only one progressive county that was not also either a Catholic, Czech, or "friends-and-neighbors" county was in the more pro-McCarthy of the two groups on the scatter diagram demonstrating the relationship between industrialization and McCarthyism. Progressive counties supported McCarthy in proportion to their ruralness, not out of proportion to it.

The Proxmire election produces similar evidence. We have seen that both Proxmire and McCarthy deviated from the traditional party vote in a progressive direction. Here again the explanation appears to be the common rural support they attracted rather than any particular progressive appeal. The counties shifting most radically from McCarthy to Proxmire were disproportionately rural, but the rural corn belt counties were more prominent in this group than were ex-progressive counties.

31. There is a possible ambiguity here. There were many more progressive than Czechoslovakian counties in the state. A slight tendency for progressive counties disproportionately to support McCarthy might have a greater total effect than a stronger tendency confined to the few Czech counties. My point is that the source of pressure to support McCarthy was apparently weakest in the progressive case.

32. Trow, "Right-Wing Radicalism and Political Intolerance: A Study of Support for McCarthy in a New England Town" (unpublished Ph.D. dissertation, Department of Political Science, Columbia University, 1957), pp. 41–45, 153–166.

33. Talcott Parsons, "Social Strains in America," in Daniel Bell (ed.), *The New American Right, op. cit.,* pp. 136–137.

34. David Riesman and Nathan Glazer, "The Intellectuals and the Discontented Classes," in Daniel Bell (ed.), *The New American Right, op. cit.,* pp. 70–71.

35. Nelson W. Polsby, "Toward an Explanation of McCarthyism," *Political Studies,* Vol. 8 (October 1960), p. 257.

36. Cf. Edgar A. Schuler and Carl C. Taylor, "Farm People's Attitudes and Opinions," in Carl C. Taylor *et al., Rural Life in the United States* (New York: Knopf, 1949), p. 505.

37. The correlations between his vote and progressive elections ran from —.3 to —.5.

38. The correlations run from .3 to .5; his relation to McCarthy's vote in the general election was no higher. Davis was stronger in German than in Scandinavian counties, though within each group there was no relation between ethnicity and the vote.

39. Cf. James Q. Wilson, *The Amateur Democrat* (Chicago: University of Chicago Press, 1962), p. 267.

40. Samuel Lubell, *The Future of American Politics, op. cit.*, p. 143.
41. Lemke did get 20 percent of the vote in a heavily German, Catholic town in Fond du Lac county in southeastern Wisconsin. Since this town responded sharply to both world wars, the German rather than the Catholic factor may well explain the high Lemke vote. Cf. Baggaley, "Religious Influence on Wisconsin Voting, 1928–1960," *op. cit.*, p. 70.

Chapter Four

1. Howard G. Williams, "Nye — A Lost Leader," *Nation,* Vol. 158 (June 24, 1947), p. 730.
2. Ross B. Talbot, "The North Dakota Farmers Union and North Dakota Politics," *Western Political Quarterly,* Vol. 10 (December 1957), pp. 879–880.
3. Peter Viereck, "The Revolt Against the Elite," in Daniel Bell (ed.), *The New American Right* (New York: Criterion Books, 1955), p. 94. Lipset recognizes the role foreign policy played in the switch. But in more cautious language than Viereck, he suggests that "liberal isolationists" now vote for "right-wing nationalists." As I suggest later, this oversimplifies and distorts the evolution. Cf. S. M. Lipset, "The Sources of the 'Radical Right,'" in Daniel Bell (ed.), *The New American Right, op. cit.*, p. 191.
4. I.e., people born in Russia, or with at least one parent born there.
5. Eighteen percent to 13 percent. When one considers third and fourth generation Norwegians, the disproportion is even greater.
6. As in South Dakota and Wisconsin, the traditional Republican vote was not significantly rural.
7. This is the best measure of agricultural wealth available in the 1890 census. In the 1910 census, this figure was not easily computed, and a longer term measure of agricultural wealth was available. Hence, in all three states the average value of land per acre was used to measure the relationship between wealth and progressivism.
8. Before 1930, the census gives no county breakdown of the percentage of the population living on farms. However, it is possible to compute the relation of farm homes to all homes. This is a good approximation to the rural-farm population. Thus, where there has been no great change in the relative ruralness of the counties, as in North Dakota between 1910 and 1930, the farm-home index for 1910 correlates .9+ with the rural-farm measure for 1930. This indicates that for a given year the two indexes would be virtually identical. I use the farm-home measure for political movements in the Dakotas that flourished before 1930. Cf. Duncan McRae, Jr., and James A. Meldrum, "Critical Elections in Illinois, 1888–1958," *Amer-*

ican Political Science Review, Vol. 54 (September 1960), p. 679n.

9. Within the Red River Valley, the best explanation of the Populist vote is that it went down as the wealth of the counties increased. The fewer the percentage of farms in the six counties, the smaller the Populist vote, but there are too few counties to be confident of this relationship. Thoughout North Dakota as a whole, there was no relationship between the percentage of farmers and the Populist vote.

10. Raymond C. Miller, "The Populist Party in Kansas" (unpublished Ph.D. dissertation, Department of Political Science, University of Chicago, 1928), pp. 141, 233, 280, 306.

11. Stanley Parsons, "Nebraska Populism Reconsidered," Paper presented at the annual meeting of the American Historical Association, 1962, pp. 13–14.

12. Benton H. Wilcox, "An Historical Definition of Northwestern Radicalism," *Mississippi Valley Historical Review,* Vol. 26 (December 1939), pp. 383–386; S. M. Lipset, *Agrarian Socialism* (Berkeley, Calif.: University of California Press, 1959), pp. 10–17.

13. Stanley Parsons, "Nebraska Populism Reconsidered," *op. cit.,* pp. 13–15, and Chapter 5.

14. Hallie Farmer, "The Economic Background of Frontier Populism," *Mississippi Valley Historical Review,* Vol. 10 (March 1924), pp. 421–422.

15. Cf., Karl Marx, *The Eighteenth Brumaire of Louis Bonaparte* (New York: International Publishers, 1963), pp. 122–128. There is a certain ambiguity in mass theory concerning this Marxian insight. The pluralists predict that the more isolated will be more easily mobilizable into mass movements. But Lipset has gone beyond this in pointing out that the most isolated are the least easily mobilizable by anyone. They vote the least and are the most apathetic. He therefore believes that a mass movement must first be organized among the more involved though still isolated groups. The "lower depths" will only be drawn into support once the movement appears powerful. Lipset has empirical evidence for this Marxian improvement of mass theory. Nazism in Germany did not receive support in its early stages in proportion to the decline in nonvoting. This rather happened after the movement was established. Similarly, Lipset reports data that skilled workers are more likely than unskilled to join nascent Communist parties. Cf. S. M. Lipset, *Political Man* (Garden City, N.Y.: Doubleday, 1960), pp. 121–126, 149–152.

16. S. M. Lipset, *Agrarian Socialism, op. cit.,* pp. 165–169.

17. Occasionally there was a Populist factor in later North Dakota elections. The vote to prohibit Sunday theater performances had a large Populist component (.5 on the original matrix and .3 on

the factor matrix). Examination of the county election returns suggests that this was the ethnic rather than the economic component of Populism: Scandinavians were against Sunday theaters, Germans and Catholics for them.

18. These correlations are by no means completely dependent on one another. With percentage Scandinavian held constant, the Progressive index is correlated $-.58$ with the percentage Russian-German; with percentage Russian-German held constant, the Scandinavian correlation is .51.

19. Cf., D. Jerome Tweton, "Sectionalism in North Dakota Politics: The Progressive Republican Revolt of 1900," *North Dakota History,* Vol. 25 (January 1958), pp, 21–27.

20. Alfred D. Chandler, "The Origins of Progressive Leadership," in Elting E. Morrison, Jr. (ed.), *The Letters of Theodore Roosevelt,* Vol. 8 (Cambridge, Mass.: Harvard University Press, 1954), pp. 1462–1465.

21. Cf., Robert L. Morlan, *Political Prairie Fire* (Minneapolis, Minn.: University of Minnesota Press, 1955), pp. 6–21.

22. Richard Hofstadter, *The Age of Reform* (New York: Knopf, 1955), p. 183; cf., pp. 175–184.

23. For the progressive and League legislation, see Roy P. Johnson, "John Burke," *North Dakota History,* Vol. 28 (Winter 1961), p. 30; Benton H. Wilcox, "A Reconsideration of the Character and Economic Basis of Northwestern Radicalism" (unpublished Ph.D. dissertation, Department of History, University of Wisconsin, 1933), pp. 93–94; Robert L. Morlan, *Political Prairie Fire, op cit.,* p. 106.

24. La Follette's 1924 vote was actually negatively correlated with his 1916 vote ($r = -.23$).

25. Cf., Victor C. Ferkiss, "Populism: Myth, Reality, Current Danger," *Western Political Quarterly,* Vol. 14 (September 1961), p. 738.

26. Robert L. Morlan, *Political Prairie Fire, op cit.,* p. 73.

27. The correlation is .42; when the Russian-German population is controlled, the correlation rises to .47.

28. Cf. G. A. Lundberg, "The Demographic and Economic Basis of Political Radicalism and Conservatism," *American Journal of Sociology,* Vol. 32 (March 1927), pp. 727–728. Since the greatest increase in population between 1910 and 1920 was in the cities, the percentage increase in population does not predict League strength. But clearly the farming areas of the west were more recently settled and in a more primitive state than those of the east.

29. Both correlations are only .3. The percentage of wheat farms in North Dakota corresponds to the percentage of cash-grain farms. General farming and wheat-and-cattle farming are more prevalent in both the richest and the poorest areas of the state.

30. Cf., Lawrence H. Larsen, "William Langer: Senator from North Dakota" (unpublished Master's thesis, Department of History, University of Wisconsin, 1955).
31. With percentage Russian-German held constant, Langer's relation to the farm vote remains .59.
32. The correlations are .63 and .6. With the farm vote held constant, the ethnic relation is .54.
33. Thus it correlated —.5 with the percentage Russian-German, but was still —.2 with rural-farm after controlling for the Russian-German vote.
34. The Smith vote correlated .64 with a referendum supporting the repeal of prohibition.
35. With the Russian-German vote held constant, his rural support was .51; the zero-order correlation was .59.
36. The correlations were .89 in 1940 and 1944, .87 in 1948, .82 in 1952 and 1956, and (with control for the Catholic vote) .73 in 1960. The off-year correlations were lower but generally approached .7.
37. Ross B. Talbot, "The North Dakota Farmers Union and North Dakota Politics," *Western Political Quarterly, op. cit.,* p. 890.
38. Martin A. Trow, "Right-Wing Radicalism and Political Intolerance: A Study of Support for McCarthy in a New England Town" (unpublished Ph.D. dissertation, Department of Political Science, Columbia University, 1951), p. 21.
39. Frank J. Kendrick, "McCarthy and the Senate" (unpublished Ph.D. dissertation, Department of Political Science, University of Chicago, 1962), pp. 256–257. And after he voted against the censure of McCarthy, Langer spoke for a group whose membership included Communist sympathizers.
40. Lawrence H. Larsen, "William Langer: A Maverick in the Senate," *Wisconsin Magazine of History,* Vol. 44 (Spring 1961), pp. 191–192.
41. *Ibid.,* p. 191.
42. Samuel Lubell, *The Future of American Politics* (New York: Harper, 1952), pp. 143–145.
43. Lemke's career after 1936 is instructive in this regard. When Lemke ran for governor in 1940, he was the candidate of the conservative opposition to the Non-Partisan League. The anti-League rich eastern counties supported him strongly. The wheat farmers who had supported him in 1936 opposed him in 1940. The regular Republican organization subsequently pushed Lemke for congress. Cf. Howard G. Williams, "Nye — A Lost Leader," *Nation, op. cit.,* p. 730.
44. Bob Faulds, "Dakota Points the Way," *New Republic,* Vol. 119 (August 16, 1948), p. 10; Henry Wallace, "Report on the Farmers," *New Republic,* Vol. 116 (June 30, 1947), p. 12.
45. On these developments, cf. Ross B. Talbot, "The North Dakota Farmers Union and North Dakota Politics," *op. cit.*

46. With ethnicity controlled, Burdick's vote correlated .57 with the percentage rural-farm, compared to less than .3 for the Democratic gubernatorial candidate in 1954.
47. John A. Crampton, " 'Yours for Humanity . . .': The Role of Ideology in the Farmers Union" (unpublished Ph.D. dissertation, Department of Political Science, University of California, 1962), pp. 39–45, 70.
48. Ross B. Talbot, "The North Dakota Farmers Union and North Dakota Politics," *op. cit.*, p. 890.

Chapter Five

1. John Gunther, *Inside U.S.A.* (New York: Harper, 1947), p. 237.
2. The intercorrelations of Populist strength vary from .63 to .87, with only the first Populist election ever falling below .8.
3. In computing the relationship between Populism and demographic variables, the 1893 Populist vote was used because it had the highest intercorrelations with the other Populist elections.
4. The Populist vote in the urban county was substantially below that in the three counties of the same ethnic background, wealth, and crop pattern which border on it. For urban desertion of the Democratic Party because of the Bryan campaign in other states, cf. Lee Benson, "Research Problems in American Political Historiography," in Mirra Komarovsky (ed.), *Common Frontiers of the Social Sciences* (Glencoe, Ill.: Free Press, 1957), pp. 177–181; V. O. Key, Jr., "A Theory of Critical Elections," *Journal of Politics,* Vol. 17 (February 1955), pp. 11–16; Duncan MacRae, Jr., and James A. Meldrum, "Critical Elections in Illinois 1888–1958," *American Political Science Review,* Vol. 54 (September 1960), pp. 673–678. Benson reports findings on New England and New York, Key on New England, MacRae and Meldrum on Illinois.
5. The exception is Minnehaha, the county with the largest city. This is further evidence of an urban vote against Populism.
6. Cf. Stanley Parsons, "Nebraska Populism Reconsidered," Paper delivered at the annual meeting of the American Historical Association, 1962, pp. 3–9; Raymond C. Miller, "The Populist Party in Kansas" (unpublished Ph.D. dissertation, Department of History, University of Chicago, 1928), pp. 141, 271–272, 305; Roscoe C. Martin, *The People's Party in Texas* (Austin, Texas: University of Texas Press, 1933), pp. 59–68, 211; J. Rogers Hollingsworth, "Populism: The Problem of Rhetoric and Reality," *Agricultural History,* Vol. 39 (April 1965), p. 83.
7. The correlation coefficient between the percentage of Scandinavians in 1910 and the Thorson vote was .52. Holding the value of land constant reduced the correlation to .33. Holding the percentage Scandinavian constant reduced the progressive relation to wealth to .58.

8. The progressive votes were for Thorson for Congress in 1910, Sterling for Senator in 1912, Crawford for Senator in 1914, and against Taft (for La Follette or Roosevelt) in the 1912 presidential primary. The only relations between these and other votes are between Crawford's 1914 vote and the 1889 prohibition referendum (.49) and between Taft's vote and the 1889 Democratic and antiprohibition votes (.41, .53). Crawford's 1908 support was unrelated to the votes on prohibition, the initiative, woman's suffrage, and the prohibition of Sunday theater performances, although most of these measures were part of his program.

9. Interestingly enough, Norbeck was far more for La Follette in 1912 than was Crawford and only supported Teddy Roosevelt reluctantly. This corresponds to his economic base, which was between Crawford's and La Follette's. Cf. Gilbert Courtland Fite, *Peter Norbeck, Prairie Statesman* (Columbia, Mo.: University of Missouri Press, 1948), p. 39.

10. The vote against Norbeck in the 1920 primary was simply a Non-Partisan League vote, although the candidate opposing Norbeck was a stalwart. Norbeck's 1916 and 1920 votes correlated .14.

11. By 1920, Germans and Russian-Germans were voting Republican more than League. The 1918 League vote tended to go in 1920 to the Farmer-Labor candidate for President. But the negative correlation between the 1918 League vote and the 1920 Republican presidential vote was low. The counties with the biggest increase in the GOP vote between 1918 and 1920 were clearly German and Russian-German.

12. The 1922 and 1918 League votes were correlated only .35. Rice found some relationship between wheat and the Non-Partisan League vote in South Dakota; wheat counties averaged 7 percent above the state average. But this finding is misleading. In 1918 and 1920, it simply reflects the concentration of Germans in the wheat belt. In 1922, it reflects League weakness in the west; wheat counties were not significantly more pro-League than corn counties that year.

   Rice also found insurgency in the early 1920's in Iowa and Nebraska weakest in the rich corn counties, a development that took place in South Dakota in the late 1920's. Cf. Stuart A. Rice, *Farmers and Workers in American Politics* (New York: Columbia University Press, 1924), pp. 169–176.

13. In the corn belt $r = 69$. The index used here to determine agricultural wealth was compiled by the Department of Agriculture. Cf. Margaret Jarmon Hagood, *Farm-Operator Family Level-of-Living Indexes for Counties of the United States: 1930, 1940, 1945, and 1950* (Washington, D. C.: United States Department of Agriculture, 1952), pp. 43–44.

14. Moreover, the correlation of the Smith vote with the Democratic vote for Senator in 1930 against McMaster was only .17

and that of F.D.R. only .09. Their correlations with the 1930 Democratic governor, whose opponent was not a progressive, were thirty points higher.

15. The relationships between wealth and the Roosevelt vote in the corn and western areas and between McMaster and wealth in the corn area would all be considerably higher were it not for the drop in the Roosevelt and McMaster strength in the poorest counties. The three poorest corn belt counties (including the only two west of the Missouri River) and the poorest western county were all less for Roosevelt and McMaster than their wealth would have predicted.

16. Actually, the Smith and first Roosevelt votes correlated $-.43$ and $-.45$ with the Republican vote of 1918. In North Dakota and Wisconsin, the unusual combination of Germans and progressives brought about by World War I also anticipated not McCarthyism but the Smith vote.

17. For comparable developments in Illinois and Indiana, cf. Duncan MacRae, Jr., and James A. Meldrum, "Critical Elections in Illinois, 1888–1958," *op. cit.,* pp. 678–681; V. O. Key, Jr., and Frank Munger, "Social Determinism and Electoral Decision: The Case of Indiana," in Eugene Burdick and Arthur J. Brodbeck (eds.), *American Voting Behavior* (Glencoe, Ill.: Free Press, 1955), pp. 288–290. The modern South Dakota Democratic vote is usually correlated below .5 with the Smith and 1932 Roosevelt votes, lower than its correlations with the 1902–1910 Democratic vote. The 1930 McMaster vote remains correlated with the modern Democratic vote ($r = .3$ to .5).

18. With the correlation between the Democratic vote in 1908 and 1948 held constant, the relationship between the number of cattle per farm and the Democratic vote changes from .45 in 1908 to $-.45$ in 1948. The change would be even more striking were it not for seven noncattle counties, also much less Democratic in 1948 than in 1908; all were highly German or Russian-German. Holding constant the number of cattle per farm, the relationship between the 1908 and 1948 Democratic votes rises from .54 to .64. The decline of Democratic strength in the west means the party is no longer stronger among native-stock than foreign-stock inhabitants.

19. Campbell, *et al.,* pp. 418–419, make the point that small farmers are in general more Democratic than large farmers. However, in view of the small number of cases they report and the absence of any distinction between types of farming, this finding is at best provisional.

20. The Democratic Party remains a clear minority party in South Dakota politics. However, in the second half of the 1950's the party increased its vote substantially and in 1958 elected the first Democratic governor since the New Deal. Farm unrest in the Plains states in the late 1950's is generally associated with

the Democratic resurgence. In South Dakota there was evidence of disproportionate farm desertion of the Republican Party within the corn belt, but not among the farmers of the state as a whole.

The 1960 presidential election did not continue the 1958 pattern. Its relationship to 1958 was less than its relation to any Democratic vote since 1942. Kennedy's vote closely resembled that given to other postwar Democratic presidential candidates, but its correlation with the percentage of Catholics was .37, some twenty points higher than was typical for the postwar Democratic vote. In 1958, rural Protestants had voted unusually Democratic. In 1960, they voted unusually Republican.

21. Taft's vote had no relation to the 1922 Non-Partisan League vote, but was correlated .33 with the 1918 League vote. The big issue in the primary was Universal Military Training. Taft backers attacked Ike for being a militarist. Cf. "Dakota's Decision," *Newsweek,* Vol. 39 (June 16, 1952), p. 39. Lubell found that in the presidential primary in Wisconsin in 1952 Taft got a German vote. Cf. Samuel Lubell, *The Revolt of the Moderates* (New York: Harper, 1956), pp. 268–269.

22. The correlation between percentage of Germans and the Republican vote for President in 1948 was .47.

23. "Too Busy to Win," *Time,* Vol. 55 (June 19, 1950), pp. 21–22.

24. Each election that might have indicated either support for McCarthy or the regular Republican vote contained idiosyncrasies. Thus, Case, previously a congressman for western South Dakota, ran disproportionately strong in a few northwestern counties. To take Mundt's vote as a measure of McCarthyism, on the other hand, may inflate support for McCarthy in the corn belt. By 1954 an agricultural recession had begun in the Middle West, and it seems to have hurt the GOP more in the wheat belt than in the corn belt. (Cf. Samuel Lubell, *The Revolt of the Moderates, op. cit.,* p. 168.) That Mundt was relatively stronger in the corn than in the wheat belt may have had nothing to do with McCarthyism.

There are also problems with measures of regular Republicanism. One cannot use presidential elections alone, since there are clear differences in the vote in presidential and off-years. In the only postwar off-year election, 1946, George Michelson was elected governor. Michelson's Scandinavian background may have given him disproportionate support among that ethnic group.

25. $r = .22$. The relation would be much higher were it not for the opposition to McCarthy among wheat belt counties with few Scandinavians.

26. Louis Bean, *Influences in the 1954 Mid-Term Elections* (Washington, D. C.: Public Affairs Institute, 1954), pp. 26–28.

27. Cf. Chapter 7 on the Farmers Union and Chapter 3 for a discussion of the Wisconsin corn counties. The Lemke vote in

South Dakota was concentrated in the corn belt, although his vote was even more scattered in South Dakota than it was in Wisconsin. In no county did Lemke get 10 percent of the vote. But six of the eleven counties in which he got 5 percent of the vote or better were the six rich counties in the southeast corner of the corn belt. These are close to the Iowa border and were probably influenced by the strength of the Farm Holiday Movement in Iowa. Dr. John L. Shover informs me that the Farm Holiday movement was strongest in northwestern Iowa in the counties adjacent to southeastern South Dakota. The largest city in the area is Sioux City, Iowa, only a few miles from the South Dakota border. Its newspapers service the neighboring South Dakota counties, and the *Sioux City Unionist and Public Ledger* supported Lemke. (As in Wisconsin and North Dakota, the Lemke vote was neither German nor Catholic.)

Chapter Six

1. Adam B. Ulam, *The Unfinished Revolution* (New York: Random House, 1960), pp. 28–57 and *passim.*
2. David W. Noble, *The Paradox of Progressive Thought* (Minneapolis, Minn.: University of Minnesota Press, 1958), pp. vi–viii, and *passim.*
3. Quoted in Norman Pollack, *The Populist Response to Industrial America* (Cambridge, Mass.: Harvard University Press, 1962), pp. 15–16, 22–25.
4. William A. Peffer, *The Farmer's Side: His Troubles and Their Remedy* (New York: Appleton, 1891), pp. 3–64, 75–123.
5. Populist and Alliance platforms can be found in John R. Hicks, *The Populist Revolt* (Lincoln, Neb.: University of Nebraska Press, 1961), pp. 427–444.
6. Richard Hofstadter, *The Age of Reform* (New York: Knopf, 1955), pp. 62–63.
7. Frederic Howe learned from his environment that individual morality was at the root of politics. His education as a reformer taught him the importance of the system. This was a common experience. Cf. Frederic C. Howe, *Confessions of a Reformer* (New York: Scribner's, 1925); C. Vann Woodward, *Tom Watson: Agrarian Rebel* (New York: Macmillan, 1938), p. 82.
8. See also the excellent and more extended comments by Norman Pollack in "Hofstadter on Populism: A Critique of 'The Age of Reform,'" *Journal of Southern History,* Vol. 26 (November 1960), pp. 482–489.
9. Richard Hofstadter, *The Age of Reform* (New York: Knopf, 1955), pp. 70–81; Walter R. Nugent, "Populism and Nativism in Kansas, 1888–1900" (unpublished Ph.D. dissertation, Department of History, University of Chicago, 1961), pp. 81–83.
10. Stanley Parsons, "Nebraska Populism Reconsidered," Paper de-

livered at the annual meeting of the American Historical Association, 1962, pp. 3–8; J. Rogers Hollingsworth, "Populism: The Problem of Rhetoric and Reality," *Agricultural History,* Vol. 39 (April 1965), p. 83.

11. Benjamin R. Twiss, *Lawyers and The Constitution* (Princeton, N.J.: Princeton University Press, 1942), pp. 141–146.

12. Richard Hofstadter, *The Age of Reform, op. cit.,* p. 80; S. M. Lipset, *Political Man* (Garden City, N.Y.: Doubleday, 1960), p. 167; Peter Viereck, *The Unadjusted Man* (Boston: Beacon Press, 1956), p. 202; Daniel Bell, *The End of Ideology* (Glencoe, Ill.: Free Press, 1960), pp. 104–107.

13. Oscar Handlin, "American Views of the Jew at the Opening of the Twentieth Century," *Publications of the American Jewish Historical Society,* Vol. 40 (June 1951), p. 338.

14. Leon W. Fuller, "Colorado's Revolt Against Capitalism," *Mississippi Valley Historical Review,* Vol. 11 (December 1934), pp. 355–357.

15. E.g., see Norman Pollack, *The Populist Response to Industrial America, op. cit.,* pp. 43–67; Roscoe C. Martin, *The People's Party in Texas* (Austin, Texas: University of Texas Press, 1933), pp. 217–218.

16. Viereck, however, retells the story to make Jewishness the focal point and then concludes that the vast popular reception for *Caesar's Column* was an example of Populist anti-Semitism at the mass level. Peter Viereck, *The Unadjusted Man, op. cit.,* p. 202.

17. Oscar Handlin, "American Views of the Jew at the Opening of the Twentieth Century," *Publications of the American Jewish Historical Society, op. cit.,* pp. 325–328.

18. Ignatius Donnelly, *Caesar's Column* (Chicago: J. Regan, n.d.), p. 36.

19. Cf. Norman Pollack, "The Myth of Populist Anti-Semitism," *American Historical Review,* Vol. 43 (October, 1962), pp. 76–80; Norman Pollack, "Hofstadter on Populism: A Critique of 'The Age of Reform,' " *op. cit.,* p. 500; Walter R. Nugent, "Populism and Nativism in Kansas, 1888–1900" *op. cit.,* pp. 86–89; John Higham "Anti-Semitism in the Gilded Age," *Mississippi Valley Historical Review,* Vol. 53 (March 1957).

20. Oscar Handlin, "American Views of the Jew at the Opening of the Twentieth Century," *Publications of the American Jewish Historical Society, op. cit.,* p. 338. In the Cross of Gold speech, Bryan used the crucifixion metaphor to attack hard-money advocates. To assume that "gold-bugs" were identified with the Jews (who killed Christ) is to assume just what has not been proved — that the Populists were anti-Semitic.

21. Cf. C. Vann Woodward, "Tom Watson and the Negro in Agrarian Politics," *Journal of Southern History,* Vol. 4 (February, 1938), pp. 16–23; C. Vann Woodward, "The Populist

Heritage and the Intellectual," *American Scholar,* Vol. 29 (Winter 1959), p. 65; William R. Gnatz, "The Negro and the Populist Movement in the South" (unpublished Master's thesis, University of Chicago, Department of History, 1961), p. 39.

22. On Populist support in the south cf. V. O. Key, Jr., *Southern Politics in State and Nation* (New York: Knopf, 1949), pp. 138–142, 232–237, and 549 for South Carolina, Mississippi, and Georgia; Melvin J. White, "Populism in Louisiana during the Nineties," *Mississippi Valley Historical Review,* Vol. 5 (June 1918), pp. 14–15; Perry H. Howard, *Political Tendencies in Louisiana 1812–1952* (Baton Rouge, La.: Louisiana State University Press, 1957), pp. 90–99; Alex Matthews Arnett, *The Populist Movement in Georgia* (New York: Columbia University Press, 1922), map facing p. 184; C. Vann Woodward, *Tom Watson: Agrarian Rebel* (New York: Macmillan, 1938), pp. 160–161, 217; Roscoe C. Martin, *The People's Party in Texas, op. cit.,* pp. 60–68, 86–111, 136–137. Virginia, where Populism was not strong, is an exception to Populist strength in the hills and weakness in the black belt. Cf. William Du Bose Shelton, *Populism in the Old Dominion* (Princeton, N.J.: Princeton University Press, 1935), pp. 86–87.

23. Cf. Walter Ellsworth Nydegger, "The Election of 1892 in Iowa," *Iowa Journal of History and Politics,* Vol. 25 (July 1927), pp. 442–444; Stanley Parsons, "Nebraska Populism Reconsidered," Paper presented at the annual meeting of the American Historical Association, 1962, pp. 11–13; Walter R. Nugent, "Populism and Nativism in Kansas, 1888–1900," *op. cit.,* pp. 204–215.

24. Richard Hofstadter, *The Age of Reform, op. cit.,* pp. 87–91.

25. Cf. Roscoe C. Martin, *The People's Party in Texas, op. cit.,* pp. 103–111, 132; Donald E. Walters, "Populism in California, 1889–1900 (unpublished Ph.D. dissertation, Department of History, University of California, 1952), pp. 70, 148–150, 289.

26. John Higham, "Anti-Semitism in the Gilded Age," *op. cit.,* pp. 565–566.

27. John Higham, *Strangers in the Land* (New Brunswick, N.J.: Rutgers University Press, 1955), pp. 95–98, 346; Walter R. Nugent, "Populism and Nativism in Kansas, 1888–1900," *op. cit.,* p. 45. Populist and Alliance platforms before 1892 contained nothing about immigration restriction.

28. Nugent writes, "It hardly helped [the farmer's] peace of mind to learn that the Sante Fe railroad was now in the hands of the Barings of London, and that Englishmen alone and in companies owned large tracts of land in Kansas, and that London bankers had close ties with both the eastern bankers, who had bought up their mortgages at bargain-basement prices, and to American statesmen, including John Sheridan and Cleveland, to whom the contraction policy was economic dogma." Walter R. Nugent, "Populism and Nativism in Kansas, 1888–1900," *op. cit.,* p. 34.

29. Walter R. Nugent, "Populism and Nativism in Kansas, 1888–1900," *op. cit.*, pp. 180–182.
30. Richard Hofstadter, *The Age of Reform, op. cit.*, pp. 89–90. Of even more dubiousness as evidence of Populist jingoism are citations from a "west-coast newspaper" (Populist?) and "the silver senator from Nevada." (The Populists ran a ticket against the silver ticket in that state.) Similarly, Hofstadter is more impressed (p. 286) by the unsubstantiated statement that some Klan members supported La Follette in 1924 than by La Follette's forthright attack on the Klan — an attack not matched by Davis and Coolidge.
31. Indeed, the charges against the Populists might better be made against the APA. In Wisconsin the APA was for the rule of the people against the special interests. The workingmen and small businessmen were alleged to be the bulwark of democracy and liberty. "The time is not far distant when class legislation will be a thing of the past, and the workingmen will have as much to say in the making of laws as the millionaire. . . ." This was to be accomplished in a purely "American" way; it would "never come about through the radical methods proposed by Populists or Socialists." Cf. Gerald K. Marsden, "Patriotic Societies and American Labor: The American Protective Association in Wisconsin," *Wisconsin Magazine of History,* Vol. 41 (Summer 1958), pp. 288–289.
32. Walter R. Nugent, "Populism and Nativism in Kansas, 1888–1900," *op. cit.,* pp. 132–136; John Higham, *Strangers in the Land, op. cit.,* pp. 80–86. In the 1870's anti-Catholicism had been strong among respectable Republicans; *ibid.,* pp. 28–29.
33. John Locke, *Of Civil Government* (New York: Dutton, Everyman's), pp. 177–179, 183–203.
34. John P. Roche, "The Curbing of the Militant Majority," *Reporter,* Vol. 29 (July 18, 1963), pp. 34–38.
35. Frederic C. Howe, *Confessions of a Reformer* (New York: Scribner's, 1925), pp. 17–18.
36. Cf. Roscoe C. Martin, *The People's Party in Texas, op. cit.,* p. 44.
37. In Texas in November 1892, there were 3,170 Populist clubs. *Ibid.,* pp. 142–149.
38. *Ibid.,* pp. 84–85, 166–167; John R. Hicks, *The Populist Revolt* (Lincoln, Neb.: University of Nebraska Press, 1961), *passim.*
39. Victor Ferkiss, "Populism: Myth, Reality, Current Danger," *Western Political Quarterly,* Vol. 14 (September 1961), pp. 737–740, and S. M. Lipset, "The Sources of the Radical Right," in Daniel Bell (ed.), *The New American Right* (New York: Criterion Books, 1955), p. 174, charge that the Populists often interfered with academic freedom. So does Peter Viereck. He cites the example of the removal of Veblen from the University of Minnesota because of the "democratic, egalitarian, Populist milieu." (*The Unadjusted Man, op. cit.,* p. 46.) In fact, the

Populists were never close to power in Minnesota. At the time of Veblen's removal, the state was in firm Republican hands.

40. The "overeducation" charge is made by Edward Shils, *The Torment of Secrecy* (Glencoe, Ill.: Free Press, 1956), p. 99. See the anti-Populist report of G. T. Fairchild, "Populism in a State Agricultural College," *American Journal of Sociology,* Vol. 3 (November 1897).

41. Prohibition and woman suffrage were allied in part because of fears by Germans and other antiprohibitionists that the women would support prohibition.

42. Cf. Glenn Lowell Brudvig, "The Farmer's Alliance and the Populist Movement in North Dakota (1884–1896)" (unpublished Master's thesis, University of North Dakota, 1956), p. 115; Walter R. Nugent, "Populism and Nativism in Kansas, 1888–1900," *op. cit.,* pp. 53, 118; Herbert S. Schell, *History of South Dakota* (Lincoln, Neb.: University of Nebraska Press, 1961), p. 232; Herman Clarence Nixon, *The Populist Movement in Iowa,* reprinted from the January 1926 number of the *Iowa Journal of History and Politics* (Iowa City, Iowa: State University of Iowa), p. 157; J. Rogers Hollingsworth, "Populism: The Problem of Rhetoric and Reality," *op. cit.,* p. 85; Roscoe C. Martin, *The People's Party in Texas, op. cit.,* pp. 80–81. The North Dakota Populist Party, which supported prohibition, generally fused with the Democrats at election time. In Wisconsin during the 1930's, the Progressive Party vote was related to the vote for prohibition, as one would expect of a Scandinavian and native-stock movement. But if this was because of the agrarian radical crusade, how to explain the even higher relationship of the Republican vote to prohibition? Cf. H. F. Gosnell, *Grass Roots Politics* (Washington, D. C.: American Council on Public Affairs, 1942), p. 56.

43. Cf. Allan F. Westin, "The Supreme Court, the Populist Movement and the Campaign of 1896," *Journal of Politics,* Vol. 15 (February 1953), pp. 3–41. "It was in this period (1876–1896) that the Supreme Court created a wide disenchantment with constitutional processes on the part of the Populist Party."

44. Cf. Benton H. Wilcox, "An Historical Definition of Northwestern Radicalism," *Mississippi Valley Historical Review,* Vol. 26 (December 1939), pp. 378–379, 394, and *passim;* Carl C. Taylor, *The Farmers' Movement 1620–1920* (New York: American Book Co., 1953), pp. 49–99 and *passim.*

45. Richard Hofstadter, *The Age of Reform, op. cit.,* pp. 46–47.

46. *Ibid.,* pp. 109–112; Richard Hofstadter, "The Psuedo Conservative Revolt," in Daniel Bell (ed.), *The New American Right, op. cit.,* pp. 43–44.

47. C. Vann Woodward, "The Populist Heritage and the Intellectual," *op. cit.,* p. 63.

48. Richard Hofstadter, *The Age of Reform, op. cit.,* pp. 96–109.

49. William Kornhauser, *The Politics of Mass Society* (Glencoe, Ill.: Free Press, 1959), pp. 39–40.

50. Cf. Allan F. Westin, "The Supreme Court, the Populist Movement, and the Campaign of 1896," *loc. cit.*

51. German fascism owed a real debt to the failure of the German revolution of 1918 to end the inaccessibility and independent power of the army, the police, and the bureaucracy.

52. William Kornhauser, *The Politics of Mass Society, op. cit.*, p. 44. Kornhauser adds that not all concern with remote objects is a manifestation of mass behavior, but he insists that all mass behavior has such concerns and that there is a tendency for remote concerns to lead to mass behavior.

53. Karl Ernest Meyer, "The Politics of Loyalty: From La Follette to McCarthy in Wisconsin: 1918–1952" (unpublished Ph.D. dissertation, Department of Political Science, Princeton University, 1956), pp. 79–116.

54. This is not to say that Populists displayed the sophistications of Karl Marx. It is emphatically to deny that the similarities between Marxism and Populism show that America was developing on the European pattern. But cf. Norman Pollack, *The Populist Response to Industrial America, op. cit.*, pp. 82–83. For the notion of Populism as a surrogate for socialism, cf. Michael N. Shute, "Populism and the Pragmatic Mystique" (unpublished manuscript, n.d.).

55. Cf. Stanley Elkins and Eric McKitrick, "A Meaning for Turner's Frontier," *Political Science Quarterly*, Vol. 114 (September 1954), pp. 324–339.

56. At the turn of the century, North Dakota, Minnesota, and Wisconsin had higher percentages of foreign-born in their population than any other rural states. In 1920, almost 60 percent of the Swedish farmers in America lived in seven midwestern states. Cf. Carl C. Taylor, "The Evolution of American Rural Society," in Carl Taylor, *et al., Rural Life in the United States* (New York: Knopf, 1949), p. 27. Norwegians were the second-largest ethnic group in the Dakotas and Wisconsin.

   Lubell has argued that progressivism in the Middle West served a function for German and Scandinavian immigrants analogous to that served in cities by the machine. This is persuasive in the Scandinavian case, but flies in the face of German opposition to progressivism. Cf. Samuel Lubell, *The Future of American Politics* (New York: Harper, 1952), p. 206.

57. The figures are from Fred A. Shannon, *The Farmer's Last Frontier: Agriculture 1860–1897* (New York: Farrar and Rinehart, 1945), pp. 350–351. Shannon points out that since 1920, when the census began to count farmers and their families as a percentage of the total population, the ratio of those living on farms to total population has been the same as the ratio of farmers to the gainfully employed. Therefore, one can use the

latter figures as a measure of the farm population before 1920.
58. Margaret Jarmon Hagood, "The Dynamics of Rural Population," in Carl Taylor, *et al., Rural Life in the United States, op. cit.,* pp. 241–243.
59. Douglas Ensminger, "Rural Neighborhoods and Communities," in *ibid.,* p. 73.
60. The phrase is in Fred Shannon, *The Farmer's Last Frontier, op. cit.,* p. 359.

Chapter Seven

1. Cf. Grant McConnell, *The Decline of Agrarian Democracy* (Berkeley, Calif.: University of California Press, 1953), pp. 1–35; Michael Rogin, "Voluntarism: The Political Functions of an Anti-Political Doctrine," *Industrial and Labor Relations Review,* Vol. 15 (July 1962), p. 523.
2. This is not to say, with Hofstadter, that the "hard" post-Populist farm organizations were practical while the "soft" Populists were not. Hofstadter achieves this result by focusing on Populist rhetoric and farm psychology in the Populist chapters and on farm organization activities later on. In fact, the Farm Bureau was practical for many of its members. But its perpetuation of the yeoman myth and its glorification of rural life surpassed Populist romanticism. Often the Farm Bureau, like manufacturers of farm products and other industrialists, utilized the agrarian myth to disguise its purposes and power. Cf. Richard Hofstadter, *The Age of Reform* (New York: Knopf, 1955), pp. 109–130; Grant McConnell, *The Decline of Agrarian Democracy, op. cit.;* C. Vann Woodward, *Tom Watson: Agrarian Rebel* (New York: Macmillan, 1938), pp. 51–137; Gilbert C. Fite, *George N. Peek and the Fight for Farm Parity* (Norman, Okla.: University of Oklahoma Press, 1954), pp. 20, 123–125, 281; Paul M. Johnstone, "Old Ideals vs. New Ideas in Farm Life," in U.S. Department of Agriculture, *Farmers in a Changing World; Yearbook of Agriculture* (Washington, D. C.: Government Printing Office, 1940), p. 165.
3. Writers like Croly and Weyl explicitly focused their analysis around the fragmenting of rural homogeneity. Cf. Walter Weyl, *The New Democracy* (New York: Macmillan, 1912); Herbert Croly, *The Promise of American Life* (New York: Macmillan, 1910).
4. Much contemporary progressive historiography centers around whether the progressives remained rooted in the moral certainties of the past or left the nineteenth century behind. Cf. Morton White, *Social Thought in America: The Revolt Against Formalism* (Boston: Beacon Press, 1957); Eric F. Goldman, *Rendezvous with Destiny* (New York: Knopf, 1952); Richard Hofstadter, *Age of Reform* (New York: Knopf, 1955); Henry F.

May, *The End of American Innocence* (New York: Knopf, 1959); Charles Forcey, *The Crossroads of Liberalism* (New York: Oxford University Press, 1961); Samuel P. Hays, *Conservation and the Gospel of Efficiency* (Cambridge, Mass.: Harvard University Press, 1959); David Noble, *The Paradox of Progressive Thought* (Minneapolis, Minn.: University of Minnesota Press, 1958); Gabriel Kolko, *The Triumph of Conservatism* (New York: Free Press, 1963); George E. Mowry, *The California Progressives* (Berkeley, Calif.: University of California Press, 1951); Sam Haber, "Scientific Management and the Progressive Movement" (unpublished Ph.D. dissertation, Department of History, University of California at Berkeley, 1961), now published as *Efficiency and Uplift* (Chicago: University of Chicago Press, 1964). Footnote references are to the dissertation.

5. Charles McCarthy, *The Wisconsin Idea* (New York: Macmillan, 1912), pp. 302–303.
6. Eric F. Goldman, *Rendezvous with Destiny, op. cit.,* pp. 306–314.
7. Hofstadter, *Age of Reform, op. cit.,* pp. 15–16.
8. Cf. Gerd Korman, "Politics, Loyalties, Immigrant Traditions, and Reform: The Wisconsin German-American Press and Progressivism 1909-1912," *Wisconsin Magazine of History,* Vol. 40 (Spring 1957).
9. Cf. Sam Haber, "Scientific Management and the Progressive Movement," *op. cit.,* pp. 108, 117, 131–133, 141–153; Charles Forcey, *The Crossroads of Liberalism, op. cit.,* p. 312; Gabriel Kolko, *The Triumph of Conservatism, op. cit.,* pp. 160–164. My interpretation here owes much to a conversation with Arthur Lipow. Note that as long as Populists were confident of winning a majority of the population to their organization, they cared little about direct democracy. These reforms occupied a prominent place in the Populist program only after 1896. It should be noted, however, that a progressive like La Follette did think of direct democracy as increasing popular control over decision makers.
10. V. O. Key, Jr., and Winston W. Crouch, *The Initiative and the Referendum in California* (Berkeley, Calif.: University of California Press, 1939), pp. 565–574.
11. Cf. Duane Lockard, *The Politics of State and Local Government* (New York: Macmillan, 1963), pp. 226–238; Charles R. Adrian, *Governing Urban America* (New York: McGraw-Hill, 1961), pp. 100–102; Charles R. Adrian, "Some General Characteristics of Non-Partisan Elections," *American Political Science Review,* Vol. 46 (September 1952), pp. 766–776; Eugene C. Lee, *The Politics of Nonpartisanship* (Berkeley, Calif.: University of California Press, 1960).
12. Cf. John Dewey, *The Public and Its Problems* (Chicago: Gate-

way Books, 1946); Mary Parker Follett, *The New State* (New York: Longmans, Green, 1918).

13. Cf. Sam Haber, "Scientific Management and the Progressive Movement," *op. cit.,* pp. 71–74.

14. Cf. George E. Mowry, *The California Progressives, op. cit.,* pp. 39–50. Hofstadter concentrates on this type of progressive; cf. *The Age of Reform, op. cit.,* pp. 200–211.

15. Cf. Sam Haber, "Scientific Management and the Progressive Movement," *op. cit.,* pp. 149–163.

16. Cf. George E. Mowry, *The California Progressives, op. cit.,* pp. 45–56, 90–94; Walton Bean, *Boss Ruef's San Francisco* (Berkeley, Calif: University of California Press, 1952), pp. 260–316.

17. Charles McCarthy, *The Wisconsin Idea, op. cit.,* p. 3.

18. AFL, *Proceedings,* 1930, p. 318.

19. Jean-Jacques Rousseau, *The Social Contract and Discourses* (New York: Dutton, Everyman's Library), pp. 13–14. Rousseau's belief was also predicated on social homogeneity and harmony of interests.

20. Cf. Henry S. Kariel, *The Decline of American Pluralism* (Palo Alto, Calif.: Stanford University Press, 1961), pp. 68–113; Marver H. Bernstein, *Regulating Business by Independent Commission* (Princeton, N.J.: Princeton University Press, 1955); Philip O. Foss, *Politics and Grass* (Seattle, Wash.: University of Washington Press, 1960); and a host of similar studies.

21. Cf. Grant McConnell, *Private Power and American Democracy* (New York: Knopf, 1966), pp. 38–50.

22. Cf. Sam Haber, "Scientific Management and the Progressive Movement," *op. cit.,* pp. 112–113, 122–125, 154, 219–220; Charles Forcey, *The Crossroads of Liberalism, op. cit.,* p. 299; Grant McConnell, *Private Power and American Democracy* (New York: Knopf, 1966), pp. 52–70. Note the active role Taft's Department of Commerce and Labor played in the formation of the Chamber of Commerce.

23. Cf. Andrew M. Scott, "The Progressive Era in Perspective," *Journal of Politics,* Vol. 21 (November 1959).

24. Cf. Arthur J. Altmeyer, "The Wisconsin Idea and Social Security," *Wisconsin Magazine of History,* Vol. 42 (Autumn 1948).

25. Pro-war Socialists like John Spargo and William English Walling also became more conservative as the Socialist Party opposed the war.

26. For a treatment of the war's impact on progressivism, cf. Henry F. May, *The End of American Innocence, op. cit.,* pp. 361–398.

27. George Mowry, *The California Progressives, op. cit.,* pp. 286–301.

28. And in each case, a brief flurry of radical political activity preceded the prosperity and normalcy of the postwar years.

29. Cf. Arthur S. Link, "What Happened to the Progressive Move-

ment in the 1920's?" *American Historical Review,* Vol. 64 (July 1959), p. 840.

30. *Ibid.,* p. 845.
31. Farm movements had favored special demands before, such as the exemption of farm coops from antitrust laws and the exemption of farm improvements from taxation. However, McNary-Haugen was the first agrarian reform measure of a special interest character to dominate agrarian reform politics.
32. Sylvia Snowiss, "Roosevelt and Congress, The First Hundred Days" (unpublished Master's thesis, Department of Political Science, University of Chicago, 1962), pp. 10–13, 29–39, 56–67, 94–95, provides statistical evidence for this assertion.
33. Grant McConnell, *The Decline of Agrarian Democracy, op. cit.*
34. There is no evidence of disproportionate Populist support for noneconomic authoritarian movements. Lipset writes that the Ku Klux Klan was a latter-day expression of provincial Populism; S. M. Lipset, *Political Man* (Garden City, N.Y.: Doubleday, 1960), p. 167. Oscar Handlin asserts that the mass of Klan members came from areas strongly radical in the 1890's: "American Views of the Jew at the Opening of the Twentieth Century," *Publications of the American Jewish Historical Society,* Vol. 40 (June 1951), p. 325. However, in his own history of the Jews in America, Handlin lists the states in which the Klan was strongest at its height — Oregon, Ohio, Indiana, and Illinois. Populism was insignificant in all but Oregon, and even this state was not a center of Populist strength. Cf. Oscar Handlin, *Adventures in Freedom* (New York: McGraw-Hill Book Co., 1954), pp. 203–204. The Great Plains, the heartland of midwestern Populism, did not support the Klan.
35. Louis J. Ducoff, "Farm Laborers," in Carl Taylor, *et al., Rural Life in the United States* (New York: Knopf, 1949), pp. 284–291; C. Vann Woodward, *Tom Watson: Agrarian Rebel* (New York: Macmillan, 1938), pp. 218–219, 401–405.
36. Evidence on farmer sensitivity to depressions is contained in Leon Epstein, *Politics in Wisconsin* (Madison, Wis.: University of Wisconsin Press, 1958), pp. 71–74; Angus Campbell *et al., The American Voter* (New York: Wiley, 1960), pp. 417–422; Samuel Lubell, *The Revolt of the Moderates* (New York: Harper, 1956), pp. 155–174.
37. Bernard Berelson *et al., Voting* (Chicago: University of Chicago Press, 1954), pp. 194–198.
38. Cf. Stuart Rice, *Farmers and Workers in American Politics* (New York: Columbia University Press, 1924), pp. 214–220.
39. Karl Marx, *The Eighteenth Brumaire of Louis Bonaparte* (New York: International Publishers, 1963).
40. Cf. Charles P. Loomis and J. Allen Beagle, "The Spread of German Nazism in Rural Areas," *American Sociological Review,* Vol. 11 (December 1946); Rudolph Heberle, *From*

Democracy to Nazism (Baton Rouge, La.: Louisiana State University Press, 1945). For a classic analysis of the petit bourgeois roots of German Nazism cf. Leon Trotsky, *What Next?* (New York: Pioneer Publishers, 1932).

In Canada, the neofascist Social Credit Party is strong in the wheat areas of Alberta, while similar Saskatchewan areas produced the social-Democratic Cooperative Commonwealth Federation.

41. Victor Ferkiss, "The Populist Influences on American Fascism," *Western Political Quarterly,* Vol. 10 (June 1959), pp. 353, 356.

42. *Ibid.,* pp. 350–351. The second of Ferkiss' arguments — that the Populist "plebiscitarian" ideology produced fascism — is better dealt with in analyzing McCarthyism. Ferkiss himself admits that the Populist economic theories are dead, but he asserts that McCarthyism proves that the Populist theories of plebiscitary democracy are still dangerous. Cf. Victor Ferkiss, "Populism: Myth, Reality, Current Danger," *Western Political Quarterly,* Vol. 14 (September 1961), p. 340.

43. Cf. David J. Saposs, "The Role of the Middle Class in Social Development: Fascism, Populism, Communism, Socialism," in *Economic Essays in Honor of Wesley Clair Mitchell* (New York: Columbia University Press, 1935).

44. Perry Howard, *Political Tendencies in Louisiana:* 1812–1952 (Baton Rouge, La.: Louisiana State University Press, 1957), pp. 90–98, 112–114, 123. Even this evidence is of dubious validity in demonstrating the authoritarian predispositions of agrarian radical supporters. At the time of his first victory, Long's antidemocratic characteristics were hardly clear. Indeed, one finds many historians who feel that the benefits Long brought to Louisiana's farmers and workers far outweigh his political strong-arm tactics at the state level. His national activities prior to his assassination are another story. But in state politics, Long was far from the typical southern demagogue: He was not a racist, and he made many concrete reforms. Cf. T. Harry Williams, "The Gentleman from Louisiana: Demagogue or Democrat," *Journal of Southern History,* Vol. 26 (February 1960).

45. Gerald R. McCoy, "The Development and Dissolution of the Wisconsin Progressive Party of 1934–46" (unpublished Master's thesis, Department of Political Science, University of Chicago, 1949), p. 68.

46. John A. Crampton, "Yours for Humanity: The Role of Ideology in the Farmers Union" (unpublished Ph.D. dissertation, Department of Political Science, University of California at Berkeley, 1962), pp. 67–68, 189–196.

47. Gerald R. McCoy, "The Development and Dissolution of the Wisconsin Progressive Party of 1934–46," *op. cit.,* p. 70.

48. Its absence of anti-Semitism was no accident in this regard. As

Lipset and others have pointed out, because the Jews are perceived to have a close relation to money and usury, an authoritarian rural economic revolt will have anti-Semitic overtones. Cf. S. M. Lipset, "The Sources of the 'Radical Right,'" in Daniel Bell (ed.), *The New American Right* (New York: Criterion Books, 1955), p. 219n.

Chapter Eight

1. Seymour Martin Lipset, *The First New Nation* (New York: Basic Books, 1963), pp. 262, 271.
2. Cf. Robert A. Dahl, *Who Governs* (New Haven: Yale University Press, 1961), pp. 321–324. Dahl runs into difficulty because at the same time that he makes this argument he recognizes that McCarthy did not have significant active support outside the political stratum. He therefore retreats to a position close to that discussed later, pp. 256–260.
3. Talcott Parsons, "Social Strains in America," in Daniel Bell (ed.), *The New American Right* (New York: Criterion Books, 1955), p. 136. Italics in original.
4. Daniel Bell, "Interpretations of American Politics," in Daniel Bell (ed.), *The New American Right, op. cit.*, p. 25.
5. Cf. Julius Turner, *Party and Constituency: Pressures on Congress* (Baltimore, Md.: Johns Hopkins Press, 1951), pp. 145–160; Ralph H. Smuckler, "The Region of Isolation," *American Political Science Review*, Vol. 47 (June 1953); Ray Allen Billington, "The Origins of Middle Western Isolationism," *Political Science Quarterly*, Vol. 60 (March 1945); Samuel Lubell, *The Revolt of the Moderates* (New York: Harper, 1956), p. 274.
6. *Congressional Quarterly*, "McCarthy's Strength Centered in West, Midwest," Vol. 12 (December 3, 1954), p. 1409.
7. Cf. Charles J. V. Murphy, "McCarthy and the Businessman," *Fortune*, Vol. 49 (April 1954). Texas was also a center of pro-McCarthy business sentiment. Cf. Charles J. V. Murphy, "Texas Businessmen and McCarthy," *Fortune*, Vol. 49 (May 1954).
8. Leslie A. Fiedler, "McCarthy," *Encounter*, Vol. 3 (August 1954), p. 15.
9. Every daily paper in the state of Georgia opposed the Populists. Cf. C. Vann Woodward, *Tom Watson: Agrarian Rebel* (New York: Macmillan, 1938), p. 242. In addition to opposing the Populists and the Non-Partisan League, the newspapers of North Dakota opposed progressive governor John Burke. Cf. Benton H. Wilcox, "A Reconsideration of the Character and Economic Basis of Northwestern Radicalism" (unpublished Ph.D. dissertation, Department of History, University of Wisconsin, 1933), p. 94.

10. James M. Burns, *The Deadlock of Democracy* (Englewood Cliffs, N.J.: Prentice-Hall, 1963), p. 188.
11. Cf. Talcott Parsons, "Social Strains in America," in Daniel Bell (ed.), *The New American Right, op. cit.,* pp. 136–137; Senator Joe McCarthy, *The Story of General George C. Marshall* (1952), pp. 132, 140–141. McCarthy's anti-British appeals did not have Populist roots so much as Irish and German roots.
12. Charles Murphy, "McCarthy and the Businessmen," *Fortune, op. cit.,* p. 180. For evidence of the consistently conservative character of McCarthy's voting record, cf. George Belknap, "A Study of Senatorial Voting by Scale Analysis" (unpublished Ph.D. dissertation, Department of Political Science, University of Chicago, 1951), pp. 49, 59, 64, 69; Miles McMillan, "Calling the Roll on McCarthy," *Progressive,* Vol. 17 (May 1954), pp. 13–16. Ferkiss, however, writes, "His voting record was, in fact, somewhat left of center on major issues of government economic intervention." Cf. Victor C. Ferkiss, "Political and Intellectual Origins of American Radicalism, Right and Left," *Annals of the American Academy of Political and Social Science,* Vol. 344 (November 1962), p. 5.
13. Charles Murphy, "Texas Businessmen and McCarthy," *Fortune, op. cit.,* pp. 100, 216.
14. By the time the Korean War ended, McCarthy controlled a Senate committee, had terrorized the Republican Party, and was front-page news daily. He had achieved such notoriety that he could not be expected to fade away immediately. Therefore, it is not surprising that a year elapsed between the end of the war and his censure.
15. Samuel A. Stouffer, *Communism, Conformity and Civil Liberties* (Garden City, N.Y.: Doubleday, 1955), pp. 57, 71.
16. Talcott Parsons, "Social Strains in America," in Daniel Bell (ed.), *The New American Right, op. cit.* Cf. also David Riesman and Nathan Glazer, "The Intellectuals and the Discontented Classes," and Peter Viereck, "The Revolt Against the Elite," in *ibid.*
17. Seymour Martin Lipset, "The Sources of the Radical Right," in *ibid.,* p. 212.
18. Daniel Bell, "Interpretations of American Politics," in *ibid.,* p. 20.
19. Daniel Bell, *The End of Ideology* (Glencoe, Ill.: Free Press, 1960), pp. 294, 373–375.
20. Since then Lipset has published a valuable analysis of survey data bearing on support for McCarthy. Cf. Seymour Martin Lipset, "Three Decades of the Radical Right: Coughlinites, McCarthyites, and Birchers (1962)," in Daniel Bell (ed.), *The Radical Right* (Garden City, N.Y.: Doubleday Anchor, 1964).
21. Cf. William F. Buckley and L. Brent Bozell, *McCarthy and His Enemies* (Chicago: Regnery, 1954), pp. 282–285, 308–330. On

page 285, for example, the authors write, "It is curious that what is widely thought of as a contemptible aspect of Senator McCarthy's method actually amounts to nothing more than his intimacy with the people."

22. Martin A. Trow, "Right-Wing Radicalism and Political Intolerance: A Study of Support for McCarthy in a New England Town" (unpublished Ph.D. dissertation, Department of Political Science, Columbia University, 1957), p. 281.

23. Nelson W. Polsby, "Towards an Explanation of McCarthyism," *Political Studies,* Vol. 8 (October 1960), pp. 269–270.

24. Martin A. Trow, "Right-Wing Radicalism and Political Intolerance: A Study of Support for McCarthy in a New England Town," *op. cit.,* p. 281 and references there cited.

25. *Memorial Services Held in the Senate and House of Representatives of the United States, Together with Remarks Presented in Eulogy of Joseph McCarthy* (Washington, D. C.: Government Printing Office, 1957), pp. 343–344.

26. Richard Rovere, *Senator Joe McCarthy* (New York: Meridian, 1960), p. 248.

27. Reported in Nelson Polsby, "Towards an Explanation of McCarthyism," *op. cit.,* p. 253.

28. Cf. Richard Rovere, *Senator Joe McCarthy, op. cit.,* pp. 167–168.

29. Frank J. Kendrick, "McCarthy and the Senate" (unpublished Ph.D. dissertation, Department of Political Science, University of Chicago, 1962), p. 33.

30. Cf. Michael Straight, *Trial by Television* (Boston: Beacon Press, 1954), pp. 146–148.

31. Similarly, it is hard to agree with Luthin that McCarthy's participation in a county picnic in Wisconsin demonstrates his demagoguery. Cf. Reinhard H. Luthin, *American Demagogues* (Boston: Beacon Press, 1954), p. 307.

32. Cf. *supra,* Chapter 2.

33. Samuel Stouffer, *Communism, Conformity and Civil Liberties, op. cit.,* pp. 26–57.

34. Cf. Herbert H. Hyman, "England and America; Climates of Tolerance and Intolerance (1962)," in Daniel Bell (ed.), *The Radical Right, op. cit.,* particularly p. 288.

35. Cf. S. M. Lipset and Nathan Glazer, "The Polls on Communism and Conformity," in Daniel Bell (ed.), *The New American Right, op. cit.* S. M. Lipset, *The First New Nation, op. cit.,* pp. 277–281, makes a parallel point about personality and politics.

36. Cf. William Kornhauser, *The Politics of Mass Society* (Glencoe, Ill.: Free Press, 1959), pp. 59–60, 102–103, 131–134; Edward Shils, *The Torment of Secrecy* (Glencoe, Ill.: Free Press, 1956), pp. 38–41, 46, 98–108, 169–184; S. M. Lipset, *The First New Nation, op. cit.,* pp. 262–271.

37. Nelson Polsby, "Towards an Explanation of McCarthyism," *op. cit.*, p. 262. Republicans comprised 46 percent of those for Mc-Carthy and 24 percent of those against him; 30 percent of those for McCarthy and 58 percent of those against him were Democrats.

38. Cf. Frank Kendrick, "McCarthy and the Senate," *op. cit.*, pp. 330–331, Nelson Polsby, "Towards an Explanation of Mc-Carthyism," *op. cit.*, pp. 258–262. The contrast between Jewish and Catholic support for McCarthy provides the only exception. That case aside, the biggest percentage point spread in this data is the 27 points separating farmers from business and pro-fessional people.

   Those who attended a Christian Anti-Communist Crusade school in Oakland, California, in 1962 were overwhelmingly Re-publican. Ninety percent had voted for Nixon in 1960. Cf. Ray-mond E. Wolfinger, *et al.*, "America's Radical Right: Politics and Ideology," in David E. Apter (ed.), *Ideology and Discontent* (New York: Free Press, 1964), pp. 267–268.

39. Cf. Angus Campbell and Homer C. Cooper, *Group Differences in Attitudes and Votes* (Survey Research Center: University of Michigan, 1956), p. 92.

40. S. M. Lipset, "Three Decades of the Radical Right: Coughlinites, McCarthyites, Birchers (1962)," in Daniel Bell (ed.), *The Radical Right, op. cit.*, p. 397. Note also that party differences are exaggerated by the lack of southern support for McCarthy. Democratic party allegiance and anti-Catholic attitudes limited support for McCarthy in the South. If one considered only northern respondents, the effect of party on attitudes toward Mc-Carthy might be considerably reduced.

41. *Ibid.*, pp. 408–410. Lipset suggests that the relations are weak, but they are as strong as the relationships between party and demographic variables and support for McCarthy. Survey data from the 1952 election further reveal that ". . . rudimentary ideological patterns on questions of foreign policy were at least as firmly crystallized as on matters of domestic policy. More-over, despite the efforts of Eisenhower and his leading followers to narrow the range of competition of foreign issues, the ideol-ogy of his supporters diverged from that of Stevenson in for-eign policy to a degree equal to, if not greater than, that encountered in domestic politics." Morris Janowitz and Dwaine Marvick, *Competitive Pressures and Democratic Consent* (Ann Arbor, Mich.: Institute of Public Administration, University of Michigan, 1956), pp. 115–116.

42. S. M. Lipset, "Three Decades of the Radical Right: Coughlinites, McCarthyites, Birchers (1962)," in Daniel Bell (ed.), *The Radical Right, op. cit.*, p. 408.

43. Martin A. Trow, "Small Businessmen, Political Intolerance, and

Support for McCarthy," *American Journal of Sociology*, Vol. 64 (November 1958), pp. 275–278.

44. S. M. Lipset, "Three Decades of the Radical Right: Coughlinites, McCarthyites, Birchers (1962)," in Daniel Bell (ed.), *The Radical Right, op. cit.*, pp. 410–411. Analysis of another national sample in the middle 1950's also indicates that among political leaders and educated followers, those with a prolabor orientation were much more opposed to congressional witch-hunts than those with a probusiness orientation. Cf. Jerry Mandel, "The Effect of Class Consciousness and Political Sophistication on Working-Class Authoritarianism" (unpublished Master's thesis, Department of Sociology, University of California at Berkeley, 1964), pp. 53–59. On the conservative issue position of those who attended the Christian Anti-Communist Crusade school in Oakland, California, cf. Raymond E. Wolfinger, *et al.*, "America's Radical Right: Politics and Ideology," *op. cit.*, pp. 271–273.

45. S. M. Lipset, "Three Decades of the Radical Right: Coughlinites, McCarthyites, Birchers (1962)," in Daniel Bell (ed.), *The Radical Right, op. cit.*, p. 400; A. Campbell and H. C. Cooper, *Group Differences in Attitudes and Votes, op. cit.*, pp. 145–149; Frank Kendrick, "McCarthy and the Senate," *op. cit.*, pp. 330–331; Immanuel Wallerstein, "McCarthyism and the Conservative" (unpublished Master's thesis, Department of Political Science, Columbia University, 1957), pp. 82–85. The exceptions are the surveys reported by Campbell and Cooper, and Kendrick; but in these, as in some of the other surveys, professionals and businessmen are classed together. Note that the clientele of the Christian Anti-Communist Crusade school in Oakland was overwhelmingly wealthy and college-educated. Cf. Raymond E. Wolfinger, *et al.*, "America's Radical Right: Politics and Ideology," *op. cit.*, pp. 268, 276–277.

46. S. M. Lipset, "Three Decades of the Radical Right: Coughlinites, McCarthyites, Birchers (1962)," in Daniel Bell (ed.), *The Radical Right, op. cit.*, p. 400; A. Campbell and H. C. Cooper, *Group Differences in Attitudes and Votes, op. cit.*, pp. 145–149; Martin Trow, "Small Businessmen, Political Intolerance, and Support for McCarthy," *American Journal of Sociology, op. cit.*, pp. 274–276. The retired, listed in only one poll, were the most pro-McCarthy group of all. (Cf. Lipset, *Radical Right*, p. 400.)

47. Nonunion members supported McCarthy no more than union members did, but they opposed him less. (More were neutral or had no opinion.) This suggests that union membership exposed workers to anti-McCarthy union leaders but not that workers without unions focused their discontent on McCarthy's targets rather than union targets. The latter interpretation would require greater support for McCarthy among nonunion workers. Cf. A. Campbell and H. C. Cooper, *Group Differences in Atti-*

tudes and Votes, op. cit., pp. 145–149; Martin Trow, "Right-Wing Radicalism and Political Intolerance: A Study of the Support for McCarthy in a New England Town," *op. cit.,* pp. 153–166.

48. S. M. Lipset, "Three Decades of Support for the Radical Right: Coughlinites, McCarthyites, Birchers (1962)," in Daniel Bell (ed.), *The Radical Right, op. cit.,* p. 400; A. Campbell and H. C. Cooper, *Group Differences in Attitudes and Votes, op. cit.,* pp. 145–149; Frank Kendrick, "McCarthy and the Senate," *op. cit.,* pp. 330–331.

49. A. Campbell and H. C. Cooper, *Group Differences in Attitudes and Votes, op. cit.,* pp. 145–149; Nelson Polsby, "Towards an Explanation of McCarthyism," *op. cit.,* p. 261; Frank Kendrick, "McCarthy and the Senate," *op. cit.,* pp. 330–331.

50. A. Campbell and H. C. Cooper, *Group Differences in Attitudes and Votes, op. cit.,* p. 149; S. M. Lipset, "Three Decades of the Radical Right: Coughlinites, McCarthyites, Birchers (1962)," in Daniel Bell (ed.), *The Radical Right, op. cit.,* p. 404.

51. S. M. Lipset, "Three Decades of the Radical Right: Coughlinites, McCarthyites, Birchers (1962)," in Daniel Bell (ed.), *The Radical Right, op. cit.,* p. 406.

52. Nelson Polsby, "Towards an Explanation of McCarthyism," *op. cit.,* p. 261; A. Campbell and H. C. Cooper, *Group Differences in Attitudes and Votes, op. cit.,* pp. 145–149; Frank Kendrick, "McCarthy and the Senate," *op. cit.,* pp. 330–331; Immanuel Wallerstein, "McCarthyism and the Conservative," *op. cit.,* pp. 75–78. The greatest educational differences are reported in John M. Fenton, *In Your Opinion* (Boston: Little, Brown, 1960), pp. 135–136, 140–141.

53. S. M. Lipset, "Three Decades of the Radical Right: Coughlinites, McCarthyites, Birchers (1962)," in Daniel Bell (ed.), *The Radical Right, op. cit.,* p. 398.

54. Martin A. Trow, "Right-Wing Radicalism and Political Intolerance: A Study of Support for McCarthy in a New England Town," *op. cit.,* p. 109.

55. S. M. Lipset, "Three Decades of the Radical Right: Coughlinites, McCarthyites, Birchers (1962)," in Daniel Bell (ed.), *The Radical Right, op. cit.,* pp. 412–414.

56. Cf. Charles D. Farris, " 'Authoritarianism' as a Political Behavior Variable," *Journal of Politics,* Vol. 18 (February 1956), pp. 69–78. Within the lower class, the more authoritarian supported Folsom more than the less authoritarian. This could be accounted for by education or income, or it may be a truly psychological factor. Within the middle class, there was no relationship between authoritarianism and support for Folsom.

Those who attended the Christian Anti-Communist Crusade school were "joiners," felt more politically efficacious than was typical for white, college-educated northerners, and were extremely active politically. Cf. Raymond E. Wolfinger, *et al.*, "America's Radical Right: Politics and Ideology," *op. cit.*, pp. 276–277.

57. Richard Hofstadter, "The Pseudo-Conservative Revolt," in Daniel Bell (ed.), *The New American Right, op. cit.*, pp. 49–50.

58. Martin A. Trow, "Right-Wing Radicalism and Political Intolerance: A Study of the Support for McCarthy in a New England Town, *op. cit.*, pp. 94–100.

59. S. M. Lipset, "Three Decades of the Radical Right: Coughlinites, McCarthyites, Birchers (1962)," in Daniel Bell (ed.), *The Radical Right, op. cit.*, pp. 414–417. Lack of support for McCarthy in the ethnocentric South does not corrupt this finding, since one reported poll excluded the southern states. On greater southern intolerance and authoritarianism, cf. Samuel A. Stouffer, *Communism, Conformity, and Civil Rights, op. cit.*, pp. 110–111, and the study reported by E. Terry Prothro and Levan Milikian, in "The California Public Opinion Scale in an Authoritarian Culture," *Public Opinion Quarterly*, Vol. 17 (Fall 1953), p. 354.

60. Reported by S. M. Lipset, "Three Decades of the Radical Right: Coughlinites, McCarthyites, Birchers (1962)," in Daniel Bell (ed.), *The Radical Right, op. cit.*, pp. 402–403.

61. Data from files of National Opinion Research Center, Chicago.

62. David Riesman and Nathan Glazer, "The Intellectuals and the Discontented Classes," in Daniel Bell (ed.), *The New American Right, op. cit.*, pp. 70–71. In his latest work, but not in his original article on McCarthyism, Lipset stresses the importance of the Communist issue. Cf. S. M. Lipset, "Three Decades of the Radical Right: Coughlinites, McCarthyites, Birchers (1962)," in Daniel Bell (ed.), *The Radical Right, op. cit.*, pp. 392–393.

63. Samuel A. Stouffer, *Communism, Conformity, and Civil Liberties, op. cit.*, pp. 230–231. In other words, 2½ percent of the population singled out McCarthy as their general, anti-Communist hero. This corresponds to the 5 percent of the population which said it would support him for President on a third-party ticket. Cf. John Fenton, *In Your Opinion, op. cit.*, p. 143.

64. S. M. Lipset, "The Sources of the Radical Right," in Daniel Bell (ed.), *The New American Right, op. cit.*, p. 214.

65. A. Campbell *et al.*, *The Voter Decides* (Evanston, Ill.: Row, Peterson, 1954), p. 52; A. Campbell *et al.*, *The American Voter* (New York: Wiley, 1960), pp. 50, 182, 198–199. The Republican's foreign policy advantage rests on the peace issue not the war issue; thus Goldwater's saber rattling lost that traditional advantage in 1964.

66. Immanuel Wallerstein, "McCarthyism and the Conservative," *op. cit.*, pp. 75–78. Even so, there was no greater tendency for the college educated to approve of McCarthy personally but oppose his methods than for the high-school educated. This

tendency was significantly more apparent among the grade-school educated, but the difference in percentage point spread should not be exaggerated. At the college level, the spread between approval of McCarthy and disapproval of his methods is 32, at the high-school level 33, and at the grade-school level 19. This interpretation differs from John Fenton, *In Your Opinion, op. cit.*, p. 136, where the figures are reported.

67. Louis Bean, *Influences in the 1954 Mid-Term Elections* (Washington, D. C.: Public Affairs Institute, 1954), pp. 22, 32–33, and *supra*, Tables 8.1 and 8.4.

68. *Ibid.*, p. 33.

69. *Ibid.*, pp. 18–21; Nelson Polsby, "Towards an Explanation of McCarthyism," *op. cit.*, pp. 265–268; *supra*, Chapters 3–5. Bean (p. 32) only found an important pro-McCarthy influence in 1950 in Maryland. In 1952, Republican moderates ran better for the senate than Republican conservatives, and were less likely to run behind Eisenhower. Cf. Louis Harris, *Is There a Republican Majority?* (New York: Harper, 1954), pp. 203–204, 223.

70. Louis Bean, *Influences in the 1954 Mid-Term Elections* (Washington, D. C.: Public Affairs Institute, 1954), p. 26; *supra*, Chapters 3, 5.

71. *Supra*, Chapter 3. According to Fiedler, the "working class districts of Kenosha, Racine, and Milwaukee, ordinarily safe for the Democrats," helped to elect McCarthy. The only basis for this assertion is that in McCarthy's 1946 primary victory workers did not vote as heavily for La Follette as they had in 1940. McCarthy carried working-class areas. But to relate this, as Fiedler does, to "the revolt of the community against its intelligence," is perverse. Because of La Follette's anticommunism, the then Communist-controlled CIO sought to defeat La Follette. In addition, many pro-La Follette workers probably did not vote in the Republican primary. It is ascribing intelligence indeed to the working class to assume that in 1946 it could perceive that McCarthy was an anti-intellectual revolutionary and hence support him. (Cf. Leslie Fiedler, "McCarthy," *op. cit.*, pp. 14, 20.)

72. A. Campbell, *et al.*, *The American Voter, op. cit.*, p. 301.

73. As Trow has pointed out, status concerns kept white-collar workers and those in the managerial hierarchy from supporting McCarthy, since he seemed to be attacking that hierarchy. Cf. Trow, "Right-Wing Radicalism and Political Intolerance: A Study of the Support for McCarthy in a New England Town," *op. cit.*, pp. 41–43, 101–102, 132.

74. This view extrapolates from Samuel Lubell's interpretations in *The Future of American Politics* (New York: Harper, 1952).

75. It could be argued that McCarthy had no strength at the polls because his followers were completely disenchanted with tra-

ditional political activity. As Lipset suggests, much of McCarthy's support may have come from people too alienated to vote. Cf. S. M. Lipset, "The Sources of the 'Radical Right,'" in Daniel Bell (ed.), *The New American Right, op. cit.,* p. 199. But if these people were too alienated to vote, they were also probably too alienated to exert influence in any other way. Voting is almost always the first step. Moreover, Lipset has shown that Nazism in Germany did not grow originally because of the support of previous nonvoters. He argues that these elements will wait until a movement has demonstrated strength before supporting it at the polls. Cf. S. M. Lipset, *Political Man, op. cit.,* pp. 121–122, 149–152. One might still argue that a totally latent McCarthy mass support could have erupted suddenly into prominence, but this would be pure speculation.

76. S. M. Lipset, *The First New Nation, op. cit.,* p. 262.

77. Cf. Paul E. Breslow, "The Relationship between Ideology and Socio-Economic Background in a Group of McCarthyite Leaders" (unpublished Master's thesis, Department of Political Science, University of Chicago, 1955), pp. 82–103.

78. Quoted in Nelson Polsby, "Towards an Explanation of McCarthyism," *op. cit.,* p. 263.

79. S. M. Lipset, *The First New Nation, op. cit.,* pp. 1–2, 262–273, 318–343.

80. There were, of course, other reasons for the absence of something similar to McCarthyism in Britain. Unlike America, Britain was not entering the world stage as a preeminent power for the first time. The Communist "menace" was much more salient in America. But McCarthyism arose out of the response of American elites to these new challenges, not primarily out of the response of American masses.

81. Cf. Donald R. Matthews, *U.S. Senators and Their World* (New York: Random House, Vintage Books, 1960), pp. 64–66, 254–255 and letter from Professor Matthews to the author.

82. Peter Viereck, "The Revolt Against the Elite," in Daniel Bell (ed.), *The New American Right, op. cit.,* p. 111.

83. Frank Kendrick, "McCarthy and the Senate," *op. cit.,* p. 145.

84. *Ibid.,* pp. 173–174; K. E. Meyer, "The Politics of Loyalty: From La Follette to McCarthy in Wisconsin: 1918–1952" (unpublished Ph.D. dissertation, Department of Political Science, Princeton University, 1956), pp. 90–91.

85. Cf. Michael Straight, *Trial by Television, op. cit.,* p. 140. Cf. also Norman A. Graebner, *The New Isolationism* (New York: Ronald Press, 1956), p. 199; Telford Taylor, *Grand Inquest* (New York: Simon and Schuster, 1955), pp. 114–123; Aaron Wildavsky, "Exploring the Content of McCarthyism," *The Australian Outlook* (June 1955).

86. Dwaine Marvick (in personal conversation) has suggested some relevant findings from survey data on members of the John

Birch Society in California. The Birchers justify their views by pointing to prestigious members of their local communities who are also Birchers. As in support for McCarthy, deference can be more important than anti-elitism.

87. Cf. Frank Kendrick, "McCarthy and the Senate," *op. cit.*, pp. 317–323; Aaron Wildavsky, "Exploring the Content of McCarthyism," *op. cit.*

88. Aaron Wildavsky, "Exploring the Content of McCarthyism," *op. cit.*

89. Quoted in *ibid.*

90. Daniel Bell, "Interpretations of American Politics," in Daniel Bell (ed.), *The New American Right, op. cit.*, p. 25; Leslie Fiedler, "McCarthy," *op. cit.*, p. 13.

91. Cf. Jack Anderson and Ronald W. May, *McCarthy the Man, The Senator, The Ism* (Boston: Beacon Press, 1952), pp. 266–270.

92. Cf. Reinhard Luthin, *American Demagogues, op. cit.*, pp. 293–294.

93. Cf. Nelson W. Polsby and Aaron B. Wildavsky, *Presidential Elections* (New York: Scribner's, 1964), pp. 40–46.

94. This point was suggested, in correspondence, by Nelson Polsby.

95. Cf. Edward Shils, *The Torment of Secrecy, op. cit.*, pp. 46–47, 102–109.

96. This argument is developed more fully in the following chapter.

97. Charles Murphy, "McCarthy and the Businessmen," *op. cit.*, pp. 100, 216.

98. Cf. William S. White, *Citadel* (New York: Harper, 1965), p. 137.

Chapter Nine

1. Cf. Karl Marx, *Eighteenth Brumaire of Louis Bonaparte* (New York: International Publishers, 1963).

2. Richard Hofstadter, *The Age of Reform* (New York: Knopf, 1955), p. 16.

3. For a form of this argument that links McCarthyism to aspects of American politics in general rather than to agrarian radicalism in particular, cf. Hans J. Morgenthau, *The Purpose of American Politics* (New York: Knopf, 1960), pp. 146–157.

4. Cf. C. Vann Woodward, *Tom Watson: Agrarian Radical* (New York: Macmillan, 1938), *passim*.

5. Richard Hofstadter, *The Age of Reform, op. cit.*, p. 5.

6. We will note later than those same contrasting attitude syndromes are found at the popular level.

7. What "homogenization" means here may be pictured by imagining what would happen to several apples placed in a powerful Waring blender. The apples would first become small particles and then turn into mush.

8. Perhaps the most influential book written in the 1950's from this point of view was John Kenneth Galbraith, *American Capitalism* (Boston: Houghton Mifflin, 1952), pp. 1–34, 89–170. One consequence is that when liberals move from complacency to concern, as Galbraith did when he wrote *The Affluent Society* (Boston: Houghton Mifflin, 1958), they see no problem of power standing in the way of their public policy goals. It is only necessary to educate the people (cf. pp. 13–14).

9. Cf. William Kornhauser, *The Politics of Mass Society* (Glencoe, Ill.: Free Press, 1959), pp. 15, 48–49.

10. This division is affected by social stratification. Educated and wealthy people tend to be close to the leadership stratum whereas those of low education, sophistication, and social class predominate in the "followers" stratum: workers, farmers, and Negroes, for example.

    Note also that classical Marxism sees social stratification as a horizontal division and minimizes the importance of horizontal *political* stratification. Pluralists argue that social stratification creates vertical cleavages in politics, since business is not significantly more powerful than labor, and so on.

11. *Supra,* Chapter 1.

12. For a developed theory of the dangers of taking issues outside the leadership stratum, cf. Robert Dahl, *Who Governs* (New Haven, Conn.: Yale University Press, 1961), pp. 80–94, 318–325. Also cf. *supra,* Chapter 1.

13. Cf. Jerry Mandel, "The Effects of Class Consciousness and Political Sophistication on Working Class Authoritarianism" (unpublished Master's thesis, Department of Sociology, University of California at Berkeley, 1964), p. 65.

14. Cf. Herbert McClosky, "Conservatism and Personality," *American Political Science Review,* Vol. 52 (March 1958), pp. 35–44.

15. Cf. Herbert McClosky, *et al.,* "Issue Conflict and Consensus among Party Leaders and Followers," *American Political Science Review,* Vol. 54 (June 1960), pp. 422–423.

16. The literature on this subect is necessarily impressionistic but of considerable substance. Cf., for example, Robert Michels, *Political Parties* (Glencoe, Ill.: Free Press, 1949); Grant McConnell, *The Decline of Agrarian Democracy* (Berkeley, Calif.: University of California Press, 1953); Philip Selznick, *T.V.A. and the Grass Roots* (Berkeley, Calif.: University of California Press, 1949); J. D. Greenstone, "Labor in Three Cities" (unpublished Ph.D. dissertation, Department of Political Science, University of Chicago, 1963); Karl Mannheim, *Ideology and Utopia* (New York: Harcourt, Brace, Harvest Books), pp. 118–119.

17. AFL, *Proceedings,* 1924, pp. 5–6.

18. Cf. Grant McConnell, *Private Power and American Democracy* (New York: Knopf, 1966), pp. 52–154. Michael Rogin, "Voluntarism: The Political Functions of an Anti-Political

Doctrine," *Industrial and Labor Relations Review,* Vol. 15 (July 1962).
19. Cf. Angus Campbell, *et al., The American Voter* (New York: Wiley, 1960), pp. 188–265.

Appendix A

1. For further explication of the techniques of correlation analysis, cf. V. O. Key, Jr., *A Primer of Statistics for Political Scientists* (New York: Thomas Y. Crowell, 1954), pp. 78–153.

Appendix B

1. For a more detailed and precise explanation of the basic principles and methods of factor analysis, see John M. Butler, *et al., Quantitative Naturalistic Research* (Englewood Cliffs, N.J.: Prentice-Hall, 1963). Cf. also, L. L. Thurstone, *Multiple Factor Analysis* (Chicago: University of Chicago Press, 1947).
2. The adequacy of this approximation can be checked by performing mathematical operations on the factor matrix. Consider a factor matrix with the following loadings for the first two rows:

row	I	II	III
1	.3	—.7	.8
2	.8	—.2	.1

One multiplies corresponding elements of the two rows together and adds: $(.3 \times .8 = .24) + (-.7 \times -.2 = .14) + (.8 \times -.1 = -.08) = .30$. The computed relationship between rows one and two can be compared with the actual relationship on the original matrix. If the two approximate each other satisfactorily, then the factor matrix has accounted for the relationship. If not, additional factors should be extracted.

In the present analysis, the fifth and sixth factors essentially loaded high on only one row each of the original matrix. Since the seventh, eighth . . . *n*th principal axes would account for progressively less of the original data, it seemed reasonable to believe that after the fourth principal axis one was extracting principal axes unique to one row of the original matrix rather than common to several rows.
3. On the concept of simple structure, cf. L. L. Thurstone, *Multiple Factor Analysis, op. cit.,* pp. 319–346.
4. Cf. John M. Butler, *et al., Quantitative Naturalistic Research, op. cit.,* Chapter 4. The first principal axis was ignored because it is an average of all the data rows. It should also be noted that in selecting data vectors around which to rotate, those with a negative loading on the first principal axis were ignored.
5. The method of this rotation is described in *ibid.,* Chapter 4 and Appendix B. First an oblique rotation was made from the

orthogonal principal axis matrix to the new matrix. This new matrix was then orthogonalized by a method that makes successive approximations to an orthogonal structure. In the present analysis, it was necessary to orthogonalize only once.

6. The usual procedure for plotting scatter diagrams is used to examine the relation of each factor to each other by pairs. This gives six graphs in an analysis with four factors such as this one.

7. On the method of graphical rotation cf. L. L. Thurstone, *Multiple Factor Analysis, op. cit.*, pp. 194–216. In the present rotation the Populist and traditional Democratic factors became intercorrelated $(r = -.33)$.

BIBLIOGRAPHY

Election Statistics

NORTH DAKOTA

Robert Byrne, Secretary of State. *Compilation of Election Returns National and State, 1914–1928*. Bismarck, N. D., 1930.

The Fargo Forum. November 5, 1958, p. 2; June 30, 1960, p. 2.

Thomas Hall, Secretary of State. *Compilation of Election Returns National and State, 1930–1944*. Bismarck, N. D., 1945.

Ben Meier, Secretary of State. *Compilation of Election Returns National and State, 1946–1954*. Bismarck, N. D., 1956.

State of North Dakota. *Legislative Manual*. Bismarck, N. D., 1912.

SOUTH DAKOTA

South Dakota Legislative Manual. Pierre, S. D., 1913–1956.

WISCONSIN

The Wisconsin Blue Book. 1887–1958.

GENERAL

Robinson, Edgar Eugene. *The Presidential Vote, 1896–1932*. Stanford, Calif.: Stanford University Press, 1934.

Scammon, Richard M. (ed.). *America Votes*. 3 Vols. Vols. I and II, New York: The Macmillan Co., 1956, 1958; Vol. III, Pittsburgh, Pa.: University of Pittsburgh Press, 1958.

The 1961 World Almanac and Book of Facts. New York: *World Telegram and Sun*, 1961.

Census Material

Department of the Interior, Census Office. *Report on the Population of United States at the Eleventh Census: 1890.* Vol. I, Part 1, Washington, D. C.: Government Printing Office, 1897.

Department of the Interior, Census Office. *Statistics of Agriculture in the United States at the Eleventh Census: 1890.* Washington, D. C.: Government Printing Office, 1895.

Department of the Interior, Census Office. *Report on Farms and Homes: Property and Indebtedness at the Eleventh Census: 1890.* Washington, D. C.: Government Printing Office, 1896.

Department of the Interior, Census Office. *Report on Statistics of Churches of the United States at the Eleventh Census: 1890.* Washington, D. C.: Government Printing Office, 1894.

Department of Commerce, Bureau of the Census. *Thirteenth Census of the United States; Vol. VII, Agriculture, 1909–1910; Report by States, Nebraska to Wyoming.* Washington, D. C.: Government Printing Office, 1913.

Department of Commerce, Bureau of the Census. *Thirteenth Census of the United States; Vol. III, Population, 1910; Report by States, Nebraska to Wyoming.* Washington, D. C.: Government Printing Office, 1913.

Department of Commerce, Bureau of the Census. *Religious Bodies, 1916; Part I, Summary and General Tables.* Washington, D. C.: Government Printing Office, 1919.

Department of Commerce, Bureau of the Census. *Fourteenth Census of the United States; Vol. III, Population, 1920; Report by States, Nebraska to Wyoming.* Washington, D. C.: Government Printing Office, 1922.

Department of Commerce, Bureau of the Census. *Fifteenth Census of the United States: 1930; Population, Vol. III, Part 2.* Washington, D. C.: United States Government Printing Office, 1932.

Department of Commerce, Bureau of the Census. *Fifteenth Census of the United States: 1930; Agriculture, Vol. II, Type of Farm; Part I, The Northern States.* Washington, D. C.: United States Government Printing Office, 1932.

United States Department of Commerce, Bureau of the Census. *Religious Bodies: 1936; Vol. I, Summary and Detailed Tables.* Washington, D. C.: United States Government Printing Office, 1941.

United States Department of Commerce, Bureau of the Census.

Census of Population: 1950; Characteristics of the Population; Part 34: North Dakota. Washington, D. C.: United States Government Printing Office, 1952.

United States Department of Commerce, Bureau of the Census. *Census of Population: 1950; Vol. II, Characteristics of the Population; Part 41: South Dakota.* Washington, D. C.: United States Government Printing Office, 1952.

United States Department of Commerce, Bureau of the Census. *Census of Agriculture: 1950; Counties and State Economic Areas; Vol. 1, Part 11: North and South Dakota.* Washington, D. C.: United States Government Printing Office, 1952.

Books

Aaron, Daniel. *Men of Good Hope.* New York: Oxford University Press, 1951.

Adorno, T. W., *et al. The Authoritarian Personality.* New York: Harper and Bros., 1950.

Anderson, Jack, and Ronald W. May. *McCarthy the Man, the Senator, the Ism.* Boston: The Beacon Press, 1952.

Arnett, Alex Matthews. *The Populist Movement in Georgia.* New York: Columbia University, 1922.

Auerbach, M. Morton. *The Conservative Illusion.* New York: Columbia University Press, 1959.

Banfield, Edward. *The Moral Basis of a Backward Society.* Glencoe, Ill.: The Free Press, 1958.

Bean, Louis. *Ballot Behavior.* Washington, D. C.: American Council on Public Affairs, 1940.

————. *How to Predict Elections.* New York: Alfred A. Knopf, 1948.

————. *Influences in the 1954 Mid-Term Elections.* Washington, D. C.: Public Affairs Institute, 1954.

Bean, Walton. *Boss Ruef's San Francisco.* Berkeley, Calif.: University of California Press, 1952.

Bell, Daniel. *The End of Ideology.* Glencoe, Ill.: The Free Press, 1960.

———— (ed.). *The New American Right.* New York: Criterion Books, 1955.

———— (ed.). *The Radical Right.* Garden City, N. Y.: Doubleday & Company, Inc., Anchor Books, 1964.

Bendix, Reinhard. *Work and Authority in Industry.* New York: John Wiley & Sons, Inc., 1956.

Benson, Lee. *The Concept of Jacksonian Democracy*. Princeton, N. J.: Princeton University Press, 1961.

———. *Merchants, Farmers, and Railroads*. Cambridge, Mass.: Harvard University Press, 1955.

Berelson, Bernard, Paul F. Lazarfeld, and William N. McPhee. *Voting*. Chicago: University of Chicago Press, 1954.

Blum, John Morton. *The Republican Roosevelt*. Cambridge, Mass.: Harvard University Press, 1954.

Bogue, Allan G. *Money at Interest: The Farm Mortgage on the Middle Border*. Ithaca, N. Y.: Cornell University Press, 1955.

Bogue, Donald J., and Calvin L. Beale. *Economic Areas of the United States*. Glencoe, Ill.: The Free Press, 1961.

Boorstin, Daniel J. *The Genius of American Politics*. Chicago: University of Chicago Press, 1953.

———. *The Lost World of Thomas Jefferson*. New York: Henry Holt and Co., 1948.

Bowers, Claude G. *Beveridge and the Progressive Era*. Boston: Houghton Mifflin Company, 1932.

Bramson, Leon. *The Political Context of Sociology*. Princeton, N. J.: Princeton University Press, 1961.

Buck, Solon Justus. *The Granger Movement*. Cambridge, Mass.: Harvard University Press, 1933.

Buckley, William F., and L. Brent Bozell. *McCarthy and His Enemies*. Chicago: H. Regnery Co., 1954.

Butler, John M., *et al. Quantitative Naturalistic Research*. Englewood Cliffs, N. J.: Prentice-Hall, 1963.

Campbell, Angus, Philip E. Converse, Warren E. Miller, and Donald E. Stokes. *The American Voter*. New York: John Wiley & Sons, Inc., 1960.

———, and Homer C. Cooper. *Group Differences in Attitudes and Votes*. Ann Arbor, Mich.: Survey Research Center, University of Michigan, 1956.

———, Gerald Gurin, and Warren E. Miller. *The Voter Decides*. Evanston, Ill.: Row, Peterson and Co., 1954.

Capper, Arthur. *The Agricultural Bloc*. New York: Harcourt, Brace and Co., 1922.

Carnegie, Andrew. *Triumphant Democracy*. New York: Charles Scribner's Sons, 1887.

Carr, Robert K. *The House Committee on Un-American Activities, 1945–1950*. Ithaca, N. Y.: Cornell University Press, 1952.

Christie, Richard, and Marie Jahoda (eds.). *Studies in the Scope*

342

and Method of The Authoritarian Personality. Glencoe, Ill.: The Free Press, 1954.

Clark, John B. *Populism in Alabama.* Auburn, Ala.: Auburn Printing Co., 1927.

Cole, Wayne S. *America First.* Madison, Wis.: University of Wisconsin Press, 1953.

Cornwall, William G. *Free Coinage from the Businessman's Standpoint.* Buffalo, N. Y.: Matthews-Northrup Co., 1891.

Crawford, Lewis F. *History of North Dakota.* Vol. I. Chicago, Ill.: American Historical Society, 1931.

Croly, Herbert. *The Promise of American Life.* New York: The Macmillan Company, 1910.

Curti, Merle, *et al. The Making of an American Community.* Stanford, Calif.: Stanford University Press, 1959.

Dahl, Robert A. *Who Governs.* New Haven, Conn.: Yale University Press, 1961.

David, Henry. *A History of the Haymarket Affair.* New York: Farrar and Rinehart, Inc., 1936.

Destler, Chester McArthur. *American Radicalism: 1865–1901.* New London, Conn.: Connecticut College, 1946.

Dewey, John. *The Public and Its Problems.* Chicago: Gateway Books, 1946.

Doan, Edward N. *The La Follettes and the Wisconsin Idea.* New York: Rinehart and Co., Inc., 1947.

Donnelly, Ignatius. *Caesar's Column.* Chicago: J. Regan and Co., n.d.

Donner, Frank J. *The Un-Americans.* New York: Ballantine Books, 1961.

Dunne, Finley Peter. *Mr. Dooley's Opinions.* New York: R. H. Russell, 1901.

Durkheim, Emile. *The Division of Labor.* Glencoe, Ill.: The Free Press, 1947.

Epstein, Leon D. *Politics in Wisconsin.* Madison, Wis.: University of Wisconsin Press, 1958.

Fenton, John M. *In Your Opinion.* Boston: Little, Brown, and Company, 1960.

Filler, Louis. *Crusaders for American Liberalism.* Yellow Springs, Ohio: Antioch Press, 1950.

Fine, Nathan. *Labor and Farmer Parties in the United States: 1828–1928.* New York: Rand School, 1928.

Fine, Sidney. *Laissez Faire and the General-Welfare State.* Ann Arbor, Mich.: University of Michigan Press, 1956.

343

Fite, Gilbert C. *George N. Peek and the Fight for Farm Parity.* Norman, Okla.: University of Oklahoma Press, 1954.

———. *Peter Norbeck, Prairie Statesman.* Columbia, Mo.: University of Missouri Press, 1948.

Follett, Mary Parker. *The New State.* New York: Longmans, Green and Co., 1918.

Forcey, Charles. *The Crossroads of American Liberalism.* New York: Oxford University Press, 1961.

Fox, Dixon Ryan (ed.). *Sources of Culture in the Middle West.* New York: D. Appleton-Century Co., 1934.

Gates, Paul W. *The Farmer's Age: Agriculture 1815–1860.* New York: Holt, Rinehart and Winston, 1960.

Goldman, Eric F. *Rendezvous with Destiny.* New York: Alfred A. Knopf, 1952.

Gore, Leroy. *Joe Must Go.* New York: Julian Messner, Inc., 1954.

Gosnell, Harold F. *Grass Root Politics.* Washington, D. C.: American Council on Public Affairs, 1942.

Graebner, Norman A. *The New Isolationism.* New York: Ronald Press Co., 1956.

Gunther, John. *Inside U.S.A.* New York: Harper and Bros., 1947.

Handlin, Oscar. *Adventures in Freedom.* New York: McGraw-Hill Book Co., 1954.

———. *The Uprooted.* New York: Grosset and Dunlap, 1951.

———, and Mary Flug Handlin. *Commonwealth.* New York: New York University Press, 1945.

Harris, Louis. *Is There A Republican Majority?* New York: Harper and Bros., 1954.

Hartz, Louis. *Economic Policy and Democratic Thought: Pennsylvania, 1776–1860.* Cambridge, Mass.: Harvard University Press, 1948.

———. *The Liberal Tradition in America.* New York: Harcourt, Brace and Co., 1955.

Hays, Samuel P. *Conservation and the Gospel of Efficiency.* Cambridge, Mass.: Harvard University Press, 1959.

———. *The Response to Industrialism 1885–1914.* Chicago: University of Chicago Press, 1957.

Heberle, Rudolf. *From Democracy to Nazism.* Baton Rouge, La.: Louisiana State University Press, 1945.

Hesseltine, William B. *The Rise and Fall of Third Parties.* Washington, D. C.: Public Affairs Press, 1948.

344

Hicks, John D. *The Populist Revolt*. Lincoln, Neb.: University of Nebraska Press, 1961.

Higham, John. *Strangers in the Land*. New Brunswick, N. J.: Rutgers University Press, 1955.

Hitchborn, Franklin. *The System*. San Francisco, Calif.: James H. Barry, 1915.

Hofstadter, Richard. *The Age of Reform*. New York: Alfred A. Knopf, 1955.

————. *The American Political Tradition*. New York: Alfred A. Knopf, 1948.

Holcombe, Arthur N. *The Political Parties of Today*. New York: Harper and Bros., 1924.

Howard, Perry H. *Political Tendencies in Louisiana: 1812–1952*. Baton Rouge, La.: Louisiana State University Press, 1957.

Howe, Frederic C. *Confessions of a Reformer*. New York: Charles Scribner & Sons, 1925.

Janowitz, Morris, and Marvick, Dwaine. *Competitive Pressures and Democratic Consent*. Ann Arbor, Mich.: Bureau of Government Institute of Public Administration, University of Michigan, 1956.

Jones, Alfred Winslow. *Life, Liberty, and Property*. New York: J. B. Lippincott Co., 1941.

Kelley, Samuel C., Jr., *et al*. *The Population, Labor Force and Income of North Dakota, 1900–1965*. Grand Forks, N.D.: Bureau of Economic and Business Research, University of North Dakota, 1954.

Key, V. O., Jr. *American State Politics*. New York: Alfred A. Knopf, 1956.

————. *A Primer of Statistics for Political Scientists*. New York: Thomas Y. Crowell, 1954.

————. *Southern Politics in State and Nation*. New York: Alfred A. Knopf, 1949.

————, and Winston W. Crouch. *The Initiative and the Referendum in California*. Berkeley, Calif.: University of California Press, 1939.

Kolko, Gabriel. *The Triumph of Conservatism*. New York: The Free Press of Glencoe, 1963.

Kornhauser, William. *The Politics of Mass Society*. Glencoe, Ill.: The Free Press, 1959.

Kraenzel, Carl Frederick. *The Great Plains in Transition*. Norman, Okla.: University of Oklahoma Press, 1957.

La Follette, Belle Case, and Fola La Follette. *Robert M. La Follette*. 2 Vols. New York: The Macmillan Co., 1953.

La Follette, Robert M. *La Follette's Autobiography*. Madison, Wis.: The Robert M. La Follette Co., 1913.

Link, Arthur S. *Woodrow Wilson and the Progressive Era*. New York: Harper and Bros., 1954.

Lipset, Seymour Martin. *Agrarian Socialism*. Berkeley, Calif.: University of California Press, 1959.

————. *The First New Nation*. New York: Basic Books, Inc., 1963.

————. *Political Man*. Garden City, N. Y.: Doubleday & Co., 1960.

Lloyd, Henry Demarest. *Wealth Against Commonwealth*. New York: Harper and Bros., 1894.

Locke, John. *Of Civil Government*. New York: E. P. Dutton and Co., Everyman's Library.

Lowenthal, Leo, and Norbert Guterman. *Prophets of Deceit*. New York: Harper and Bros., 1949.

Lubell, Samuel. *The Future of American Politics*. New York: Harper and Bros., 1952.

————. *The Revolt of the Moderates*. New York: Harper and Bros., 1956.

Luthin, Reinhard H. *American Demogogues*. Boston: The Beacon Press, 1954.

McCarthy, Charles. *The Wisconsin Idea*. New York: The Macmillan Co., 1912.

McCarthy, Senator Joe. *McCarthyism: The Fight for America*. New York: The Devin-Adair Co., 1952.

————. *The Story of General George C. Marshall*. New York: The Devin-Adair Co., 1952.

McCloskey, Robert Green. *American Conservatism in an Age of Enterprise*. Cambridge, Mass.: Harvard University Press, 1951.

McConnell, Grant. *The Decline of Agrarian Democracy*. Berkeley, Calif.: University of California Press, 1953.

MacKay, Kenneth Campbell. *The Progressive Movement of 1924*. New York: Columbia University Press, 1947.

MacRae, Duncan, Jr. *Dimensions of Congressional Voting*. Berkeley, Calif.: University of California Publications in Sociology and Social Institutions, University of California Press, 1958.

Martin, Roscoe C. *The People's Party in Texas*. Austin, Tex.: University of Texas, 1933.

Matthews, Donald R. *U.S. Senators and Their World*. New York: Random House, Inc., Vintage Books, 1960.

346

Maxwell, Robert S. *La Follette and the Rise of the Progressives in Wisconsin.* Madison, Wis.: State Historical Society of Wisconsin, 1956.

May, Henry F. *The End of American Innocence.* New York: Alfred A. Knopf, 1959.

Mayer, George H. *The Political Career of Floyd B. Olson.* Minneapolis, Minn.: University of Minnesota Press, 1951.

Mecklin, John Moffatt. *The Ku Klux Klan.* New York: Harcourt, Brace and Co., 1924.

Memorial Services Held in the Senate and House of Representatives of the United States, together with Remarks Presented in Eulogy of Joseph Raymond McCarthy. Washington, D. C.: United States Government Printing Office, 1957.

Meyers, Marvin. *The Jacksonian Persuasion.* New York: Vintage Books, 1960.

Miller, Perry. *Jonathan Edwards.* New York: Meridian Books, 1959.

Mills, C. Wright. *White Collar.* New York: Oxford University Press, 1956.

Morlan, Robert L. *Political Prairie Fire.* Minneapolis, Minn.: University of Minnesota Press, 1955.

Mowry, George E. *The California Progressives.* Berkeley, Calif.: University of California Press, 1951.

――――. *The Era of Theodore Roosevelt.* New York: Harper and Bros., 1958.

――――. *The Progressive Movement 1900–1920: Recent Ideas and New Literature.* Washington, D. C.: Service Center for Teachers of History, 1958.

――――. *Theodore Roosevelt and the Progressive Movement.* Madison, Wis.: University of Wisconsin Press, 1946.

Murray, Robert K. *Red Scare.* Minneapolis, Minn.: University of Minnesota Press, 1955.

Nelson, Bruce. *Land of the Dacotahs.* Minneapolis, Minn.: University of Minnesota Press, 1946.

Neprash, Jerry Alvin. *The Brookhart Campaigns in Iowa 1920–26.* New York: Columbia University Press, 1932.

Newman, William J. *The Futilitarian Society.* New York: George Braziller, Inc., 1961.

Nixon, Herman Clarence. *The Populist Movement in Iowa.* Reprinted from the January 1926 Number of the Iowa Journal of History and Politics. Iowa City, Iowa: State Historical Society of Iowa.

Noble, David W. *The Paradox of Progressive Thought*. Minneapolis, Minn.: University of Minnesota Press, 1958.

Nye, Russel B. *Midwestern Progressive Politics*. East Lansing, Mich.: Michigan State College Press, 1951.

Palamountain, Joseph Cornwall. *The Politics of Distribution*. Cambridge, Mass.: Harvard University Press, 1955.

Parsons, Talcott. *Structure and Process in Modern Societies*. Glencoe, Ill.: The Free Press, 1960.

Peffer, William A. *The Farmer's Side: His Troubles and Their Remedy*. New York: D. Appleton and Co., 1891.

———. *Government Control of Money*. Washington, D. C.; Senate of the United States, 1892.

———. *The Way Out*. Topeka, Kan.: Kansas Farmers Co., 1890.

Pollack, Norman. *The Populist Response to Industrial America*. Cambridge, Mass.: Harvard University Press, 1962.

Pye, Lucian. *Guerilla Communism in Malaya*. Princeton, N. J.: Princeton University Press, 1956.

Ranulf, Svend. *Moral Indignation and Middle Class Psychology*. Copenhagen, Denmark: Levin and Munksgaard, 1938.

Rice, Stuart A. *Farmers and Workers in American Politics*. New York: Columbia University Press, 1924.

———. *Quantitative Methods in Politics*. New York: Alfred A. Knopf, 1928.

Riesman, David, with Nathan Glazer, and Ruel Denney. *The Lonely Crowd*. Garden City, N. Y.: Doubleday & Co., Anchor Books, 1953.

Rorty, James, and Moshe Dechter. *McCarthy and the Communists*. Boston: The Beacon Press, 1954.

Rosenberg, Bernard, and David Manning White (eds.). *Mass Culture: The Popular Arts in America*. Glencoe, Ill.: The Free Press, 1957.

Rovere, Richard H. *Senator Joe McCarthy*. New York: Meridian Books, 1960.

Saloutos, Theodore, and John D. Hicks. *Agricultural Discontent in the Middle West, 1900–1939*. Madison, Wis.: University of Wisconsin Press, 1951.

Schaar, John H. *Loyalty in America*. Berkeley, Calif.: University of California Press, 1957.

Schell, Herbert S. *History of South Dakota*. Lincoln, Neb.: University of Nebraska Press, 1961.

Schumpeter, Joseph A. *Capitalism, Socialism, and Democracy*. New York: Harper and Bros., 1950.

Selznick, Philip. *T. V. A. and the Grass Roots.* Berkeley, Calif.: University of California Press, 1949.

Shafer, Joseph. *A History of Agriculture in Wisconsin.* Madison, Wis.: State Historical Society of Wisconsin, 1922.

Shannon, Fred A. *American Farmers' Movements.* Princeton, N. J.: D. Van Nostrand Co., Inc., 1957.

———. *The Farmer's Last Frontier: Agriculture 1860–1897.* New York: Farrar and Rinehart, Inc., 1945.

Shelton, William Du Bose. *Populism in the Old Dominion.* Princeton, N. J.: Princeton University Press, 1935.

Shils, Edward A. *Torment of Secrecy.* Glencoe, Ill.: The Free Press, 1956.

Simkins, Francis Butler. *The Tillman Movement in South Carolina.* Durham, N. C.: Duke University Press, 1926.

Smith, Henry Nash. *Virgin Land.* New York: Random House, Inc., Vintage Books, 1959.

Smith, J. Allen. *The Spirit of American Government.* New York: The Macmillan Co., 1907.

Stedman, Murray S., Jr., and Susan W. Stedman. *Discontent at the Polls.* New York: Columbia University Press, 1950.

Stember, Charles Herbert. *Education and Attitude Change.* New York: Institute of Human Relations Press, 1951.

Stouffer, Samuel A. *Communism, Conformity, and Civil Liberties.* Garden City, N. Y.: Doubleday & Co., 1955.

Straight, Michael. *Trial by Television.* Boston: The Beacon Press, 1954.

Talmon, Jacob. *The Origins of Totalitarian Democracy.* London: Secker and Warburg, 1952.

Taylor, Carl C. *The Farmers' Movements 1620–1920.* New York: American Book Co., 1953.

———, et al. *Rural Life in the United States.* New York: Alfred A. Knopf, 1949.

Taylor, Telford. *Grand Inquest.* New York: Simon and Schuster, Inc., 1955.

Thurstone, Louis Leon. *Multiple Factor Analysis.* Chicago: University of Chicago Press, 1947.

de Tocqueville, Alexis. *Democracy in America.* 2 Vols. New York: Random House, Inc., Vintage Books, 1959, 1960.

Turner, Frederick Jackson. *The Frontier in American History.* New York: Henry Holt and Co., 1920.

Turner, Julius. *Party and Constituency; Pressures on Congress.* Baltimore, Md.: The Johns Hopkins Press, 1951.

349

Twiss, Benjamin R. *Lawyers and the Constitution.* Princeton, N. J.: Princeton University Press, 1942.

Ulam, Adam B. *The Unfinished Revolution.* New York: Random House, Inc., 1960.

Viereck, Peter. *The Unadjusted Man.* Boston: The Beacon Press, 1956.

Webb, Walter Prescott. *The Great Plains.* New York: Ginn and Co., 1931.

Weber, Max. *From Max Weber: Essays in Sociology.* H. H. Gerth and C. Wright Mills (eds.). New York: Galaxy Books, 1958.

————. *The Protestant Ethic and the Spirit of Capitalism.* New York: Charles Scribner's Sons, 1958.

Wechsler, James A. *The Age of Suspicion.* New York: Random House, Inc., 1953.

Weyl, Walter. *The New Democracy.* New York: The Macmillan Co., 1912.

White, Morton. *Social Thought in America: The Revolt Against Formalism.* Boston: The Beacon Press, 1957.

Wisconsin Citizens' Committee on McCarthy's Record. *The McCarthy Record.* Madison, Wis., 1952.

Wood, Robert C. *Suburbia.* Boston: Houghton Mifflin and Company, 1959.

Woodward, C. Vann. *Tom Watson: Agrarian Rebel.* New York: Macmillan Co., 1938.

Articles

Abrams, Richard M. "Paradox of Progressivism: Massachusetts on the Eve of Insurgency," *Political Science Quarterly,* Vol. 75 (September 1960), pp. 379–399.

Adrian, Charles R. "The Origins of Minnesota's Nonpartisan Legislature," *Minnesota History,* Vol. 33 (Winter 1952), pp. 155–163.

Allinsmith, Wesley, and Beverley Allinsmith. "Religious Affiliation and Politico-Economic Attitudes," *Public Opinion Quarterly,* Vol. 12 (Fall 1948), pp. 377–389.

Altmeyer, Arthur J. "The Wisconsin Idea and Social Security," *Wisconsin Magazine of History,* Vol. 42 (Autumn 1948), pp. 19–25.

Apter, David E. "The Role of Traditionalism in the Political Modernization of Ghana and Uganda," *World Politics,* Vol. 13 (October 1960), pp. 45–68.

Baggaley, Andrew R. "Patterns of Voting Change in Wisconsin Counties, 1952–1957," *Western Political Quarterly,* Vol. 12 (March 1959), pp. 141–144.

————. "Religious Influence on Wisconsin Voting, 1928–1960," *American Political Science Review,* Vol. 56 (March 1962), pp. 66–70.

————. "White Collar Employment and the Republican Vote," *Public Opinion Quarterly,* Vol. 20 (Summer 1956), pp. 471–473.

Bailey, Thomas A. "The West and Radical Legislation 1890–1930," *American Journal of Sociology,* Vol. 38 (January 1933), pp. 603–611.

Baker, Oliver E. "Agricultural Regions of North America," *Economic Geography,* Vol. 2 (October 1926), pp. 459–493; Vol. 3 (January 1927), pp. 50–86; Vol. 3 (July 1927), pp. 309–339; Vol. 3 (October 1927), pp. 447–466; Vol. 4 (January 1928), pp. 44–73; Vol. 4 (October 1928), pp. 399–433.

Barnes, James H. "Myths of the Bryan Campaign," *Mississippi Valley Historical Review,* Vol. 34 (December 1947), pp. 367–401.

Barnhart, John D. "Rainfall and the Populist Party in Nebraska," *American Political Science Review,* Vol. 19 (August 1925), pp. 522–540.

Bates, J. Leonard. "Fulfilling American Democracy: The Conservation Movement 1907–1921," *Mississippi Valley Historical Review,* Vol. 44 (June 1957), pp. 29–57.

Becker, Karl Lotus. "Kansas," in *Essays in American History Dedicated to Frederick Jackson Turner.* New York: Henry Holt and Co., 1910, pp. 85–112.

Bell, Daniel. "The Theory of Mass Society," *Commentary,* Vol. 22 (July 1956), pp. 75–83.

Benson, Lee. "Research Problems in American Historiography," in Mirra Komarovsky (ed.). *Common Frontiers of the Social Sciences.* Glencoe, Ill.: The Free Press, 1957, pp. 113–183.

Billington, Ray Allen. "The Origins of Middle Western Isolationism," *Political Science Quarterly,* Vol. 60 (March 1945), pp. 44–64.

Bowers, William J. "The Fruits of Iowa Progressivism 1900–1915," *Iowa Journal of History,* Vol. 57 (January 1959), pp. 34–60.

Briggs, Harold E. "Early Bonanza Farming in the Red River

Valley of the North," *Agricultural History*, Vol. 6 (January 1932), pp. 26–37.

———. "The Development and Decline of Open Range Ranching in the Northwest," *Mississippi Valley Historical Review*, Vol. 20 (March 1934), pp. 521–536.

Bunzel, John H. "The General Ideology of American Small Business," *Political Science Quarterly*, Vol. 70 (March 1955), pp. 87–102.

Caldwell, Martha B. "The Woman Suffrage Campaign of 1912," *The Kansas Historical Quarterly*, Vol. 13 (1943), pp. 300–318.

Canning, Ray R., and James M. Baker. "Effect of the Group on Authoritarian and Non-Authoritarian Persons," *American Journal of Sociology*, Vol. 64 (May 1959), pp. 579–581.

Carleton, William G. "Isolationism and the Middle West," *Mississippi Valley Historical Review*, Vol. 33 (December 1946), pp. 377–390.

Case, Herman M. "Guttman Scaling Applied to Center's Conservatism-Radicalism Battery," *American Journal of Sociology*, Vol. 48 (March 1953), pp. 556–563.

Chandler, Alfred D. "The Origins of Progressive Leadership," in Elting Morison, Jr. (ed.). *The Letters of Theodore Roosevelt*. Vol. VIII. Cambridge, Mass.: Harvard University Press, 1954.

Chapman, Philip C. "The New Conservatism: Cultural Criticism vs. Political Philosophy," *Political Science Quarterly*, Vol. 75 (March 1960), pp. 17–34.

Colletta, Paolo E. "Tempest in a Teapot? Governor Ponter's Appointment of William V. Allen to the United States Senate," *Nebraska History*, Vol. 38 (June 1957), pp. 155–163.

———. "The Morning Star of Reformation: William J. Bryan's First Congressional Campaign," *Nebraska History*, Vol. 37 (June 1956), pp. 103–120.

———. "The Nebraska Democratic State Convention of April 13–14, 1892," *Nebraska History*, Vol. 39 (December 1958), pp. 317–334.

Congressional Quarterly, "The McCarthy Censure," Vol. 12 (December 3, 1954), pp. 1404–1407.

———. "McCarthy's Strength Centered in West, Midwest," Vol. 12 (December 3, 1954), p. 1409.

Danker, Donald F. "Nebraska and the Presidential Election of 1912," *Nebraska History*, Vol. 37 (December 1956), pp. 283–310.

Diamond, William. "Urban and Rural Voting in 1896," *American Historical Review,* Vol. 46 (January 1941), pp. 281–305.

Doster, James F. "Were Populists Against Railroad Corporations? The Case of Alabama," *Journal of Southern History,* Vol. 20 (1954), pp. 395–399.

Duffus, Robert L. "The Ku Klux Klan in the Middle West," *World's Work,* Vol. 46 (August 1923), pp. 363–372.

Edwards, Everett E. "American Agriculture — The First 300 Years," in United States Department of Agriculture, *Farmers in a Changing World. Yearbook of Agriculture.* Washington, D. C.: Government Printing Office, 1940, pp. 171–276.

————."Middle Western Agricultural History as a Field of Research," *Mississippi Valley Historical Review,* Vol. 24 (December 1937), pp. 315–328.

Elkins, Stanley, and Eric McKitrick. "A Meaning for Turner's Frontier," *Political Science Quarterly,* Vol. 64 (September 1954), pp. 321–353.

Emerick, C. F. "Analysis of Agrarian Discontent in the United States," *Political Science Quarterly,* Vol. 11 (September 1896), pp. 433–463; (December 1896), pp. 601–639.

Engberg, George B. "The Knights of Labor in Minnesota," *Minnesota History,* Vol. 22 (December 1941), pp. 367–390.

Fairchild, G. T. "Populism in a State Education Institution, The Kansas State Agricultural College," *American Journal of Sociology,* Vol. 3 (November 1897), pp. 392–404.

Farris, Charles D. "A Method of Determining the Ideological Groupings in the Congress," *Journal of Politics,* Vol. 20 (May 1958), pp. 308–338.

————. " 'Authoritarianism' as a Political Behavior Variable," *Journal of Politics,* Vol. 18 (February 1956), pp. 61–82.

————. "Selected Attitudes on Foreign Affairs as Correlates of Authoritarianism and Political Anomie," *Journal of Politics,* Vol. 22 (February 1960), pp. 50–67.

Farmer, Hallie. "The Economic Background of Frontier Populism," *Mississippi Valley Historical Review,* Vol. 10 (March 1924), pp. 406–427.

Faulds, Bob. "Dakota Points the Way," *New Republic,* Vol. 119 (August 16, 1948), pp. 9–10.

Ferkiss, Victor C. "Political and Intellectual Origins of American Radicalism, Right and Left, *Annals of the American Acad-*

353

emy of Political and Social Science, Vol. 344 (November 1962), pp. 1–12.

―――. "The Populist Influences on American Fascism," *Western Political Quarterly,* Vol. 10 (June 1957), pp. 350–373.

―――. "Populism: Myth, Reality, Current Danger," *Western Political Quarterly,* Vol. 14 (September 1961), pp. 737–740.

Fiedler, Leslie A. "McCarthy," *Encounter,* Vol. 3 (August 1954), pp. 10–21.

Findley, James C. "Cross-Filing and the Progressive Movement in California Politics," *Western Political Quarterly,* Vol. 12 (September 1959), pp. 699–701.

Fite, Gilbert C. "The Agricultural Issue in the Presidential Campaign of 1928," *Mississippi Valley Historical Review,* Vol. 37 (March 1951), pp. 653–672.

―――. "Republican Strategy and the Farm Vote in the Presidential Campaign of 1896," *American Historical Review,* Vol. 45 (June 1960), pp. 787–806.

Fletcher, Ralph, and Mildred Fletcher. "Consistency in Party Voting from 1896–1932," *Social Forces,* Vol. 15 (December 1936), pp. 281–285.

Francis, Clara. "The Coming of Prohibition to Kansas," *Collections of the Kansas State Historical Society,* Vol. 15 (1919–1922), pp. 192–227.

Friedrich, Carl J. "The Agricultural Basis of Emotional Nationalism," *Public Opinion Quarterly,* Vol. 1 (April 1937), pp. 50–61.

Fuller, Leon W. "Colorado's Revolt against Capitalism," *Mississippi Valley Historical Review,* Vol. 21 (December 1934), pp. 343–360.

Gilman, Rhoda R. "Ramsey, Donnelly, and the Congressional Campaign of 1868," *Minnesota History,* Vol. 36 (December 1959), pp. 300–308.

Glazer, Nathan. "The Method of Senator McCarthy," *Commentary,* Vol. 15 (March 1953), pp. 244–256.

Goffman, Irwin W. "Status Consistency and Preference for Change in Power Distribution," *American Sociological Review,* Vol. 22 (June 1957), pp. 275–281.

Gosnell, Harold F., and Norman N. Gill. "An Analysis of the 1932 Presidential Vote in Chicago," *American Political Science Review,* Vol. 29 (December 1935), pp. 967–984.

Gusfield, Joseph R. "Mass Society and Extremist Politics,"

American Sociological Review, Vol. 27 (February 1962), pp. 19–30.

Halich, Wasyl. "Ukranian Farmers in the United States," *Agricultural History,* Vol. 10 (January 1936), pp. 25–39.

Handlin, Oscar. "American Views of the Jew at the Opening of the Twentieth Century," *Publications of the American Jewish Historical Society,* Vol. 40 (June 1951), pp. 323–344.

Harrington, Elbert W. "A Survey of the Political Ideas of Albert Baird Cummins," *Iowa Journal of History and Politics,* Vol. 39 (October 1941), pp. 739–786.

Herberg, Will. "Government by Rabble-Rousing," *New Leader,* Vol. 37 (January 18, 1954), pp. 13–16.

Hicks, John D. "The Legacy of Populism in the Western Middle West," *Agricultural History,* Vol. 23 (October 1949), pp. 225–236.

———. "The People's Party in Minnesota," *Minnesota History,* Vol. 5 (November, 1924), pp. 531–560.

———. "The Third Party Tradition in American Politics," *Mississippi Valley Historical Review,* Vol. 20 (June 1933), pp. 3–28.

Higham, John. "Anti-Semitism in the Guilded Age," *Mississippi Valley Historical Review,* Vol. 43 (March 1957), pp. 559–578.

Hill, Perry C. "Wisconsin Votes for President," *Wisconsin Magazine of History,* Vol. 36 (Autumn 1952), pp. 11–16.

Holbo, Paul S. "Wheat or What? Populism and American Fascism," *Western Political Quarterly,* Vol. 16 (September 1961), pp. 727–736.

Hollingsworth, J. Rogers. "Populism: The Problem of Rhetoric and Reality," *Agricultural History,* Vol. 39 (April 1965), pp. 81–85.

Horton, John E., and Wayne E. Thompson. "Powerlessness and Political Negativism: A Study of Defeated Local Referendums," *American Journal of Sociology,* Vol. 67 (March 1962), pp. 485–493.

Huntington, Samuel P. "The Electoral Tactics of the Nonpartisan League," *Mississippi Valley Historical Review,* Vol. 36 (March 1950), pp. 613–632.

Janowitz, Morris, and Dwaine Marvick. "Authoritarianism and Political Behavior," *Public Opinion Quarterly,* Vol. 17 (Summer 1953), pp. 185–201.

Jarchow, Merril E. "King Wheat," *Minnesota History,* Vol. 29 (March 1948), pp. 1–28.

Johnson, Roy P. "John Burke," *North Dakota History,* Vol. 28 (Winter 1961), pp. 29–31.

Johnson, Walter. "Politics in the Midwest," *Nebraska History,* Vol. 32 (March 1951), pp. 1–17.

Johnstone, Paul H. "Old Ideas Versus New Ideas in Farm Life," in United States Department of Agriculture. *Farmers in a Changing World. Yearbook of Agriculture.* Washington, D. C.: Government Printing Office, 1940, pp. 111–170.

————. "Turnips and Romanticism," *Agricultural History,* Vol. 12 (July 1938), pp. 224–255.

Kennedy, Padriac M. "Lenroot, La Follette, and the Campaign of 1908," *Wisconsin Magazine of History,* Vol. 42 (Spring 1959), pp. 163–174.

Kern, Jean B. "The Political Career of Horace Boies," *Iowa Journal of History,* Vol. 47 (July 1949), pp. 214–246.

Key, V. O., Jr. "A Theory of Critical Elections," *Journal of Politics,* Vol. 17 (February 1955), pp. 3–18.

————, and Frank Munger. "Social Determinism and Electoral Decision: The Case of Indiana," in Eugene Burdick and Arthur J. Brodbeck (eds.). *American Voting Behavior.* Glencoe, Ill.: The Free Press, 1955.

Korman, Gerd. "Politics, Loyalties, Immigrant Traditions, and Reform: The Wisconsin German-American Press and Progressivism 1909–1912," *Wisconsin Magazine of History,* Vol. 40 (Spring 1957), pp. 161–168.

Lamphere, George N. "History of Wheat Raising in the Red River Valley," *Collections of the Minnesota Historical Society,* Vol. 10 (February 1905), pp. 1–33.

Lane, Robert E. "Politics, Personality, and Electoral Choice," *American Political Science Review,* Vol. 49 (March 1953), pp. 173–190.

Larsen, Lawrence H. "William Langer: A Maverick in the Senate," *Wisconsin Magazine of History,* Vol. 44 (Spring 1961), pp. 189–198.

Link, Arthur S. "What Happened to the Progressive Movement in the 1920's?" *American Historical Review,* Vol. 64 (July 1959), pp. 833–851.

Lipset, Seymour Martin. "A Changing American Character," in Seymour Martin Lipset and Leo Lowenthal (eds.), *Culture and Social Character.* Glencoe, Ill.: The Free Press, 1961, pp. 136–171.

————. "Socialism — Left and Right — East and West," *Confluence,* Vol. 7 (Summer 1958), pp. 173–192.

356

————. "Social Stratification and 'Right-Wing' Extremism," *British Journal of Sociology*, Vol. 10 (December 1959), pp. 346–382.

————, *et al.* "The Psychology of Voting," in G. Lindzey (ed.), *Handbook of Social Psychology*. Vol. II. Cambridge, Mass.: Addison-Wesley Publishing Co., Inc., 1954.

Lodge, Henry Cabot. "The Meaning of The Votes," *North American Review*, Vol. 165 (January 1897), pp. 1–11.

Loomis, Charles P., and J. Allan Beegle. "The Spread of German Nazism in Rural Areas," *American Sociological Review*, Vol. 11 (December 1946), pp. 724–734.

Lowitt, Richard. "George Norris, James J. Hill, and the Railroad Rate Bill," *Nebraska History*, Vol. 40 (June 1959), pp. 137–146.

————. "George Norris and Agricultural Relief During the Twenties," *Nebraska History*, Vol. 36 (September 1955), pp. 173–182.

————. "Populism and Politics: The Start of George W. Norris' Political Career," *Nebraska History*, Vol. 42 (June 1961), pp. 75–94.

Lundberg, George A. "The Demographic and Economic Basis of Political Radicalism and Conservatism," *American Journal of Sociology*, Vol. 32 (March 1927), pp. 719–732.

Luthin, Reinhard H. "Smith Wildman Brookhart of Iowa: Insurgent Agrarian Politician," *Agricultural History*, Vol. 25 (October 1951), pp. 187–197.

Lynn, Erwin L. "The Influence of Liberalism and Conservatism on Voting Behavior," *Public Opinion Quarterly*, Vol. 8 (Summer 1949), pp. 299–309.

Macmahon, Arthur W. "Political Parties and Elections: Presidential Vote," *Political Science Quarterly*, Supplement, Vol. 40 (1925), pp. 51–56.

MacRae, Duncan, Jr. "Occupations and the Congressional Vote, 1940–1950," *American Sociological Review*, Vol. 20 (June 1955), pp. 332–340.

————, and James A. Meldrum. "Critical Elections in Illinois, 1888–1958," *American Political Science Review*, Vol. 54 (September 1960), pp. 669–683.

McClosky, Herbert. "Conservatism and Personality," *American Political Science Review*, Vol. 52 (March 1958), pp. 27–45.

————, *et al.* "Issue Conflict and Consensus among Party Leaders and Followers," *American Political Science Review*, Vol. 54 (June 1960), pp. 406–427.

McCoy, Donald R. "The National Progressives of America, 1938," *Mississippi Valley Historical Review*, Vol. 54 (June 1957), pp. 75–93.

McGovern, George. "Mission to the Hungry," *Progressive*, Vol. 26 (March 1962), pp. 19–22.

McMillan, Miles. "Calling the Roll on McCarthy," *Progressive*, Vol. 17 (May 1954), pp. 13–16.

McVey, Frank L. "The Populist Movement," *Economic Studies*, Vol. 1 (August 1896), pp. 135–209.

McWilliams, Carey. "North Dakota Showdown," *Nation*, Vol. 178 (March 1952), pp. 295–296.

Mahler, Ludwig. "Ideology and History in America," *New Politics*, Vol. 1 (Fall 1961), pp. 132–143.

March, James G. "McCarthy Can Still Be Beaten," *Reporter*, Vol. 7 (October 22, 1952), pp. 17–19.

Margulies, Herbert F. "The Background of the La Follette-McGovern Schism," *Wisconsin Magazine of History*, Vol. 40 (Autumn 1956), pp. 21–29.

————. "The Election of 1920 in Wisconsin: The Return to 'Normalcy' Reappraised," *Wisconsin Magazine of History*, Vol. 41 (Autumn 1957), pp. 15–22.

————. "The La Follette-Phillip Alliance of 1918," *Wisconsin Magazine of History*, Vol. 37 (Summer 1955), pp. 248–249.

Marsden, K. Gerald. "Patriotic Societies and American Labor: The American Protective Association in Wisconsin," *Wisconsin Magazine of History*, Vol. 41 (Summer 1958), pp. 287–294.

Merton, Robert. "Social Structure and Anomie," *American Sociological Review*, Vol. 3 (October 1938), pp. 672–682.

Miller, Raymond Curtis. "The Background of Populism in Kansas," *Mississippi Valley Historical Review*, Vol. 11 (March 1925), pp. 469–489.

Mitau, G. Theodore. "The Democratic-Farmer-Labor Party Schism of 1948," *Minnesota History*, Vol. 34 (Spring 1955), pp. 187–194.

Murphy, Charles J. V. "McCarthy and the Businessman," *Fortune*, Vol. 49 (April 1954), pp. 156–158, 180–194.

Murray, Stanley N. "Railroads and the Agricultural Development of the Red River Valley of the North, 1870–1890," *Agricultural History*, Vol. 31 (October 1957), pp. 57–66.

National Farmers Union Washington Newsletter, Vol. 8 (November 17, 1961), p. 1.

————. "Farm Bureau Drags God into Debate," Vol. 8 (December 15, 1961), p. 1.

Nettler, Gwynne. "Cruelty, Dignity, and Determinism," *American Sociological Review,* Vol. 24 (June 1959), pp. 375–384.

New Republic. "North Dakota Barometer," Vol. 142 (April 11, 1960), pp. 6–7.

Newsweek. "Dakota's Decision," Vol. 39 (June 16, 1952), pp. 27–28.

————. "Duel in North Dakota," Vol. 11 (June 27, 1938), p. 12.

————. "The Governor To Be," Vol. 43 (June 14, 1954), p. 29.

Niebuhr, Reinhold. "Beria and McCarthy," *New Leader,* Vol. 37 (January 4, 1954), pp. 3–4.

Nixon, Herman Clarence. "The Economic Basis of The Populist Movement in Iowa," *Iowa Journal of History and Politics,* Vol. 21 (July 1923), pp. 373–396.

Nydegger, Walter Ellsworth. "The Election of 1892 in Iowa," *Iowa Journal of History and Politics,* Vol. 25 (July 1927), pp. 359–449.

O'Connor, James R. "National Farm Organizations and United States Tariff Policy in the 1920s," *Agricultural History,* Vol. 32 (January 1958), pp. 32–43.

Ogburn, William F., and Lolagene C. Combs. "The Economic Factor in the Roosevelt Elections," *American Political Science Review,* Vol. 34 (August 1940), pp. 719–727.

————, and Estelle Hill. "Income Classes and the Roosevelt Vote in 1932," *Political Science Quarterly,* Vol. 50 (June 1935), pp. 186–193.

————, and Abe J. Jaffe. "Independent Voting in Presidential Elections," *American Journal of Sociology,* Vol. 42 (September 1936), pp. 186–201.

————, and Delum Peterson. "Political Thought of Social Classes," *Political Science Quarterly,* Vol. 31 (June 1916), pp. 300–317.

————, and Nell Snow Talbot. "A Measurement of the Factors in the Presidential Election of 1928," *Social Forces,* Vol. 8 (December 1929), pp. 175–183.

O'Neill, W. M., and Daniel J. Levinson. "A Factorial Exploration of Authoritarianism and Some of Its Ideological Concomitants," *Journal of Personality,* Vol. 22 (June 1954), pp. 449–463.

Pollack, Norman. "Hofstadter on Populism: A Critique of 'The

Age of Reform,'" *Journal of Southern History,* Vol. 26 (November 1960), pp. 478–500.

———. "The Myth of Populist Anti-Semitism," *American Historical Review,* Vol. 68 (October 1962), pp. 76–80.

Polsby, Nelson W. "Towards an Explanation of McCarthyism," *Political Studies,* Vol. 8 (October 1960), pp. 250–271.

Prothro, E. Terry, and Levan Melikian. "The California Public Opinion Scale in an Authoritarian Culture," *Public Opinion Quarterly,* Vol. 17 (Fall 1953), pp. 353–363.

Ridge, Martin. "Ignatius Donnelly: Minnesota Congressman 1863–69," *Minnesota History,* Vol. 36 (March 1959), pp. 173–183.

———. "Ignatius Donnelly and the Granger Movement in Minnesota," *Mississippi Valley Historical Review,* Vol. 42 (March 1956), pp. 693–709.

Roberts, Alan H., and Milton Rokeach. "Anomie, Authoritarianism, and Prejudice: A Replication," *American Journal of Sociology,* Vol. 61 (January 1956), pp. 355–358.

Robinson, Edgar Eugene. "Recent Manifestations of Sectionalism," *American Journal of Sociology,* Vol. 19 (January 1914), pp. 446–467.

Robinson, Elwyn B. "The Themes of North Dakota History," *North Dakota History,* Vol. 26 (Winter 1959), pp. 5–24.

Robinson, Daniel M. "Tennessee Politics and the Agrarian Revolt 1886–1896," *Mississippi Valley Historical Review,* Vol. 20 (December 1933), pp. 365–380.

Ronald, Malcomb B. "The Dakota Twins," *Atlantic Monthly,* Vol. 158 (September 1936), pp. 359–365.

Ruggles, Clyde O. "The Economic Basis of the Greenback Movement in Iowa and Wisconsin," *Proceedings of the Mississippi Valley Historical Association,* Vol. 6 (1912–1913), pp. 142–165.

Russ, William A., Jr. "Godkin Looks at Western Agrarianism: A Case Study," *Agricultural History,* Vol. 19 (October 1945), pp. 233–234.

Saposs, David J. "The Role of the Middle Class in Social Development: Fascism, Populism, Communism, Socialism," in *Economic Essays in Honor of Wesley Clair Mitchell.* New York: Columbia University Press, 1935, pp. 393–424.

Schell, Herbert S. "Adjustment Problems in South Dakota," *Agricultural History,* Vol. 14 (April 1940), pp. 65–75.

———. "The Granges and the Credit Problem in Dakota Territory," *Agricultural History,* Vol. 10 (April 1936), pp. 59–73.

Schmidt, Louis Bernard. "The Agricultural Revolution in the Prairies and the Great Plains of the United States," *Agricultural History,* Vol. 8 (October 1934), pp. 169–195.

———. "The Internal Grain Trade of the United States 1860–1890," *Iowa Journal of History and Politics,* Vol. 19 (April 1921), pp. 196–245; Vol. 19 (July 1921), pp. 414–455; Vol. 20 (January 1922), pp. 70–131.

———. "The Role and Technique of Agrarian Pressure Groups," *Agricultural History,* Vol. 30 (April 1956), pp. 49–57.

———. "Some Significant Aspects of the Agrarian Revolution in the United States," *Iowa Journal of History and Politics,* Vol. 17 (July 1920), pp. 271–295.

———. "The Westward Movement of the Corn-Growing Industry," *Iowa Journal of History and Politics,* Vol. 21 (January 1923), pp. 112–141.

———. "The Westward Movement of the Wheat-Growing Industry in the United States," *Iowa Journal of History and Politics,* Vol. 18 (July 1920), pp. 396–412.

Scott, Andrew M. "The Progressive Era in Perspective," *Journal of Politics,* Vol. 21 (November 1959), pp. 685–701.

Shenton, James P. "The Coughlin Movement and the New Deal," *Political Science Quarterly,* Vol. 73 (September 1958), pp. 352–373.

Sherman, Richard B. "The Status Revolution and Massachusetts Progressive Leadership," *Political Science Quarterly,* Vol. 78 (March 1963), pp. 59–65.

Shils, Edward. "Daydreams and Nightmares: Reflections on the Criticism of Mass Culture," *The Sewanee Review,* Vol. 75 (1957), pp. 587–608.

———. "Populism and the Rule of Law," The Law School of the University of Chicago, Conference on Jurisprudence and Politics, April 30, 1954, pp. 91–107.

Smith, Guy-Harold. "Notes on the Distribution of the German-Born in Wisconsin in 1905," *Wisconsin Magazine of History,* Vol. 13 (1929–1930), pp. 107–120.

———. "Notes on the Distribution of the Foreign-born Scandinavian in Wisconsin in 1905," *Wisconsin Magazine of History,* Vol. 14 (1930–1931), pp. 419–436.

Smuckler, Ralph H. "The Region of Isolation," *American Political Science Review,* Vol. 47 (June 1953), pp. 386–401.

Steckler, Gerard G. "North Dakota Versus Frederick Jackson

Turner," *North Dakota History,* Vol. 28 (Winter 1961), pp. 33–43.

Stevenson, George M. "Nativism in the Forties and Fifties, with Specific Reference to the Mississippi Valley," *Mississippi Valley Historical Review,* Vol. 9 (December 1922), pp. 185–202.

Stewart, Ernest D. "The Populist Party in Indiana," *Indiana Magazine of History,* Vol. 14 (December 1918), pp. 332–367.

Talbot, Ross B. "The North Dakota Farmers' Union and North Dakota Politics," *Political Science Quarterly,* Vol. 10 (December 1957), pp. 875–901.

Throne, Mildred. "The Grange in Iowa, 1868–1875," *Iowa Journal of History and Politics,* Vol. 47 (October 1949), pp. 289–324.

Time. "Eighteenth Year," Vol. 43 (June 19, 1944), p. 20.

———. "Fourteen Delegates," Vol. 69 (June 16, 1952), p. 23.

———. "Too Busy to Win," Vol. 55 (June 19, 1950), pp. 21–22.

———. "Trouble for Gerald," Vol. 44 (October 16, 1944), p. 21.

Tinsley, James A. "Texas Progressives and Insurance Regulation," *Southwest Social Science Quarterly,* Vol. 36 (December 1955), pp. 237–247.

Tracy, Frank Basil. "The Rise and Doom of the Populist Party," *Forum,* Vol. 16 (October 1893), pp. 241–250.

Trow, Martin. "Small Businessmen, Political Intolerance, and Support for McCarthy," *American Journal of Sociology,* Vol. 64 (November 1958), pp. 270–281.

Tryon, Warren S. "Agriculture and Politics in South Dakota 1889–1900," *South Dakota Historical Collections,* Vol. 13 (1926), pp. 284–310.

Tucker, William P. "Populism Up-to-Date, The Story of the Farmers Union," *Agricultural History,* Vol. 21 (October 1947), pp. 198–208.

Tweton, D. Jerome. "North Dakota in the 1890's: Its People, Politics, and Press," *North Dakota History,* Vol. 24 (April 1957), pp. 113–118.

———. "Sectionalism in North Dakota Politics: The Progressive Republican Revolt of 1900," *North Dakota History,* Vol. 25 (January 1958), pp. 21–28.

Wallace, Henry. "Report on the Farmers," *New Republic,* Vol. 116 (June 30, 1947), pp. 12–13.

Warner, Donald F. "The Farmers' Alliance and the Farmers' Union. An American-Canadian Parallelism," *Agricultural History*, Vol. 23 (January 1949), pp. 9–19.

———. "Prelude to Populism," *Minnesota History*, Vol. 32 (September 1951), pp. 129–146.

Washington Correspondent. "The Progressives of the Senate," *American Mercury*, Vol. 16 (April 1929), pp. 385–393.

Watson, Richard L., Jr. "Woodrow Wilson and His Interpreters," *Mississippi Valley Historical Review*, Vol. 44 (September 1957), pp. 207–236.

Westin, Alan Furmin. "The Supreme Court, The Populist Movement, and the Campaign of 1896," *Journal of Politics*, Vol. 15 (February 1953), pp. 3–41.

White, Melvin J. "Populism in Louisiana During the Nineties," *Mississippi Valley Historical Review*, Vol. 5 (June 1918), pp. 3–19.

Wiebe, G. D. "The Army-McCarthy Hearings: The Public Conscience," *Public Opinion Quarterly*, Vol. 22 (Winter 1958–1959), pp. 490–502.

Wilcox, Benton H. "An Historical Definition of Northwestern Radicalism," *Mississippi Valley Historical Review*, Vol. 26 (December 1939), pp. 377–394.

Wildavsky, Aaron. "Exploring the Content of McCarthyism," *The Australian Outlook* (June 1955).

Williams, Howard G. "Nye — A Lost Leader," *Nation*, Vol. 158 (June 24, 1947), pp. 730–731.

Williams, T. Harry. "The Gentleman from Louisiana: Demagogue or Democrat," *Journal of Southern History*, Vol. 26 (February 1960), pp. 3–21.

Woodburn, James Albert. "Western Radicals in American Politics," *Mississippi Valley Historical Review*, Vol. 13 (September 1926), pp. 143–168.

Woodward, C. Vann. "The Populist Heritage and the Intellectual," *American Scholar*, Vol. 29 (Winter 1959), pp. 55–72.

———. "Tom Watson and the Negro in Agrarian Politics," *Journal of Southern History*, Vol. 4 (February 1938), pp. 14–33.

Wrong, Dennis. "Theories of McCarthyism — A Survey," *Dissent*, Vol. 1 (Autumn 1955), pp. 385–392.

Zucker, Norman L. "George W. Norris: Nebraska Moralist," *Nebraska History*, Vol. 42 (June 1951), pp. 95–124.

Department of Agriculture Pamphlets

Agricultural Research Service. *Farming in the Great Plains.* Washington, D. C.: United States Department of Agriculture, 1961.

Durost, Donald D. *Index Numbers of Agricultural Production by Regions, 1939–1958.* Washington, D. C.: Agricultural Research Service, United States Department of Agriculture, 1960.

Generalized Types of Farming in the United States. Washington, D. C.: United States Department of Agriculture, 1960

Hagood, Margaret Jarmon. *Farm-Operator Family Level-of-Living Indexes for Counties of the United States 1930, 1940, 1945, and 1950.* Washington, D. C.: Bureau of Agricultural Economics, United States Department of Agriculture, 1952.

McElveen, Jackson V. *Family Farms in a Changing Economy.* Washington, D. C.: Agricultural Research Service, United States Department of Agriculture, 1957.

Strand, Edwin G., and Earl O. Heady. *Productivity of Resources Used on Commercial Farms.* Washington, D. C.: Technical Bulletin No. 1128, United States Department of Agriculture, 1955.

Strickler, Paul E., and Charles A. Hines. *Numbers of Selected Machines and Equipment on Farms.* Washington, D. C.: Agricultural Research Service and Agricultural Marketing Service, Statistical Bulletin No. 258, United States Department of Agriculture, 1960.

Unpublished Material

Balknap, George. "A Study of Senatorial Voting by Scale Analysis." Unpublished Ph.D. dissertation, Department of Political Science, University of Chicago, 1951.

Breslow, Paul E. "The Relationship Between Ideology and Socio-Economic Background in a Group of McCarthyite Leaders." Unpublished Master's thesis, Department of Political Science, University of Chicago, 1955.

Brudvig, Glenn Lowell. "The Farmers' Alliance and Populist Movement in North Dakota (1884–1896)." Unpublished Master's thesis, University of North Dakota, 1956.

Crampton, John A. " 'Yours for Humanity . . . ': The Role of Ideology in the Farmers Union." Unpublished Ph.D. dissertation, Department of Political Science, University of California, 1962.

Gnatz, William R. "The Negro and the Populist Movement in the South." Unpublished Master's thesis, Department of History, University of Chicago, 1961.

Haber, Sam. "Scientific Management and the Progressive Movement, 1910–1929." Unpublished Ph.D. dissertation, Department of History, University of California, 1961.

Huntington, Samuel Phillips. "The Politics of the Non-Partisan League." Unpublished Master's thesis, Department of Political Science, University of Chicago, 1948.

Kendrick, Frank J. "McCarthy and the Senate." Unpublished Ph.D. dissertation, Department of Political Science, University of Chicago, 1962.

Larsen, Lawrence Harold. "William Langer, Senator from North Dakota." Unpublished Master's dissertation, Department of History, University of Wisconsin, 1955.

Mandel, Jerry. "The Effects of Class Consciousness and Political Sophistication on Working Class Authoritarianism." Unpublished Master's thesis, Department of Sociology, University of California at Berkeley, 1964.

McCoy, Donald R. "The Development and Dissolution of the Wisconsin Progressive Party of 1934–46." Unpublished Master's thesis, Department of Political Science, University of Chicago, 1949.

Meyer, Karl Ernest. "The Politics of Loyalty: From La Follette to McCarthy in Wisconsin: 1918–1952." Unpublished Ph.D. dissertation, Department of Political Science, Princeton University, 1956.

Miller, Raymond Curtis. "The Populist Party in Kansas." Unpublished Ph.D. dissertation, Department of History, University of Chicago, 1928.

Naftalin, Arthur. "A History of the Farmer-Labor Party of Minnesota." Unpublished Ph.D. dissertation, Department of Political Science, University of Minnesota, 1948.

Nugent, Walter R. "Populism and Nativism in Kansas, 1888–1900." Unpublished Ph.D. dissertation, Department of History, University of Chicago, 1961.

Parsons, Stanley. "Nebraska Populism Reconsidered." Paper presented at the Annual Meeeting of the American Historical Association, Washington, 1962.

Parzen, Herbert. "A Comparative Study of the Progressive Presidential Campaigns of 1912 and 1924." Unpublished Master's thesis, Department of Political Science, Columbia University, 1926.

Snowiss, Sylvia. "Roosevelt and Congress: The First Hundred Days." Unpublished Master's thesis, Department of Political Science, University of Chicago, 1962.

Thorndal, Otto Nelson. "La Follette's Record in Congress 1885–1891." Unpublished Master's thesis, Department of History, University of Chicago, 1925.

Trow, Martin A. "Right-Wing Radicalism and Political Intolerance: A Study of Support for McCarthy in a New England Town." Unpublished Ph.D. dissertation, Department of Political Science, Columbia University, 1957.

Wallerstein, Immanuel Maurice. "McCarthyism and the Conservative." Unpublished Master's thesis, Department of Political Science, Columbia University, 1954.

Wilcox, Benton Harold. "A Reconsideration of the Character and Economic Basis of Northwestern Radicalism." Unpublished Ph.D. dissertation, Department of History, University of Wisconsin, 1933.

INDEX

INDEX

Handlin, Oscar, 6, 173
Hartz, Louis, 35–36, 37
Haymarket Affair, 173
Herberg, Will, 6, 44
Hitler, Adolf, 217
Hofstadter, Richard, 5, 17, 20, 26, 27, 66, 70, 80, 81, 97, 98, 118, 169, 172, 173, 183–184, 195n, 265–266
  quoted, 183, 240–241
Homogeneity
  and pluralists, 270, 273–274, 280
  and progressives, 193–196, 199
Hoover. J. Edgar, 242
House Un-American Activities Committee, 161
Howe, Frederic, quoted, 178–179
Hull, Merlin, 134

Income tax, 51–52
Industrialization, 10–15, 32, 169–171, 208–210, 264–267, 269, 272
Initiative and referendum, 198n
Iowa, 98, 214
  Populists in, 175
Isolationism, 79, 269
  and McCarthyism, 223
IWW, 56

Jackson, Andrew, 48, 51
Jefferson, Thomas, 36, 41, 42, 47, 48
Jingoism, Populists and, 176–177
Johnson, Hiram, 207
Johnson, Lyndon, 267

Kansas, 172
  Populism in, 114n, 175, 176
Kansas State Agricultural College, 181
Kennedy, E. E., 213–214
Kennedy, John F., 81, 84, 246, 284
Kihss, Peter, 255, 256
Knights of Labor, 176, 192
Kolko, Gabriel, 203n
Korean War, 100, 224–225, 243, 247, 259
Kornhauser, William, 6, 10, 16–17, 20, 185
Ku Klux Klan, 180, 208–209

Labor, *see* Working class
Labor unions
  membership and McCarthy support, 236
  progressives and, 200n
La Follette, Phil, 75, 214
La Follette, Robert, 6, 65–103 *passim*, 117, 126, 137, 151, 194n, 200n, 204, 213, 215n, 217, 222
  agricultural wealth and vote for, 70
  coalition in Wisconsin, 65
  difference between Roosevelt and, 71n, 71–72
  difference between Wilson and, 71n, 71–72
  election of 1904, 68–70
  election of 1900, 66–67, 69
  and McCarthy, 4n–5n, 59–60

and Republican primary election of 1922, 73
  support for in South Dakota, 137
La Follette, Robert, Jr., 86, 134, 208n, 213, 262
Lamont, Corliss, 130
Langer, William, 214, 252
  and agrarian radicalism, 106, 135
  and McCarthy, 104, 136
  and the Non-Partisan League, 125–131
Laski, Harold, 11
Lease, Mary Ellen, 173
Lehman, Herbert, 130
Lemke, William, 102–103, 105, 131–133, 135, 212, 213
  see also Lubell, Samuel, on Lemke (Union Party) vote
Lenroot, Irving, 73
Lippman, Walter, 256
Lipset, Seymour Martin, 5, 17, 29, 97, 98, 173, 226, 233, 234, 240, 251
  quoted, 218
Lloyd, Henry Demarest, 172–173
Locke, John, 40, 178
Lockean consensus, 35–38, 51, 178, 193
  and industrialization, 32–58
Lockean liberalism
  and class legislation, 49
  and industrialization, 36
Lockean moralism and conservative ideology, 32–58
Lodge, Henry Cabot, quoted, 55
Long, Huey, 212, 213
Louis Napoleon, 211
Lubell, Samuel, 96, 103, 131
  on Lemke (Union Party) vote, 103, 131
  on progressivism, 75, 79–84
Lucas, Scott W., 161
Luddites, 21

MacArthur, Douglas, 214
McCarthy, Charles, 200
  quoted, 194–195
McCarthy, Joseph, 1–2, 186, 227–231, 245, 251–252
  political pattern of, 251–252
  rhetoric of, 230–231
  in Wisconsin
    analysis of relation to progressive tradition, 84–99
    bases of support, 86, 89
    Catholic vote for, 91–92, 94, 97
    and communism issue, 97
    corn belt vote for, 94, 97–99
    Czechoslovakian vote for, 91–92, 94
    as destroyer of group base of politics, 59–60, 97
    friends-and-neighbors effect in vote for, 91, 94, 99
    German vote for, 72, 99
    middle-class vote for, 93–94
    Polish vote for, 93–94
    rural support for, 89, 91, 99